Elderly people and
the environment

$42.50

DATE			

Elderly People and the Environment

Human Behavior and Environment

ADVANCES IN THEORY AND RESEARCH

Elderly People and the Environment

EDITED BY
IRWIN ALTMAN
University of Utah
Salt Lake City, Utah

M. POWELL LAWTON
Philadelphia Geriatric Center
Philadelphia, Pennsylvania

JOACHIM F. WOHLWILL
Pennsylvania State University
University Park, Pennsylvania

PLENUM PRESS • NEW YORK AND LONDON

Library of Congress Cataloging in Publication Data

Main entry under title:

Elderly people and the environment.

(Human behavior and environment: advances in theory and research; v. 7)
Includes bibliographical references and index.
1. Aged—United States—Dwellings. I. Altman, Irwin. II. Lawton, M. Powell (Mortimer
Powell), 1923–   . III. Wohlwill, Joachim F. IV. Series: Human behavior and environ-
ment; v. 7.
BF353.H85 vol. 7   155.9s [363.5′9]   83-26700
[HD7287.92.U6]
ISBN 0-306-41429-5

672 17278

©1984 Plenum Press, New York
A Division of Plenum Publishing Corporation
233 Spring Street, New York, N.Y. 10013

Printed in the United States of America

Contributors

IRWIN ALTMAN • College of Social and Behavioral Science, University of Utah, Salt Lake City, Utah

ABRAHAM CARP • The Wright Institute, Berkeley, California

FRANCES M. CARP • The Wright Institute, Berkeley, California

J. KEVIN ECKERT • Department of Anthropology, Case Western Reserve University, Cleveland, Ohio

MARTIN V. FALETTI • Stein Gerontological Institute, Miami Jewish Home and Hospital for the Aged, Miami, Florida

STEPHEN M. GOLANT • Department of Geography, University of Florida, Gainesville, Florida

MICHAEL E. HUNT • Institute for Social Research and College of Architecture and Urban Planning, University of Michigan, Ann Arbor, Michigan

M. POWELL LAWTON • Philadelphia Geriatric Center, Philadelphia, Pennsylvania

SONNE LEMKE • Social Ecology Laboratory and the Geriatric Research, Education, and Clinical Center, Veterans Administration and Stanford University Medical Center, Palo Alto, California

ROBERT W. MARANS • Institute for Social Research and College of Architecture and Urban Planning, University of Michigan, Ann Arbor, Michigan

RUDOLF H. MOOS • Social Ecology Laboratory and the Geriatric Research, Education, and Clinical Center, Veterans Administration and Stanford University Medical Center, Palo Alto, California

MARY ITTMAN MURREY • Department of Anthropology, Case Western Reserve University, Cleveland, Ohio

SANDRA J. NEWMAN • Public Policy Program, The Johns Hopkins University, Baltimore, Maryland

GRAHAM D. ROWLES • Department of Geology and Geography, West Virginia University, Morgantown, West Virginia

RAYMOND STRUYK • The Urban Institute, Washington, D.C.

KATHLEEN L. VAKALO • Institute for Social Research and College of Architecture and Urban Planning, University of Michigan, Ann Arbor, Michigan

JOACHIM F. WOHLWILL • Division of Individual and Family Studies, Pennsylvania State University, University Park, Pennsylvania

JAMES ZAIS • The Urban Institute, Washington, D.C.

Preface

The present volume in our series follows the format of the immediately preceding ones in dealing with a topical theme of considerable importance in the environment and behavior field. In view of current and projected demographic trends, it is a certainty that a broad-ranging set of issues concerned with the elderly and the physical environment will continue to be of focal pertinence—if not of increasing importance—in the remaining decades of this century.

The present volume also follows in the tradition of earlier volumes in the series in being eclectic with respect to content, theory, and methodology and in including contributions from a variety of disciplines, such as anthropology, economics, psychology, geography, and urban and regional planning. To have encompassed the whole array of disciplines and topics in this emerging field in a single volume would have been impossible. We trust that the sample of contributions that we have selected is provocative and that it will illustrate the range of problems and topics and point to promising areas of study and analysis.

We are pleased to have M. Powell Lawton as a guest co-editor for this volume. His broad-ranging expertise, perceptive judgment, and fine editorial talents have contributed enormously to the volume.

We regret to inform readers that, with this volume, Jack Wohlwill terminates his role as co-editor of *Human Behavior and Environment*. A set of newly emerging scholarly interests and involvements are proving increasingly difficult to reconcile with his obligations toward our series, making it inadvisable for him to continue as co-editor. From the beginning, our relationship as co-editors has been intellectually satisfying, personally productive, and extraordinarily congenial. We have learned a great deal from one another, as well as from the more than four dozen authors with whom and about whom we have communicated and collaborated in the seven volumes of this series. Therefore, we end this period of a close working relationship with considerable regret but also with a real sense of satisfaction in the fruits of our joint venture and of confidence in the prospects for the future of the series, which will continue under the primary editorship of Irwin Altman. It will follow the same goals and policies as heretofore, with guest co-editors invited to participate in individual volumes as circumstances and topics warrant.

Volume 8 of this series, *Home Environments*, is presently in preparation and will deal with the topic of home and residential environments.

IRWIN ALTMAN
JOACHIM F. WOHLWILL

Contents

Chapter 1

Dimensions of Environment–Behavior Research: Orientations to Place, Design, Process, and Policy

M. POWELL LAWTON
IRWIN ALTMAN
JOACHIM F. WOHLWILL

Chapter 2

Housing Older America

SANDRA J. NEWMAN
JAMES ZAIS
RAYMOND STRUYK

CHAPTER 3

RETIREMENT COMMUNITIES

ROBERT W. MARANS
MICHAEL E. HUNT
KATHLEEN L. VAKALO

CHAPTER 4

ALTERNATIVE MODES OF LIVING FOR THE ELDERLY: A
CRITICAL REVIEW

J. KEVIN ECKERT
MARY ITTMAN MURREY

CHAPTER 5

AGING IN RURAL ENVIRONMENTS

GRAHAM D. ROWLES

CHAPTER 6

SUPPORTIVE RESIDENTIAL SETTINGS FOR OLDER PEOPLE

RUDOLF H. MOOS
SONNE LEMKE

Chapter 7

Human Factors Research and Functional Environments for the Aged

Martin V. Faletti

Chapter 8

The Effects of Residential and Activity Behaviors on Old People's Environmental Experiences

Stephen M. Golant

CHAPTER 9

A COMPLEMENTARY/CONGRUENCE MODEL OF WELL-BEING OR MENTAL HEALTH FOR THE COMMUNITY ELDERLY

FRANCES M. CARP
ABRAHAM CARP

Dimensions of Environment–Behavior Research

ORIENTATIONS TO PLACE, DESIGN, PROCESS, AND POLICY

M. POWELL LAWTON, IRWIN ALTMAN, AND JOACHIM F. WOHLWILL

INTRODUCTION

This collection of papers on environment and aging comes more than 20 years after formally designated research in the area first began. Rather than serving as a comprehensive review of research, the present volume has two major purposes: to integrate knowledge on promising research topics and to identify and fill in some of the empirical and theoretical gaps in environmental-gerontological research that have become evident as knowledge has accumulated over the years. These two goals, if achieved, should point to promising directions of future research and should add an increment to our understanding of the relationship between elderly people and the physical environment.

Since the book was not designed as a comprehensive statement of knowledge in the field, it is important to define how the separate chap-

M. POWELL LAWTON • Philadelphia Geriatric Center, Philadelphia, Pennsylvania 19141.   IRWIN ALTMAN • College of Social and Behavioral Science, University of Utah, Salt Lake City, Utah 84112.   JOACHIM F. WOHLWILL • Division of Individual and Family Studies, Pennsylvania State University, University Park, Pennsylvania 16802.

ters fit into the totality of the topic now known as person–environment relations. Gerontology is an unusually broad and multidisciplinary field of study, and the present volume recognizes this by having authors from a broad spectrum of disciplines, including anthropology, economics, geography, psychology, and urban planning. Had space permitted, it would have been easy to expand the representation of disciplines beyond this array to include contributions from scholars in architecture, interior design, political science, and family and consumer studies. The diversity of points of view on gerontological topics reaches deeply into the value systems, philosophy, research, and theoretical orientations of these disciplines, yielding a field of considerable complexity and richness. The heterogeneity of the field is further reflected in the fact that these disciplines adopt several orientations to environments and the elderly. It is in relation to a framework of these differing orientations that the contributions in the present volume can be best understood.

Several years ago Altman (1973) described the environment and behavior field in terms of three orientations differentially adopted by researchers and practitioners: orientation to place, orientation to psychological and social processes, and orientation to design and practice. To these dimensions we now propose to add a fourth, namely, orientation to environmental policy.

Orientation to place involves a focus on specific places or settings—homes, neighborhoods, communities, parks, and the like. This is a natural interest of environmental designers and practitioners, as they face the task of modifying, creating, and building specific places and settings.

Orientation to design focuses on the creation and shaping of the setting and objects used by people. The place orientation and the design orientation together reflect the activities engaged in by the practicing environmental designer. The traditional, theory-oriented or basic researcher is rarely involved in design activities, although this has begun to change in the last decade. A recent volume by Zeisel (1981) deals explicitly with an analysis of the design process and the research process, describes their similarities and differences, and attempts to provide theoretical and working principles for linking design and research.

The orientation to social and psychological processes is a primary interest of researchers in the behavioral and social sciences, as they attempt to develop a body of knowledge and theory concerning social and psychological processes in relation to the environment. As Altman noted, the difference in the orientation of researchers to processes and practitioners to places often leads to difficulties in communication and to a less than satisfactory translation of research knowledge into usable design concepts.

As exhibited by certain of the chapters in this volume and in other writings in the field, a fourth orientation has emerged, that of policy studies, policy planning, policy implementation, and policy assessment. *Policy orientation* is strategic and involves the development and assessment of broadly based national or regional plans and strategies regarding environments. Traditionally, neither environmental designers nor environmental researchers have contributed very much to policy studies although this has begun to change in recent years. Obviously strategic policy studies are crucial, since they define the political and social parameters (including resource allocation by governmental and community agencies) of environment–behavior studies and practice. Thus contributions to environmental policy by researchers and practitioners in the environment and behavior field will be increasingly important in the coming years.

The remainder of this chapter describes representative research in the gerontological literature that emphasizes one or more of these different orientations. Since, naturally, many studies have more than a unidimensional orientation, any attempt at rigid classification is tenuous and inappropriate. In the course of the discussion we will indicate how the various chapters in the present volume are different and similar in their orientations to place, design, social and psychological processes, and policy.

ORIENTATION TO PLACE

The special place and setting needs of older people were recognized early by gerontologists as being of primary interest, particularly residential institutions and retirement housing. Older people in such locations have been studied periodically in descriptive terms; for example, there was a stream of research devoted to determining the differences between older people living in institutions and those living in the community (Davidson & Kruglov, 1952; Fox, 1950). Although its purpose was partly policy-oriented, one of the best descriptions of institutional environments for the elderly was Townsend's (1964) study of English homes for the aged. This work not only addressed policy questions but also considered social processes and services in institutional environments, and it portrayed in the best of descriptive-scientific traditions many aspects of the milieu in which these social processes occurred.

Retirement communities in warm climates began to appear in the 1920s, and descriptions of them were frequent in the gerontological literature. Here again, although the emphasis was on retirement places as multifaceted settings, various analyses necessarily focused on selected social processes that characterized these environments. For example, Peterson and Larson (undated) found that residents of retirement communities had fewer living children than did older people in general; their documentation of the high level of social interaction in these communities suggested that the move to such environments may have been motivated by social needs. In a French retirement community, Ross (1977) demonstrated how a substantial amount of the social life was based on social satisfaction in terms of procommunist and anticommunist political ideologies.

The first true conceptual framework that directly and systematically classified environments for the elderly was proposed by Kleemeier (1959). As a cognitive and perceptual psychologist performing research at Moosehaven, an institutional retirement complex in Florida sponsored by the Moose Lodges, Kleemeier proposed a transactional view of behavior in such environments, in which places and processes were considered as an integral unity. His articulation of three social-physical dimensions of institutions is still used today. A *congregate* dimension reflects the extent to which similar activities are performed by all residents of the place at the same time. A *segregate* dimension refers to the extent to which the environment is set apart, physically and socially, from ordinary community environments. A *control* dimension is based on the degree of resident as opposed to staff and administration decision-making and behavioral regulation. Although Kleemeier did not use quantitative data in developing these ideas, he demonstrated that a place orientation could be used as a vehicle for the initiation of research and design in the gerontological literature.

Neighborhoods as places where people play out their lives have also been a focus for research. Rosenberg's (1970) study of the local friendships of older people demonstrated how the block face in urban areas was a resource for social interchange. Carp's (1976) studies of transportation as a mediator between older persons and resources expanded the geographic area of concern to the community as a whole. Regnier, Eribes, and Hansen (1973) studied the way older residents of Los Angeles perceived their neighborhoods and how many of them who lived in single-room hotels used a nearby park as their "living rooms."

A very influential place-oriented study was the research evaluation of Victoria Plaza in San Antonio by Carp (1966). The assessment of this public housing environment, one of the first built exclusively for older people, demonstrated a variety of favorable effects for those residing in this project, compared with applicants who did not move into Victoria Plaza. Although the research was place-oriented in its evaluation of a specific environment, Carp made a number of qualitative observations that stimulated design-oriented hypotheses regarding the physical characteristics of such housing.

ORIENTATION TO DESIGN

Traditional behavioral research is difficult to perform on design issues. For example, Lawton and Nahemow (1979) interviewed 1,000 older people in 150 planned housing environments that differed widely in physical design characteristics and in the degree of satisfaction and psychological well-being of the residents. However, they concluded that the amount of knowledge gained that would be useful for design purposes was less than what might have been obtained by other means. By contrast, in a companion piece to the same research, Howell (1980) used two qualitative approaches: asking older tenants to talk in open-ended fashion about how they used features of their environment and unobtrusively observing them using public spaces of housing environments. These approaches succeeded particularly well in highlighting both barriers and facilitators to the use of environments and to the understanding of the multiplicity of needs that may be served by any given space. For example, watching people try to see what was going on in a space before committing themselves to entering the space led Howell to recommend building in "pre-viewing" designs, that is, a window or an opening that would allow the potential user to appraise the environment in terms of its suitability for meeting current needs long before the user would be required actually to enter it.

Much more often than not, however, the design orientation to environments for the elderly has proceeded with reasoning by analogy rather than being based on behavioral and social science research. Typically, a set of guiding principles for maximizing the need satisfaction of older people has been abstracted from the body of gerontological knowledge on physical health, individual behavior, and social processes. These principles in turn have been used to formulate prescriptions for environmental design whose results are hypothesized to lead to desired behavior (Zeisel, Epp, & Demos, 1978). Such design hypotheses are thus capable of being tested through qualitative observation and interviewing of people. Research of this type has produced such results as a design guide for institutions (Koncelik, 1976) and a concept for a prosthetic environment for patients with senile dementia (Liebowitz, Lawton, & Waldman, 1979).

Design-oriented books on housing for the elderly have resulted from the collection of both formal and informal observations of functioning housing environments (Green, Fedewa, Johnston, Jackson, & Deardorff, 1975; Lawton, 1975). Carp (1976) examined neighborhoods in terms of how well basic needs of older people could be met by a variety of neighborhood variables such as transportation, the location of resources, and the configuration of pathways. The "product environment" (Koncelik, 1982) is a highly creative treatment of how currently available hardware, furniture, and materials may be used to compensate for a variety of perceptual, motor, and social impairments common among the very old and institutionalized elderly.

The design process for producing new environments for older people shows signs of being affected by environmental research. For example, locational criteria for public housing for older people developed through surveys of managers of such housing (Niebanck, 1965) have been utilized by the United States Department of Housing and Urban Development in judging building proposals. However, research is badly needed to determine how such knowledge diffuses and how it is utilized by various participants in the design process.

ORIENTATION TO SOCIAL AND PSYCHOLOGICAL PROCESSES

Theory development in gerontology has evolved sporadically and has usually been borrowed from classic approaches in psychology or environmental psychology (Barker, 1968; Lewin, 1935; Murray, 1938). For example, Lawton and Nahemow (1973) and Lawton (1982) offered a competence-press model in which adaptive behavior and positive affect are treated as outcomes of environmental demands that are commensurate with the biobehavioral competence of the person. A corollary, the "environmental docility hypothesis," suggests that as competence decreases, behavior becomes increasingly determined by factors outside the person.

A second theoretical framework is that of "person–environment congruence," an environmental process elaborated by Kahana (1982). In her view, psychological well-being is an outcome of congruence between personal needs and perceived environmental dimensions. She presented data showing that these outcomes varied as a function of the particular dimensions of congruence, for example, privacy, order, and affiliation and also as a function of whether incongruence was in the direction of oversupply or undersupply.

Schooler (1982) applied Lazarus's (1966) cognitive theory of stress to explain and elaborate the process of coping with environmental change exhibited by older people. New directions in merging stress theory with environmental process have been offered by Moos and Billings (1981); advances have been made in applying behavioral reinforcement concepts (Baltes & Zerbe, 1976), environmental cognition (Regnier, 1976; Rowles, 1978; Weisman, 1982), environmental dispositions (Windley, 1982), ecological psychology (Windley and Scheidt, 1982), linguistics (DeLong, 1982) and other principles of environment and behavior research.

The modern history of research on environment and behavior, having evolved out of parent disciplines in the social and behavioral sciences, has followed the tradition of those fields by focusing primarily on psychological and social processes and has shown less concern with special places and special populations, such as the elderly, or with environmental design and environmental policy formulation. In the light of this history, it is perhaps no surprise that place-oriented and design-oriented gerontological environmental researchers found relatively little direct knowledge to draw upon from the environment and behavior fields. Yet there are a variety of heavily researched concepts and processes that are applicable to an understanding of the elderly in relationship to the physical environment. (See reviews of this literature by Craik, 1973; Russell & Ward, 1982; Stokols, 1978; and the more than dozen volumes of the *Proceedings of the Environmental Design Research Association*.)

One of the oldest and most thoroughly researched areas in the field deals with the perceptions and cognitions of the large-scale environment of neighborhoods, cities and regions (Downs & Stea, 1973; Moore & Golledge, 1976). Studies of environmental knowledge, locations, way-finding, use of various environmental cues, and the cognition of the environment have been conducted for the past two decades. Volumes of information have been collected about human cognitions, information processing, and perceptions in different environments and for different people. An enormous amount of this work has dealt with children's cognition and perceptual development, whereas very little work has been concerned with the elderly. Exceptions include Regnier's work (1976, 1981; Regnier *et al.*, 1973), which has demonstrated that older people's uses of space is highly conditioned by personal factors such as health, income, sex, and length of residence. Another example of such work focuses on the autobiography of environments and deals with elderly populations (see, for example, Rowles' chapter in the present volume). The promise of work in this field is reflected in the emerging studies of different age groups in respect to cognitions, perceptions, beliefs, and feelings about present and past environments.

Environment and behavior researchers have also been very much concerned with the social processes of privacy, personal space, territoriality, and crowding (Altman, 1975) and other aspects of spatial behavior. For example, the study of personal spacing has long been a popular topic area of the field, with studies examining spatial intrusion and spacing habits and practices of people in different cultures and from different demographic backgrounds. Again, however, one finds relatively little interest in this topic by gerontological researchers and few attempts by environmental researchers to examine systematically the spacing practices of the elderly. As another example, research on crowding was one of the popular topics in the environment and behavior field in the 1970s, although the volume of research in this area has tapered off recently. The bulk of this research has been concerned with reactions to and coping with density by college students in laboratory or dormitory settings. Despite qualitative observations that older people enjoy clustering in the lobbies of housing and institutional environments, one finds almost no studies concerned with reactions to crowding and density among the elderly.

Territoriality, or the identification with and control of objects and places, is another topic of study pertinent to elderly populations. With the exception of occasional ethnographic studies (DeLong, 1970), one finds relatively few examples of gerontologically oriented research on territoriality. However, there is increased concern with place identity and place attachment in the field as a whole, and it is likely that this as yet untapped area will open as a promising one for study in relationship to the elderly. Finally, the regulation of privacy, which deals with variations in accessibility of people to one another, is likely to become an area of primary concern to gerontological research in the coming years. With the development of a spectrum of living arrangements, residential settings, and new communities, the management of privacy among the elderly (indeed for the population as a whole) will become a salient topic.

There are many other issues and concepts in the environment and behavior field that have considerable relevance to the elderly and that bear directly upon design and place, for example, aesthetics, environmental complexity, environmental certainty and uncertainty, and regulation of external stimulation. Matters pertaining to human engineering features of environment also cry out for research in respect to the elderly (see the chapter by Faletti in this volume). Indeed, the general area of human factors, including studies of noise, temperature, lighting, and so forth, is of crucial importance, yet is underresearched in relationship to elderly populations. The list is long, the applications are few, the basic research is lacking. Yet, the potential is great and we look forward to increasing study of fundamental person–environment processes in relationship to the elderly.

To treat the history of research in environment and aging in any greater detail would turn this chapter into a literature review, which is not what it is meant to be. In retrospect, however, the gerontological literature appears to have been rich in place-oriented research that has netted, either incidently or deliberately, a substantial amount of design-relevant knowledge about such topics as dwellings, cluster housing, neighborhoods, communities, transportation, relocation, and institutions. And there seems to be an increasing concern with policy-related issues in respect to various places. On the other hand, the literature has provided only a few general theoretical models applicable to the elderly. Although useful, these models have not yet received sufficient elaboration or generated very much empirical research to test and extend them. Moreover, with some exceptions, environmental gerontological research has not been paced by, contributed to, or influenced by research on fundamental environmental processes. Thus, there are substantial gaps in our understanding of some of the mechanisms that underlie the design and functioning of places.

ORIENTATION TO ENVIRONMENTAL POLICY

There are natural links between place, process, design, and policy orientation, because environmental policy almost always represents an institutional (national, state, local government) decision about the forms that places should assume and the rules that govern their use. Thus the first guiding principle of the Federal Housing Act of 1937 was that adequate housing was the right of all Americans. The implementation of this policy statement has led to many researchable issues. The research as actually performed has dealt variously with mixtures of place, process, and design orientation. In one way, then, policy may be viewed as superordinate to or cutting across the other orientations. However, because policy determination is often the explicit reason for conducting research, it deserves consideration as a separate perspective on environment–behavior relations and the elderly.

A classic example of research that has strongly affected policy also affords an illustration of how a single project can address all four orientations. Rosow (1967) set out to investigate the consequences of age-mixing in urban apartment buildings at a time when the first age-segregated housing designed for older people was being occupied. While the successful examples furnished by private age-segregated retirement communities had led federal policymakers to feel that age segregation was a viable alternative for some older people, no hard data were available at the time. Ideologically there was reason to question whether segregation in any form should be fostered in a national program, in light of the Housing Act's guiding principle as stated above. Rosow inquired about the amount of social interaction associated with different age mixes in a large sample of apartment houses in Cleveland. His findings were very clear: The higher the concentration of age peers in one's building, the greater the level of social contact that an older tenant experienced. Although this finding does not settle every issue regarding age segregation (nor have all such issues by any means been settled even up to the present), it was an extremely influential factor in the growth of the age-segregated housing programs to their current level of nearly one million units. In the process, of course, Rosow produced a great deal of knowledge about apartment housing as a place for older people to live, particularly about the social life in such housing: with whom tenants interacted and how often, their attitudes toward helping, and other forms of social relationships. The fact that Rosow's research began with a strong emphasis on social process (that is, a richly elaborated theory of age stratification) unquestionably sharpened his ability to measure productive constructs and to emerge with such clear-cut findings relevant to place, design, and policy orientations. Finally, the design orientation was served to the extent that the rules relating physical proximity to social interaction on both the microlevel (distance between dwelling units) and the macrolevel (location within a city) became better understood and therefore more easily incorporated into the structure and siting decisions of future housing.

There have been a number of other policy-oriented research projects in person–environment relations, the import of which can be only briefly indicated here. A long series of evaluations on the effects of involuntary relocation of vulnerable older people had led to the general consensus that, at the very least, mass transfer of nursing home patients constituted a risk to the health of residents (the evidence was most recently reviewed by Coffman, 1981). Case-study research on the process by which this knowledge was disseminated and finally implemented in far-reaching national policy and judicial action was documented by Archea and Margulis (1979); this report stands as a model of how such a difficult research goal can be attained.

Finally, a study of a large sample of older homeowners (Rabushka & Jacobs, 1980) revealed that these owner-occupants recognized only about half of the physical defects in their homes that were identified when trained housing inspectors assessed the same houses' physical quality. This instance is particularly interesting in showing that policy-relevant research is, at best, neutral with respect to values and ideology. The authors interpreted their findings to mean that older people knew better than "experts" what pleased them and that therefore no national program for home-maintenance assistance was necessary. A representative of the sponsor of the research (HUD), however, cited these data as support for the establishment of such a program, on the grounds that some older people were selectively prone to ignore problems and defer maintenance to the overall detriment of the quality of the housing stock (Struyk & Soldo, 1980).

A great many other areas require research that is at least partly designed to speak to environmental policy questions, for example:

- What incentives should be established for older people to remain with family rather than go to an institution?
- Should affective attachment to home be a factor in policies relating to such large-scale phenomena as condominium conversions, renewal programs, or regentrification?
- How strongly should alternative housing programs of the kind discussed by Eckert and Murrey in Chapter 4 be pursued?

ORGANIZATION OF THE VOLUME

To a considerable extent the chapters in the present volume reflect the current state and the past history of environmental research in relationship to elderly people. The majority of the chapters focus directly on environmental places that are relevant to the elderly, from small- to large-scale settings. Thus the chapters span the range of places from small-scale levels of kitchens and meal preparation areas, to homes and residences, to congregate and institutional settings, to neighborhoods and towns, to regional communities and to national analyses of housing stock.

In addition to their emphasis on places, a number of chapters examine psychological and social processes in various settings. The processes investigated encompass a broad range, typical of what one would find in the literature of the several fields in the social and behavioral sciences. Social and psychological processes include overt behavioral actions such as daily living activities, task and intellectual performance, social interaction, physical and physiological coping, adaptation, and adjustment. In addition, more subjective psychological processes examined in the various chapters include cognitions and perceptions concerning aspects of the physical environment, social-environmental processes of satisfaction, well-being, place attachment and object attachment, group and community cohesion, and social bonding. Most of the chapters that deal with social and psychological processes do so in the context of specific places, for example, feelings of satisfaction and place attachment in small rural towns or in institutional settings. However, the chapters by Golant and Carp and Carp focus largely on social processes in a generic sense, independent of particular or specific settings. In the same way, the single chapter that directly addresses policy issues, by Newman, Zais, and Struyk, necessarily deals with home environments and places of the elderly, but its primary focus is on demographic features and economic conditions of the elderly in the United States, the quality and availability of housing, and so forth in relationship to issues of national policy. Although this chapter is the only one that deals directly with policy matters as its central focus, one can discern policy implications for the design of homes, neighborhoods, and communities in almost all of the chapters. In the same way, although none of the chapters deals primarily with design issues as a central theme, several chapters have both direct and indirect implications for environmental design.

The following three chapters of the volume address broad-ranging policy or policy/place questions. In Chapter 2, Newman *et al.* examine a number of strategic issues regarding housing environments in relationship to the demographic characteristics of the elderly, their economic and health status, housing costs, and current governmental policies in the United States. From this broad ranging strategic level, Marans, Hunt, and Vakalo (Chapter 3) propose a taxonomy and description of different types of retirement communities and residential arrangements, in terms of scale, population characteristics, services, financial sponsorship, and the like. In Chapter 4, Eckert and Murrey examine a range of alternative housing forms for the elderly such as communes and cooperatives, mobile homes, condominium and rental apartments, hotels and single room occupancy arrangements. In many respects, these three chapters outline the parameters of present living environments for the elderly, demographics of the elderly population, and their financial and health circumstances. As such, they point directly and indirectly to policy, place, and process issues.

The next three chapters, by Rowles (Chapter 5), Moos and Lemke (Chapter 6), and Faletti (Chapter 7), similarly emphasize places and settings but also address directly questions of psychological and social processes in relationship to places. On the widest scale, Rowles examines a variety of psychological and social processes of the rural elderly in their towns and homes. He considers the cognitions and perceptions of the rural elderly, their personal and social activities, psychological attachments, and feelings of well-being in relationship to their town, neighborhood, and homes. Moos and Lemke offer a conceptual framework and measuring instruments to assess the linkage of architectural and design features of residential environments, especially congregate housing arrangements, in relation to a variety of psychological qualities of residents and their psychological and behavioral adaptation and coping. At the smallest scale of analysis, Faletti describes human factors research in relationship to kitchen and meal preparation places. In his chapter Faletti summarizes fine-grained analyses of performance and sensory and perceptual skill requirements in selected aspects of the meal preparation process.

The last two chapters of the volume place their primary emphasis on the development of theoretical models of psychological and social processes. Golant (Chapter 8) examines the relationship of behavioral and social activities of the elderly to a variety of experiential outcomes, including attachment, familiarity, and satisfaction. In Chapter 9, Carp and Carp review existing theoretical models of the relations of the elderly to the physical environment and propose a comprehensive and broad-ranging model based on their prior and ongoing work.

The field of environmental gerontology has been a productive and growing one for two decades. The chapters in this volume summarize some of the ongoing work that we consider to have particular promise. The various contributions also point to substantial gaps in the literature that require attention. It is to the further development of environments for the elderly as a field of investigation, and to the enhancement and creation of appropriate and high-quality environments for older people, that the present volume is dedicated.

REFERENCES

Altman, I. Some perspectives on the study of man–environment phenomena. *Representative Research in Social Psychology*, 1973, *4*, 109–126.

Altman, I. *The environment and social behavior.* Monterey, Calif.: Brooks/Cole, 1975 (New York: Irvington, 1982).

Archea, J., & Margulis, S. T. Environmental research inputs to policy and design programs. In T. O. Byerts, S. C. Howell, & L. A. Pastalan (Eds.), *The environmental context of aging.* New York: Garland STPM Press, 1979, 217–228.

Baltes, M. M., & Zerbe, M. B. Independence training in nursing home residents. *Gerontologist*, 1976, *16*, 428–432.

Barker, R. G. *Ecological psychology.* Stanford, Calif.: Stanford University Press, 1968.

Carp, F. M. *A future for the aged.* Austin, Tex.: University of Texas Press, 1966.

Carp, F. M. Urban life-style and life-cycle factors. In M. P. Lawton, R. J. Newcomer, & T. O. Byerts (Eds.), *Community planning for an aging society.* Stroudsburg, Pa.: Dowden, Hutchinson & Ross, 1976, pp. 19–40.

Coffman, T. L. Relocation and survival of institutionalized aged: A re-examination of the evidence. *Gerontologist,* 1981, *21,* 483–500.

Craik, K. Environmental psychology. *Annual Review of Psychology,* 1973, *24,* 403–422.

Davidson, H. H., & Kruglov, L. Personality characteristics of the institutionalized aged. *Journal of Consulting Psychology,* 1952, *16,* 5–12.

DeLong, A. J. The microspatial structure of the older person. In L. A. Pastalan & D. H. Carson (Eds.), *Spatial behavior of older people.* Ann Arbor, Mich.: University of Michigan Press, 1970, pp. 68–87.

DeLong, A. J. Synthesis and synergy: Developing models in man–environment relations. In M. P. Lawton, P. G. Windley, & T. O. Byerts (Eds.), *Aging and the environment: Theoretical approaches.* New York: Springer, 1982, pp. 19–32.

Downs, R. M., & Stea, D. *Image and environment.* Chicago: Aldine, 1973.

Fox, C. The intelligence of old indigent persons residing within and without a public home for the aged. *American Journal of Psychology,* 1950, *63,* 110–112.

Green, I., Fedewa, B. E., Johnston, C. A., Jackson, W. M., & Deardorff, H. L. *Housing for the elderly: The development and design process.* New York: Van Nostrand, 1975.

Howell, S. C. *Designing for aging: Patterns of use.* Cambridge, Mass.: MIT Press, 1980.

Kahana, E. A congruence model of person–environment interaction. In M. P. Lawton, P. G. Windley, & T. O. Byerts (Eds.), *Aging and the environment: Theoretical approaches.* New York: Springer, 1982, pp. 97–121.

Kleemeier, R. W. Behavior and the organization of the bodily and the external environment. In J. E. Birren (Ed.), *Handbook of aging and the individual.* Chicago: University of Chicago Press, 1959, pp. 400–451.

Koncelik, J. *Designing the open nursing home.* Stroudsburg, Pa.: Dowden, Hutchinson & Ross, 1976.

Koncelik, J. A. *Aging and the product environment.* Stroudsburg, Pa.: Dowden, Hutchinson & Ross, 1982.

Lawton, M. P. *Planning and managing housing for the elderly.* New York: Wiley-Interscience, 1975.

Lawton, M. P. Competence, environmental press, and the adaptation of older people. In M. P. Lawton, P. G. Windley, & T. O. Byerts (Eds.), *Aging and the environment: Theoretical approaches.* New York: Springer, 1982, pp. 33–59.

Lawton, M. P., & Nahemow, L. Ecology and the aging process. In C. Eisdorfer & M. P. Lawton (Eds.), *Psychology of adult development and aging.* Washington, D.C.: American Psychological Association, 1973, pp. 619–674.

Lawton, M. P., & Nahemow, L. Social science methods for evaluating the quality of housing for the elderly. *Journal of Architectural Research,* 1979, *7,* 5–11.

Lazarus, R. S. *Psychological stress and the coping process.* New York: McGraw-Hill, 1966.

Lewin, K. *Dynamic theory of personality.* New York: McGraw-Hill, 1935.

Liebowitz, B., Lawton, M. P., & Waldman, A. A prosthetically designed nursing home. *American Institute of Architects Journal,* 1979, *68,* 59–61.

Moore, G. T., & Golledge, R. G. (Eds.), *Environmental knowing.* Stroudsburg, Pa.: Dowden, Hutchinson & Ross, 1976.

Moos, R. H., & Billings, A. G. Conceptualizing and measuring coping resources and processes. In L. Goldberger & S. Breznitz (Eds.), *Handbook of stress: Theoretical and clinical aspects.* New York: Macmillan, 1981, pp. 212–230.

Murray, H. A. *Explorations in personality.* New York: Oxford, 1938.

Niebanck, P. *The elderly in older urban areas.* Philadelphia: University of Pennsylvania Institute for Environmental Studies, 1965.

Peterson, J. A., & Larson, A. Social-psychological factors in selecting retirement housing. In F. M. Carp (Ed.), *Patterns of living and housing of middle-aged and older people.* Washington, D. C.: U.S. Government Printing Office, undated.

Rabushka, A., & Jacobs, B. *Old folks at home.* New York: Free Press, 1980.

Regnier, V. A. Neighborhoods as service systems. In M. P. Lawton, R. J. Newcomer, and T. O. Byerts (Eds.), *Community planning for an aging society.* Stroudsburg, Pa.: Dowden, Hutchinson & Ross, 1976, pp. 240–259.

Regnier, V. Neighborhood images and use. In M. P. Lawton and S. L. Hoover (Eds.), *Community housing choices for older Americans.* New York: Springer, 1981, pp. 180–197.

Regnier, V. A., Eribes, R. A., & Hansen, W. *Cognitive mapping as a concept for establishing neighborhood service delivery locations for older people.* Proceedings of the eighth annual Association for Computing Machinery symposium, New York, 1973.

Rosenberg, G. S. *The worker grows old.* San Francisco: Jossey-Bass, 1970.

Rosow, I. *Social integration of the aged.* New York: Free Press, 1967.

Ross, J. K. *Old people, new lives: Community creation in a retirement residence.* Chicago: University of Chicago Press, 1977.

Rowles, G. D. *Prisoners of space?* Boulder, Colo.: Westview Press, 1978.

Russell, J., & Ward, L. Environmental psychology. *Annual Review of Psychology,* 1982, *33,* 651–688.

Schooler, K. K. Response of the elderly to environment: A stress-theoretic perspective. In M. P. Lawton, P. G. Windley, & T. O. Byerts (Eds.), *Aging and environment: Theoretical approaches.* New York: Springer, 1982, pp. 80–96.

Stokols, D. Environmental psychology. *Annual Review of Psychology,* 1978, *29,* 253–295.

Struyk, R. J., & Soldo, B. J. *Improving the elderly's housing.* Cambridge, Mass.: Ballinger, 1980.

Townsend, P. *The last refuge.* London: Routledge & Kegan Paul, 1964.

Weisman, J. Developing man–environment models. In M. P. Lawton, P. G. Windley, & T. O. Byerts (Eds.), *Aging and the environment: Theoretical approaches.* New York: Springer, 1982, pp. 69–79.

Windley, P. G. Environmental dispositions: A theoretical and methodological alternative. In M. P. Lawton, P. G. Windley, and T. O. Byerts (Eds.), *Aging and the environment: Theoretical approaches.* New York: Springer, 1982, pp. 60–68.

Windley, P. G., & Scheidt, R. J. An ecological model of mental health among small-town elderly. *Journal of Gerontology,* 1982, *37,* 235–242.

Zeisel, J., Epp, G., & Demos, S. *Low-rise housing for older people: Behavioral criteria for design.* Washington, D. C.: Office of Policy Development and Research, U.S. Department of Housing and Urban Development, 1978.

Zeisel, J. *Inquiry by design: Tools for environment—behavior research.* Monterey, Calif.: Brooks/Cole, 1981.

2

Housing Older America

SANDRA J. NEWMAN, JAMES ZAIS, AND RAYMOND STRUYK

INTRODUCTION

An underlying goal of government involvement in the housing sector is to promote the well-being of the population. This goal, which became a legislative mandate with the call for "a decent, safe, and sanitary dwelling for every American" in the 1937 Housing Act, is based on the presumption that housing conditions have significant effects on the health and welfare of the citizenry. The implied logic of this relationship is that if deleterious conditions are identified, government programs can be developed to eliminate or counteract them. Efforts to achieve this goal have taken many forms. Two prominent examples are construction and rehabilitation programs to improve housing conditions and rent subsidy programs that reduce the burden of housing costs for the poor.

The elderly constitute one subgroup that has received special attention from government housing programs. Part of the rationale for special housing assistance programs for the elderly rests on two factors: differences in housing needs of older as opposed to younger households and the disproportionate prevalence of housing problems among the elderly. The advent of several major changes that accompany aging—retirement, reduced income, widowhood, and health problems—makes it legitimate to look at the housing situation of the elderly as a group and

SANDRA J. NEWMAN • Public Policy Program, The Johns Hopkins University, Baltimore, Maryland 21218. JAMES ZAIS and RAYMOND STRUYK • The Urban Institute, Washington, D.C. 20037.

also provides some evidence that their housing needs are likely to be distinct from those of other households.

Yet, for the elderly as for other groups, the transition between identifying needs and developing effective programs to address them is not smooth. Conceptually, for example, it is difficult to convert indicators of need into standards of what is desirable or undesirable, acceptable or unacceptable (Baer, 1976). Empirical measurement of needs also presents problems. But the ultimate obstacle is that despite vast improvements in our knowledge about the elderly and their housing, the linkages between household characteristics, housing attributes, and well-being are not completely understood.

These dilemmas are central to housing policy research. They are, therefore, reflected throughout this chapter, which reviews the housing situation of the elderly and evaluates government efforts to improve it.

Since housing needs are determined by the characteristics of the household, we begin by examining these attributes and how they shape housing needs. This discussion also presents basic information on the elderly's housing and neighborhood conditions and suggests some directions for future research. The third section reviews current housing programs for the elderly and evaluates them in light of what we know about the elderly's housing needs and problems. The final section speculates about changes in United States housing policy and the likely effects of these proposed shifts on the elderly.

HOUSING NEEDS, CONDITIONS, AND PROBLEMS OF THE ELDERLY

POPULATION CHANGE

Changes in the age structure of the population have been, and will continue to be, dramatic over this century. While in 1900 only 4% of the population was over 65, this proportion has risen to slightly more than 11% today, or 25.5 million people. Diseases such as diphtheria and tuberculosis that once killed many people before they passed through middle age have been controlled; more and more people survive into their 60s and 70s. The most dramatic increase in the population of older Americans has been among the very old. Over the last two decades, the population 85 and older has doubled. By 2010, those 75 and over (the "old-old") may constitute more than 40% of the elderly population. By the same year, when the generation of the postwar baby boom reaches retirement age, one set of census estimates shows that almost a quarter of the population will be 55 and over. By the simple fact of demographic change, old age has become a major preoccupation (Cherry & Cherry, 1974).

This information on population change contains two important implications for housing. One is that the proportion of aggregate housing consumption in the nation accounted for by the elderly will steadily increase. The other is that the nature of housing consumption will change, since it is among the very old—the group that is growing the fastest—that serious problems of aging are concentrated: low incomes and accumulations of multiple health impairments.

HOUSEHOLD STATUS

Whether an older individual lives with others or lives alone also affects housing needs. By forestalling or even eliminating the need for institutional care, living with others may affect aggregate housing demand. Living with others may also influence the nature of the housing bundle that can adequately fulfill the older person's needs; the importance of special features, dwelling layout, service availability, and the like may be less vital than if an older person is in need of care and lives alone.

The best estimates on the current proportion of single versus multiple person households headed by elderly persons and how this proportion has changed over time can be found in the Annual Housing Survey. Over the decade of the 1970s, the proportion of elderly-headed households that included more than one member declined from 60% to 55% (U.S. Bureau of the Census, 1981a). This increase in the number of older people living alone is even sharper if we examine the household sizes of all elderly persons—both those who head their own households and those who live in households where the head is younger than 65 (primarily those living with their adult children). Between 1971 and 1978, the proportion of the population 65 years and over living alone increased from 26% to more than 30% (U.S. Bureau of the Census, 1971, 1979a). The decline in multiple-person households may become even more pronounced in the future as other demographic and social trends come into play: smaller family sizes, higher rates of divorce, and greater geographic mobility.

At least in the short run, the fact that the increase in single-person households is due almost entirely to an increase in the proportion of women living alone may be significant for housing policy.[1] On average, current cohorts of late middle-aged and older women may be not so well

---

[1]That is, elderly males are about as likely to live alone or with others as they have been for the last several decades.

TABLE 1

SEX, HOUSING TENURE, AND HOUSEHOLD SIZE OF HOUSEHOLDS WITH HEAD 65
YEARS AND OVER, 1970 AND 1979[a]

	1970	1979
Female head of household:		
Owns, lives with other	17.3	14.4
Owns, lives alone	41.6	47.9
Rents, lives with others	7.4	5.4
Rents, lives alone	33.7	32.3
	100.0	100.0
Male head of household:		
Owns, lives with others	65.0	69.7
Owns, lives alone	8.4	9.4
Rents, lives with others	18.5	13.1
Rents, lives alone	8.2	7.8
	100.1	100.0

[a]Source: U.S. Bureau of the Census, 1981a. Figures given are in percentages, which do not always add
to 100 due to rounding.

educated and less interested and experienced in housing repair and
upkeep compared to men. They may also be more apprehensive about
contracting with others for services. Home maintenance and repair help
targeted to elderly female-headed households may, therefore, be
appropriate.

Also significant is the relationship between household size, sex of
household head, and housing tenure. Table 1 shows that the most substantial shift over the decade has been toward a larger proportion of
elderly women who live alone in their owned homes. Overall, the
largest proportion of older women in both 1970 and 1979 lived with their
husbands in their owned homes. But regardless of whether married
women are included or excluded from the denominator in these calculations, the only significant trend over the decade remains the increase in
female owners living alone (19% to 24%).

Table 2 presents data on housing tenure status for successive older-
age cohorts. The dramatic differences in proportions of elderly owners
and renters regardless of age make housing tenure a very important
characteristic by which to subgroup the elderly. There appears to be a
shift from owning to renting as age increases.[2] Since the fraction of older
renters who are either heads of families or are males living alone de-

[2]Assuming cohort and period effects are insignificant.

TABLE 2
HOUSING TENURE, SEX, AND HOUSEHOLD SIZE OF HOUSEHOLDS WITH HEAD 55
YEARS AND OVER, BY AGE GROUPS[a]

	Age groups		
	55–64	65–74	75+
Tenure			
Owner	77.6	73.9	69.2
Renter	22.4	26.1	30.8
Total	100.0	100.0	100.0
Owners			
In families	83.2	67.0	52.5
Living alone:[b]			
Males	4.3	6.1	10.8
Females	12.5	26.9	37.0
Total	100.0	100.0	100.0
Renters			
In families	52.5	37.0	30.0
Living alone:			
Males	17.5	15.7	13.6
Females	30.0	47.3	56.4
Total	100.0	100.0	100.0

[a]Source: U.S. Bureau of the Census, 1979b. Figures are in percentages.
[b]This category corresponds to the census category "primary individuals" which includes both those living alone and those living with nonrelatives. The former, however, comprise more than 96% of the category.

clines with aging, the increase in renters may be associated with the large number of women living alone, primarily widows, who shift to rental units as they age (Zais, Struyk, & Thibodeau, 1982). This shift is large enough so that at the oldest ages, the majority of all renters live alone. For homeowners, although the trend is in the same direction, the majority of the "old-old" still live in families.

INCOME AND POVERTY STATUS

Income status is a prime determinant of housing consumption not just for the elderly but for all individuals. Limited finances restrict options; for the elderly, this may mean not only an inability to purchase basic necessities but also to make necessary adjustments in housing and living arrangements in response to major life changes in older age (Struyk & Soldo, 1980).

But in the case of the elderly, examining only current income may be particularly misleading. Major purchases, including purchasing a home, have already been made. This may mean that postretirement income needs are not as great as they were before retirement. It also suggests that many elderly have accumulated a stock of assets—home equity—that could be drawn on if necessary.

A simple distribution of all older persons by income category shows that more than half of all elderly individuals had incomes below $5,000 in 1979 (U.S. Bureau of the Census, 1981b). Yet, the majority of even the very low income elderly-headed households own their homes, a fact that distinguishes them dramatically from other households (Zais et al., 1982).

Nevertheless, among both the elderly and the nonelderly, and for both blacks and whites, homeowners have higher incomes than renters. As shown in Table 3, this disparity is associated with household size and the sex of the household head: families have higher incomes than persons living alone, and female heads of households are persistently the worst off of both household groups.[3] Thus the group that appears to be growing the most over time (i.e., female owners) and the group that increases substantially over the life cycle (i.e., female renters) also have the highest concentrations of the lowest income elderly-headed households.

Information on the poverty status of elderly-headed households reinforces the distinctions in income levels of tenure, family status, and sex subgroups. As shown in Table 4, elderly renters are twice as likely to fall below the poverty line as are owners. But this should not be interpreted to mean that elderly owners are well-off: other census data show that families headed by elderly persons constitute the largest proportion of all families in owned homes whose income falls below the poverty level (Newman, 1981a). Living in a family cuts the proportion below poverty by more than a factor of two for both owners and renters. Female heads of households, again, emerge with the highest rates of poverty.

Any discussion of the income and poverty status of the elderly is incomplete without at least brief mention of two longstanding controversies. First, only money income is included in the calculations of the official poverty level. Noncash benefits from food stamps, Medicaid, public housing, and the like are not considered. Thus, the "true" incidence of poverty among the elderly may be overestimated. Furthermore, if the elderly receive a disproportionate share of noncash benefits relative to the nonelderly, then the proportion of the poverty population

[3]Adjustments for family size affect the numbers but not the conclusions.

TABLE 3
1979 MEDIAN INCOME (IN DOLLARS) BY TENURE, SEX, AND HOUSEHOLD TYPE
(HOUSEHOLDS WITH HEAD 65 YEARS OR OVER)[a]

Household type	Owners	Renters
Households of 2 or more persons		
Husband–wife families	11,900	9,200
Other male head	12,200	6,700
Other female head	9,600	7,200
One-person households		
Male	6,600	5,400
Female	5,700	5,100

[a]Source: U.S. Bureau of the Census, 1981c.

that they represent under the current definition may actually be inappropriately high (Fendler & Orshansky, 1980). Even if the argument for including noncash income is convincing, the difficulty of valuing many of these benefits remains. In addition, since younger people get many significant benefits that do not apply to most elderly (such as employer-paid health insurance premiums and interest deductions on home mortgages), any overstatement of the poverty rate may apply with greater force to younger age groups.

Second, the official poverty figures are based on total family income. Thus, in calculating the poverty rates for older people who live with their adult children, the older person's income is combined with

TABLE 4
1979 POVERTY STATUS BY TENURE, FAMILY STATUS AND SEX
(HOUSEHOLDS WITH HEAD 65 YEARS OR OVER)[a]

	Owners	Renters
Percentage below poverty level:		
Total	14.7[b]	28.0[b]
	(N = 11965)	(N = 4184)
In families	8.0	14.7
Not in families		
Males	19.5	31.7
Females	27.1	35.2
Living alone	25.5	34.3

[a]Source: Calculated from U.S. Bureau of the Census, 1981d.
[b]Corresponding percentage for the nonelderly are 6.1 for owners and 19.3 for renters.

the total income of the child's family. If only the cash income of the older person is counted while the income of others living in the same household is not, then the fraction of the elderly who are poor rises from 14% to 21% (Orshansky, 1979).

HEALTH LIMITATIONS

Besides being affected by status and income, the housing situation of the elderly is significantly influenced by the greater incidence of health limitations in this group. According to the 1980 National Health Interview Survey, roughly 45% of the noninstitutional population 65 and older had a health limitation that restricted activities (U.S. Public Health Service, 1981). National panel data show that individuals who were between 65 and 74 years of age in 1980 reported, on average, twice as many health limitations in that year as they had reported a decade earlier (Newman, 1981a). By 1980, more than half of those 75 years or older reported that health problems limited the kind or amount of activity they could perform. Since more than half of this group lives alone, there is a basis for concern about how the needs of many of these individuals are being met. These needs include not only health and personal care but also the maintenance and repair of the housing unit and even its day-to-day upkeep. For homeowners, the problem may be especially serious: health problems may limit not only the work they would otherwise do for themselves but also their willingness or ability to contract with others to work for them.

RESIDENTIAL MOBILITY

The elderly comprise one of the most immobile segments of the population. As shown in Table 5, homeowners 65 years of age and older were four times less likely to change residences between 1979 and 1980 than either younger homeowners or elderly renters. Mobility rates for elderly renters were nearly three times lower than for nonelderly renters. Among owners who do move, about 40% shift to rental units but only 15% of renters shift to homeownership. Thus uneven flows have the effect of increasing the size of the elderly renter population, a trend that was noted earlier.

Unlike other groups in the population, the lower incidence of residential mobility among the elderly does not seem to reflect a disproportionate fraction of desired moves that were prevented by circumstances beyond one's control: as shown in Table 6, when a nationally representative sample of elderly homeowners was asked whether they desired to

TABLE 5
INCIDENCE OF RESIDENTIAL MOBILITY, BY AGE AND HOUSING TENURE[a]

	Percentage that moved between		
	1979–1980	1978–1980	1975–1980
Less than 65 years of age			
Owners	12.1	21.9	41.3
Renters	45.9	62.6	79.2
65–74 years of age			
Owners	3.5	6.6	17.6
Renters	15.1	25.8	44.9
75 years of age or older			
Owners	3.7	6.2	12.6
Renters	17.0	27.2	57.7

[a]Source: Panel Study of Income Dynamics, 1980 Merged Individual Tape, Survey Research Center, The University of Michigan. Includes individuals who were heads of households or spouses of heads of households. For a description of the survey, see M. Hill *et al.* (1981).

move, only about half as many elderly as nonelderly in each tenure class answered "yes."

There are three main reasons for concern about the fact that the elderly rarely move. First, we know that as people age they are likely to experience a number of important changes that can affect their well-

TABLE 6
DESIRE TO MOVE, BY AGE AND HOUSING TENURE[a]

	Fraction desiring to move (year)	
	1971	1978
Less than 65 years of age		
Owners	20.0	22.6
Renters	49.1	50.2
65–74 years of age		
Owners	12.2	11.7
Renters	16.6	18.5
75 years of age or older		
Owners	9.7	11.8
Renters	17.1	16.3

[a]Source: 1971 and 1978 National Quality of Life in America Studies, Survey Research Center, The University of Michigan.

being. Comparable major changes at younger ages often precipitate decisions to move. Since the elderly do not adjust to often dramatic life changes by moving, the questions are: What happens to them? Do their residences become increasingly ill-suited to their needs? Do they take some actions to make their housing units more suitable?

Second, the serious imbalance between housing demand and supply in many areas across the country has prompted some to argue for a government policy encouraging residential moves by those elderly persons who live in large single-family homes. The proponents of this view argue that such moves would increase the supply of suitable housing from the existing stock for younger and larger families.

Third, few old people own any assets of greater value than their homes (Storey, 1981). Liquidating an owned home could pull a substantial proportion of the elderly out of poverty and provide financial support for their basic needs (Juster, 1981).

The most consistent result from the large body of empirical research on residential mobility is the inverse relationship between age and mobility (Butler, Chapin, Hemmens, Kaiser, Stegman, & Weiss, 1969; Kain & Quigley, 1975; Morrison, 1967; VanArsdol, Sabagh, & Butler, 1968). This result has been interpreted in several ways: (1) strong psychic attachment to the current residence as a result of spatial and social relationships built over over many years (Morrison, 1967; Tomassen, 1979; VanArsdol, *et al.*, 1968); (2) lack of knowledge concerning housing alternatives or inability to search for new housing due to poor health or no transportation (Beyer & Nierstrasz, 1967); (3) the absence of suitable housing alternatives within the search space defined by the household (Speare, Goldstein, & Frey, 1974); (4) incorrect assessment of the costs of current housing due to undervaluation of the opportunity costs (i.e., unused or underused portion of the house equity) (Carliner, 1973). Even though several studies have focused on the residential mobility of the elderly (Golant, 1972; Goldscheider, VanArsdol, & Sabagh, 1966; Lawton, Kleban, & Carlson, 1973), no compelling evidence for any of these hypotheses has been set forth. Part of the problem has been the lack of good data. Data from national samples of the general population tend to contain insufficient numbers of observations of elderly households and particularly of those who move. On the other hand, findings from studies of the elderly in particular locales may not be generalizable.

HOUSING COSTS

Consistent with the high rates of poverty among the elderly is the relatively high fraction of income that many elderly devote to housing costs. The small aggregate difference between the elderly and nonelderly in this ratio is not particularly meaningful since more than half of elderly heads of households are owners who have paid off their mortgages. (Among the nonelderly, almost an equal proportion—41% versus 44%—rent or own with mortgage debt.) Large expense burdens are, therefore, concentrated among the roughly one-third who rent and the 10% who still hold a mortgage.

The most recent tabulations documenting these ratios were presented by Struyk and Soldo (1980) and are reproduced, in part, in Table 7. According to the current standard used by the Department of Housing and Urban Development to determine what a household "needs" for housing assistance—30% or more of income devoted to housing—more than 48% of elderly renters and more than 38% of elderly owners with mortgages have "excessive" housing cost burdens. These rates are several times as high as those for the corresponding groups of nonelderly. The fact that those who live alone are especially likely to be heavily burdened reflects the higher rates of poverty among this group. It should also be remembered that the largest fraction of elderly living alone are females and that the proportion of single-person households is growing over time.

TABLE 7

1976 HOUSING EXPENSE BURDENS, BY TENURE AND HOUSEHOLD TYPE[a]

Tenure and household type	Percentage of income to housing:	
	.30 or less	.31 or greater
Renters		
Nonelderly	71	29
Elderly	52	48
Husband–wife	61	39
Single person	47	53
Other	58	42
Owner with mortgage		
Nonelderly	87	13
Elderly	61	39
Husband–wife	69	31
Single person	40	60
Other	58	42
Owner without mortgage		
Nonelderly	94	6
Elderly	86	14
Husband–wife	93	7
Single person	77	23
Other	88	12

[a]Source: 1976 Annual Housing Survey tabulations by Struyk and Soldo, 1981, Tables 3–11.

Other data indicate that as the pre-old age cohort enters older age, its housing cost to income ratio rises. Those who were 65 to 74 in 1980 had housing cost to income ratios that were between 6 and 12 percentage points higher than they had been a decade earlier. These increases continue, although they are less sharp, after age 75 (Newman, 1981a). A critical question is whether, in order to remain in their homes, these households cut back on vital nonhousing consumption to the point where their health and well-being is threatened (Reschovsky, 1980).

The actual housing expenditure levels of the elderly indicate that single-person households are, again, the most disadvantaged. According to Struyk and Soldo (1980), nearly half of all older renters living alone spent only $100 or less per month for rent in 1976. Since this is also the group with high housing cost to income ratios, this low absolute amount means that many of these households are near or below the poverty level. For the remainder, these low housing costs probably translate into low housing quality.

Estimates of the market value of owned homes as provided by the owners themselves can also be used as proxies for quality. These data are subject to more measurement error than rents, however, since the owner may be out of touch with the market—a characteristic that may be especially apt for the many older owners who have lived in the same home for many years. Bearing this in mind, such respondent reports during the 1970s indicated that the elderly appear to own homes with lower market values than younger owners (U.S. Bureau of the Census, 1981a; Baer, 1976). Moreover, among elderly owners, properties owned free and clear carry lower values than those that are still mortgaged, although this relationship is stronger for the young-old than the old-old (Newman, 1981a). Although the increases in house value that characterized the last decade also affected the homes of the elderly, the increase appears to be less dramatic: between 1976 and 1978, for example, homeowners 45 to 64 years of age experienced a 44% increase in average house value; for those 65 or older, the increase was 32%. Whether reporting error contributed to this discrepancy is not known.

The value of the homes owned by the elderly is also important for what it tells us about the amount of wealth that could be drawn upon to cover operating expenses on the home. The only adequate data to address this question apply to elderly owners without mortgage debt. While the housing assets of this group as a whole are substantial, with a 1980 median value of more than $35,000, it is considerably lower among owners with housing problems—the group whose upkeep needs are the greatest (Mayer & Lee, 1980).

Lower house values, however, are not associated with lower ratios of property taxes to incomes. In 1978, the average gross property tax as a percentage of family income was 3.7%; the corresponding figures for homeowners 65 to 74 years of age and those 75 and older were 4.4% and 5.1%, respectively (Morgan, Ponza, & Imbruglia, 1981). Between 1976 and 1978, average property taxes increased for homeowners 65 and older, but their average incomes fell. The result was a 20% increase in the ratio of average property tax to income.

Utility costs are particularly high for the very old homeowner not only in terms of the cost burden they represent relative to income but also compared to the utility costs paid by younger age groups. There may be many reasons why this is so—the tendency for the very old to live in older houses that may not be well insulated or that may have old and inefficient heating systems, for example. In fact, according to the Annual Housing Survey, heating deficiencies are among the housing problems most frequently reported by elderly respondents. They are also less likely than other age groups to have central heating systems.

As with housing cost to income ratios, utility costs for owners (i.e., heat, electricity, and water charges) appear to increase with aging at the latter stages of the life cycle. With an adjustment for inflation over the decade 1970–1980, owners who were 65 to 74 years of age in 1980 experienced nearly a $200 increase in utility costs over what they paid in 1970; those 75 years of age or older in 1980 experienced increases of a similar magnitude over the same time period (Newman, 1981a). This may suggest that home energy conservation measures are not being adopted by the elderly or that their homes are not as well suited to such adjustments.

HOUSING CONDITIONS

Like the definition of poverty adopted more than 10 years ago by the federal government as the basis for its poverty estimates and "drawing criticism ever since," alternative definitions of *deficient, flawed* or *substandard* housing have also generated considerable controversy (Fendler & Orshansky, 1980). The issue is not just academic: If housing assistance programs consider current housing condition in their determination of who is eligible for aid, assistance to a particular household may hinge on the housing standard that is used. A recent report by HUD on the housing adequacy of the elderly demonstrates this point clearly (U.S. Department of Housing and Urban Development, 1979). Sixteen variables measuring physical housing characteristics such as plumbing, electrical, and heating were grouped into eight sets of defects. This approach yielded a rate of flawed housing occupied by elderly households that is roughly the same as that for all occupied housing. Yet, if just the simple incidence each of these same 16 defects is calculated for housing occupied by older and younger households, the elderly have a higher incidence of nearly all of these defects (Newman, 1981a).

Part of the conceptual problem in housing research is the inherent complexity of the underlying concepts. Much of this complexity arises because housing denotes not only shelter but also a range of housing services and a social and environmental setting. Thus a basic question is which components of the "housing bundle" should be measured?

Almost regardless of which components are measured, however, there is also the second problem of selecting empirical indicators that best represent each component. Key constructs such as "housing adequacy" and "housing quality," for example, are not based on completely explicit criteria and have no precise, quantifiable definitions of where "bad" ends and "good" begins. A third conceptual issue is whether housing constructs are more accurately assessed through as objective a set of measures or attributes as possible or through subjective reports about those attributes.

Measurement problems would remain even if there were unanimous agreement on the concepts and attributes to be measured. The seemingly most objectively measurable attributes or observable facts involve some estimation or judgment by either respondent or interviewer (Newman, 1981b).

Information on the general characteristics of the housing occupied by elderly-headed households provides a good basis for a discussion of housing quality regardless of the definition that is chosen. If the housing units occupied by the elderly and the nonelderly are largely similar, any difference in housing quality is likely to be more directly associated with aging or its correlates rather than determined simply by the self-selection of older persons into housing units that are dissimilar from those of younger households.

For owners, the most dramatic difference is in length of residence: nearly 60% of elderly owners have lived in the same house for about 20 years or longer; the comparable fraction for nonelderly owners is 20%. This attribute is consistent with another distinctive characteristic of the elderly—their low rates of residential mobility—that was discussed earlier. This characteristic is very significant since it suggests that for many older people housing adjustments undertaken in response to changes in life circumstances must occur in place, if they occur at all.

The housing units occupied by elderly owners are also considerably older than those of younger owners. While age of house is far from a perfect correlate of quality, extenuating circumstances that are more prevalent among the elderly (such as health limitations, female heads of households living alone, and very low disposable incomes) may mean that maintenance and repair needs that are more likely to arise in older homes are also less likely to receive adequate attention.

The housing characteristics of elderly renters are largely similar to those of younger renters. One interesting difference is that the elderly are less likely to rent single-family homes, perhaps because of the greater maintenance burdens of such units (Struyk & Soldo, 1980).

Since a single generally accepted standard of physical adequacy is not available, we will compare the housing conditions of elderly and nonelderly occupied units along several indicators that measure the flow of services provided by a dwelling (Struyk & Soldo, 1980). These indicators also have good external validity since they are among the criteria that are actually used by the nation's largest housing assistance program, the Section 8 Housing Assistance Payment Program. These six indicators are:

- *Plumbing:* Either unit lacks complete plumbing facilities or household must share their use.
- *Kitchen:* Either unit lacks a complete kitchen or household must share its use.
- *Sewage:* One or more of the following three services was unavailable or completely unusable for six or more hours at least three times during the past 90 days: (1) running water, (2) sewage system, (3) toilet.
- *Heat:* The heating system was completely unusable for six or more hours at least three times during the past winter.
- *Maintenance:* Two or more of the following four conditions exist: (1) leaking roof, (2) substantial cracks or holes in walls and ceiling, (3) holes in floor, (4) broken plaster or peeling paint in areas larger than one square foot.
- *Public Halls:* The unit is in a building with public hallways and stairs, and two or more of the following three conditions exists: (1) missing light fixtures, (2) stair railings are missing or poorly attached, (3) missing, loose, or broken steps.

Regardless of tenure, the elderly have rates of plumbing and kitchen inadequacies that are twice as high as those of the nonelderly. For the other indicators, the differences are generally insignificant.

Among the elderly, there is little difference between the young-old and the old-old, but differences by household type can be observed: husband–wife families, whether owner or renter, are less likely to report the presence of most of these deficiencies compared to other house-holds. The only sociodemographic characteristics that are consistently associated with higher rates of housing problems for all six indicators are poverty status and race.

Recently, we have taken a conceptually distinct approach to es-timating the housing adequacy of the elderly. Since some dwellings may have only temporary inadequacies that are repaired over time, our defi-nition was restricted to units that have persistently exhibited deficien-cies over time. Although the full details of this work are presented elsewhere (Newman, Struyk, & Manson, 1982), it is worth noting here that elderly renters, in particular those in rural areas, tend to occupy housing units that have some major physical deficiencies year after year compared to both nonelderly renters and to homeowners in both age groups and locations.

NEIGHBORHOOD CONDITIONS

The "bundle of services" referred to when describing housing con-sumption includes characteristics of the environment beyond the prop-erty line. From a policy perspective, we are interested in the effects which the neighborhood environment has on its elderly residents and whether particular types of neighborhoods are associated with es-pecially beneficial outcomes.

Unfortunately, the conceptual and measurement problems associ-ated with examining housing characteristics and quality are magnified when we shift our attention to neighborhoods. At a fundamental level, there is no generally accepted definition of neighborhood. Recent work in the Detroit metropolitan area, for example, indicates that residents varied widely in the way they define the size of their neighborhoods (Rodgers, 1975). Other studies, including the Annual Housing Survey, have provided a single definition to respondents prior to the battery of neighborhood questions, presumably under the assumption that this frame of reference will be applied throughout the remainder of the inter-view. It is questionable, however, whether an individual's divergent sense of neighborhood space can be changed so easily (Newman, 1981b). Given these problems, research on the neighborhood conditions of the elderly must must be viewed with extra care.

Generalizations regarding the basic characteristics of the elderly's neighborhoods come from analysis of national-level data using census tracts to represent neighborhoods. This research suggests that the el-derly are disproportionately represented in older central cities of major metropolitan areas and in small rural towns (Struyk & Soldo, 1980). On average, these areas appear to be fragile: they contain older housing of lower quality and smaller size and above-average vacancy rates.

Research on the social characteristics of the elderly's neighborhoods is based largely on particular locales, making generalizations hazardous. There is, however, the suggestion that older people living in neighborhoods with high concentrations of their peers interact with these neighbors and that the frequency of this interaction is associated with better morale and greater knowledge of available services (see Lawton, 1976). However, since other neighborhood characteristics were not taken into account, it is impossible to say how the other basic attributes were correlated with, or affected, these patterns.

DIRECTIONS FOR FUTURE RESEARCH

This chronicle demonstrates that our repository of information about the elderly and their housing is impressive. But it also reveals that there are significant gaps in our knowledge which ultimately diminish our ability to choose among alternative strategies to relieve the housing problems faced by older people. Since the list of policy research needs is large, we briefly discuss two examples that have enduring interest.

One area in which additional research is sorely needed is the conceptualization and measurement of housing quality and standards. Such research has potentially great practical significance. Currently, Census Bureau counts of a variety of physical housing defects are often relied upon to demonstrate the status of the housing stock including whether housing quality has improved or declined over time. This information is eventually translated into normative judgments about whether housing assistance is necessary. But with basic conceptual and measurement questions regarding housing quality and needs unresolved, such judgments may be seriously flawed. This problem is particularly troublesome in the case of housing policy development for the elderly since the housing unit plays an especially important role in the lives of older persons.

Another area of inquiry concerns links between demographic and housing characteristics and the need for housing assistance. These links are by no means straightforward and are marked by substantial variation across households. Yet political realities demand that we become better informed about the characteristics of the elderly who are most in need of assistance and how we can best identify them. As we will amplify later in our policy discussion, rationing of government resources has become mandatory. Since it is clear that rationing is going to occur, it is vital that we develop guiding principles for the equitable allocation of the resources that are available. Research can contribute toward developing these principles. Such research would be particularly useful if it included estimated outcomes associated with alternative definitions of need and analysis of the interrelationships and overlaps of government programs for the elderly.

GOVERNMENT RESPONSE

The governmental role in housing has been a complex one—attested to by President Reagan's appointing the President's Commission on Housing in his first months in office. A variety of means has been used to respond to the perceived housing needs of various groups, including the elderly. These approaches have included tax incentives for both consumers and producers of housing, regulatory control of housing development, subsidy programs, and the construction of public housing, among others. Many times all of these approaches are used in the same community, because federal, state and local jurisdictions all play some role in housing. Thus any description of the system has to be an oversimplification. Even streamlining and simplifying, however, does not fully eliminate the impression of fragmentation in housing program purposes and execution.

In general, government response can be categorized into two forms—supply-side and demand-side programs. Supply-side programs attempt to increase directly the supply of housing through construction of housing, subsidizing construction by the private sector, or assistance to financial and other institutions that provide housing. Demand-side programs, on the other hand, augment the effective demand for housing by financial assistance to consumers, such as through rent subsidies or tax breaks for home purchasers.

In the material below, we will concentrate on federal programs, and we will distinguish between programs intended to assist renters and those intended to assist homeowners. As we shall see, the federal government has been mainly concerned with renters through its various renter assistance programs, and its chief approach to homeowners has been the facilitation of home purchase through tax deductions for mortgage interest and local property tax payments. Since home purchase usually occurs in early stages of the life cycle, and since these provisions favor those who still have mortgage debt, elderly homeowners, with a few exceptions, receive relatively less benefit from these provisions. Other direct programmatic attention from the federal government is also quite limited. Elderly renters, on the other hand, appear to be served in a proportion greater than their share of the eligible population (Zais *et al.*, 1982).

The federal government's housing programs are not based on entitlement; that is, not everyone who is eligible is entitled to benefits. Instead, the housing assistance system is one of limited slots, with an estimated 3.8 million renters to be served by the end of 1983. For many years, additional units were added each year to the assistance programs, but this pattern has apparently come to an end, as we shall discuss below. What appears to be persistent is the general thrust of federal housing policy to make eligibility basically dependent on the financial circumstances of households.

Prior to 1981, the two major programs of federal assistance—public housing and Section 8—were handled differently with respect to eligibility criteria. In Section 8, local administering agencies were to restrict admission to the program to those households with incomes below 80% of the housing market area median income, adjusted for household size. Public housing, on the other hand, afforded considerable discretion to local authorities, although the Department of Housing and Urban Development routinely approved income limits that were within 80–90% of the Section 8 limits for the area.

The 1981 legislative year brought uniformity to the two programs, and it is likely that this is the beginning of an attempt to treat all households alike. New program participants must now be at or below 50% of the area median income. A recent study shows that this way of targeting program resources to more needy households actually favors the elderly because elderly headed households are more likely to be at the lower end of the income spectrum (Zais *et al.*, 1982).

Although income is the basic criterion for eligibility, HUD programs are not directed at all household types. In general, three groups of households are served: (1) households of two or more persons, (2) single individuals who are handicapped or disabled, and (3) single elderly individuals. The omitted group consists of single-person, nonelderly households. Thus these rules also favor the elderly (who are eligible regardless of their household composition, provided their incomes are low enough) because they do not have to compete against nonelderly individuals for program slots.

Beyond these rules which act in favor of elderly participation, two other programmatic features suggest that the elderly are a group whose housing has been of special concern to national policymakers. One example of age targeting is the Section 202 programs, discussed below, which restricts admission to the elderly and to handicapped or disabled individuals. A second example is public housing and other new construction subsidy programs, in which developers are frequently encouraged to submit plans for special designs for elderly projects. These features all provide clear evidence that the elderly have been given special attention in terms of government response.

In the following sections, we review and evaluate the main thrusts of government policy toward the elderly renter and homeowner. In one sense, much of what appears here is historical because the system of housing assistance is undergoing major changes.

A comprehensive evaluation of housing programs would require an analysis of multiple criteria including cost efficiency, equity, administrative simplicity, housing preservation, and freedom of choice (Olsen & Rasmussen, 1979). Since such an extensive review is beyond the scope of this chapter, we have chosen instead to describe briefly each program and then focus on two of the more generic and fundamental criteria for housing assistance to the elderly: equity in the allocation of housing assistance resources to the elderly relative to the nonelderly and efficient targeting to the poor. Where data are readily available or a secondary analysis project has already been undertaken, we also address some of the other criteria. After reviewing the programs and policies, we will outline what appears to be the main direction of future policy.

Renter Programs

The federal government has assisted elderly renters through a variety of programs since the Second World War. At the end of 1980, approximately 40% of all rental-assisted units were occupied by the elderly (Zais et al., 1982). However, statistics for these programs are not always of the quality required for systematic analysis, and the complex nature of assistance programs demands caution. For example, as we shall see, there is often a danger of overcounting, since some households are assisted by more than one program, typically a supply-side subsidy and a rent subsidy. This section reviews the three major programs of the late 1970s and early 1980s and then provides information on the types of elderly households served by them.

Public Housing

The oldest and largest federally supported housing program, launched in 1937, is low-rent housing. Begun with such anti-Depression objectives as generating jobs and eliminating slums, its present mission is almost exclusively to assist poor households to live in adequate housing. Some public housing projects are specially designed for the elderly.

Public housing units are owned and operated by local housing authorities which are usually distinct from local governments. The federal government pays for development costs for constructing the units and now also pays a portion of the operating expenses. Local authorities must meet the remainder of the operating costs out of rents and utility charges collected from tenants. The local authorities also have all of the management responsibilities for developing, operating, and maintaining projects.

In the largest cities, public housing typically constitutes between 5% and 8% of the entire rental housing stock. Some cities have percentages exceeding 10 (Struyk & Soldo, 1981). By the end of fiscal year 1980, there were about 1.2 million federally supported units of public housing, and it is estimated that about 37% of the units were occupied by elderly-headed households (Zais *et al.*, 1982).

Section 8

The fastest growing program in recent years has been the so-called Section 8 program. After many supply-side programs mushroomed in the 1960s and early 1970s, Congress enacted the landmark 1974 Housing and Community Development Act, which established Section 8. The intent of the law was to allow local governments the flexibility to provide housing assistance consistent with local market conditions, using both demand-side and supply-side approaches. In a very tight market, with little prospect of the private market relieving the pressure of low vacancy rates, the city could choose a strategy favoring new construction. Where opposite conditions prevail, the city could choose to rely more heavily on the existing stock.

By the end of fiscal year 1980, the Section 8 Program was, in the aggregate, larger than the public housing program with 1.1 million units occupied and several hundred thousand units under development. But whether Section 8 is viewed as assisting the elderly depends on what segment of the program is considered. Section 8 actually consists of four distinct elements: Existing, Moderate Rehabilitation, Substantial Rehabilitation, and New Construction. Moderate Rehabilitation is administered along with the Existing Program and accounts for only a few units. Similarly, Substantial Rehabilitation is administered with the New Construction Program. Thus discussions of Section 8 can be simplified by referring to the experience of Section 8 Existing in contrast to New Construction.

Nearly 70% of all currently occupied Section 8 units are accounted for by the Existing segment of the program. This segment assists households in leasing units from the standing stock of privately owned units which meet certain physical standards. The government pays the landlord the difference between the actual market rent for a unit, up to a maximum called "fair market rent." The household pays the other share of the rent, calculated now at 30% of adjusted gross income.

The Existing Program offers households substantial freedom in choosing their own units. The household may elect to stay in its current unit or find another one, provided that the dwelling meets housing quality standards for the program and is within the rent limitation. In general, approximately half of the program's participants have stayed in their pre-program dwelling, although this is true for about 65% of elderly participants (Zais et al., 1982).

The New Construction component of Section 8 is quite different. It provides a guaranteed rental stream to developers who build or rehabilitate units under the program. HUD signs a 20- or 30-year annual contributions contract with the developer, obligating HUD to pay the difference between a tenant's rental contribution and the full rent for the units in the project. Developers obtain mortgage financing privately, or from HUD through the Government National Mortgage Association, or from a state or local agency which raises funds by selling tax-exempt bonds.

Section 202

The Section 202 Program was created by the Housing Act of 1959 but has been changed frequently since then. In several key respects it is unique among the federal programs that have subsidized new construction. First, the program is restricted to serving the elderly and handicapped or disabled. Second, the program relies exclusively on nonprofit sponsors to develop and operate projects. Third, the projects are financed by a direct loan to the sponsor (unlike the Section 8 New Construction program); this relieves the sponsor of the need to seek private financing. Section 202 projects are expected to provide more than shelter, although there are sharp limits on the health care facilities and services to be provided in each project.

In 1974, the program underwent a major change. Because it was felt that too many low-income households were excluded because of rent levels they could not afford, the applicable interest rate was defined as the United States Treasury's long-term borrowing rate (as opposed to 5% above that rate). In addition, a Section 8 subsidy was set aside for each unit built under Section 202 to ensure that at least 20% of participants were lower-income households. Now, most Section 202 projects also receive Section 8 subsidies.

The Section 202 program accounts for only a fraction of all units under HUD programs. By the end of 1980, an estimated 50,000 units were occupied. Unfortunately, no adequate data exist on the types of households that are being served by the program, particularly since the 1974 changes became law. However, the percentage of program participants who are elderly, 80%, is the highest of any of HUD's renter assistance programs.

Elderly Participants

In the late 1970s and early 1980s, the major programs in terms of number of units for elderly renters were public housing, Section 8 Existing, and Section 8 New Construction. Fortunately, special data collections were undertaken at the end of the decade for each of these programs so that we are able to compare the characteristics of elderly households served within SMSAs. Table 8 provides these comparisons.

The figures indicate that Section 8 New Construction serves the highest percentage of elderly-headed households—68%—while the other two programs serve around one-third. While there are not many differences in household composition (e.g., sex of head, household size, couples versus singles), other characteristics show substantial differences. Public housing appears to serve the greatest percentage of black elderly and also a larger fraction of those 75 years of age or older. This age difference may, in fact, be explained by "aging in place" of public housing tenants, but it raises significant questions about whether such elderly households will be provided with adequate services to meet their needs in public housing as they and their projects continue to age.

HOMEOWNER PROGRAMS

Rehabilitation and Repair Loans and Grants

The data recently collected as part of HUD's Community Development Strategies Evaluation (CDSE) provide some important background information for a discussion of housing rehabilitation and repair programs that have benefited the elderly. This study reviewed a wide variety of home improvement loan and grant programs in nine cities. These programs ranged from city-run and subsidized programs to state housing finance agency programs to federal programs.

TABLE 8
PROFILE OF ELDERLY HOUSEHOLDS SERVED IN THREE MAJOR
FEDERAL HOUSING PROGRAMS[a]

		Section 8	
Household characteristic	Public housing	Existing	New construction
Race of head (in percentages)			
White	51	70	89
Black	42	27	8
Hispanic	5	2	1
Other	3	[b]	1
Sex of head (in percentages)			
Male	28	25	24
Female	72	75	76
Household size (in percentages)			
1 person	78	80	84
2 persons	17	18	16
3+ persons	5	2	0
Household composition (in percentages)			
Single, no children	78	80	84
Couples, no children	13	16	15
Other	9	4	1
Major sources of income (in percentages)			
Social Security	75	75	84
SSI	13	9	5
Earnings	4	1	3
Other	8	15	7
Age of head (in percentages)			
62–74 years	55	70	72
75 years or older	45	30	28
Average Annual Income (in dollars)	3496	4118	4229
Percentage of participants who are elderly	37	33	68

[a]Source: Zais et al., 1982. Profiles are for participants in SMSAs only.
[b]Less than 0.5%.

There appear to be large differences across cities in the percentage of assisted households headed by an elderly individual, in some cases exceeding the percentage of the elderly in the population and in other cases underrepresenting the elderly. Thus aggregate totals of the number of elderly served by the various programs discussed below hide substantial geographic variation (Ginsberg, Pack, Gale, & McConney, 1980).

Section 312 Rehabilitation Loan Program (Department of Housing and Urban Development). The Section 312 Program provides below-market interest rate loans to property owners to finance the cost of rehabilitation. Although 312 loans were available for rental properties, the large majority of all loans went to owner-occupants (Struyk & Soldo, 1980). To receive these federal dollars, two main conditions must be met: the houses must be located in neighborhoods that have been targeted for other government assistance (e.g., code enforcement or urban homesteading), and the owner must be unable to obtain a comparable rehabilitation loan from other sources. Priority is given to low- and moderate-income owners who will occupy the property once the rehabilitation work is completed (Mayer & Lee, 1980).

Using a definition of homeowner housing needs based on a comparison of the needs of the elderly relative to those of a control group of nonelderly, Mayer and Lee (1980) estimated that between 1976 and 1978 the elderly who had high housing cost burdens and inadequate housing units received just about their fair share of 312 loans. But those who had low incomes and inadequate units were underrepresented by a significant margin (about 16%). However, since the total size of the program is small—only 47,500 loans were made through fiscal year 1976—the actual number of elderly owners who have been assisted is very small.

The now unused Section 115 program, which was largely similar to 312 but offered funding through grants rather than loans, had previously been administered along with the 312 program. Mayer and Lee (1980) found that switching from grants (or grants and loans) to loans only seriously hurt participation of the elderly in rehabilitation, and particularly hurt the low-income elderly. They conclude that "many elderly homeowners with low current incomes are in some combination unable and unwilling to involve themselves in a repair program requiring added debt."

Community Development Block Grant Program (CDBG) (Department of Housing and Urban Development). The main goal of the CDBG Program, which replaced or consolidated several categorical programs in 1974, has been to provide localities with greater flexibility in dealing with the problems of urban blight and decay. Most monies are allocated to eligible cities and urban counties according to formulae based on population size, poverty, crowding, age of housing stock, and other characteristics that are assumed to measure need for assistance. While the block grant funds must be used mainly to help low- and moderate-income households, the assistance need not be restricted only to badly deteriorated geographic areas (Struyk & Soldo, 1980; Mayer & Lee, 1980).

Communities have taken a variety of approaches toward funding repair and rehabilitation activities using their CDBG allocations. Some have offered financing for this work through grants, loans, loan guarantees, and interest subsidies. Others have provided the repair and re-habilitation work directly through home maintenance and repair pro-grams, rehabilitation aid, and the like.

The CDBG Program is HUD's principal initiative to help local gov-ernments address their community needs: in the seven years between 1975 and 1981, Congress appropriated more than $23.3 billion for the CDBG Program (U.S. Department of Housing and Urban Development, 1981). More than one quarter of these funds were targeted to housing-and rehabilitation-related activities, with the largest percentage of dol-lars going toward the rehabilitation of private single-family houses.

According to HUD's CDBG Evaluation Data Base, roughly 40% of all CDBG-funded housing assistance dollars to entitlement communities were projected to go to the elderly and handicapped as compared to small families or large families. Roughly 30% of CDBG housing as-sistance dollars were projected to be directed to renters while 70% were to go to homeowners. The elderly and handicapped were expected to receive roughly one-third of the renter assistance and about 43% of the assistance for homeowners.

These data are not adequate for addressing the question of whether the programs funded by CDBG respond to the needs of the elderly. Because the programs are developed and implemented at the local level, information on the variation in specific approaches to housing assistance is enormous and the best data must be collected locally. The data that are available also present problems for our other purpose of evaluating whether the elderly are receiving a proper share of housing assistance dollars under CDBG. Two problems are most serious: First, the elderly and handicapped are grouped into one category, making it impossible to determine the size of the elderly recipient population, even in the aggre-gate. Second, these data are based on projected expenditures, not actual ones. How many of these plans eventually turn into action is not known.

Keeping these weaknesses in mind, we can turn again to Mayer and Lee's estimate of housing needs among elderly homeowners and com-pare them to the projections for CDBG housing assistance. The owner group with the highest incidence of need—those with low incomes and deficient housing units—were expected to receive just about their fair share of assistance dollars directed toward owners. Since the proportion of elderly owners with high housing-cost burdens and housing deficien-cies is considerably lower than the low-income and housing deficiency group, the aggregate proportions suggest that their needs should be more than adequately served.

Section 502 and 504 (Farmer's Home Administration, Department of Agri-culture). The Section 502 Rural Housing Loan Program provides direct loans to owners at reduced interest rates for the purchase, construction, or repair of a dwelling or site. The major objective of the program, however, is housing purchase. Applicants must be low- or moderate-income, as defined by FmHA for each state, and unable to get financing from a private institution. At the same time, eligibility also depends on the ability to meet the routine costs of homeownership—taxes, insurance, routine maintenance, and the like—and to repay the 502 loan.

In some sense, Section 504 picks up where Section 502 stops: households who are too poor to meet the "sufficient income" requirement of Section 502 are eligible for Section 504 grants or loans. Section 504 provides grants and reduced interest loans to underwrite the costs of housing improvements, additions, or repairs.

As with CDBG, funds are allocated under both of these programs on the basis of a needs formula; but unlike CDBG, only owner-occupants in rural areas are eligible. Entitlement to loans under either program is not based on age, but only the elderly are eligible for Section 504 grants.

Again, using Mayer and Lee's housing needs calculations, this time adjusted to represent the rural elderly, it appears that in fiscal 1978, the elderly received a smaller proportion of allocations under both 502 and 504 combined than their share of rural housing needs (Mayer & Lee, 1980). There is considerable variation among these programs, however: an extremely small proportion of Section 502 loan recipients are elderly, whereas more than half of 504 recipients are elderly, and, of course, all 504 grant recipients are elderly by definition.

These programs are quite small: combined, only an estimated 5,500 elderly households had been served by the end of fiscal 1977 (Mayer & Lee, 1980).

Title XX (Department of Health and Human Services). Under the Title XX Program as it existed up until FY1982, the federal government provided matching funds to states for a wide variety of social service programs. Although the states and localities had considerable discretion in the types of programs they could fund with Title XX support, these programs were required to meet certain legislated national goals. Two which are particularly apt for the present discussion were fostering self-sufficiency and preventing inappropriate institutionalization. From the perspective of the housing needs of the elderly, these goals have been translated mainly into home maintenance and repair programs.

Although a minimum number of services and programs had to be provided for the very poor, states were allowed to serve households regardless of their income. They were also allowed to charge fees for services.

Gilbert, Specht, and Nelson's data (1979; also see Mayer & Lee,

1980) suggest that only about one percent of the total Title XX expenditures in 1976 and 1977 that were directed at the elderly was spent on housing repair services. In addition, by Mayer and Lee's definition of the elderly's housing needs, the share of Title XX housing assistance dollars received by the elderly for such services falls far short of the level required. This conclusion may be somewhat misleading, however, since Title XX data are reported in terms of dollars expended on the elderly rather than households served. Thus a large number of households could have received some assistance though the size of that assistance would necessarily be quite small.

Starting in FY1982, the Title XX program became a social services block grant. Since Title XX funds previously went directly to the states, the main effects of this change will most likely be the greater discretion allowed the states regarding the design and funding of programs. The new regulations for the social services block grant provide a clear indication of this new flexibility: "social services block grants funds may be transferred to support health services, health promotion and disease prevention activities . . . including block grants administered by other Federal departments" (45CFR Parts 16, 74, and 96). Since funding for social services has also been cut back severely, it will be difficult to distinguish between reactions by states that are motivated by the smaller number of restrictions on the use of social service dollars and those caused by reduced funding.

Title III (Department of Health and Human Services). Title III Grants for State and Community Programs on Aging, administered through the Administration on Aging, provides matching grants through the states to local agencies for a wide range of services for persons 60 years and older. The 1978 reauthorization of the Older Americans Act, which is the enabling legislation for Title III, indicated that the highest priority groups for most Title III funded programs and services are the very old with economic and social needs. This targeting has been softened considerably in the 1981 amendments. Lawton *et al.* (1980) provide the most up-to-date estimates of the size of the Title III repair and renovation programs. In fiscal 1978, roughly $3.2 million of the total Title III allotment to state agencies, or 2.1%, was spent on housing repair or renovations. If the more positive estimates of Struyk and Soldo (1980) based on the second quarter of FY1978 are adjusted by these final estimates, the total number of older persons aided by these Title III monies was less than 100,000 nationwide.

Because the nature of Title III programs is determined at the local level, calculating the size of particular programs or average expenditures per recipient for states, regions, or the nation can provide seriously misleading estimates for a given locality's program. This feature of Title III programs is clearly demonstrated in the analysis by Lawton *et al.* (1980). The four states of Pennsylvania, Virginia, West Virginia, and Maryland encompass 88 Area Agencies on Aging and virtually every one of these Agencies approaches the question of repair services differently.

Disaggregated data on the program approaches of the more than 700 Area Agencies on Aging are not readily available. Recognizing this problem of uneven distribution of program size and cost within states, we can examine the data that do exist on mean size and cost by state that are presented in Struyk and Soldo (1980). It appears that most expenditures were very small and that major repairs were rarely undertaken. The cost per recipient exceeded $150 in only 5 states. In addition, the average number of recipients per state was less than 1,500. These numbers suggest that, as with several other programs that we have reviewed, Title III repair and renovation programs make only a small contribution toward meeting the housing needs of older citizens. The lack of disaggregate data prevents us from addressing the important question of whether the neediest elderly are being served.

Housing Expense Burden Relief

Property Tax Relief Programs. A number of state programs have been introduced over the last dozen years that attempt to deal directly with the property tax burden on elderly homeowners.[4] The most common approach is the property tax circuit breaker, which exists in some form in more than half the states (Advisory Commission on Intergovernmental Relations, 1981). Under this type of program, a state underwrites some proportion of the property tax levy on the homes of elderly owners. Eligibility is often limited to those with incomes falling below some established threshold. This threshold varies widely across the states: it is set at $20,000 in the District of Columbia, for example, but at $5,000 in West Virginia. Generally, the higher the tax burden or the lower the income, the greater the tax relief. The benefit usually takes the form of a credit on state personal income taxes, but several states provide payments from their general revenues.

Closely related relief programs that exist in many of the states that have circuit breakers and in all of those that do not are the homestead exemption and credit. Homestead exemptions are a dollar amount or

---

[4]Many states also provide relief for renters since it is believed that landlords pass on much of the property tax to their tenants.

percent share of property valuation that is exempt from property taxes. Homestead credits are dollar or percentage reductions in taxes on property. In Alaska, for example, elderly property owners are fully exempted from property taxes whereas in Iowa, homeowners receive a credit for the actual levy on the first $4,850 of valuation.

Circuit breaker-type programs are considered to be an efficient and relatively inexpensive way to reduce the tax burdens of low-income elderly homeowners (Advisory Commission on Intergovernmental Relations, 1973). One drawback, however, is that higher average payments (or the value of exemptions and credits) go to households with higher house values within any income class since more valuable houses are likely to have higher assessments and, therefore, higher property taxes (See Gold, Kutza, & Marmor, 1973). The disparity in eligibility requirements for circuit breaker programs across the states also raise questions of equity. Michigan, for example, does not use an income threshold to determine eligibility and had over one million claimants in 1977. In contrast, Missouri, a state which has a somewhat smaller population 65 years and over but which uses an income ceiling of $7,500, had only about 56,000 claimants (U.S. Bureau of the Census, 1980; Advisory Commission on Intergovernmental Relations, 1979). Equity considerations also arise because of the differential reliance across jurisdictions on the property tax as a source of state and local revenue.

Home Equity Conversion. Home equity conversion plans, which range from simple deferral or forbearance of property taxes to the complicated split-equity mortgage, enable older homeowners to consume part of their home equity while they continue to live in their homes (Scholen & Chen, 1980; Tuccillo, 1981). They represent a response to four dominant characteristics of the elderly population: the very high incidence of homeownership generally, and particularly ownership free of mortgage debt; the great reluctance of homeowners to move; and the growth in housing-related costs which the elderly must meet out of fixed incomes. All of these plans are designed to provide some relief from the costs incurred by the homeowners or to use accumulated equity to increase income flow. As of the present time, only a few, mainly experimental, equity conversion programs have actually been launched. Those initiated under the auspices of private banks have been described as "sporadic and short-lived" (Harney, 1981).

While the premises and goals of these plans are appealing, they suffer from several drawbacks. First, the potential audience for these plans is likely to be small since the current situation of high mortgage interest rates and lower annuity interest rates make it infeasible for anyone but the very old or very wealthy to participate. According to one set of empirical estimates, the median payments from reverse annuity mortgages for poor elderly homeowners across the United States, given an annuity interest rate of 12% and a mortgage interest rate of 15%, is only $241 per year (Jacobs, 1980).

Second, there are likely to be significant legal, marketing, and tax barriers to development: for example, most of the plans are complex and difficult to explain in simple terms; the bequest motive may work against acceptance; and any income generated may reduce eligibility for other government transfer income such as Supplemental Security Income (SSI).

Federal Income Tax Subsidies to Homeowners.[5]   As with many provisions of the tax code, the tax advantages to homeowners vary considerably across socioeconomic groups (Aaron, 1972). While only about one third of all households now file itemized returns, owners with very low incomes are especially unlikely to benefit very much both because they are less likely to itemize their deductions and because, even if they do itemize, their marginal tax rate is relatively low. These two characteristics apply with particular force to the elderly, thereby reducing the value of these deductions to them. However, the fact that the elderly tend to have paid off more of their mortgage debt compared to younger taxpayers may contribute even more toward lowering the benefits to be derived from these deductions for the aged.

Several of these characteristics can be observed in Table 9. Only 1.5 million elderly homeowners (roughly 15% of all elderly homeowners) filed itemized returns and claimed property tax or mortgage interest deductions in 1979—a reduction of more than one million returns from 1970 due to a number of changes in the Revenue Act that increased the percentage of adjusted gross income allowable with a standard deduction, created low income tax credits, and the like. The regressivity of the deductions is clear from the rise in the value of the subsidy with increases in income. It is this feature that has led at least one housing economist to characterize these provisions as "housing allowances for the non-poor" (Quigley, 1982). The fact that less than half as many elderly took advantage of the mortgage interest provision as the proper-

[5]See Baer (1976) for a similar discussion for 1970. Perhaps the most significant program of subsidies to homeowners regardless of age is embodied in three provisions of the Internal Revenue Code: the absence of a requirement to declare imputed income from ownership, the deductibility of property taxes, and the deductibility of mortgage interest payments. The value of the latter deduction has grown markedly over the last decade because of the dramatic rise in interest rates. According to the Department of Housing and Urban Development, the revenue cost of allowing property tax and mortgage interest deductions was more than $29 billion in 1981 (Office of Management and Budget, 1982a).

TABLE 9
ESTIMATED AVERAGE FEDERAL INCOME TAX SUBSIDY FOR HOMEOWNERS 65 YEARS
AND OLDER WHO ITEMIZE, BY INCOME CLASS AND TYPE OF DEDUCTION, 1979[a]

	Elderly homeowner deductions					
	Property tax			Mortgage interest		
		Average subsidy[b] (in dollars)			Average subsidy[b] (in dollars)	
Adjusted gross income classes (in dollars)	Number of elderly	After deductions	Before deductions	Number of elderly	After deductions	Before deductions
2,000–5,999[c]	87,528	0	57	39,928	0	100
6,000–9,999	171,808	33	81	81,354	67	161
10,000–15,999	303,491	108	134	120,360	175	215
16,000–24,999	340,365	160	187	153,850	250	291
25,000–49,999	415,804	301	335	149,808	443	514
50,000–99,999	165,290	607	669	49,518	786	889
100,000 and over	72,195	1892	1956	19,999	2935	2104
Total	1,556,481			614,817		

[a]Source: U.S. Internal Revenue Service, Statistics of Income, 1979, Table 4.2 and Tax Rate Schedule.
[b]Based on average tax rates for elderly persons filing separately. Lower estimate assumes deduction is taken *after* all other deductions have been taken; higher estimate assumes deduction is taken *before* all other deductions have been taken.
[c]Lower bracket deleted due to insufficient observations.

ty tax provision is probably explained by the large proportion of elderly owners (more than two-thirds) with little or no remaining mortgage debt.

Nevertheless, more than one million elderly homeowners benefited by these provisions in 1979; the total amount of deductions for both of these provisions was $2.7 billion. Therefore, despite several characteristics of the elderly that make them less likely to derive as much value from these deductions as their younger counterparts, these provisions remain the largest homeowner subsidy program, even for the elderly.

One provision of the Internal Revenue Code that is the exclusive preserve of older homeowners is the one-time exclusion from gross income of up to $125,000 of gain realized on the sale of a principal residence. This provision applies to taxpayers 55 years or older. Estimated tax losses from this provision in 1981 are about $450 million (Office of Management and Budget, 1982b). The main purpose of this provision was tax relief, but it may also be expected to induce at least some changes in mobility rates and residential choices that would not have occurred otherwise. Since the original provision (granting a $100,000 exclusion) was passed only very recently (1978), we do not yet know whether such changes have actually occurred.

Weatherization Assistance.   Federal, state, and local programs have existed for several years that focus exclusively on improving the weatherization of dwellings. Such assistance has the potential of achieving two goals: lowering utility cost burdens on owners and improving dwelling quality. While our discussion focuses on recent federal programs, state and local activities will likely gain prominence in the future as federal involvement is cut back or folded into local programs.

The Weatherization Assistance Program (WAP) that has been administered by the Department of Energy has provided for installation of insulation, storm windows and doors, and other energy efficiency improvements for housing occupied by low-income families.[6] Both homeowners and renters have been eligible for assistance, but only about 11% of the dwellings that have received services have been rental units. Nearly 200,000 dwellings of both the elderly and nonelderly had been weatherized by August 1980 (U.S. Department of Energy, 1980).

The credit on federal income tax returns for energy conservation expenditures differs from the WAP in four ways. First, under the WAP, agency personnel made the weatherization improvements, whereas under the tax credit system the household has been responsible for this work. Second, the WAP was targeted on low-income families but income tax credits have been available only to those with sufficient income to make itemization worthwhile. Third, although WAP provided a 100% subsidy up to $1,000 in materials, the energy tax credits have provided a 15% subsidy on the first $2,000 of materials and labor. Finally, tax credits have encompassed a broader range of activities than have been allowable under the WAP.

Information on participation rates is not readily available. Two related aspects of participation, however, have been cited in the literature: first, about 38% of the total dwellings assisted under the WAP have been estimated to contain an elderly individual. Second, the majority of those who file for the tax credit have moderate or high incomes. Combining the two forms of assistance, it has been estimated that roughly 20% of all lower-income homeowners have received some relief (Struyk, undated). What portion of these homeowners are elderly, however, has not been estimated.

---

[6]Defined as families with incomes less than 125% of the poverty line or with a member who received AFDC or SSI during the 12 months prior to application to the program.

In addition to the WAP and tax credits, Congress has, in the past, written emergency legislation to provide direct monetary relief for low-income households faced with high energy bills. This "crisis intervention" relief has been available at various times to both homeowners and renters and has taken the form of either monetary or in-kind assistance. In 1977, for example, the Special Crisis Intervention Program (SCIP) was created; in 1978, supplemental appropriations were approved for the Emergency Energy Assistance Program (EEAP). In each of these years, $200 million was authorized to cover the costs of these programs. Each program was administered by the Community Services Administration which allocated monies to the states or to substate areas to underwrite up to $250 of the energy costs of needy households. According to one evaluation of these programs, somewhat less than half of all households receiving some help from each of these programs were elderly (Campbell, 1979).

FUTURE PROSPECTS

Government programs, including housing assistance, were the objects of increasing concern during the 1970s. Possibly the overriding issue was how to control government spending. Another issue involved the degree of authority and responsibility for programs at the federal, state, and local levels and the distribution of authority between these levels of government. A third issue was how to shift from intrusive government programs to a form of assistance that would rely more heavily on private market processes and the autonomy of individual consumers. Finally, government assistance had become increasingly universalized, possibly at the risk of forfeiting some services to the poor and contributing to spiraling costs.

Although these issues gained prominence in the 1970s, they are clearly fundamental and enduring. Aspects of each of these four issues are reflected in current proposals to alter housing policy for the elderly. The future of housing policy remains uncertain, but the few major themes that have emerged during the early tenure of the current administration signal some significant shifts from past directions.

The Administration's proposal for dismantling the Department of Energy includes recommendations for reducing or phasing out energy conservation grants to state and local governments (Office of Management and Budget, 1982c). As part of the 1982 effort to consolidate categorical programs into block grants to the states, the emergency energy assistance programs are to be united into one block grant program and targeted to states most in need based on their climatic conditions.

With respect to the assistance of renters, the most important development is a new proposal to hold the number of assisted units at the Office of Management and Budget estimate of 3.6 million rather than add new units each year. This means that the number of households in "need," as specified by income eligibility criteria, will continue to be several times greater than the number of households actually assisted.

A second general thrust is a greater, if not exclusive, reliance on the existing stock as opposed to new construction. One of the major arguments on behalf of this approach is that it is less costly. Indeed, the type of program most often discussed is a housing voucher program, not unlike Section 8 Existing, but with fewer restrictions on household behavior. Households will have greater incentives to shop for lower rent units but will pay the rents on the units they ultimately find, even if they exceed the "fair market rent."

A recent evaluation of the Reagan administration's voucher program proposal indicates that since comparatively low subsidy levels are involved, elderly participation as a percentage of participation by all age groups is expected to increase. This conclusion was based mainly on the observation that the elderly appear to be relatively insensitive to payment levels (Zais et al., 1982). Since the elderly have such low mobility rates, most who participate in the program will likely receive assistance in their current housing units. One by-product of this immobility is that their housing consumption will not increase very much, if at all. The program, then, will have its major effects on housing affordability, although the maximum amount of subsidy per household will be considerably smaller than under current programs.

Two of the most worrisome aspects of this type of voucher program for the elderly are the lack of a direct attack on physical housing problems and the absence of a strong outreach component. A voucher does not solve the persistent housing problems of elderly renters. Since it is much less likely that an elderly individual will be willing or able to search for another housing unit compared to a younger renter, it is not clear that those elderly in the worst housing conditions will be helped to upgrade their housing. There is also concern about how well connected the elderly are to sources of information about housing assistance. Receiving their fair share of vouchers obviously requires that they are aware of the program. At the present time, no special outreach efforts for elderly or disabled households have been discussed as an integral part of the voucher proposal.

A third general thrust in housing policy under the current administration is the desire to target housing assistance to the "truly needy." The main concern with such revisions in targeting is whether the concept will be defined to maximize equity in assistance. In some of our other work, we have examined the notion of persistent poverty (i.e., falling into poverty in the majority of years in a given time period) as an equitable definition of greatest need (Newman *et al.*, 1982). Persistent income problems and persistent housing deficiencies are particularly likely to characterize the situation of the elderly. The present approach to the definition, however, is strictly a single-year, relative poverty standard set at 50% of the area's median income.

Using the 50% of median definition of need, estimates for 1983 participation rates in SMSAs indicate that more than half of the elderly renters who are income eligible for assistance are already receiving some help: of the 1.9 million elderly households that will be eligible by income for assistance, 1.1 million will already be participating (Zais *et al.*, 1982). Homeowner programs do not use this definition of need. However, if they did, few would qualify for assistance since homeowners' incomes are higher than those or renters.

Since so much of the federal effort on behalf of elderly homeowners is channeled through the CDBG program, the major question is how federal cutbacks in funding will affect the size and focus of services. CDBG underwent a 13% reduction in budget authority in FY1982, but no budget change is proposed for FY1983. In terms of design, the program remains targeted to low- and moderate-income residents, but the amount of information that cities were required to provide to the federal government in order to qualify for these funds has been reduced dramatically. The effects of this deregulation of CDBG are hard to predict.

In part, the outcome will depend on whether the elderly have a strong political base in their local communities and whether they can lobby effectively for needed services. But even with politics and advocacy on their side, the smaller overall federal allocations place programs for the elderly in a precarious position. Whether we will be able to assess how well these and other programs manage in this new environment is itself not clear since the federal government plans little or no monitoring of its new federalism.

REFERENCES

Aaron, H. *Shelter and subsidies*. Washington, D. C.: The Brookings Institution, 1972.
Advisory Commission on Intergovernmental Relations. Big breakthrough for circuit-breaker. *Bulletin* No. 73–2, Washington, D. C., 1973.

Advisory Commission on Intergovernmental Relations. *Significant features of fiscal federalism, 1978–79.* Washington, D. C.: ACIR, 1979.

Advisory Commission on Intergovernmental Relations. *Significant features of fiscal federalism, 1980–81.* Washington, D. C.: ACIR, 1981.

Baer, W. Federal housing programs for the elderly. *In* M. P. Lawton, R. Newcomer, & T. Byerts (Eds.), *Community planning for an aging society.* New York: McGraw-Hill, 1976.

Baer, W. The evolution of housing indicators and housing standards: Some lessons for the future. *Public Policy,* 1976, 24.

Beyer, G., & Nierstrasz, F. *Housing the aged in western countries.* New York: Elsevier, 1967.

Butler, E., Chapin, F., Hemmens, G., Kaiser, E., Stegman, M., & Weiss, S. *Moving behavior and residential choice: A national survey.* Washington, D. C.: Highway Research Board, 1969.

Campbell, T. *Emergency energy assistance programs: SCIP and EEAP service relative to need and the impact of state policies on service in SCIP.* Working paper 1197–1. Washington, D. C.: The Urban Institute, 1979.

Carliner, G. Income elasticity of housing demand. *Review of Economics and Statistics,* 1973, 55.

Cherry, R., & Cherry, L. Slowing the clock of age. *The New York Times Magazine,* May 20, 1974, 20–92ff.

Fendler, C., & Orshansky, M. Improving the poverty definition. *1979 Proceedings of the American Statistical Association Social Statistics Section,* 1980, 640–645.

Gilbert, N., Specht, H., & Nelson, G. *Social services to the elderly: Title XX and the aging network.* Washington, D. C.: U.S. Department of Health, Education, and Welfare, 1979.

Ginsberg, R., Pack, J., Gale, S. & McConney, M. *Household survey I: Interim report.* Philadelphia: University of Pennsylvania, 1980 (mimeo).

Golant, S. *The residential location and spatial behavior of the elderly.* Chicago: University of Chicago, Department of Geography, 1972.

Gold, B., Kutza, E., & Marmor, T. U.S. social policy on old age: Present patterns and predictions. In B. Neugarten & R. Havighurst (Eds.), *Social policy, social ethics, and the aging society.* Washington, D. C.: U.S. Government Printing Office, 1976, pp. 9–22.

Goldscheider, C., VanArsdol, M., & Sabagh, G. Residential mobility of older people. In F. Carp (Ed.), *Patterns of living and housing of middle aged and older people.* Washington, D. C.: U.S. Government Printing Office, 1966, pp. 65–82.

Harney, K. Help for house-rich, income-poor elderly. *The Washington Post,* December 19, 1981, E1.

Jacobs, B. The potential antipoverty impact of RAMs and property tax deferral. In H. Scholen & Y. P. Chen (Eds.), *Unlocking home equity for the elderly.* Cambridge, Mass.: Ballinger, 1980, pp. 50–60.

Juster, L. *Current and prospective financial status of the elderly population.* Ann Arbor: Institute for Social Research, 1981 (mimeo).

Kain, J., & Quigley, J. *Housing markets and racial discrimination.* New York: National Bureau of Economic Research, 1975.

Lawton, M. Housing and living environments of the elderly. In R. Binstock & E. Shanas (Eds.), *Handbook of aging and the social sciences.* New York: Van Nostrand Reinhold, 1976.

Lawton, M., Kleban, M., & Carlson, D. The inner-city resident: To move or not to move. *Gerontologist,* 1973, 13, 443–448.

Mayer, N., & Lee, O. *The effectiveness of federal home repair and improvement programs in meeting elderly homeowner needs*. Contract Report 1283–1. Washington, D. C.: The Urban Institute, April, 1980.

Morgan, J., Ponza, M., & Imbruglia, R. Trends in residential property taxes. In M. Hill, D. Hill, & J. Morgan (Eds.), *Five thousand American families—Patterns of economic progress*. Ann Arbor, Mich.: Institute for Social Research, 1981, pp. 391–404.

Morrison, P. Duration of residence and prospective migration: The evaluation of a stochastic model. *Demography*, 1967, *IV*, 533–561.

Newman, S. Testimony. *Housing and the elderly: Present problems and future considerations*. Hearing before the Subcommittee on Housing and Consumer Interest of the House Select Committee on Aging, 97th Congress, 1st session, July 29, 1981a, 108–116.

Newman, S. *Residential crowding: A study of definitions*. Ann Arbor, Mich.: Institute for Social Research Working Paper, 1981b.

Newman, S., Struyk, R., & Manson, D. *Poverty, housing deprivation and housing assistance*. Washington, D. C.: The Urban Institute, 1982.

Office of the Federal Registrar, National Archives and Record Service. *Code of Federal Regulation* (Title 45). Washington, D. C.: U.S. Government Printing Office, 1980.

Office of Management and Budget. *Budget of the United States, fiscal year 1983*. Washington, D. C.: U.S. Government Printing Office, 1982. (a)

Office of Management and Budget. *Tax expenditures: Special analysis g*. Washington, D. C.: U.S. Government Printing Office, 1982. (b)

Office of Management and Budget. *Major themes and additional budget details, fiscal year 1983*. Washington, D. C.: U.S. Government Printing Office, 1982. (c)

Olsen, E., & Rasmussen, D. Section 8 existing: A program evaluation. *Occasional papers in housing and community affairs*, 1979, 6, 1–32.

Orshansky, M. *Report to the National Commission on Social Security*. Washington, D. C., 1979 (mimeo).

Quigley, J. *Taking housing allowances seriously as a national program: A budgetary perspective*. Paper presented at the University of the District of Columbia Conference on Neighborhood Development and Public Finance, Washington, D. C., April 6, 1982.

Reschovsky, J. *Causes and effects of life-cycle lock-in*. Ann Arbor, Mich.: Institute for Social Research, 1980 (mimeo).

Rodgers, W. *The quality of urban life in the Detroit metropolitan area: Documentation*. Ann Arbor, Mich. Institute for Social Research, 1975.

Scholen, K., & Chen, Y. *Unlocking home equity for the elderly*. Cambridge, Mass.: Ballinger, 1980.

Speare, A., Goldstein, S., & Frey, W. *Residential mobility, migration, and metropolitan change*. Cambridge, Mass.: Ballinger, 1974.

Storey, J. *The future of income, assets, and consumption*. Discussion paper prepared for the National Institute on Aging, Washington, D. C., 1981 (mimeo).

Struyk, R. *Home energy costs and the housing of the poor and of the elderly*. Washington, D. C.: The Urban Institute, undated (mimeo).

Struyk, R., & Soldo, B. *Improving the elderly's housing*. Cambridge, Mass.: Ballinger, 1980.

Tomassen, S. Current breaking and life-cycle lock-in. *National Tax Journal*, 1979, 31, 59–65.

Tuccillo, J. Review of *Unlocking home equity for the elderly*, by K. Scholen & Y. Chen. *Journal of the American Planning Association*, 1981, 47, 474.

U.S. Bureau of the Census. *Current population reports*, Series P–20, no. 225—Marital status and living arrangements: March 1971. Washington, D. C.: U.S. Government Printing Office, 1971.

U.S. Bureau of the Census. *Current population reports*, Series P–20, no. 338—Marital status and living arrangements: March 1978. Washington, D.C.: U.S. Government Printing Office, 1979. (a)

U.S. Bureau of the Census. *Current population reports,* Series P–23, no. 85—Social and economic characteristics of the older population, 1978. Washington, D. C.: U.S. Government Printing Office, 1979. (b)

U.S. Bureau of the Census. *State and metropolitan area data book, 1979.* Washington, D. C.: U.S. Government Printing Office, 1980.

U.S. Bureau of the Census. *Annual housing survey: 1979, Part A.* Washington, D. C.: U.S. Government Prining Office, 1981. (a)

U.S. Bureau of the Census. *Current population reports,* Series P–60, no. 129—Money income of families and persons in the U.S., 1979. Washington, D. C.: U.S. Government Printing Office, 1981. (b)

U.S. Bureau of the Census. *Annual housing survey: 1980, Part C.* Washington, D. C.: U.S. Government Printing Office, 1981. (c)

U.S. Bureau of the Census. *Current population reports,* Series P–60, no. 130—Characteristics of the population below the poverty level: 1979. Washington, D. C.: U.S. Government Printing Office, 1981. (d)

U.S. Department of Energy. *Residential energy consumption survey: Conservation.* Washington, D. C.: U.S. Government Printing Office, 1980.

U.S. Department of Health and Human Services. *Vital & health statistics,* Series 10, no. 139—Current estimates from the national health interview survey, United States, 1980. Washington, D. C.: National Center for Health Statistics, 1981.

U.S. Department of Housing and Urban Development. *How well are we housed? Elderly.* Washington, D. C.: U.S. Government Printing Office, 1979.

U.S. Department of Housing and Urban Development. *Sixth annual community development block grant report.* Washington, D. C.: HUD, July 1981.

U.S. Internal Revenue Service. *Statistics of income—1978 individual income tax returns.* Washington, D. C.: U.S. Government Printing Office, 1981.

Van Arsdol, M. Sabagh, G., & Butler, E. Retrospective and subsequent metropolitan residential mobility. *Demography,* 1968, *5,* 249–267.

Zais, J., Struyk, R., & Thibodeau, T. *Housing policy for the elderly renter: Implications of the Reagan Program.* Washington, D. C.: The Urban Institute, 1982.

3

Retirement Communities

ROBERT W. MARANS, MICHAEL E. HUNT, AND KATHLEEN L. VAKALO

INTRODUCTION

For the millions of older Americans who will retire during the next decade and who are functionally independent, various housing and living arrangements are available. However, if past figures on residential mobility are any indication of future trends, most new retirees will remain in the homes and apartments they occupied while part of the labor force. Among the noninstitutionalized elderly in the United States, less than one in five people over 65 years of age changed their place of residence between 1975 and 1979, compared to two in five in the general population (Soldo, 1980). Of older Americans who will change residence, some will move to a smaller home requiring less time, energy, and money to maintain it, while others will move in with willing children, relatives, and friends. Still others will opt for entirely new living arrangements either within the same community or elsewhere in the country. These latter moves are most likely to occur among people less than 70 years of age, and for many they are likely to be toward destinations offering a mild climate and recreational and scenic attractions.

During the past decade, a number of studies have demonstrated that retirement is not the most important reason for seeking a new residence. In a survey of Detroit area residents, half of the respondents

ROBERT W. MARANS, MICHAEL E. HUNT, and KATHLEEN L. VAKALO • Institute for Social Research and College of Architecture and Urban Planning, University of Michigan, Ann Arbor, Michigan 48106.

considered moving after suffering a serious disability and more than nine out of ten of these actually changed their residence. Of the same group, 13% considered a move at the death of a spouse and only 12% at retirement (Newman, 1976). In a national study of mobility, the most frequently mentioned reason for changing residence given by people 55 years of age was to be closer to family, followed closely by retirement and then climate (Long & Hansen, 1979). While long distance moves to destinations offering an entirely new life style and a new environmental setting are often precipitated by retirement, moves of shorter distance, usually within the same community, are undertaken for health and family reasons.

The choice of a place to move to involves two closely related decisions, one dealing with the selection of a dwelling and the other involving the setting or community in which that dwelling is located. In choosing a community, those who move after retirement must consider whether they wish to remain where they lived before retirement. For those who decide to move elsewhere, the question becomes one of first choosing a region of the country and then selecting the particular community within that region offering the greatest number of attributes capable of fulfilling individual goals. In making these decisions, consideration must be given to the attractions and limitations of living in an age-integrated setting or one which is intended to attract a predominantly older population.

In this chapter, the retirement community option is considered. In doing so, we first examine retirement communities from a historic perspective and review past research on the topic. Next, we present a theoretical framework for considering relationships between retirement communities, their populations, and their surroundings. We then review a 1982 national study on changing properties of retirement communities, supported through an Administration on Aging (AOA) grant. As part of that review, a typology for classifying retirement communities is presented along with a characterization of each type. Finally, the future of retirement communities in the United States and thoughts on future research are discussed.

RETIREMENT COMMUNITY RESEARCH—A REVIEW

Intentional retirement communities, as they are commonly referred to, are not recent phenomena in the United States. Some date back to the 1920s, when various labor, fraternal, and religious organizations acquired relatively inexpensive property in Florida with the intent of creating a supportive living environment for their retiring members. Moosehaven, for example, was established by the Loyal (fraternal) Order of Moose as a means of caring for its retired members while at the same time demonstrating the fraternal claims of the Order (Gottschalk, 1975). Other sponsored communities in Florida were created for benevolent purposes until a series of catastrophes, culminating with the stock market crash of 1919, brought their development to a standstill (Duncan, Streib, LaGreca, & O'Rand, 1978).

The post-World War II period represented a new era of retirement community development, as private builders in Florida and in other parts of the United States became aware of the potential for marketing homes to a growing population of older Americans. Despite their success in attracting home buyers, planned residential developments catering to relatively homogeneous age groups have been viewed with skepticism by a number of social critics. Margaret Mead characterized such developments as "golden ghettos," while Lewis Mumford argued that such large scale organized living quarters for older persons were socially unnatural and should be avoided at all cost (1956).

The proliferation of retirement communities during the 1950s was accompanied by a rash of retirement community research, designed to examine some aspect of life in these residential settings. While the studies for the most part were intended to test the advisability of older persons living in an age-concentrated community, many examined relationships between the elderly and their surroundings. In one early retirement community study, Hoyt (1954) found that most residents (88%) preferred to live "in a community such as this, where everyone is retired, rather than one in which people were working." Reasons given for preferring the age-concentrated environment dealt with the possibilities for association with others, the mutual assistance in time of illness, and the desirability of being in a quiet, child-free setting. Similar findings were reported by Hamovitch and Larson (1966) in their study of Leisure World, California. The researchers found that three-quarters of the residents had been pleased with their move, and most (87%) said they would never consider moving out. In still another retirement community study in central Florida (Aldridge, 1959), a highly supportive environment was reported by residents who saw this as important to their well-being, while a California study of six retirement housing sites showed that residents' perceptions of community support were a function of the services available and the linkages between the housing site and its surroundings (Sherman, 1975). More recently, researchers at the University of North Carolina who examined residents' attitudes in two retirement communities and compared them with attitudes of older people in planned new towns, concluded that age-segregated communities were more supportive. They provided more opportunity for social contact and more protection from social isolation than did age-integrated new communities or conventional communities occupied by older people (Burby & Weiss, 1976).

Much of the research suggests that retirement communities are successful in their ability to support the needs of their elderly residents. The research also suggests that the type and level of support differ from one community to another as do the specific needs of their populations. Furthermore, there are indications that the links and exchanges between different types of retirement communities, the people within them, and the external environment vary greatly. However, the exact nature of these links and how they change over time has not been specified. In order to understand them better, relationships between the elderly and their environments should be viewed within a theoretical framework. Similarly, the limits and scope of what constitutes a retirement community should be defined.

A FRAMEWORK FOR EXAMINING PERSON–ENVIRONMENT RELATIONS

The concept of person–environment congruence or fit is offered as a means of examining links between retirement communities, their residents and their surroundings. In her work on environmental transactions of the elderly, Kahana (1980) suggests that people vary in the types and relative strengths of their needs, while environments vary in their capacity to satisfy these needs. A good fit, or congruence, occurs when the environment is able to satisfy individual needs. Conversely, when the environment is unable to satisfy these needs, there is a poor fit, or incongruence, between the person and the environment.

Another model of person–environment fit offered by French and his associates also bears on relationships between retirement communities and their populations (French, Cobb, & Rodgers, 1974; Harrison, 1978). The suggestion is made that there are two kinds of fit between the individual and the environment. One is represented by the degree to which the environment provides resources or supplies to meet individual needs. The second kind of fit considers the capabilities and resources of the individual in meeting the demands and requirements of the environment. A misfit or incongruence of either kind is seen as threatening to the individual's well-being.

In the context of our discussion, the environment of the elderly is seen as operating at two levels: the retirement community itself (internal environment) and the larger community in which the retirement community is located (exterior environment). The resources and services of these two environments could include various public and private facilities and programs ranging from health care and shopping to parks and transportation. Social support systems (family, friends, organizations) and opportunities for productive activity (employment, volunteer work) can also be viewed as resources.

The abilities and resources of the elderly have been conceptualized by Lawton (1972) as a set of competencies in the domains of biological health, sensorimotor functioning, cognitive skills, and ego strength. The financial status of the elderly might also be considered a resource. Finally, the requirements of the environment, or its "demand character," as described by Lawton and Nahemow (1973), can be viewed in terms of a retirement community's physical characteristics (steep slopes to negotiate, long distances between dwellings and services or facilities), the cost and availability of services, rules and regulations (no visitors after 11:00 P.M.), and social norms (dress codes, respect for privacy).

In addition to the links and exchanges that occur between the elderly and their interior and exterior environments, reciprocal relationships exist between retirement communities and their surroundings. For instance, tax revenues can flow from retirement communities to their host municipalities, which in turn provide various public services. Similarly, retirement communities can provide employment opportunities while at the same time contributing to the local economy. These reciprocal relationships are considered for different types of retirement communities later in this chapter.

DEFINING AND CLASSIFYING RETIREMENT COMMUNITIES

The empirical research discussed earlier has been conducted in settings ranging from mobile home parks and hotels to enclaves containing various housing arrangements and support services. Clearly, the term *retirement community* has assumed different meanings among researchers. Some consider retirement communities to be relatively self-contained, small entities, spatially separated from large population centers. Others have used the concept to refer to any communal living arrangement composed entirely or primarily of retired people. Whether or not a community is located in an isolated setting, the common ingredient of the places examined is the population, which, for the most part, is not employed or actively working in a regular occupation.

PAST EFFORTS—DEFINITION

An early attempt to define retirement communities systematically was made by Webber and Osterbind (1961), who classified retirement housing by the degree to which it involves congregate, segregate, institutional living. One class of housing was the retirement village, which was described as "a small community relatively independent, segregated, and non-institutional, whose population was mostly older people, separated more or less completely from their regular or career occupations in gainful or non-paid employment." The retirement village was viewed as noninstitutional, in the sense that the population was largely free of the regimen imposed by common food, common rules, common quarters, and common authority (p. 4).

More recent definitions also discuss the concept of independence and a relatively active older population living in a segregated setting. In a study of retirement communities in California, for example, retirement communities were defined as planned, low-density developments of permanent buildings designed to house active adults over the age of 50 and equipped to provide extensive services and leisure activities (Barker, 1966). Similarly, a study of retirement communities in New Jersey considered planned, low-density, age-restricted developments, constructed by private capital, and offering extensive recreational services and relatively low-cost housing for purchase (Heintz, 1976). Lawton (1980) refers to retirement communities as one form of planned housing for the elderly and characterizes them as privately developed and self-contained, imposing on age limitation on their residents and containing purchased homes and shopping, medical, and active leisure services. Longino (1980), on the other hand, takes a broader perspective and defines retirement communities as any subsidized or nonsubsidized living environment to which most of the residents have moved since they retired.

These definitions share several features. The practice of age segregation is noted in all, but the degree to which a community is segregated by age can vary. Some definitions imply absolute segregation, whereas others state that residents are *mainly* older people. All definitions suggest that the older people are physically well and active, and some may even be employed part-time or full-time. Finally, the concept of a planned or intentional community for older people is imbedded in most definitions.

Despite these common features, definitions of retirement communities as discussed in the literature vary in inclusiveness. Some definitions consider community attributes such as size, density of development, sponsorship, levels of service, tenure arrangements for residents, and location, whereas others ignore these attributes. With such diversity, it has been suggested that rather than relying on a single definition, a classification system or typology of retirement communities is needed in order to describe better this particular living arrangement for the elderly.

Past Efforts—Classification

Nearly 20 years ago, Burgess (1961) classified retirement communities according to their sponsorship, location, the type of services they offered, and their housing design. Others have described retirement communities according to their size, financial arrangements, architecture, and provision for leisure activities. Webber and Osterbind (1961), for example, classified retirement villages in three groups: real estate developments, supervised planned communities, and full-care homes and communities. Supervised and planned communities were further classified as trailer parks, dispersed dwelling communities, and retirement hotels. Planned retirement communities have been viewed by Longino and his colleagues (1980) as either subsidized or nonsubsidized, while they consider *de facto* or unintentional retirement communities as a third class. For others, however, retirement communities or villages are simply one of several classes of housing available to the noninstitutionalized elderly (Mangum, 1978; Walkley, Mangum, Sherman, Dodds, & Wilner, 1966).

There appears to be as much variation in the classification of retirement communities as there is in attempts to define them. Some classifications have been more exclusive than others, and rarely has a class or type of community within any classification system been clearly specified as to the boundaries or limits of what kinds of living arrangements would be considered within it. Furthermore, retirement communities have been treated as static environments, with no provision made for considering them as dynamic entities the definitions of which may change over time. It is clear from both the research and the popular literature that retirement communities and the populations within them have changed over the years: communities have grown in size, their physical structures and populations have aged, and in many cases new services to support the aging population have been introduced while others have been curtailed or even eliminated.

CLASSIFYING RETIREMENT COMMUNITIES—A BROADER PERSPECTIVE

As part of a 1982 Administration on Aging study of retirement communities in the United States, efforts were made to identify and classify such communities as a prelude to examining their changing properties.[1] Within the multipurpose study, retirement community identification was achieved through the development of a comprehensive directory, compiled from various public, nonprofit, and commercial sources published between 1964 and 1979. The comprehensive directory identifies all retirement communities by state and presents detailed information on community location, size, housing types, and sponsorship (Feldt, Hindert, & Vakalo, 1981).[2] Data from the directory have been used in satisfying another study objective—the estimation of the number of retirement communities throughout the United States, the size of the population living in these communities, and their geographic distribution (Marans, Feldt, Pastalan, Hunt, & Vakalo, 1982). Finally, in order to determine the extent and nature of change in retirement communities over time, case studies have been conducted on a small sample of communities selected from the directory. Within each of 18 retirement communities, an ethnographic approach was used in developing the case studies. The approach included on-site visits, an examination of archival records, and individual and group interviews with managers, developers, service personnel, local government officials, and residents.

The classification of retirement communities considered the need for variability on each of four community attributes: the scale of the community, its population characteristics, the level of services, and the sponsorship or auspices under which the community was built.

Scale

The scale attribute refers to the size of the retirement community population. To be considered a community, housing units must be available for at least 100 residents. Three size categories were defined using information gathered for the directory. Small retirement communities are places with 100 to 999 residents; medium-sized retirement commu-

[1]The study was conducted at the University of Michigan's Institute of Gerontology under Grant No. 90AR-0011/02. Co-principal investigators were Allan G. Feldt, Robert W. Marans, and Leon A. Pastalan.
[2]The directory was published as part of the final report and is available through the National Policy Center on Housing and Living Arrangements for Older Americans, College of Architecture and Urban Planning, The University of Michigan.

nities house 1,000 to 5,000 residents; large retirement communities are those containing populations of more than 5,000 residents.

Population Characteristics

The housing units in the community must be planned for people who for the most part are over 50 years old, independently healthy, and retired. Three resident groups typically characterize planned retirement communities. One consists of retirees who are healthy and no older than 75 years of age. A second contains retirees who tend to be older than 75 and generally healthy. A third group consists of a mix of healthy and frail retirees who are predominantly over 75. Large concentrations of frail elderly are likely to be found in nursing homes, which would not be considered retirement communities.

It should be noted that there are retirement communities that contain populations which are not altogether old, healthy, or retired. Retirement communities can house people under 50 years of age and older persons still actively engaged in the labor market. They might also provide nursing care for their frail elderly, although this group, by definition, would represent less than half of the total population.

Level of Services

The service attribute considers the type and quantity of health, recreational/leisure, social, and commercial services and facilities. At least one of these services or facilities must be available as part of the housing aggregation. Retirement community facilities and services related to health care include hospitals, nursing homes, clinics, doctors' offices, or special home care programs. Outdoor recreation facilities consist primarily of golf courses, swimming pools, tennis courts, and marinas, whereas indoor facilities range from meeting rooms to club houses and libraries. Services can also be represented by programs such as arts and crafts, classes, and outings to local area attractions. A commercial service can vary from a shopping center with an array of stores to a gift shop or a privately operated snack bar in a single building housing elderly retirees. Health care and outdoor recreation are viewed as the most important dimensions of the service attribute, and together with a combination of other services (social programs and facilities, commercial, housekeeping, maintenance), form five basic service packages found in retirement communities: extensive health, outdoor recreational, and other services; limited health and extensive outdoor recreational and other services; limited health, outdoor recreational, and other services; limited health and outdoor recreational services with an extensive array of other services; limited outdoor recreational services with extensive health and other services.

Sponsorship

Retirement communities can be built by one of two groups of sponsors or developers. One is represented by a private building or development company operating as a profit-making venture; the other is the nonprofit sponsor such as a church group, fraternal organization, or trade union. Many retirement communities in the latter group have been built with subsidies under various U.S. Department of Housing and Urban Development programs.

In sum, retirement communities are defined as aggregations of housing units, intentionally planned for at least 100 residents who for the most part are over 50 years of age, healthy, and retired. Moreover, they can be built under various forms of sponsorship and must provide their residents with a minimal level of services.

FIVE TYPES OF RETIREMENT COMMUNITIES

Any retirement community can be classified using various combinations of the four attributes. It should be recognized, however, that these attributes can change over time. For example, the residents may age and become increasingly frail, the population may grow, community sponsorship may change, or the service package may be altered. Hence a classification system or typology which takes into account the changing nature of retirement communities is viewed as essential to defining and understanding them.

Five types depicted in Table 1 are most representative of retirement communities in the United States today. These are retirement new towns, retirement villages, retirement subdivisions, retirement residences, and continuing-care retirement centers. A characterization of each type is presented in the following paragraphs, with special consideration given to their service characteristics, population, and links between residents, their communities, and the surrounding environment. The material, unless otherwise noted, is drawn from the case studies conducted as part of the AOA study.[3]

[3]A detailed discussion of the 18 retirement community case studies is presented in Hunt *et al.* (1984).

TABLE 1
CHARACTERISTICS OF FIVE TYPES OF RETIREMENT COMMUNITIES

Type of community	Scale	Resident characteristics	Level of services	Sponsorship
Retirement new town	Large	Young, predominantly healthy	Extensive health, outdoor recreational, and other	Profit
Retirement village	Medium	Young, predominantly healthy	Limited/no health; extensive outdoor recreational and other	Profit
Retirement subdivision	Large, medium, or small	Young, predominantly healthy	Limited/no health, outdoor recreational, and other	Profit
Retirement residence	Small	Old, predominantly healthy	Limited/no health, outdoor recreational; extensive other	Nonprofit
Continuing-care retirement center	Small	Old, mixed healthy and frail	Extensive health; limited outdoor recreational; extensive other	Nonprofit

RETIREMENT NEW TOWNS

These communities are designed for young, healthy retirees interested in a leisurely but active life style within a self-contained community setting. As privately built developments, they contain various health services and an extensive network of outdoor recreational facilities and leisure programs. New towns are most commonly located in the sunbelt and western states because the climate is conducive to year-round outdoor activity. They are the largest of the retirement communities, having a population of at least 5,000 residents. Many are considerably larger, however. The 1981 populations of two well-publicized retirement new towns, Arizona's Sun City and Leisure World at Laguna Hills, California, were 47,500 and 42,000 respectively. Although new towns represent only 1% of the retirement communities in the United States, they house approximately 30% of the entire retirement community population.[4]

[4]These estimates and those that follow are based on data compiled as part of the AOA study. They represent communities included in the directory and exclude publicly man-

Service Characteristics

Since retirement new towns are designed to be virtually self-contained communities, they contain a wide range of support services and
facilities. In fact, when compared to other types of retirement communities, new towns offer the most extensive network of recreational, medical, commercial, and financial services and of housing types. Opportunities are available for both outdoor and indoor recreational pursuits
ranging from golf and swimming to drama, arts and crafts, billiards, and
bridge tournaments.

Retirement new towns also contain full health care and medical
facilities. Hospitals are often present, while clinics, doctors' offices, and
laboratories are always available. The communities may even contain
nursing homes or continuing care retirement centers. For example, there
are two continuing care centers within Sun City, Arizona, and two more
are adjacent to the community. Sun City Center, Florida, contains a
sheltered care facility, and Leisure World at Laguna Hills contains a new
retirement residence. Finally, shopping facilities, banking, and opportunities for dining out are abundant, making it convenient for residents
to conduct personal affairs without having to leave the community.

Various housing options are available to prospective new town residents. Single-family homes, 2- and 4-plex housing, and townhouses
abound. High-rise buildings designed for residents seeking security and
continuing health care may also be found in retirement new towns. In
addition to fee simple ownership, rental units, condominiums, and cooperative living arrangements are available.

Population Characteristics

Retirement new towns tend to attract young and active retirement-
aged people. The average age of the resident population is likely to be
less than 75. However, the population in some places is much younger.
For example, the typical resident in Sun City Center is 64 years old.
Households for the most part consist of couples having a moderately
comfortable retirement income. Many maintain another house or apartment in a northern state and use it during the summer months. Others
travel extensively. Although fewer than one-third of the residents work
either full or parttime, many are involved in voluntary activity within
the retirement community.

---

aged retirement living arrangements such as public housing for the elderly. For a complete discussion of the directory, the procedures for generating it, and the types of living
arrangements excluded, see Feldt *et al.* (1981) and Marans *et al.* (1983).

Person–Environment Relations

Residents of retirement new towns live in highly supportive environments. Retirees who seek a challenging, active life style are supplied with an array of recreational facilities and programs, and opportunities for less active leisurely pursuits are also abundant. Residents are served by privately provided medical services and institutional health care, although in some cases these services may be located beyond community boundaries. Numerous classes and organizations offer opportunities for the elderly to socialize, while a sense of safety and security is often fostered by perimeter walls, patrols, and security gates restricting access to the community. In contrast to the closed, impermeable community, some retirement new towns (Sun City Center, Florida, and Sun City, Arizona) are open and undifferentiated from their surroundings. In these instances, feelings of security may not be as pronounced.

As in other types of retirement communities, new town populations include aging segments. Many communities, built during the 1960s, house long-term residents who moved in before retirement and are now in their 70s or 80s. In some places, this aging process has been accompanied by a general trend toward an increasingly older population. Whereas the average age of residents was 60 years at one time, it is now 75. In other places, however, the average age of residents has remained constant over time or has even declined. In part, a declining average age has been the result of an influx of a younger population. Yet most new towns house long-term residents who have aged there.

Within the aging population, some have reduced their involvement in community affairs as they experience declining health. Generally, these aging residents are less mobile than they had once been. At the same time, their need for various supportive services has changed, particularly with respect to housing, health care, transportation, and social and recreational activities.

Among the different types of retirement communities, new towns have been most accommodating to these changing needs. With respect to health care, new hospitals and programs such as homemaker services have been introduced, often at the instigation of the residents (Sun City, Arizona, Leisure World at Laguna Hills, California). In some cases, the private sector has responded to changing needs, either within or adjacent to the new towns. Private developers and nonprofit groups have built retirement residences (Leisure World, California) and continuing care centers (Sun City, Sun City Center), designed to accommodate the need for more sheltered living arrangements, smaller independent housing units, health care, and, in general, a more supportive living environment. Physicians and nursing homes have also responded by opening offices and facilities within or near retirement new towns.

The aging of the retirement new town population has prompted some residents to play increasingly supportive roles in their own communities. In one place (Leisure World, California) citizens groups have volunteered to look in on their less healthy neighbors, do their shopping, and provide transportation. In another new town, the aging population was recognized by a local governmental unit which introduced a dial-a-ride service in the community.

External Relations

Various reciprocal relationships exist between retirement new towns and their residents on the one hand and the surrounding environment on the other. As large-scaled, privately sponsored communities offering a variety of services, retirement new towns contribute substantially to the local economy through tax revenues and the consumption and saving patterns of their elderly residents. The introduction of a retirement new town is likely to improve the tax base of the local governmental unit and school district in which it is placed. Tax-base improvement comes directly from new retirement housing and other forms of development added to the tax rolls, and indirectly through adjacent land development attracted in part by the presence of the retirement community. Elderly residents, many of whom are affluent, are consumers of various goods and services and support sizeable amounts of retail, institutional, and office space which in turn are taxed by the host community.

Using data from a New Jersey retirement communities study, Heintz (1976) found that the tax revenues generated by the presence of retirement communities were far greater than the local public expenditures necessary to meet the needs of the elderly population. Similarly, the AOA study reports lower public service expenditures for retirement new towns than for nearby, comparably sized residential developments housing younger populations (Hunt, Vakalo, Marans, Feldt, & Pastalan, 1984). Several new towns characterized by their extensive security systems police themselves; others have volunteer fire departments. All contribute tax dollars to the local school without using them. In some places, developers have built community roads and installed utility systems, which in turn have been sold or deeded to the local governmental unit.

Data from the New Jersey study also show that the voting behavior of the elderly is no different from that of the nonelderly in the surrounding communities (Heintz, 1976). If, for instance, the general population is supporting or rejecting a bond issue, the retirement community would tend to vote in the same manner. In other cases, however, new town residents have voted in opposition to the general population; for example, the residents in one new town were instrumental in the defeat of a local school millage (Hunt *et al.*, 1984).

Few residents of retirement new towns are likely to become involved in local area government. Although some participate as elected officials, or as members of policy-making boards and advisory committees, most who are inclined to participate in community affairs do so within the retirement community. Similarly, there is little social contact between residents of retirement new towns and their peer groups in the wider community. The social life of most residents tends to be concentrated within their age-segregated setting. The little contact with the outside world that does take place occurs through ties with family members or through voluntary work at nearby schools, churches, or hospitals.

RETIREMENT VILLAGES

These medium-sized communities are designed to house a young, healthy retirement and preretirement population in a secure setting offering a wide assortment of outdoor recreational facilities and programs. Unlike the retirement new towns, they contain limited commercial facilities, and if health care is available, it is sparse and unobtrusive. Most retirement villages are privately developed, although historically a number have been built under union or church sponsorship. Villages are smaller than retirement new towns; they generally range in size from 1,000 to 5,000 people. And unlike new towns, retirement villages are not planned to be self-contained communities. Rather, they are located in urbanizing areas having a full range of services from which the community and its population can draw. Although they are commonly found in sunbelt states, villages have also been built in several northern states. Current population estimates indicate that villages represent 11% of all retirement communities and house approximately 81,000 residents.

Service Characteristics

Retirement villages house an active older population and have an extensive network of recreational and communal facilities. Indoor facilities typically include a clubhouse with rooms for meetings, performances, crafts, games, and an assortment of classes. Outdoor facilities include swimming pools, golf courses, shuffleboard courts, and tennis courts. In short, the recreation and leisure facilities of the retirement village often rival those associated with retirement new towns.

Because retirement villages are not planned to be self-contained, autonomous communities, the extent to which they provide shopping facilities either on site or on the perimeter of the village can vary. Some, such as Leisure World in Maryland, contain a few private businesses, while others have commercial establishments adjacent to their property. Still others, such as Hawthorne near Leesburg, Florida, have neither on-site nor nearby commercial facilities.

Similarly, the provision of health care facilities varies among villages. Most offer only emergency medical service. Leisure World, Maryland, on the other hand, contains a fully staffed medical clinic, laboratory facilities, a pharmacy, and a home-visiting service.

The mixture of housing type, quantity, and density also varies, both within and between retirement villages. Options include single detached homes, 2 to 8 plexes, low-rise and high-rise apartment buildings, and mobile homes. Leisure World Maryland, Leisure Village West in New Jersey, and the Leisure Village in Camarillo, California, each contain a mix of housing units. In contrast, Country Village Apartments near Riverside, California, and Hawthorne offer only one type of housing—low-rise apartment buildings and mobile homes, respectively.

Variability exists in the form of housing tenure as well. In addition to traditional fee simple ownership, cooperative and condominium arrangements (Leisure World Maryland, Leisure Village, and Leisure Village West), rentals (Country Village Apartments), and mobile home ownership combined with lot rental (Hawthorne) are available. Regardless of tenure arrangements, residents typically pay a monthly fee to cover the operating costs of recreational facilities and other community services.

Population Characteristics

As in the case of new towns, retirement villages tend to attract a young, active, and generally healthy population. Occupancy is typically limited to adults who are at least 50 years old, although some communities are age-integrated. For the most part, the population consists of retired couples in their late sixties, college-educated, and financially independent. Not all retirement villages, however, house an affluent and educated population. In one instance, social security is the major source of income for nearly half of the residents. and many have no more than a high school education. Nonetheless, retirement villages have tended to attract an increasingly affluent population as these communities mature. In part, the changing financial status of residents is a function of rising service costs. As these costs increase, monthly fees are raised or a fee-for-service charge instituted for services and activities previously included as part of the monthly charge. As a result, it has become increasingly expensive for retirees on limited and fixed incomes to live in retirement villages.

Person–Environment Relations

The degree to which retirement villages have been supportive of resident needs varies from community to community. Whereas most villages are able to satisfy the recreational and leisure interests of their populations, few are able to serve residents who require medical or nursing care. Similarly, many villages provide a safe environment, isolated from outsiders by virtue of walls and/or security gates. At the same time, they require residents to leave the enclave in order to shop or conduct personal business.

Retirement villages also vary in the degree to which they are willing and able to accommodate the changing needs of their aging populations. Developers of one retirement community may gradually alter the service package as the population ages. In another village, the developer may strive to maintain a stable environment by not introducing new services for the aging residents. Similarly, they may offer a limited choice in housing, thereby eliminating opportunities to move to a smaller or larger dwelling as the need arises.

Housing and leisure facilities and services are generally geared to one group—healthy older people. Many aging residents whose needs change are forced to move from the community when extensive care is required and they are no longer able to function within their dwellings. In these instances, the changing needs of the population are typically met outside the community where nursing homes, continuing-care centers, and other support services are available. Other villages may provide supportive housing within the community, often in the form of congregate housing offering meals and maid service. In most cases, however, the aging populations in retirement villages have to rely on support services from the external environment.

In general, retirement villages tend to be less supportive than new towns, largely because they are less autonomous and more restrictive in their use of land for developing new unplanned facilities. That is, unless land for facilities and/or programs for the future are contemplated or planned at the inception of the retirement village development, the facilities or programs are unlikely to be provided at a later date.

External Relations

As in the case of retirement new towns, there are a number of reciprocal arrangements between retirement communities and their surroundings. Improvements to the governmental tax base are likely to be great as a result of new housing development. Similarly, growth on adjacent land, partly with commercial and medical services supporting the retirement village, increases the tax revenues of the host community. In some instances, supportive services geared to a retirement village population have been the impetus for additional residential developments catering to other retirement populations.

Public expenditures to support retirement villages are generally low since the communities make little use of police and fire protection, parks, and recreational or educational services. Residents from villages using nearby health care services pose no more of a burden than the elderly living elsewhere in the area (Heintz, 1976). Even if retirement village residents do require extensive medical services, most of the costs are borne by Medicare rather than by the local governmental unit.

With respect to voting behavior and participation in governmental affairs, retirement village residents are no different from those people living in retirement new towns. The extent of social contact with the outside world is comparably limited. The social life of most village residents tends to be concentrated within the retirement community. However, the degree to which there are links between village residents and outside services, friends, and relatives can vary and is an individual matter rather than one influenced by village characteristics.

RETIREMENT SUBDIVISIONS

These privately built residential environments, planned for a predominantly independent and healthy elderly population, have limited outdoor recreational facilities and support services. Retirement subdivisions vary in size and are intentionally planned to be an integral part of the fabric of the surrounding community, which is usually rich in services and other amenities. The larger community is viewed as the major attraction for prospective residents who seek a predominantly elderly population and a living arrangement unencumbered by a costly infrastructure. Retirement subdivisions, therefore, tend to be located within urban areas of Florida and other sunbelt states so as to take advantage of the favorable climate, the proximity to other elderly, and the services necessary to support them. Despite their being characterized as retirement communities which house a predominantly over-50 population, subdivisions are often age-integrated. Data from the AOA study indicate that subdivisions comprise about 10% of the universe of retirement communities and house an estimated 87,000 people.

Service Characteristics

Compared to retirement new towns and villages, services and facilities within subdivisions are limited. Outdoor recreational opportunities typically include shuffleboard courts and, if the community is near water, a beach area and/or a marina. A community building combining a card room, a meeting area, and/or laundry facilities may also be available. However, commerical, medical, and nursing facilities are unlikely to be incorporated in the subdivision infrastructure. Such services are part of the external environment.

Retirement subdivisions are characterized by either one or two types of housing—conventionally built single-family homes or mobile homes. In subdivisions containing conventionally built homes, such as Orange Gardens in Kissimmee, Florida, residents own their dwellings. Tenure arrangements vary in mobile home developments, however. In some places, the home and lot are both owned by the occupant, whereas at other sites the mobile home is purchased while the lot is leased from the developer.

Population Characteristics

Although many retirement subdivisions pose limitations on the age of prospective residents, others do not or restrict occupancy to adults 18 years of age or older. For example, residents of a mobile home park near Phoenix, Arizona, must be at least 50 years old, whereas a Florida mobile home development is referred to as an adult community and prohibits residents under 18 years of age. Still other subdivisions have sections of the development set aside for young couples while at least one (Orange Gardens) permits families with school-age children. Most retirement subdivisions, however, house a predominantly older population; the majority of their residents are retired and were attracted to the community by its relatively homogenous elderly population and the modest cost of living. Even Orange Gardens, which has no age limitation, has maintained a predominantly over-50 population for more than 25 years.

Older residents in retirement subdivisions are similar in many respects to residents in retirement new towns and villages. Households typically consist of married couples in their seventies and in good health. However, residents tend to be less affluent than their counterparts in retirement new towns and villages. Since the subdivisions contain fewer services and, in general, lower housing costs, they are more affordable then other types of large-scale retirement communities. Retirement subdivisions have been referred to as the "bargain" retirement communities of the south.

Person–Environment Relations

Compared to other types of retirement communities, subdivisions represent the least supportive form of retirement living. Opportunities for pursuing recreational and other leisure interests are limited. Health care is nonexistent, and shopping and other essential services are located beyond the boundaries of the community.

Particularly problematic is the inability of retirement subdivisions to accommodate the changing needs of residents as they age. Most residents move to more supportive environments when their health begins to deteriorate. This phenomenon is most likely to occur in mobile-home subdivisions where access to the housing unit is a serious problem for the increasingly frail elderly. Under the circumstances, subdivisions are best characterized as constant environments, rarely introducing new facilities, housing, and/or programs which enable their populations to age in place.

External Relations

Retirement subdivisions and their residents are intrinsically linked to their surroundings. As privately built residential developments, subdivisions significantly improve the property tax base of the municipality in which they are located. Their residents are consumers of nearby goods and services ranging from groceries to medical care. Many also use local public services, such as parks and recreation facilities, libraries, and public transportation. Several residents work full-time or part-time outside the subdivision, and unlike those living in new towns and villages, many are socially and politically active in the host community. This pattern of residential involvement outside as well as within the community is more natural and is consistent with original development goals of the retirement subdivision: to be an integral part of the external environment.

RETIREMENT RESIDENCES

These small retirement communities are typically designed to accommodate independent, older retired persons at a moderate cost.

Many are characterized as congregate housing, a living arrangement offering its residents meals in a common dining room and other shared services. They are likely to be built under the sponsorship of nonprofit organizations, such as church groups, fraternal orders, or service clubs. In many cases, federal assistance programs such as Section 202 are used in the development process so as to enable residences to house moderate-income retirees. Nonetheless, several are privately sponsored and cater to an affluent elderly population.

Retirement residences are not associated with any particular region. In most parts of the country they are located in urban areas near public transportation, shopping, and medical services. Estimates from the AOA study indicate that nearly half (47%) of all retirement communities in the country are residences, which together house roughly 175,000 people.[5]

Service Characteristics

To a large extent, residences are small communities of older people, housed in a single high-rise building. They contain fewer than 500 dwelling units, most of which are apartments rented on a monthly basis. Charges to residents cover meals and sometimes services such as laundry and transportation. Besides dining facilities, where residents are required to eat at least one meal per day, retirement residences often contain communal rooms such as lounges, a meeting room, and a library. These and other new facilities enable residents to engage individually or collectively in an array of sedentary activities. Few, if any, opportunities exist for active outdoor recreational pursuits, while commercial uses are either limited or nonexistent. Finally, residences are unlikely to contain health facilities, although a number of congregate housing environments make limited provision for medical care to tenants.

Population Characteristics

The population in residences tends to be older than that found in retirement new towns, villages, and subdivisions. The typical resident is a single woman in her late 70s, white, and living on a modest income. She, like her neighbors, is generally in good health and able to live independently. She leaves the residence when she wishes and rarely

---

[5]These estimates are admittedly conservative and do not take into account "communities" for the elderly built under federal sponsorship but not inventoried as part of the AOA study.

seeks assistance from the staff. She was attracted to the residence by its relatively modest cost, the services and security it offered, and potential for finding a socially supportive environment.

Person–Environment Relations

Most retirement residences are supportive environments catering to older healthy retirees interested in maintaining an independent life. Although they are billed as places for independent older people, a number of residences in practice serve less independent retirees than the more common genre, "independent housing." Residences offer the combination of shelter and a package of services at a relatively modest cost, although some congregate housing can be very expensive. A sense of security is fostered by the availability of on-site services, a protective physical environment, and the proximity of other elderly whose life styles are compatible. However, many retirement residences are unable or unwilling to support their aging populations as their health care and social service needs change over time. In an effort to maintain the original character of the community and its residents, while at the same time minimizing the rate of increase in operating costs, some residences have established policies aimed at creating a stable or nonchanging environment. In doing so, their increasingly dependent residents are forced to seek alternative living arrangements. For many residents, the move is emotionally disruptive. In contrast to these retirement communities operating under a constant model, other residences have established policies aimed at accommodating the changing requirements of their tenants (Lawton, Greenbaum, & Liebowitz, 1980; Spector, Moss, & Lawton, 1982). Accommodation occurs through physical modification of the facility or through policy or programmatic changes. In one New York City residence, for example, the elderly were permitted to hire live-in nursing assistants rather than be forced to seek nursing care in another residential setting.

In addition to accommodating the changing needs of the elderly through management decisions, accommodation has also occurred at several retirement residences through outside intervention. In some places, public agencies have introduced special housekeeping, counseling, and other social services on-site, while in other residences, public and/or nonprofit service organizations have offered assistance to tenants at nearby locations (Spector *et al.*, 1982). Although the younger members of the community maintain a degree of independence involving shopping, social contacts, and voluntary activity outside the retirement residence, there is a tendency for aging tenants to become increasingly dependent on the services provided within the facility (Lawton, 1976). In some places, the provision of off-site services has helped to counteract this growing dependency, while at the same time fostering closer ties between the retirement residence and the external environment.

External Relations

Not surprisingly, retirement residences have a significantly smaller impact on the local economy than retirement new towns, villages, or subdivisions. In residences such as congregate housing where meals and sundry items are available, the consumptive behavior of occupants in the outside community is limited. Similarly, when residences are built as nonprofit entities, their tax-exempt status precludes their contributing to the tax base of the local governmental unit. Public expenditures associated with retirement residences are generally comparable to those associated with age-integrated apartment complexes of the same size. Expenditures are lower where various social and health programs, shopping, and meal programs are available within the facility. Depending on their health and mobility and the degree to which the external environment is viewed as safe or hostile, residents may venture outside the community to visit family and friends, conduct personal business, attend religious services, or perform volunteer work at nearby schools or hospitals. With the introduction of increasingly rich on-site service packages, contacts with the external environment tend to diminish.

CONTINUING-CARE RETIREMENT CENTERS

These small-scale retirement communities provide a highly supportive environment, based on a concept of continuing care. They provide multiple levels of housing under the same administrative umbrella with an independent living arrangement as a starting point for new residents. Various levels of nursing care are also available.

Continuing care centers offer retirees numerous structured programs and opportunities for passive leisurely pursuits. However, few if any contain outdoor recreational facilities, and if commercial services are available, they are limited in number and scope.

Continuing-care retirement centers generally operate under nonprofit sponsorship. They tend to be located in urban areas, although some are found in rural settings. As in the case of retirement residences, these communities are located in all parts of the country. They represent about a third of the retirement communities in the country and contain an estimated population of 124,000 retirees.

Residents of continuing care retirement centers are housed in either a building complex or multicare campus, or in a single structure. Campuses typically contain a mix of residential buildings, dining facilities, meeting rooms, and medical facilities. Residential structures range from congregate apartment buildings to free-standing cottages and town-houses. If the center is housed in a single structure, all medical facilities, dwellings, and support services are housed under one roof.

Service Characteristics

Full health and medical services are offered to older persons from their early, independent retirement years to a period when they are totally dependent. These communities enable an older person to have a completely independent life while being assured that health care and other support services are available later within the building or complex.

Continuing-care retirement centers offer three levels of nursing care: skilled, intermediate, and personal or sheltered.[6] They may also contain an infirmary for temporary nursing care. To staff these facilities, an assortment of health-care professionals is available, including nurses, physical therapists, social workers, and physicians. Because of the wide range of supportive services, continuing care retirement centers have the highest resident-to-staff ratio of the five types of retirement communities.

In addition to medical and social services, continuing-care centers offer residents the opportunity to pursue various social and recreational interests. Many have facilities and programs for arts and crafts, games, classes, billiards, and choral groups. As in the case of the retirement residences, they rarely have facilities for active outdoor sports such as golfing, tennis, and swimming. Most continuing-care communities contain a congregate dining area, a snack bar, a library, a chapel, a beauty shop and barber shop serviced at specified times throughout the week, lounges for informal gathering, and sometimes a gift shop and small convenience grocery.

---

[6]Skilled nursing care is defined as a full range of 24-hour direct medical, nursing, and other health services. Intermediate care also involves 24-hour service, but with physicians and nurses in a supervisory role. Personal or sheltered care is offered to residents having no serious health problems but who nonetheless have chronic or debilitating conditions requiring assistance with daily activities.

Many continuing-care retirement centers require residents to enter into a life-care contractual arrangement. This contract guarantees an independent living unit to residents at admission and access to nursing care whenever it is needed. The life care contract typically involves an initial endowment or founder's payment, and a monthly fee. The endowment is either nonrefundable or only partially refundable if the resident decides to leave or dies within a specified short period. The amount of the endowment varies considerably between and within communities and depends on the regional location and the size, type, and placement of the living unit. A few years ago, it was not uncommon to find endowments ranging from $10,000 to $75,000, while monthly maintenance fees varied from $200 to $2,000 (Hunt *et al.*, 1984).

Continuing-care retirement centers have more restrictive admissions requirements than other retirement communities. Applicants must have reached a minimum age, usually over 50, and must meet specified health and financial standards. In most cases, prospective residents must demonstrate at entry an ability to live independently for a period of time, say 3 to 5 years, and to afford the endowment and monthly fees.

Population Characteristics

People attracted to retirement centers tend to be older and less physically active than residents of other age-segregated communities. A significant number are frail. The typical resident is an elderly woman in her late 70s or early 80s, widowed, and from either a middle- or upper-middle-class background. Couples occupy a small proportion of the independent living units, and in rare cases the husband continues to work outside the community, usually on a part-time basis. However, few residents leave the site for prolonged periods of time.

Person–Environment Relations

Continuing-care retirement centers are highly supportive environments geared to older persons who seek medical and financial security during their retirement years. Within centers, there are opportunities for residents to live independently while partaking of a wide range of community affairs. They do so knowing that they will be cared for in spite of future housing and medical costs. Several levels of nursing and medical care are available to support retirees from the time they enter the center to the period when they become totally dependent. Furthermore, a number of centers offer housekeeping and meal services and a variety of planned programs catering to residents' interests and needs.

Inherent in continuing-care centers is their ability to adapt and continue to support the needs of their residents as they age. To a large extent, centers are adaptive because of the diversity of nursing and medical services available and the relative ease with which new services can be added as the communities grow. At the same time, many offer a range of housing and living accommodations enabling residents to move from one dwelling to another within the community as their housing needs change. In doing so, the elderly are unencumbered by problems associated with relocation, such as the need to adapt to a new housing environment (Bourestom & Pastalan, 1981).

External Relations

As in the case of retirement residences, continuing-care retirement centers have little direct impact on the local area economy. Although residents living in independent housing may be active consumers of nearby goods and services, others, particularly the frail elderly in nursing units, have a limited home range and consequently are unlikely to engage in business activity outside the community. At the same time, the full range of services needed to support these people requires a sizable staff, resulting in substantial employment opportunities for the local area population.

Since most continuing-care centers are operated under nonprofit sponsorship, they do not contribute tax dollars to their host municipalities. But neither does their presence impose a burden on local government by substantially raising public expenditures for transportation, police and fire protection, health care, or social services.

Contacts between the continuing care-centers and the outside world are largely dependent upon the health and home range of the population and the particular setting within which the centers are located. Among residents living in independent housing units and owning an automobile, many visit regularly with friends and family, run errands for their less mobile neighbors, volunteer at nearby schools, hospitals, and churches, or work part-time outside the community. These contacts are most likely to occur at the centers located in safe urban neighborhoods rather than at geographically isolated sites. For the frail elderly and those with limited mobility, links to the outside are restricted to visits by family members and outings arranged by the center. At some centers within urban areas, outreach or day-care programs are available to the elderly living in the surrounding community. Older people living alone or with working children in the vicinity of a Chicago retirement center attend programs at the center, use its facilities, or are housed there daily (Hunt *et al.*, 1984).

OVERVIEW

There appears to be a high overall level of person–environment congruence between the needs of most elderly residents and their respective communities. To a large extent, these needs are met by resources supplied by the internal environment. When internal resources are unavailable, congruence is maintained with a supply of resources from the external environment. In retirement new towns and villages where the populations are relatively young, active, and healthy, the resources supplied to them include outdoor and indoor recreational facilities and programs conducive to a challenging and active life style. Other resources include organizations and service personnel capable of fulfilling various supportive and affiliative needs. In subdivisions containing populations similar to those found in new towns and retirement villages, recreational, organizational, and other resources are less likely to be available internally and are generally found in the external environment.

The populations of retirement residences and continuing-care centers are older on average than residents of the larger communities and are inclined to lead a more passive life. Although many are healthy, residents are likely to participate in arts and crafts and board games rather than in activities such as golf or tennis. In continuing-care centers, segments of the population are frail and served by the internally supplied medical and other health care resources.

Internally placed medical resources are also available to residents of retirement new towns. However, few exist within retirement villages and residences, and none exist in retirement subdivisions. In some instances, health care has been introduced at retirement residences and villages so as to accommodate the medical needs of their populations as they age (Lawton, 1976; Spector *et al.*, 1982; Hunt *et al.*, 1984). In most instances, however, retirement villages, subdivisions, and residences have operated under a constant model, and the medical needs of the aging residents are usually met by outside resources. In rare cases where both the internal and external environments are unable to support the medical needs of the population, there is a mismatch or incongruent person–environment fit which threatens the well-being of residents.

The fit between the environment and residents' needs for security from intruders is reflected in the physical design of several retirement villages and new towns which feature security walls and limited points of entry. Controlled access is also characteristic of retirement residences and continuing-care retirement centers. Most retirement communities police themselves, although some (e.g., retirement subdivisions) rely on the external environment for police protection.

In general, the populations in each of the five types of retirement communities have the necessary abilities and resources to meet the demands of their respective environments.[7] As this review has indicated, most residents of retirement new towns, villages, and subdivisions are biologically healthy, financially able to maintain their homes and pay for services, geographically mobile, and compatible with their social and organizational environments. Many of the elderly in retirement residences and continuing-care centers are restricted in their mobility, but their environments pose fewer demands by providing easy access to services. Within these environments, the elderly are financially able to pay for the package of services they seek and use. They are also able to adapt to the organizational and social constraints imposed by their respective communities.

In retirement communities such as subdivisions where the interactions and exchanges between the population and the exterior environment are great, the degree to which environmental demands match resident resources is indicative of the level of person–environment congruence. For example, where shopping is inconveniently located and residents either do not have automobiles or are no longer able to drive, the level of person–environment congruence will be low.

To recapitulate retirement communities can be divided into two somewhat overlapping groups according to the nature of their person–environment congruence. One group, composed primarily of retirement new towns and continuing care centers, is initially supportive of their populations and supportive during later periods when the residents and their needs change. This group of communities also includes retirement villages and residences which are adaptive and able to accommodate to the changing requirements of their aging populations. The second group includes all retirement subdivisions and villages and

---

[7]Because of the ethonographic approach used in conducting the case studies, detailed data covering the abilities and resources of retirement community residents and their needs were not obtained. The match suggested by the authors between these resident attributes and the different environments is based on study observations, and the empirical findings of others (Lawton, 1969; Sherman, 1972; Longino, 1980).

residences that are initially supportive but nonadaptive or constant in their supply of resources. Although communities in the second group are able to satisfy needs initially, they are relatively unresponsive to residents as their needs change over time. To a limited extent, some of the changing requirements of the community's aging population are met by resources from the exterior environment. In most cases, however, the person–environment match becomes increasingly incongruent as the population ages.

This chapter has also described a number of reciprocal exchanges between the communities and their external environments. As we have indicated, the nature of these exchanges varies greatly and is dependent upon the characteristics of the retirement community population, the community's internal resources, and those available in the surroundings. For instance, all retirement communities contribute to the economy of the host community, but the nature of economic contributions differs from place to place. Most retirement new towns, villages, and subdivisions are privately developed and generate substantial tax revenues for the local governmental units and school districts within which they are located. Retirement residences and continuing-care centers, on the other hand, are typically built under nonprofit sponsorship and are therefore exempt from paying property taxes.

Retirement new towns, villages, and subdivisions, and to a less extent retirement residences house populations who also contribute to the local economy through consumer purchases and bank deposits. The populations of continuing-care retirement centers are less likely to spend and save locally, but their contributions to the local economy take on a different form. These communities are rich in medical and other services and have a high staff–resident ratio, creating employment opportunities for the local area population. Retirement new towns and some retirement villages are also service-rich and offer jobs ranging from construction and maintenance to security and recreation and leisure programming.

Although few retirement community residents are employed inside or outside their communities, a number engage in voluntary activity within their communities and at nearby schools, churches, and hospitals. In doing so, they are providing a service to institutions in the host community which, if deemed essential, would otherwise have to be purchased. Other retirement communities such as continuing-care centers service the local area by offering outreach programs such as day care for the unattended elderly living alone or with children.

In exchange for the various contributions it receives, the external environment supplies the retirement community with numerous public and private services and other resources. The degree to which retirement communities rely on the external environment for support is an important dimension of community autonomy and varies between and within the five types of communities.[8] For example, retirement new towns demonstrate a high degree of autonomy and independence, relying mostly on internal resources to serve their populations. On the other hand, a full range of public and private services from the external environment are necessary to support the less autonomous and more dependent retirement subdivisions.

Even though most retirement new towns have their own commercial, recreational, and medical services and in some cases police and fire protection and transportation, some are served by selected resources from the external environment. Regional shopping centers, parks, and hospitals are used when internally provided commercial, recreational, and medical facilities are unavailable or unable to meet specific needs of the new town population. Police and fire departments of the host community are also used when internal protection is limited or unavailable, and area-wide social service agencies offer a range of services available to new town residents. Many of these external resources are likely to flow into retirement villages as well, and all are crucial to the support of retirement subdivisions.

For retirement residences, a number of services available in the external environment, such as medical care, are required for community and resident support. However, because the people in residences are older and less active than the those in the larger retirement communities, less extensive external services are required.

As in the case of retirement new towns, most of the service requirements of continuing-care retirement centers and their residents are available internally, and consequently there is little need to use resources from the external environment. However, nearby shopping, public transportation, and recreational and cultural resources often serve the more mobile residents and those living in the independent housing units of the retirement community.

THE FUTURE OF RETIREMENT COMMUNITIES

At the beginning of this chapter, we noted that a variety of housing opportunities are available to older Americans contemplating retire-

---

[8]The concept of community autonomy is also viewed as a function of the locus of decision making which affects various aspects of retirement community life. This concept is discussed in Duncan, Streib, LaGreca, & O'Rand, 1978 and Streib, LaGreca, & Fotts, 1982.

ment. One set of options rests within the five types of planned retirement communities. Yet, despite considerable attention given to these communities in the popular press, they have attracted only a small segment of the retirement market. According to our estimates, there are less than one million older people living in retirement communities, even as we have broadly defined them. Although the study described above did not deal with communities of less than 100 persons, publicly supported and managed retirement residences (public housing), or continuing-care centers for veterans, we suspect that no more than 10% of older Americans are currently living in an age-segregated residential environment.

Most older people, given the choice, prefer to remain in their homes during their retirement years. Although in the future many new retirees will contemplate moving to another location, few will do so until such time as their housing becomes a financial burden or they are unwilling or unable to live independently. The majority will continue to live in places they occupied during their preretirement years.

The retirement community option, however, will continue to be available and may in fact become more viable in the future. Several factors point in this direction. First, there are increasing numbers of older Americans retiring with sizeable accumulated assets, largely derived from participation in pension programs and equity build-up through home ownership. New legislation allowing a once-in-a-lifetime $100,000 tax exemption when selling a house is viewed as particularly attractive to older people and is expected to increase the number of them who change their residence. These trends are being recognized by the home building industry. Second, residential developers, public policy makers, and older people themselves are being sensitized to the specific health care needs of people over 50 and to the fact that these needs can be met within the context of carefully designed new living arrangements. Finally, there is increasing recognition by many that security, social support, and productive activity, factors so important to the well-being of the elderly, can be found within an age-segregated setting.

PROSPECTS FOR NEW RETIREMENT COMMUNITIES

Although more retirement communities are likely to be available later in this century, new developments should differ in several respects from those created in the past. It is unlikely, for instance, that large "new towns" such as Sun City, Arizona, will be added to the stock of retirement communities. Such developments require sizeable tracts of land, and community builders have found it increasingly difficult and costly to assemble such tracts. Similar problems were experienced by builders of the age-integrated planned communities in the 1960s. Without federal programs aimed at easing the financial burden and, concomitantly, a dramatic reduction in interest rates and construction costs, the building of either age-integrated or age-segregated new towns no longer will be a viable option for developers. Rather, we expect that new retirement community development will focus on smaller-scale villages, subdivisions, residences, and continuing-care retirement centers.

As a means of reducing development and operating costs, builders of retirement villages may offer fewer and/or less costly amenities. Golf courses, for example, may be replaced by lawn bowling greens, tennis courts, and jogging trails as a means of more efficiently utilizing land while meeting new consumer interests. Similarly, higher-density developments will enable builders to reduce the overall construction cost per dwelling unit. Other village and subdivision builders will use manufactured housing units, such as mobile homes on small, low-maintenance lots, in order to minimize development costs while at the same time, attracting less affluent retirees.

Many retirement community builders will market various health care services so as to attract both older retirees and the young elderly who are sensitive to the fact that their needs will change over time. The number of continuing-care retirement centers should expand to meet the demands of the longer-living elderly who will seek a protective environment guaranteeing them continuing health care.

New retirement communities will also reflect changes in life styles of the future elderly. Although golfing will continue to be a popular sport among older people, other forms of recreation will be needed to accommodate new generations of retirees who have developed the physical skills and motivations for exercise and physical activity. We noted the provision of jogging trails and tennis courts as a means of efficiently using land. These facilities will also be required to serve older people who were jogging and playing tennis in their 20s, 30s, and 40s and who will want to continue doing so in later years. Similarly, national survey data show that downhill and cross-country skiing, hiking, camping, and fishing have become increasingly popular activities for Americans over 45 years of age (Bevins & Wilcox, 1980). If these trends continue and are recognized by retirement community builders, new retirement communities are likely to appear in places readily accessible to recreational and resort areas offering these activities.

It is also possible that new retirement communities may no longer reflect a sharp distinction between work and leisure. Many retirees in the future will want or need to combine both and could be attracted to places which allow them to do so. High rates of inflation and a desire to remain active in the labor market, together with new laws against age discrimination and forced retirement, will be factors contributing to the growing proportion of older Americans who combine part-time work and retirement. Many new retirees will continue working as they had in earlier years but with a possible reduction in hours, and others will seek out new career opportunities. These patterns suggest a need for creating retirement communities near employment centers, many of which are located outside the sunbelt states. Whereas most of today's retirement villages and subdivisions are found in the south, these classes of retirement communities could begin to appear in other parts of the country. Marketing efforts will aim at attracting older people who will retire in name only. Similarly, retirement villages, subdivisions, and continuing-care centers could become available in urban areas of the north in order to attract older people who want a new social environment and life style while remaining close to family, friends, and familiar settings.

Prospects for Existing Retirement Communities

Within existing retirement communities, a number of changes are likely to occur in the future. The AOA study has shown that in several communities pressures have been placed on developers, managers, and local governmental units to adjust to the health care needs of the aging populations where medical services are limited or nonexistent. In all likelihood, such pressures will continue and intensify, particularly in communities currently housing a predominantly young elderly population that will not want to move. Paralleling demands for various forms of health care within communities will be increases in the cost of providing other services, such as recreation programs, transportation, and general community maintenance. In turn, increasing operating costs will place a greater financial burden on community residents. Many will move as monthly assessments rise, while those who remain will either bear the financial burden or experience a reduction in the quantity and quality of services offered to them. In some cases, the changing demand for services may be placed on the governmental unit within which the retirement community is located.

It should be clear that these forces will result in changes in the character of several existing retirement communities and their populations. With the introduction of health care services, retirement residences could evolve into continuing-care centers, and villages could grow and become new towns. Similarly, subdivisions which add recreational facilities could take on the character of retirement villages. They may even become age-integrated communities over time as their older residents are replaced by younger families.

Many of the changes that have occurred in the past in the evolution of retirement communities will no doubt be experienced by other retirement communities as they move through similar evolutionary stages. At the same time, unanticipated changes are likely to occur in their evolution which, together with the changes outlined above, could threaten the lives of residents. An awareness of the nature of these changes for the different types of retirement communities will be a first step toward maintaining a satisfactory fit between retirees and their environments.

SOME DIRECTIONS FOR FUTURE RESEARCH

This chapter has presented an overview of retirement communities within the context of a multidimensional typology. The typology has been offered as a means of defining and classifying the wide range of planned living arrangements for older people. Although this typology is perhaps more inclusive than previous efforts to define and classify retirement communities, it is not without limitations. It might be argued that planned, publicly supported housing for older people is another form of retirement communities, while concentrations of elderly residents in selected neighborhoods of large cities and in small towns and rural areas of the country represent unintentional retirement communities. In the future, these two types of living arrangements should be examined in order to understand further two fundamental questions addressed by the AOA study: How do retirement communities change over time, and how have the communities responded to the needs of their aging populations? Specifically, consideration should be given to the manner in which older residents of public housing are supported as they age. The conditions under which national and local policies foster accommodation to their changing needs or ignore them is worthy of investigation. At the same time, studies of unintentional retirement communities might consider how these communities have evolved and how local units of government have served their elderly residents over time.

More detailed study of communities within each class of the typology is also warranted. For example, understanding the development process of both privately built and nonprofit communities can be useful to those in the public and private sector interested in creating new retirement communities. Similarly, the experiences of benevolent groups in their efforts to create supportive living arrangements for their members or other specific populations can offer lessons to groups of unaffiliated elderly who seek a shared living arrangement during their retirement years.

Within each type of retirement community, both elderly residents and individuals from the surrounding area worked in the retirement community on a voluntary basis. The degree to which volunteerism is crucial to the economic success of the communities needs further exploration. Similarly, since voluntary activity as a form of productive behavior is gaining interest among developmental psychologists and older Americans, the concept must be more thoroughly understood from a sociopsychological perspective.

More detailed study is warranted within each group of communities on the social and psychological needs of residents. The investigation reported in this chapter was qualitative: a limited sample of communities was examined using an ethnographic approach. Data collection focused on the community rather than on the community resident. Consideration should be given to more detailed and systematic examination of the people in retirement communities, including their rationale for being there, their experiences in dealing with changes in their health and the environment around them, and their plans for the future. More detailed studies of residents and management within retirement communities can be useful in refining the typology offered here, while at the same time providing the insights necessary for the better planning of housing environments for future generations of elderly.

Finally, we believe that new, experimental age-segregated and age-integrated living arrangements for the less affluent retiree must be designed and tested. Important examples of such arrangements include the "share-a-home" movement, the introduction of "granny shacks" and similar family-integrated units, and arrangements for the elderly which have and are being attempted in many utopian communities. These experiments could be designed for older people who are interested in moving into a supportive environment but are unable to afford the amenities and services offered by the present stock of retirement communities.

REFERENCES

Aldridge, C. Informal social relationships in a retirement community. *Marriage and Family Living*, 1959, *21*, 70–72.

Barker, M. *California retirement communities*. Berkeley, Calif.: The Center for Real Estate and Urban Economics, Institute of Urban and Regional Development, University of California, 1966.

Bevins, M. I., & Wilcox, D. P. *Outdoor recreation participation—Analyses of national surveys, 1959–1978. Vermont Agricultural Experiment Station Bulletin* 686, 1980.

Bourestom, N. C., & Pastalan, L. The effects of relocation on the elderly. *Gerontologist*, 1981, *21*, 4–8.

Burby, R. J., & Weiss, S. F. *New communities U.S.A.* Lexington, Mass.: D.C. Health, 1976.
Burgess, E. (Ed.). *Retirement villages.* Ann Arbor: Division of Gerontology, University of Michigan, 1961.
Duncan, C. J., Streib, G., LaGreca, A., & O'Rand, A. M. *Retirement communities: Their aging process.* Paper presented at the 31st Annual Meeting of the Gerontological Society, Dallas, Texas, November, 1978.
Feldt, A. G., Hindert, T. T., & Vakalo, K. (Eds.) *A directory of retirement communities in the U.S.* Ann Arbor: National Policy Center on Housing and Living Arrangements, College of Architecture and Urban Planning, University of Michigan, 1981.
French, J. R. P., Jr., Cobb, S., & Rodgers, W. L. A model of person–environment fit. In G. V. Coelho, D. A. Hamburg, and J. E. Adams (Eds.), *Coping and adaptation.* New York: Basic Books, 1974, pp. 316–333.
Gottschalk, S. S. *Communities and alternatives: An exploration of the limits of planning.* New York: Halsted Press, 1975.
Hamovitch, M. B., & Larson, A. E. *The retirement village.* Paper presented at the Institute for for State Executives in Aging at the University of Southern California, Idyllwild Campus, February, 1966.
Harrison, R. V. Person–environment fit and job stress. In C. P. Cooper & R. Payne (Eds.), *Stress at work.* New York: Wiley, 1978, pp. 175–205.
Heintz, K. M. *Retirement communities: For adults only.* New Brunswick, N.J.: The Center for Urban Policy Research, Rutgers-The State University of New Jersey, 1976.
Hoyt, G. C. The life of the retired in a trailer park. *American Journal of Sociology,* 1954, *59,* 361–370.
Hunt, M., Vakalo, K., Marans, R. W., Feldt, A. G., & Pastalan, L. *Retirement communities: An American original.* New York: Haworth Press, 1984.
Kahana, E. A congruence model of person–environment interaction. In M. P. Lawton, P. G. Windley, & T. O. Byerts (Eds), *Aging and the environment: Directions and perspectives.* New York: Springer Press, 1982, pp. 97–121.
Lawton, M. P. Supportive services in the context of the housing environment. *Gerontologist,* 1969, *9,* 15–19.
Lawton, M. P. Assessing the competencies of older people. In D. Kent, R. Kastenbaum, & S. Sherman (Eds.), *Research, planning, and action for the elderly.* New York: Behavioral Publications, 1972, pp. 122–143.
Lawton, M. P. The relative impact of congregate and traditional housing on elderly tenants. *Gerontologist,* 1976, *16,* 237–242.
Lawton, M. P. *Environment and aging.* Monterey, Calif.: Brooks-Cole, 1980.
Lawton, M. P., & Nahemow, L. Ecology and the aging process. In C. Eisdorfer & M. P. Lawton (Eds.), *Psychology of adult development and aging.* Washington, D. C.: American Psychological Association, 1973, pp. 619–674.
Lawton, M. P., Greenbaum, M., & Liebowitz, B. The lifespan of housing environments for the aging. *Gerontologist,* 1980, *20,* 56–64.
Long, L. M., & Hansen, M. A. Reasons for interstate migration: Jobs, retirement, climate and other influences. In *U.S. Bureau of the Census, Current Population Report, Series P-23,* No. 81. Washington, D. C.: U.S. Government Printing Office, 1979, pp. 1–29.
Longino, C. F., Jr. Retirement communities. In F. J. Berghorn and D. E. Schafer (Eds.) *The dynamics of aging: Original essays on the processes and experience of growing old.* Boulder, Colo.: Westview Press, 1980, pp. 391–418.
Mangum, W. P. Retirement villages: Past, present and future issues. In P. Wagner and J. M. McRae (Eds.), *Back to basics food and shelter for the elderly.* Gainesville: University Presses of Florida, 1978, pp. 88–97.

Marans, R. W., Feldt, A. G., Pastalan, L. A., Hunt, M. E., & Vakalo, K. L. *Changing properties of retirement communities*. In Urban Land Institute (Eds.), *Housing for a maturing population*. Washington: Urban Land Institute, 1983.

Mumford, L. For older people—Not segregation but integration. *Architectural Record*, 1956, *119*, 193–197.

Newman, S. J. Housing adjustments of the disabled elderly. *Gerontologist*, 1976, *16*, 312–317.

Sherman, S. R. Satisfaction with retirement housing: Attitudes, recommendations and moves. *Aging and Human Development*, 1972, *2*, 339–366.

Sherman, S. R. *The retirement community setting: Site permeability, service availability, and perceived community support*. School of Social Welfare, SUNY at Albany, 1975.

Soldo, B. J. America's elderly in the 1980s. *Population Bulletin*, 1980, *35*(4).

Spector, A., Moss, M. S., & Lawton, M. P. *Changing patterns of formal service provision at five housing sites for older people*. Duplicated report. The Philadelphia Geriatric Center, 1982.

Streib, G. F., La Greca, A., & Fotts, W. E. *The life history of retirement communities: Comparative studies of thirty communities*. Paper presented at the 77th Annual meeting of the American Sociological Association, San Francisco, California, September, 1982.

Walkley, R. P., Mangum, W. P., Jr., Sherman, S. R., Dodds, S., & Wilner, D. M. *Retirement housing in California*. Berkeley, Cal.: Diablo Press, 1966.

Webber, I., & Osterbind, C. C. Types of retirement villages. In E. Burgess (Ed.), *Retirement villages*. Ann Arbor: University of Michigan, 1961, pp. 3–10.

4

Alternative Modes of Living for the Elderly

A CRITICAL REVIEW

J. KEVIN ECKERT AND MARY ITTMAN MURREY

INTRODUCTION AND MACROSOCIAL ANALYSIS

This chapter will review critically literature and issues surrounding alternative housing for the elderly. It will focus on three central objectives:

1. To clarify what is meant by the concept of *alternative housing*. In the past it has been a murky and diffuse concept of limited heuristic value. In our analysis alternative housing will be viewed from two related yet different perspectives. First, a housing type will be considered alternative if it represents an alternative to institutonalization in a nursing home or other extended-care facility. Second, an alternative will include housing types which are considered atypical, newly emerging, or generally ignored in the literature.
2. To suggest a conceptual framework for organizing research and discussion. Thus far research on and discussion of alternative housing has been devoid of a guiding conceptual framework. For example, important levels of analysis such as macrosocial forces

J. KEVIN ECKERT and MARY ITTMAN MURREY • Department of Anthropology, Case Western Reserve University, Cleveland, Ohio 44106.

have not been taken into consideration or given adequate attention.

3. In general terms, to outline areas for future research and discussion.

What Is Alternative Housing?

Alternative housing most commonly refers to either (a) alternatives to institutionalization, that is, nursing homes, or (b) exceptions to the more common and traditional housing arrangements. The basic dimension underlying alternatives to institutionalization is the level and degree of social and medical support required. These alternatives provide a level of support enabling the older person to live in a community environment. The range of alternatives lies on a continuum of support between independent living without any support to institutionalization in a nursing home; housing along this continuum of increasing support includes housing built especially for the elderly and handicapped, congregate housing, and life-care communities which provide continued care, from independent apartment dwelling to skilled nursing care within the same facility.

Alternative housing also can be understood as an exception to the norm, describing housing arrangements which are more uncommon. Alternative housing based on "statistical rarity" is designed to "serve individuals whose needs fall through the cracks of more traditional forms" (Lawton, 1981a, p. 65). This view is valuable because it is based on the assumption that older people are not a homogeneous group but rather are as diverse as the younger population and that housing should reflect these varying interests, preferences, and needs. Looking at alternatives in this way also enables us to understand and gain insights into the varied and often creative ways in which older people adapt to the demands of aging as well as to their own preferences for housing.

Lawton mentions five broad categories of residential types: (a) community residence, (b) planned housing, (c) congregate housing, (d) domiciliary and personal care housing, (e) nursing homes. Within each of these broad categories, it is possible to differentiate between the more common or widely known traditional housing arrangements and those which are considered atypical, newly recognized, or recently documented (alternative) housing arrangements. The specific housing arrangements can be roughly organized along a support continuum from highly independent to ever increasing degrees of dependent living. Under the residential category of community housing, six alternative modes of living have been identified. While some of these alternatives have existed for decades, interest in them and research on them is recent. For example, the concept of the cooperative apartment has been with us for some time, as have single-room-occupancy hotels, yet serious discussion of these arrangements has only recently emerged. Some other alternatives are gaining in importance as they become more widely known and publicized, for example, home-sharing and foster homes. Two types of alternative can be included in the congregate housing category, as well as two specific housing arrangements in the domiciliary/personal care category—the Share-A-Home and community housing concepts and the boarding Home and foster Home.

DETERMINANTS OF HOUSING CHOICE

An important question arises at this point regarding the availability of housing designated as either traditional or alternative. What must be emphasized is that *traditional* refers to the housing form and not necessarily its ready availability. For example, planned housing for the elderly is a form of housing which may be considered traditional but is relatively rare and in high demand. Newly constructed subsidized housing has rehoused approximately 1.2 million older persons representing just under 5% of the older population (U.S. Department of Housing and Urban Development, 1976). This is not adequate to meet the housing needs of the elderly (Carp, 1978). Retirement and life-care communities, considered alternatives by some, for the most part serve only the more affluent. Therefore, when we discuss housing of any type, two major determinants of housing choice must be considered and kept in mind: enablement and preference (Lawton, 1981a). Enablement includes income, geography of residence, organizational membership, and supply of housing. Preference is based on a variety of needs including independence, privacy, security, and an appropriate social milieu.

One class of alternative housing is based primarily on lack of enablement. These alternatives, such as foster and boarding homes, are developed for and used by older people who cannot avail themselves of the more traditional and desirable housing arrangements such as congregate housing, retirement centers, or even well equipped apartments, because they do not have the financial resources or because there is a shortage of such housing. Changes occurring in the physical capability of the individual or in the social environment (for instance, gentrification) may force older people to choose new housing accommodations. Because there is not enough adequate and decent rental housing stock or congregate housing, or because there is only limited community assistance, many may be forced into one of these commonly recognized but less desirable alternatives.

Other alternatives such as communes, house-sharing, retirement centers, and in some cases mobile homes can be seen to result primarily from preference for a particular kind of housing arrangement, which may be somewhat less commonly available or used. As Lawton points out (1981a), it should be remembered that only when enablement requirements are met and support is congruent with needs does preference predominate. For the most part, these alternatives are limited to those older persons who have the financial resources to obtain it.

Many housing decisions, however, are a complex mix of enablement and preference; the SRO hotel exemplifies this complexity. For some of those who use these hotels enablement is the key decision-making factor, whereas for others preference is primary. For example, some residents of these hotels mention lack of financial or familial resources as a reason for living in hotels rather than in more desirable housing arrangements. Those residents who emphasize preference as a reason for selecting hotels maintain that the living environment of a hotel best matches their preferences for privacy, socialization, and security.

Although the importance of what could be termed enabling factors is recognized in the literature, there is a tendency for these determinants to recede into the background and for preference factors—individual psychological, physiological, and social attributes—to assume primacy in discussions of housing alternatives. The person–environment fit model exemplifies this approach and tendency (cf. Kahana, 1980; Moos & Lemke, 1979). Although larger social, political, and economic forces may be mentioned, they are not well developed or integrated into the decision model, where individual choice, adaptation and functioning in a particular microenvironment predominate. This one-sided approach blurs the vast differences between housing that arise primarily from lack of resources and a limited range of choices (SRO hotels, boarding and foster homes) and that based primarily on preference and resources (communes, house-sharing, congregate housing, life-care communities). It also neglects the importance of housing as a profit-making industry in shaping and determining the range of housing choices available. It is important not to blur the differences between housing such as congregate housing that is custom-built to serve the needs of older persons because there are sufficient funds from the government or a consumer market and housing such as boarding homes which, though prof-

itable to the owners, are far less likely to serve the needs of the elderly
who are forced to live in them.

There is a need to expand the approach to housing choices and
options from one based primarily on the individual as the basic unit of
analysis to one emphasizing social events, forces, and processes that
transcend the individual and order the very existence and range of housing alternatives from which older people must choose.

ECOLOGICAL HOUSING MODEL

The conceptual model for this paper views the individual elderly
person nested in multiple interrelated environmental systems. The basic
premise is that a person's behavior and psychological state can be better
understood with knowledge of the contexts in which that person be-

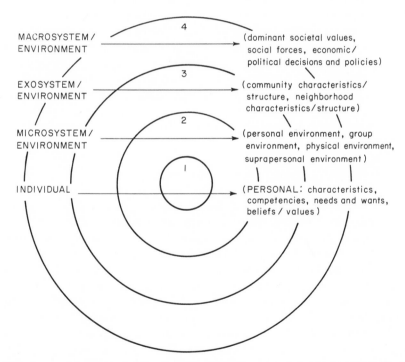

Figure 1. An ecological model of housing illustrating the various levels that influence
choice of housing arrangement.

haves (Lawton, 1980a). The framework used here to conceptualize alternative modes of living for the elderly goes beyond the microcontext, in which behavior is enacted, to encompass the larger context of community and societal systems. Alternatives can emerge from at least two extreme vantage points. First, they can emerge from the preferences of the elderly themselves. However, preference does not operate in isolation but is determined as well by perceived options and constraints. Thus what is perceived as an option and what is available are determined by forces operating in the larger social and political system, as in the case of legislation that provides for the development and planning of certain kinds of living arrangements and structures and not for others. Our ecological model has four separate and interrelated components (Figure 1).

THE INDIVIDUAL

Here the concern is with the individual characteristics such as life history and past behavior, physical and mental competencies, and various other personal demographic factors. A major question here is what to include in the concept *person*. Lawton and Nahemow (1973) have tried to view the person in terms of "competencies" in the domains of biological health, sensorimotor functioning, cognitive skills, and ego strengths. As noted by Lawton (1980a), these domains are basic to all others, they are relatively enduring and to some degree measurable.

THE MICROSYSTEM

The concern here is for the immediate environmental context in which the individual is embedded. Aspects of the microsystem/environment can be expressed in several different ways. From a psychological viewpoint, this level of the system can be seen as exerting a pressure or demand on the individual (Murray, 1938). Personal competencies and environmental demands interact along a continuum with a resultant positive or negative outcome for the individual in terms of behavior and affect. Positive affect and adaptive behavior represent a point at which environmental "press" is "average" for whatever level of competence the person in question possesses (Lawton & Nahemow, 1973). Kahana's concept of person–environment congruence is the rough equivalent of Lawton and Nahemow's concept of balanced competence and press; that is, people vary in their types and relative strengths of need, and environments vary in the extent to which they satisfy these needs.

The environment at the microlevel can also be seen as consisting of other meaningful dimensions. Lawton (1980a) has reviewed at least four:

1. The *personal environment* consists of significant persons in the life of the subject, such as parents, spouse, children, friends, and fellow employees.
2. The *group environment* (Altman & Lett, 1970) refers to the pressures attributable to the behaviors of individuals active as a group in some structural relationship to the subject. Included here are such phenomena as group pressures and social norms.
3. The *suprapersonal environment* consists of aggregate characteristics of individuals in physical proximity to the subject. Average income, age of neighbors, and ethnic composition are expressions of this dimension.
4. The *physical environment* refers to the natural or built environment.

At the microsystem level, Moos has developed the most sophisticated system of measurement and assessment. Through the use of various scales, Moos and his colleagues are able to assess environments in terms of physical, organizational, human-aggregate, behavior-setting, and social climate dimensions (Moos, Gauvin, Lemke, Max, & Mehren, 1977). As noted by Lawton (1980a), the future direction of this work may allow one to assess the separate contributions of personal, suprapersonal, social, and physical aspects of environment to the total stimulus value of institutional settings.

THE EXOSYSTEM

This is the level of the local community or neighborhood. The concept of community is elusive, yet aspects of it deserve mention. First is the territorial aspect of community, a recognizable and bounded domain. Useful in this regard is Sjoberg's (1964) definition of community as "a collectivity of actors sharing a limited territorial area as the base for carrying out the greatest share of their daily activities" (p. 114). The second aspect of the community is the collection of institutions with physical, personal, and social components that provide life-supporting and life-enriching services to individuals (e.g., stores, banks, social agencies, local government) (Lawton, 1980a).

The collection of community-based institutions creates a structure. That is to say, social, economic, and physical components of the environment are organized in different and discernible ways (Berry, 1972). At this level of our ecological model, therefore, we are concerned with structural characteristics of communities as they affect people at the local level. An excellent study involving this level of analysis is Barker and Barker's (1961) structural view of how the elderly behave in two quite different small-town environments.

The exosystem also may be expressed in terms of neighborhood, a unit of smaller scale than community (Lawton, 1980a). The neighborhood environment is of critical importance for the elderly. It may be a source of basic resources and services, physical security or threat, social interaction and entertainment, and many other satisfiers of human needs and wants. The transactions between older persons and their neighborhoods have been considered from several different vantage points including how the neighborhood is defined by different people (Lee, 1970; Regnier, Eribes, & Hansen, 1973); what people know about their neighborhoods (Regnier et al., 1973; Regnier, 1976); how people use their neighborhoods to support their needs (Chapman & Beaudet-Walters, 1978; Eckert, 1980; Kendig, 1976; Newcomer, 1976; Rosenberg, 1970); the effects of the suprapersonal or aggregate characteristics of people who inhabit the neighborhood (Bell, 1967; Cowgill, 1978; Lawton, Nahemow, & Yeh, 1980; Rosenberg, 1970; Rosow, 1976); and factors influencing perceptions of satisfaction with neighborhoods (Lawton, 1980a; Lawton & Hoover, 1979; Lawton & Yaffe, 1979; Lebowitz, 1975; McAuley, 1977; Peterson, Hamovitch, & Larson, 1973).

THE MACROSYSTEM

The global context of our ecological model is concerned with the political processes, economic forces, and all social events and processes which operate within and as part of a capitalist society and state and which influence almost every level and sphere of life. For example, the economic logic of capitalism, whether in housing, medicine, or manufacturing, necessitates the maximization of profit as the primary goal and priority. At the level of political decision making and policy formation, decreased federal regulation of industry and business, tax structures, and cuts in social spending are examples of the forces which affect the quality of life for all of us.

Gentrification, condominium conversion, the character of the housing stock, the economic position of the elderly, and changes in the economy are examples of such political decisions and policy. These political and economic forces have profound and widespread impact on the social environment and thus on housing choices; yet for the most part they are beyond the control of individuals.

ALTERNATIVE HOUSING MODES

The ideal would be to discuss findings on each alternative at each level of the ecological framework, but this is impossible. In most cases research knowledge of alternative housing arrangements is limited to only one or two levels of the framework. Typically, alternative housing is discussed in terms of the immediate environmental context in which the individual is embedded with little attention given to exosystem or macrosystem variables. Where possible, however, we will use the proposed framework as a setting for describing areas needing further study and exploration.

ALTERNATIVES WITHIN THE COMMUNITY RESIDENCE CATEGORY

Communes and Cooperatives

Several articles in recent years have discussed cooperative and communal style living for the elderly (Lawton, 1981a; McConnell & Usher, 1979; Streib & Streib, 1975). It is apparent that the number of elderly who are involved in or who might be interested in this particular alternative arrangement is extremely small. As Lawton noted, there are no firm estimates of the number of people of any age who live in true communal style. Such utopian communities seemed to have reached their peak in the 1960s and early 1970s. They corresponded with other social movements of that era and were centered particularly in the values of the young adult cohorts of that time. Pooling of financial resources, sharing household tasks, providing mutual support, and experimentation with supposedly untried ways of life were all characteristics of original communal arrangements. Cooperative and communal arrangements exist today in which older adults do live, but they are hard to document and little if any research has been done in such contexts. One example is provided by Maggie Kuhn, the founder of the Grey Panthers, who has converted her own home and another one nearby into a cooperative. In Lawton's words, "Life there is totally independent, always stimulating, and embodies every ideal of affective and instrumental exchange among people of all ages. But there are few Maggie Kuhns" (Lawton, 1981a). This statement is especially apropos since it points to a key factor in the success of such arrangements—the need for a strong charismatic leader and persons who share unique personal qualities. This particular housing arrangement puts a premium on individual characteristics and values and relies heavily on individual preference as a factor in choice.

While many gerontological planners and policy makers may herald the ideal of communal and cooperative living as a good idea for older people, it does not seem to be a particularly attractive alternative to present cohorts of older adults. For example, a three-year demonstration project in Kansas City was unable to open a communal house because older people could not be found who were willing to share space and household responsibilities. A total of more than 3,000 older persons were contacted about the program, yet only 100 were interested enough to request additional information, and almost none were willing actually to move into the home. Lawton (1981a) cited another expensive project on retirement cooperatives funded by the Administration on Aging (October 1978). He noted that the product of this project amounted to a grandiose plan for a national network of living, social, and employment cooperatives with little data to support the feasibility of the idea.

Comments of Streib and Streib (1975) on the improbability of widespread development of truly communal living for the elderly are well taken and reflect factors operating at several levels of our ecological framework. Their prediction is based on three factors: (a) the structural constraints of contemporary society which result in a fear on the part of most community residents of unconventional or "unnatural" family types; (b) the conditions and attitudes of the elderly themselves relevant to maintaining freedom, autonomy, and privacy; and (c) the relatively negative attitudes of the young communards towards including older people in their communities.

We need to know a great deal more about the feasibility and internal organization of communes and cooperatives. Better information on the prevalence of this arrangement would be most helpful with special attention directed toward regional and local differences in values and attitudes. For example, one might predict that such arrangements could flourish in some cosmopolitan areas of the United States. Future research should also address changes in attitudes toward communalism among adjacent cohorts of the elderly.

House-Sharing

House-sharing can take two forms: either renting a room to another person or converting a portion of a home into an apartment. The most typical form is to rent a room without remodeling. In such cases kitchen privileges are allowed as well as use of other living spaces. House-sharing is different from other rooming home arrangements in that it has emerged as a planned activity conducted by social agencies with the expressed purpose of convening owners and tenants. McConnell (1979) states that sharing a home develops from at least three factors operating at the individual level and related to enablement: financial status, companionship, and health. In a study done in Los Angeles county, McConnell reported that home owners rated "help in emergency" and "companionship" as the most important advantages of house sharing. Gillan (1976) notes that in college towns it has been typical for older persons, mostly women, to take in a college student as a roomer. In the past, matching of tenant to homeowner was done informally. More recently, intermediaries have been developed to interview and screen both owners and applicants, matching them against criteria voiced as important by both sets of clients. These arrangements may entail a simple verbal rental agreement or an elaborate communal contract in which all expenses, chores, and facilities are shared equally (McConnell, 1979).

McConnell and Usher (1979) provide data on several home-sharing programs in operation in the United States. Project Share, based in the Family Service Association of Nassau County, New York, is the largest project of its kind. This OAA Title III funded project deals with both short- and longer-term finances. Recent data on this project show that as of March 1982, 1,083 owners and tenants had been served, 541 of whom were together as of that time (Inz, personal communication, 1982). As noted by Lawton (1981a), home-sharing meets short-term as well as longer-term residency needs and problems. The number of turnovers points to the need for short-term residencies to meet transitory housing problems like eviction or late occupancy. McConnell (1979) provides information on other house-sharing programs in San Jose, California (Project Match); and in San Francisco (Project Share). Further information can be obtained on sharing housing from the Shared Housing Resource Center located in the Grey Panther headquarters in Philadelphia.

The potential for house-sharing seems great. Inz (personal communication, 1982) reports that since Project Share was initiated over 1,000 requests for information have been made. Approximately 70% of persons 65 and over are home owners and 97% of them live in "uncrowded" units (Wallin, 1972). However, this vast potential for house sharing must be weighed against the attractiveness of this arrangement to the present cohort of elderly. As noted by Lawton and Bader (1970), the importance of privacy increases with age. At the level of individual preference the loss of privacy brought on by house-sharing may be its greatest liability. In the future, however, factors operating at the macrosocial level, such as the possibility of reduced funds for home maintenance programs and other assistance, may turn more elderly to house-sharing as a last resort.

Reliable information concerning this alternative is increasing with the development of the Shared Housing Resource Center in Phila-delphia. At this point research is needed on macrosocial forces which might foster or inhibit the future growth of this alternative. As well, a further exploration of cohort differences in individual values such as privacy and independence must be undertaken. While we espose these values at the macrosocial or cultural level, successive numbers of elderly may show increased variability in the personal importance they attach to these values.

Mobile Homes

The mobile home is a rapidly growing alternative to home owner-ship. In this chapter, *mobile home* refers to a freestanding and stationary housing form usually anchored to a plot of land. These units provide completely furnished housing in one package; and newer mobile homes have concealed wiring, sockets in each room, insulation, and modern plumbing. They are compact and function much like an efficiency apart-ment and allow for independent living (Elrod, 1979). Rausch and Hoov-er (1980) provide very important data on the structural characteristics of mobile homes and the elderly who reside in them. A considerable por-tion of the 65-year-old and over population live in mobile homes. In 1975, 17% of the population occupying mobile homes were elderly; as of 1976, 4.9% of all people over 65 lived in mobile homes. A key factor for the increase in mobile home occupancy appears to be the opportunity they afford for home ownership, still a highly valued role in our society (Meeuwig, 1970). The vast majority of elderly living in mobile homes own their units (92%), with 61% of them having paid cash for them (Rausch, 1979). Modern mobile homes can be purchased with FHA loans either by contacting the lender directly or by going through a mobile home dealer approved by the lender (Elrod, 1979). Initial lower cost, however, may be offset by site rentals, higher financing charges, and higher depreciation (Weitzman, 1976).

Approximately half of all mobile homes are located on individual plots of land in small groups, while the remaining half are in groups of six or more and are referred to as mobile home parks (Rausch & Hoover, 1980). Monthly lot rentals in these parks can range from $50 and up-ward. As a rule, utilities are extra, as are clubhouse and recreational fees in the newer parks (Elrod, 1979). Residents of units located in the larger groups have greater access to utility and service systems (Rausch & Hoover, 1980), which might be a function of the larger groups' being located closer to public utility, water, and sewer systems. However, because of their peripheral or rural locations, mobile homes generally have poorer access to municipal services than other housing types.

The durability and quality of construction of mobile homes is an important variable in assessing this type of housing. Newer and more expensive units built after 1965 are not necessarily of higher quality than older units. Hazardous heating and electrical system breakdowns occur in greater proportion in these units and present serious hazards to all age groups. Rausch and Hoover (1980) point to the need for more uniform codes to regulate the manufacture of mobile homes. Distance from resources coupled with other utility problems suggests that everyday environmental demands are greater for mobile home dwellers (Lawton, 1981a).

Mobile home communities have been shown to possess unique social environments, and several studies exist which address the micro-level dimensions, the individual and social characteristics, of these environments for older persons in particular (Fry, 1977; Hoyt, 1954; Johnson, 1971). Both Johnson and Fry estimate that age-graded mobile home parks have mushroomed around urban centers primarily in states with warm climates. Fry has conducted the most recent field studies of two small age-graded mobile home communities which differed in terms of degree of risk related to land tenure and the role of the developer. In the first community, Casa Del Oro, the role of the developer was marked by default; whereas the developer for the second community, Equus Estates, continued to be a patron and sponsor. The two communities also differed in terms of three other features: (a) more white-collar workers lived in the former and more blue-collar workers in the latter; (b) Casa Del Oro was located 10 miles outside Tuscon, Arizona, whereas Equus Estates was within city limits; (c) Casa Del Oro residents owned their lots, whereas those in Equus Estates rented theirs.

In both communities the basic social unit was a household marked by the absence of children. The households were integrated into the community through informal cliques and organized programs centered in a recreation hall. Cliques formed on the basis of residential proximity, mutual interest activities, and geographic origin. However, the social life at Casa Del Oro was more intense and complex than at Equus Estates. Fry attributes this intensity and complexity to the greater responsibility on the part of Casa Del Oro residents to protect, manage, and maintain their investment. At Equus Estates one's investment was limited to monthly rent plus utilities and the cost of moving the mobile home if things did not work out. In general, the commitment to community life was not as great. Fry's study points to the interaction between sociality (an aspect of the microsystem) and modes of ownership (a feature of the exosystem) in small-scale, age-graded communities. She suggests that the degree and quality of interaction among community residents will be in part determined by the type of investment (renting or owning) they have made in the setting. The greater the investment, the greater the degree of interaction and organization. Despite the need to examine how functional these communities would be as their residents' physical capabilities decline, it is apparent that the attractiveness of this alternative as a source of moderately priced housing is likely to increase in the future.

Condominiums and Cooperative Apartments

Condominiums differ from cooperatives. Cooperative apartments typically are organized on a corporate basis. A corporation is formed which buys the land and building; then a mortgage is taken out on the property and shares are sold to tenants (Kratovil, 1974), who purchase long-term leases from the corporation and pay rent to the corporation for the right to possession. The rent covers a pro-rata share of amounts needed to cover the mortgage debt, taxes, and operating expenses (Elrod, 1979). In the case of a condominium, on the other hand, the purchaser buys and receives a deed to his apartment unit or townhouse and an individual nonpartitionable interest in the common areas (Kratovil, 1974). The buyer obtains a mortgage in a manner similar to that involved in buying a house. FHA financing is available for condominium purchase. Units are taxed separately and an association enforces rules and regulations.

Both condominiums and cooperatives can offer advantages to the elderly with the financial resources to purchase them. They combine features of rental living, such as freedom from exterior home maintenance and yardwork, with the benefits of home ownership-tax benefits and equity (Elrod, 1979). The closeness of neighbors can meet needs for social interaction and safety.

On the negative side, condominiums and cooperatives are not cheap. When the monthly maintenance fees and mortgage payments for condominiums and lease rental fees for cooperatives are taken into consideration, they cost as much as, and in some cases more than, conventional housing and yield less space. Inflation causes these expenses, especially maintenance fees, to rise steadily. For persons on fixed incomes such increases could rise to a point at which the condominium or cooperative is no longer affordable (Elrod, 1979). In addition, condominium and cooperative owners are much more dependent upon one another for preservation of their interests than are renters or homeowners (Henry & Wittie, 1978). As Fry (1977) discovered for mobile home park residents who owned their land, increased risk and interdependence can stimulate the formation of social groups and interaction—a positive feature for some people.

As we mentioned elsewhere in this article, conversion of rental apartments to either condominiums or cooperatives can have a dramatic negative impact on the elderly. They often live in buildings which are prime targets for conversion, and they are the least able to cope with it, both economically and psychologically. Conversion takes valuable rental units off the market in urban areas with depressed construction of new replacement units (Wood, 1977). Furthermore, it displaces people who can afford a monthly apartment rent but do not have the capital necessary to purchase a condominium or cooperative. Elrod (1979) notes that the cost for a condominium unit may be 150 times the monthly rent for an apartment, and maintenance costs and taxes may cause 35% higher monthly payments for a rental unit converted to a condominium unit. The United States Department of Housing and Urban Development (1975) predicts, however, that pressure for condominium conversion will probably continue.

One critical area needing further research is the human cost of converting apartments to either condominiums or cooperatives. For example, to what extent are the elderly being displaced through conversions, where do they go if displaced, and what are the human costs in terms of deteriorated morale, health status, and overall quality of life?

For the elderly who have the initial capital to purchase a condominium or cooperative, we need to know the impact of rising inflation rates on their quality of life. How do people without income growth potential cope and adjust to rapidly increasing living costs?

Hotels and Rooming Houses

Of the 6.8 million elderly who live in urban areas, approximately 397,000 live on a relatively permanent basis in accommodations which are referred to in the literature as "single-room occupancy." This type of housing includes three kinds of living units: (a) partial single-room units, (no access or shared access to kitchen facilities and/or bath); (b) single-room units (renter-occupied one-room housing units); (c) renter-occupied housing units in a residential hotel, rooming house, or a permanent unit in a transient hotel (Haley, Pearson, & Hull, 1981).

The populations found in these units are not homogeneous but represent the gamut in terms of age, income, social connectedness, sex distribution, and so on. For example, some case studies of SRO units have tended to support the stereotype that persons living in these environments are loners (Stephens, 1976) outside the mainstream of society, who are "socially terminal" (Siegal, 1977) or marked by maladaptation (Shapiro, 1966, 1971). Some other case studies have pointed to the heterogeneity of the SRO population in terms of housing quality and type, personal biography, age, health, modes of adjustment, and so on (Eckert, 1979, 1980; Erickson & Eckert, 1977; Sokolovsky & Cohen, 1978). At present, data are lacking to construct a comprehensive profile of elderly hotel and rooming-house dwellers and their housing. We know that, as the SRO category is defined formally, it could include small boarding residences where a single bedroom is rented by the week or month as well as converted houses and apartment buildings in urban areas where rental payments cover a room, but where residents must eat meals in local restaurants and cafeterias (Goode, *et al.*, 1980). Central to the SRO category are the hotels, which can vary dramatically in size, condition, rent, and social climate.

As noted by Goode *et al.* (1980), much of the research concerning the elderly residents of hotels and rooming houses has been narrowly focused on specific subgroups, most often differentiated by characteristics of the accommodation. Albrecht (1969) and Teski (1979) focused on retirement hotels; Kowall (1970, 1973, 1976), Sokolovsky and Cohen (1978), Eckert (1979, 1980, 1982), Erickson and Eckert (1977), Stephens (1976), and Ehrlich (1976), have concerned themselves with small and large inner-city SRO type hotels; some others have concentrated on skid-row or tenement accommodations (Ehrlich, 1976; Erickson and Eckert, 1977; Siegal, 1977; Shapiro, 1971); at least one researcher, Zorbaugh (1929), focused on the unique social situation afforded by rooming houses, a situation that was more common in the early years of this century (Hareven, 1976).

As we noted above, research on some types of SRO housing and subpopulations has been quite prolific over the past decade. Several common conclusions about SRO accommodations, living arrangements, and social life run through this body of research. Numerous researchers have noted that hotels and rooming-house environments provide formal and informal supports for their older residents (Albrecht, 1969; Eckert, 1979, 1980; Ehrlich, 1976; Erickson and Eckert, 1977; Kowall, 1976; Shapiro, 1971; Sokolovsky & Cohen, 1978; Stephens, 1976). These supports are provided in a way that allows for reciprocal social exchanges which tend to maintain one's sense of autonomy, control and self-respect (Eckert, 1979; Kowall, 1976; Shapiro, 1971). Many SRO accommodations are located in or near urban commercial zones which provide convenient and important services (restaurants, shops, transportation) to meet their older residents' needs (Eckert, 1979, 1980, 1983; Erickson & Eckert, 1977; Goode et al., 1980).

When one decides to live in a hotel or rooming house, one receives more than just a room. Basic housekeeping services are usually included in the rent along with furniture, linens, and heat. Desk clerks, resident managers, maids, or owners act as security personnel, watching out for the residents themselves as well as controlling the presence of outsiders. In times of emergency these persons sometimes provide direct support to or a liaison function for residents. Living close to other older persons of similar background or circumstances can create a climate in which mutually supportive and beneficial social relationships emerge (Eckert, 1979; Sokolovsky & Cohen, 1978). As summarized by Goode et al. (1980), this nontraditional housing has to varying degrees many of the features considered important in planned housing for the elderly. More important, it exists, and it appears to meet the housing needs of some older people.

Case studies and studies based on census data indicate that older people who live in SRO accommodations are different from those living elsewhere (Ehrlich, 1976; Erickson & Eckert, 1977; Stephens, 1976; Tissue, 1971). Lawton (1981a) reports that residents in hotels and rooming houses are characteristically male; 3.4% have never married, 3.0% are widowers, and 6.0% are divorced or separated. An overall profile of the elderly who live in hotels and rooming houses reveals that, in comparison to older people living elsewhere in the community, they are more likely to be never married or widowed, living alone, over 75, and living in poverty (Goode et al., 1980). These findings suggest that a significant proportion of this population is probably not only frail but at risk both physically and socially (Erickson & Eckert, 1977, 1979; Goode et al., 1980).

Life course trajectories that lead to living in SRO accommodations vary, but it appears that a relatively large proportion of older persons chose this housing during an earlier stage in life. The choice was determined partly by the existence of few other low cost housing alternatives and partly by a style of life and personal conditions that made housekeeping responsibilities difficult to assume (Eckert, 1980; Kowall, 1976). With functional health reasonably intact, such environments provide a niche for some individuals, at a lower cost, than other environments could. Some others are in SRO accommodations because there is no available alternative, for example, the very old who moved into a hotel because they had outlived all relatives and friends and had no other place to turn or those who have been discharged from an extended-care mental hospital or prison. For these individuals multiple problems and marginal social adjustment may make life miserable.

Public and private development efforts pose a serious threat to SRO establishments and the people who live in them. Public misunderstanding and disdain for this housing, housing policies indifferent to the needs of SRO residents, urban renewal, gentrification, and historical preservation have led to a depletion of valuable SRO housing stock and alterations in key neighborhood services so critical to supporting this residential way of life (Eckert, 1979; Ehrlich, 1976; Kowall, 1970, 1973; Levy, 1968). Hotels and rooming houses must be viewed as an integral part of their larger neighborhoods and local communities. Without the infrastructure of services available in these environments, the needs of older residents will not be satisfied.

At present, research is under way to assess the effects of forced relocation and environmental change on the elderly living in SRO hotels in a west coast city (Eckert, 1983). This study is the first to consider the consequences of relocation and urban change on the elderly hotel resident. It employs a quasi-experimental research design comparing measures of mental and physical health status, social networks and supports, and psychological adjustments before and after moving for an experimental and comparison group of older persons. Those in the comparison group were randomly selected from hotels similar in characteristics and contiguous to those being destroyed.

In general, the group experiencing relocation showed little negative change in measures of health and well-being before and after moving. However, a subpopulation of people who rated their health as poor appeared vulnerable to relocation stress. These persons were at risk in terms of selected physical health measures prior to relocation and continued to be at risk after being relocated. This finding points to the importance of disaggregating elderly persons in terms of their health status. Those in poor health are at risk; they must be identified and assisted through special services (Eckert, 1983). Data from this research further point to the importance of the infrastructure of supports both within the hotel and the local neighborhood for older urban residents.

At the macrosocial level, federal housing policy is the major stumbling block to improving the housing conditions of the single poor (Levy, 1968; Fielding, 1972; Kowall, 1973). As Kowall (1976) so cogently notes, HUD regulations requiring self-contained units—that is, private use of complete bathroom and kitchen facilities—in existing housing preclude SRO tenants and management from housing assistance programs necessary to arrest the deteriorating buildings.

At the national level, the impact of urban change, be it renewal and development or deterioration and decay, on the elderly is not known. Research in various cities and localities throughout the United States indicates that there is a problem. Large-scale national research, although unlikely to gain funding at present, is nonetheless called for.

ALTERNATIVES WITHIN THE CONGREGATE HOUSING CATEGORY

Another broad category of residential type in which alternatives can be identified is known as *congregate housing*. Although the term has no satisfactorily accurate definition, *congregate* will be used here to refer to housing that offers a minimum service package that includes on-site meals served in a common dining room, plus one or more services such as on-site medical or nursing service, personal care, or housekeeping (Lawton, 1976). The precise number of available congregate units is not known, but what is known indicates that they are in short supply and are in great demand. Lawton (1981a) offers the estimate that their numbers do not exceed 30,000 to 40,000 units including both assisted and nonassisted housing. This housing attracts both those who are fully independent and those with some limitations in physical capability.

The typical resident in congregate housing is white, female, and single or widowed. Unlike SRO hotels and rooming houses, this housing has far more women than men. In a study done by Urban Systems Research and Engineering, Inc. (1976), it was found that 75% of the residents were 75 years of age or older and 7% were black. Residents in congregate housing said that they had moved from their own houses or apartments to congregate quarters as a security against the uncertainties of old age.

The elements of congregate housing such as on-site meals plus services can be seen in recently developing smaller-scale alternatives. Brody (1979) has distinguished the congregate category (which she refers to collectively as group homes) into two levels: small congregate group homes and high-support group homes. Two emerging alternatives will be discussed which fit this category: Share-a-Home and community housing.

Share-a-Home

The Share-a-Home concept can be categorized under what Brody calls small congregate homes. These arrangements provide some mix of hired help to shop and cook; maintenance and housekeeping; and social service consultation. All appear to be under the auspices of some organization. The original Share-a-Home idea was started in 1969 by James

Gillies when a group fo 20 elderly persons jointly leased a 27-room house and facilities. Since that time the concept has grown, and at least ten additional "families" live in a variety of housing, ranging from a former Catholic convent to a spacious mansion. In 1972 Gillies established a nonprofit tax-exempt organization to assist in the formation of new families and to coordinate their ongoing operation. The organization performs "a kind of surrogate parent role for the ten families now in operation" (Streib, 1978).

In Gillies's words,

> Any senior adult may live in Share-a-Home. The only requirement is that members be ambulatory and able to manage their own personal care. There are no initiation fees—no founders fees—no contracts. Members pay only their fair share of expenses monthly, excluding personal items like clothing and medical expenses. (Gillies, 1979)

From a sociological perspective, the Share-a-Home model represents a new kind of social group in American society which blends in one location both familial and bureaucratic functions (Streib, 1978). Although it is not a traditional family, it has some of the affective and support characteristics of families and has been considered a family on some legal grounds (Sussman, 1976). It also has some of the characteristics typical of bureaucratic organizations, such as a board of directors and formal rules of operation. As "amalgam" groups, Share-a-Home families try to deal with both the uniform and nonuniform tasks and needs of some older Americans (Streib, 1978).

With programs in operation throughout the country, the Share-a-Home model is receiving considerable attention as an alternative mode of living for the elderly. For an ever-growing number of elderly men and women who do not wish to live alone, it is a way of life which allows people to retain self-respect and a degree of autonomy in an atmosphere of caring without institutional restraints (Gillies, 1979).

The concept of Share-a-Home presents several interesting research questions. First, if such groups do demonstrate qualities of families how do they cope and adjust to the loss and replacement of members over time? Second, what are the personal characteristics of people who opt for Share-a-Home, and what are the characteristics which are seen as desirable in others? Third, what problems arise as members of a Share-a-Home decline in capability and greater support services are required?

Community Housing

Another form of alternative housing which fits into the broad congregate category is what Brody (1978) refers to as intermediate or community housing. Similar to the Share-a-Home model, community housing utilizes existing housing stock with the provision of back-up services to maintain an individual's independence and autonomy. The original community housing model was developed and sponsored by the Philadelphia Geriatric Center (PGC) to provide innovative options for older persons. As described by Brody (1979), it consisted of nine one-family, semidetached homes located in a residential neighborhood adjacent to the PGC campus. Purchase and conversion of each house to contain three private efficiency apartments and a shared living room was accomplished with the aid of mortgages insured through the section 236 Rehabilitation Program of the Federal Housing Administration. Rent supplements to eligible persons allowed the apartments to be rented at reduced rates.

Basic rental fees include institutional assistance with janitorial and building maintenance; cleaning of the common areas; a "hot line" phone connected to the PGC switchboard for medical or other emergencies; access to the Centers' group recreational, religious, and social activities; social services at application and moving phases (Brody, 1978). Residents are expected to do their own shopping, cooking, and housekeeping. However, home-delivered frozen main meals and light housekeeping could be purchased from PGC. Medical care is not provided, and tenants retain their own personal physicians (Brody, Kleban, & Lebowitz, 1975).

Brody (1978) found that a major motivation for older people who moved into this housing was fear, isolation, and loneliness because of the high crime rate in the neighborhoods in which they lived. Deteriorated housing stock and depletion of family and friends living nearby was another related stimulant.

Despite the deliberate design of the environment for independence, the tenants who moved in were less healthy than a comparison group who did not move; their social needs were reflected in that the housing appealed almost exclusively to those who lived alone (Lawton, 1981a). The overall evaluation of the housing has been positive (Brody, 1978).

This kind of housing holds promise if existing agencies can be encouraged to expand their programs to handle small residences (Lebowitz, 1978). Relying on existing housing stock, community housing offers familiarity, independence, security, social opportunities, and the group support of the sponsoring organization (Lawton, 1981a).

A factor at the level of the exosystem limiting the development of the above-mentioned alternatives is restrictive zoning ordinances in many communities against the occupation by unrelated persons of a single-family residence. Although neighborhood residents may not object to a group of unrelated elderly living together, they may fear that any unconventional arrangement of people might set a precedent for other unrelated groups which they would see as undesirable. However, Elrod (1979) reports that several states have permitted unrelated persons to occupy a single-family residence notwithstanding an ordinance prohibiting such occupancy.

ALTERNATIVES WITHIN THE DOMICILIARY AND PERSONAL CARE RESIDENTIAL CATEGORY

The National Center of Health Statistics defines domiciliary and personal care residence as follows: a residence is considered domiciliary care if it offers one or two of eight named personal care services (e.g., help with eating, bathing, toileting, grooming); it is personal care if three or more of these services are offered (National Center for Health Statistics, 1976). Domiciliary and personal care can be seen as a hybrid residential type which offers personal care services but not medical/nursing services (Lawton, 1981a). Estimates are that 500,000 to 1,500,000 elderly, disabled, and mentally ill citizens live in over 300,000 domiciliary residences nationally (Report of the House Select Committee on Aging, 1979). The vast majority of these facilities are private, for profit enterprises. The primary source of payment is Supplemental Security Income (SSI), although other sources include social security, veterans benefits, and federal funds under alcohol and drug abuse programs (Report of the House Select Committee on Aging, 1979).

A particularly thorny issue regarding any discussion of this residential type revolves around nomenclature. Domiciliary facilities are known in different locations by different names, such as foster homes, board and care homes, and sheltered care homes (U.S. General Accounting Office, 1979a). Many states recognize several categories of adult care homes, applying a variety of standards to the different categories. An "adult foster home" in one state is referred to as an "adult congregate living facility" in another state. Furthermore, social service agencies differ in criteria, with some defining a boarding home as any facility which houses four or more SSI recipients not related by blood or marriage (National Citizens' Coalition for Nursing Home Reform Report, 1981). At the level of residential type, Lawton (1981a) provides some help by stating that domiciliary facilities differ from congregate housing in that they are more institutional, containing shared bedrooms and few options for independent function. Congregate housing usually has a private dwelling-unit with either private or public cooking and dining facilities. Congregate housing is more often under nonprofit sponsorship and houses more residents.

Although there are certain characteristics at the level of the individual which may be ascribed to boarding home residents in general—they are often elderly, poor (SSI recipients), mentally impaired, and without close family ties—there are wide variations. Some are elderly and sick; others are younger, retarded, deinstitutionalized patients. Some have criminal records (NCCNHR Report, 1981). The most vulnerable are the sick elderly who have been deinstitutionalized from state hospitals (NCCNHR Report, 1981).

Although there are some reputable and well-run boarding homes, a considerable number appear to provide poor care clearly contrary to the mental and physical health of their residents. Poor sanitation, inadequate provision for medical care, unavailable social services, housing and safety code violations, and inadequate diet are some of the problems contributing to a marginal quality of life for boarding home residents (NCCNHR Report, undated).

Some states have required licensing of boarding homes, but the standards are minimal and enforcement almost nonexistent. Enactment of the Keyes amendment to the Social Security Act (1976) requires states to establish, maintain, and insure enforcement of standards covering such matters as admission policies, safety, sanitation, and protection of civil rights. However, there are several major obstacles to enforcement: no provision for financial assistance to implement enforcement or inspection of homes; a misdirected penalty of reduced SSI payments to recipients who reside in a facility that does not meet state standards. Standing alone as the only penalty, this provision punishes the victim rather than the operator.

Foster Care Homes

Within the domiciliary and personal care category, the concept of *foster home* deserves special attention. As with other variations in this category, definition is a problem. For example, what is considered a foster home varies between and within states. Variation in definition within a state can depend upon the supervisory or regulatory body of government. In New York State, for instance, there are several types of foster care programs sponsored by the Department of Mental Hygiene, Department of Social Welfare, or Veterans' Administration (Sherman & Newman, 1977). Definitions of the characteristics of a foster home, as well as of the personal characteristics of residents, differ substantially between these sponsoring departments (Newman & Sherman, 1979).

Lawton (1981a) provides two general defining criteria of foster homes: (a) a single-family household, with (b) no more than four nonrelatives living in a household as paying residents. Another central crite-

rion which several authors specify as highly desirable (Sherman & Newman, 1977; Silverstone, 1978) is the creation of an atmosphere in which
patients or residents are treated as family members and participate in
normal family activities. The concept of a family-like primary group is a
key factor differentiating foster care from "mere boarding homes" (Sherman & Newman, 1977). A decent foster family living arrangement
should offer an adult in need of care—over and above basic essentials—
relatively permanent primary group relations wherein his or her individualized, affectional, and unpredictable needs are met. In such a context the resident is expected to reciprocate by trying to meet these needs
for other primary group members. The foster family potentially offers
closer links to the community of which the foster family is a part and
independence from the conforming tendencies of institutional populations (Silverstone, 1978).

Variation in type and quality of foster homes is great, and caution
must be exercised in assuming that security, social, and privacy needs
are actually met. Lawton (1981a) notes that it cannot be assumed simply
because they are part of the community and small in scale that foster
homes offer a style of life that is any richer than that offered by some
institutions.

In terms of community attitudes toward foster homes, their small
size contributes to the likelihood of their going unnoticed and therefore
being reasonably well accepted. Sherman and Newman (1977) warn
against saturating any community with too many family care homes to
protect against visibility and consequent hostility. The potential for foster care homes and other domiciliary care facilities will most likely remain high, based on (a) the number of old people with chronic health
problems and (b) the rise in the number of people who live alone.

Several research efforts are currently underway which should significantly add to our understanding of domiciliary care nationally. For
example, the Hebrew Rehabilitation Center for the Aged (HRCA) is
presently completing a study which will determine the availability and
cost of domiciliary care (i.e., board and care) and the services that are
provided to older persons is supportive residential settings. The research objectives of this study address issues at all four levels of our
ecological housing model. The stated objectives of the study include the
following:

- To determine the supply of different types of domiciliary care for
  the elderly
- To determine the costs of each type of domiciliary care for the
  elderly

- To assess the impact of federal and state policies on the supply of supportive residential settings, including funding sources and regulations, licensing requirements, and limits on entry of service providers
- To determine how elderly persons enter these facilities
- To identify types of services provided to elderly residents of such facilities
- To identify the extent and types of linkages between these facilities and other community providers
- To assess the appropriateness, adequacy, and quality of domiciliary care services, based on the needs of elderly residents, provided by such facilities
- To identify the characteristics and levels of impairment of elderly persons who are best suited to be served in each type of facility

Another grant has been awarded to the Denver Research Institute to review board and care homes and the various systems that have been developed for managing services to the elderly residents in homes that require some level of protective services. The central objectives of this study are to review state standards and regulations for board and care homes, with special attention given to the enforcement and effectiveness of the Keyes amendment. The study will also provide recommendations for enforcement mechanisms at the state and national levels.

SPECIFIC PHENOMENA AT THE MACROLEVEL

Although it is important to talk about specific types of housing arrangements, one must not isolate them from larger societal forces which are constantly changing their existence, form, and user population. Several factors operating at the macro- or societal level of our ecological model affect the development of new housing modes for the elderly. Gentrification, a crisis in available rental units, erosion of the income of the elderly through inflation, and proposed cutbacks in federal housing programs and human services all impact alternative housing for the elderly.

The upgrading of the class composition and housing stock within a neighborhood is called *gentrification*. Between the middle and late 1970s, this phenomenon was evident when a movement of upper middle class and wealthy into certain inner city areas occurred. A 1975 survey estimated that privately initiated renovation efforts were underway in 70% of the American cities with populations over 250,000 (Myers, 1978). The

reason for the shift is complex but includes such factors as fewer numbers of couples with children requiring schools and suburban environments, increased appreciation of the cultural attractions in the city, proximity to work, and the relative housing bargain available as compared to
the suburbs. The new residents occupy either renovated housing structures or newly built condominiums or apartments built especially for the
higher-priced market. The surrounding environment also may undergo
dramatic change as new shops, restaurants and other businesses that
cater to the new market move in. With development usually comes
displacement of the working-class or poorer residents, who cannot afford to buy their converted apartments or to pay increased rents and
property taxes for their housing, be it apartment, rented hotel room, or
private home. It has been demonstrated that gentrification is more likely
to occur in tracts that house more elderly. A general out-migration occurring simultaneously with gentrification of older households from the
inner city, increasing as one moves closer to the center, indicates that
the elderly are being displaced by the shift (Henig, 1981).

For the elderly who own their own homes, gentrification usually
means increased property taxes as well as increased maintenance costs.
These added costs are often too much to bear for people on fixed incomes, who are forced to move or in some cases to take in borders, thus
stimulating indirectly the development of the house-sharing alternatives. In addition there have been reports of realtors' pressuring older
people to sell at prices lower than market, value taking advantage of
their lack of knowledge of the current market (Myers, 1978).

Renters of apartments or hotel rooms are especially hard hit by
gentrification. The renovation of older apartment structures or hotels for
occupation by upper-income tenants or other uses raises rents far beyond what they have previously been. Some apartments become converted into condominiums while some hotels are destroyed or converted
into office space. In the case of condominium conversion, current
renters usually have first option on buying their apartments, but costs of
$30,000 and more are prohibitive to older persons on fixed incomes. In
1977, 30% of all elderly households were renters. Of this group 40% had
incomes below $5,000; another 32.6% had incomes between $4,500 and
$10,000; and only 8% had incomes above $20,000. Forty-two percent of
all elderly renters live in apartments which rent for at least $150. These
are the rental units which tend to be converted. A majority of elderly are
already paying over 25% of their incomes to live in units renting for from
$150 to $250 (Select Committee on Aging, 1981a, p. 48). Thus the conversion of apartments into condominiums potentially affects a large number of elderly who cannot afford further rent increases. The owner-

occupants of converted buildings clearly tend to be young professionals. Nearly two thirds are individuals who hold a professional or managerial position; about one half are 35 or younger, whereas only one fifth are over 55 and only 9% are over 65 (Select Committee on Aging, 1980a). What happens to the older displaced tenants? Although federally funded high-rises have been built for a small number of them, these are not adequate to house the vast majority. For those people who are not lucky enough to be housed in new or public housing, a move into a poor and more dangerous neighborhood may be their only choice (Myers, 1978). A large national study found that one half of all former residents of converted buildings had some difficulty in finding housing, with elderly, nonwhite and lower-income former tenants reporting more difficulty (in Select Committee on Aging, 1980a, p. 99).

The reasons for the unfortunate fates of large numbers of the elderly who are displaced are better understood when placed in the context of the current rental crisis. The nation's lowest recorded rental housing vacancy rate and shortages of affordable rental units have resulted in this crisis. The primary causes are the low level of moderately priced, new private construction and the losses of existing stock to conversions to condominiums and abandonments (U.S. General Accounting Office, 1979). A call by the current administration for the replacement of subsidized housing construction by the government, the traditional means of assistance, by a system of vouchers or certificates to be used on the open market will only add to this crisis by failing to stimulate the building of new low-cost housing. In addition, without mandated changes in the existing housing stock and market (i.e., rent control, stricter landlord–tenant laws), the poor have little choice but to remain or to move to poor-quality housing.

Although slightly more than 70% of older persons own their own homes, the structures tend to be older, in poorer condition, and of lower value than the rest of owner-occupied housing (Carp, 1978; Baer, 1976). In addition, elderly homeowners tend to be poor, with a vast majority having incomes under $4,000 (Select Committee on Aging, 1980a, p. 48), although they tend to pay a proportionately higher amount of their income in property taxes (Baer, 1976). There is need to provide mortgage, insurance, and maintenance supports to enable older people to remain in their homes and enjoy a comfortable quality of life. If the elderly can stay in their own homes, the likelihood of house-sharing will remain a viable housing alternative.

Recent trends to reduce the federal government's financial and administrative involvement in housing and human service programs will have both a direct and indirect impact on the development of alternative housing for the elderly. For example, expanded rent subsidy programs under Section 8 requiring the elderly to pay only 25% of their income for rent could have provided much needed assistance to persons living in SRO units. However, proposed budget cuts may reduce by 33% the number of presently subsidized units. Section 236, which provided rent supplements for persons living in the community housing alternative, could be similarly affected.

The quality of housing available for the share-a-home alternative may be affected through reduced funding for the Community Development Block Grants (CDBG) and consolidation of Section 312 loans, Weatherization and Urban Development Action Grant Programs. Section 312 provided loans for repairs when CDBG grant funds did not cover complete costs. Without additional funding, the only source for low-interest, home-repair loans will be eliminated.

The development of less desirable housing alternatives for the elderly could be influenced through decreases in medical payments. Expanding needs, tightening eligibility, and lowered reimbursement could stimulate the development of low-quality board and care homes—in effect, a "bootleg" nursing-home industry.

The development of innovative housing alternatives for the elderly demands a commitment by policy makers at the local, state, and federal levels of government. The possible elimination of very promising alternative housing, such as the congregate housing demonstration program, signals a distressing future trend.

In summary, the negative factors include the lower quality of the elderly's housing and the reduction of funds for home maintenance, housing subsidies, and government-sponsored housing. The call of a replacement of construction with vouchers will force elderly to find their own housing on an open private market which is unresponsive to the needs of the poor. There is no solution offered for people at risk of being displaced by the processes of gentrification, relocation for private redevelopment and renewal, and condominium conversion. Property taxes may be rising, often in response to gentrification. Increases in fuel costs because of gas and oil deregulation, as well as cuts in energy assistance and weatherization, will force many older people to make choices among decent housing, adequate nutrition, or keeping warm.

FUTURE RESEARCH AND CONCLUSION

Alternative housing for the elderly encompasses a broad range of residential types and specific housing arrangements. To date, research exploring alternative housing has been diverse in method and objective.

Research in the future would benefit from clearer specification of research problems, theoretical and conceptual frameworks, and attempts at anchoring these in an ecological framework. There is a need for research on alternative housing which explores the interaction between levels in our ecological model. Although such research is complex, of a large scale, and expensive, it is nonetheless necessary. Research of this type will begin to consolidate and order the bits and pieces of data we now possess and assist in theory building. Although it is sometimes easier to conduct research on individuals within their immediate environmental context, factors operating at the level of the local neighborhood and larger society should not be ignored.

The making of choices among possible alternative housing arrangments is a result of complex multilevel factors ranging from political and economic forces (macrolevel) to psychological and cultural characteristics (microlevel) of the individual. However, the larger social, political, and economic forces and processes within a particular changing society are the primary determinants in explaining and accounting for the existence and range of housing alternatives and in the variation in choice between groups of elderly, as well as the changes in these housing options over time.

An insightful review of housing literature (Eribes, 1979) reveals that the most common and persistent problem is the "inability of public policy in aligning national goals with the needs of shelter of the especially disadvantaged." This inability of public policy to meet the housing needs of the disadvantaged is not altogether suprising since housing is a private industry with an inherent interest in making profit. Although the federal government has attempted to provide subsidized housing, only a small portion of the needy were served; and now even these meager attempts are threatened. The power of political and economic forces can be demonstrated in the complete and unhesitating elimination of congregate housing in the face of years of research demonstrating its benefits. To address the housing needs and problems of the elderly, then, we must directly face and change these forces, which are the source of the major problems.

REFERENCES

Albrecht, R. Retirement hotels in Florida. *University of Florida Institute of Gerontology Series.* 1969, *18*, 71–82.

Altman, I., & Lett, E. E. The ecology of interpersonal relationships: A classification system and conceptual model. In J. E. McGrath (Ed.), *Social and psychological factors in stress.* New York: Holt, Rinehart & Winston, 1970, pp. 177–201.

Baer, W. C. Federal housing programs for the elderly. In M. P. Lawton, R. J. Newcomer, &

T. O. Byerts (Eds.), *Community planning for an aging society: Designing services and facilities.* Stroudsburg, Pa.: Dowden, Hutchinson & Ross, 1976, pp. 81–98.

Barker, R. G., & Barker, L. S. The psychological ecology of old people in Midwest, Kansas, and Yoredale, Yorkshire. *Journal of Gerontology,* 1961, *16,* 144–149.

Bell, W. Urban neighborhoods and individual behavior. In M. Sherif & C. W. Sherif (Eds.), *Problems of youth: Transition to adulthood in a changing world.* Chicago: Aldine, 1967, pp. 235–264.

Berry, B. J. L. (Ed.), *City classification handbook.* New York: Wiley, 1972.

Brody, E. M. Community housing for the elderly: The program, the people, the decision-making process, and the research. *The Gerontologist,* 1978, *18,* 121–129.

Brody, E. M. Service-supported independent living in an urban setting: The Philadelphia Geriatric Center's community housing for the elderly. In T. O. Byerts, S. C. Howell, & S. A. Pastalan (Eds.), *Environmental context of aging.* New York: Garland STPM Press, 1979.

Brody, E. M., Kleban, M. H., & Liebowitz, B. Intermediate housing for the elderly: Satisfaction of those who moved in and those who did not. *The Gerontologist,* 1975, *15,* 350–356.

Carp, F. M. Housing organization and designs for the elderly. Prepared for the *AAS intergovernmental research and development project workshop on health and human resources: The elderly.* Warrenton, Va.: Airlie House, December 12–14, 1978.

Chapman, N. J., and Beaudet-Walters, M. *Predictors of environmental well-being for older adults.* Paper presented at the Annual Meeting of the Gerontological Society, Dallas, November, 1978.

Cowgill, D. O. Residential segregation by age in American metropolitan areas. *Journal of Gerontology,* 1978, *33,* 446–453.

Eckert, J. K. Urban renewal and redevelopment: High risk for the marginally subsistent elderly. *The Gerontologist,* 1979, *19,* 496–502.

Eckert, J. K. *The unseen elderly: A study of marginally subsistent hotel dwellers.* San Diego: Campanile Press, 1980.

Eckert, J. K. Dislocation and relocation of the urban elderly: Social networks as mediators of relocation stress, *Human Organization,* 1982, (42)1, 39–45.

Ehrlich, P. A. Study of the "invisible elderly": Characteristics and needs of the St. Louis downtown SRO elderly. In *The invisible elderly.* Washington, D. C.: The National Council on the Aging, 1976, pp. 7–14.

Elrod, L. H. Housing alternatives for the elderly. *Journal of Family Law,* 1979, *18,* 723–759.

Eribes, R. The housing puzzle: Do the pieces fit? *Public Administration Review,* 1979, *5,* 945–499.

Erickson, R. J., & Eckert, J. K. The elderly poor in downtown San Diego hotels. *The Gerontologist,* 1977, *17,* 440–446.

Fielding, B. Low-income, single-person housing: What's happening as a result of the "congregate housing" provisions of the 1970 Act? *Journal of Housing,* 1972, *29,* 133–136.

Fry, C. L. The community as a commodity: The age graded case. *Human Organization,* 1977, *36,* 115–123.

Gillan, R. B. Zoning for the elderly. In M. P. Lawton, R. J. Newcomer, & T. O. Byerts (Eds.), *Community planning for an aging society: Designing services and facilities.* Stroudsburg, Pa.: Dowden, Hutchinson & Ross, 1976, pp. 99–105.

Gillies, J. W. Share-a-Home—A new lease on life. *Generations,* 1979, 3(3), 26.

Goode, C., Lawton, M. P., & Hoover, S. L. *Elderly hotel and rooming house dwellers: The population and its housing.* Philadelphia: Philadelphia Geriatric Center, 1980.

Haley, B. A., Pearson, M., & Hull, D. A. *Urban elderly residents of single room occupancy housing (SRO's), 1976–1980.* Paper presented at the 34th Annual Meeting of the Gerontological Society of America, Toronto, Canada, November, 1981.

Hareven, T. K. The last stage: Historical adulthood and old age. *Daedalus,* 1976, (4), *105,* 13–27.

Henig, J. Gentrification and displacement of the elderly: An empirical analysis. *The Gerontologist,* 1981, *21,* 67–75.

Henry, L. J., & Wittie, R. A. Uniform Condominium Act: Key issues. *Real Property, Probate and Trust Journal,* 1978, *13,* 437–539.

Hoyt, G. C. The life of the retired in a trailer park. *American Journal of Sociology,* 1954, *59,* 361–371.

Inz, J. Personal communication, April 1982.

Johnson, S. K. Idle haven: Community building among the working-class retired. Berkeley: University of California Press, 1971.

Kahana, E. A. A congruence model of person–environment interaction. In M. P. Lawton, P. G. Windley, & T. O. Byerts (Eds.), *Aging and the environment: Directions and perspectives.* New York: Garland STPM Press, 1980, pp. 97–121.

Kendig, H. Neighborhood conditions of the aged and local government. *Gerontologist,* 1976, *16,* 148–156.

Kowall, C. *New housing for furnished room inhabitants.* Mimeograph. New York: Office of Special Purpose Housing, Housing and Development Administration, 1970.

Kowall, C. *SRO housing—A national need* (Mimeograph). New York: Office of Special Purpose Housing and Development Administration, 1973.

Kowall, C. *The federal housing program and its response to the needs of the SRO elderly residents.* A position paper for the 2nd Conference on the Invisible Elderly. St. Louis: St. Louis University, Institute of Applied Gerontology, 1976.

Kratovil, R. Condominiums and co-ops. *Real Estate Law,* 1974 (3), 381.

Lawton, M. P. The relative impact of congregate and traditional housing on elderly tenants. *The Gerontologist,* 1976, *16,* 237–242.

Lawton, M. P. *Environment and aging.* Monterey, Calif.: Brooks/Cole Publishing Company, 1980. (a)

Lawton, M. P. Housing the elderly: Residential quality and residential satisfaction. *Research on Aging,* 1980, *2,* 309–328. (b)

Lawton, M. P. Alternative housing. *Journal of Gerontological Social Work,* 1981, *3,* 61–80. (a)

Lawton, M. P. An ecological view of living arrangements. *The Gerontologist,* 1981, *21,* 59–66. (b)

Lawton, M. P., & Bader, J. Wish for privacy by young and old. *Journal of Gerontology,* 1970, *25,* 48–54.

Lawton, M. P., & Hoover, S. L. *Housing and neighborhood: Objective and subjective quality,* Philadelphia: Philadelphia Geriatric Center, 1979.

Lawton, M P., & Nahemow, L. Ecology and the aging process In C. Eisdorfer and M. P. Lawton (Eds.), *Psychology of adult development and aging.* Washington, D. C.: American Psychological Association, 1973, pp. 619–674.

Lawton, M. P., Nahemow, L., & Yeh, T. Neighborhood environment and the well-being of older tenants in planned housing. *Journal of Aging and Human Development,* 1980, *11,* 211–227.

Lawton, M. P., & Yaffe, S. *Victimization of the elderly and fear of crime.* Philadelphia: Philadelphia Geriatric Center, 1979.

Lebowitz, B. *Age and fearfulness: Personal and situational factors. Journal of Gerontology,* 1975, *30,* 696–700.

Lebowitz, B. Implications of community housing for policy and planning. *The Gerontologist*, 1978, *18*, 138–143.

Lee, T. Urban neighborhood as socio-spatial schema. *In* H. M. Proshansky, W. H. Ittelson, & L. G. Rivlin (Eds.), *Environmental psychology*. New York: Holt, Rinehart & Winston, 1970. Pp. 349–370.

Levy, H. Needed: A new kind of single room occupancy housing. *Journal of Housing*, 1968, *25*, 572–580.

McAuley, W. J. *Age, desired characteristics of the residential environment, and likelihood of residential mobility*. Paper presented at the Annual Meeting of the Western Gerontological Society, Denver, March 1977.

McConnell, S. R. House sharing: An alternative living arrangement for the elderly. *Generations*, 1979, *3*(3), 24–25.

McConnell, S. R., & Usher, C. E. *Intergenerational house-sharing*. Los Angeles: University of Southern California, Andrus Gerontology Center, 1979.

Meeuwig, M. J. Housing and activities of the elderly. *Journal of Home Economics*, 1970, *62*, 592–597.

Moos, R. H., & Lemke, S. Multiphasic environmental assessment procedure: Preliminary manual. Palo Alto, Calif.: *Social Ecology Laboratory, Stanford University School of Medicine*, 1979.

Moos, R. H., Gauvin, M., Lemke, S., Max, W., & Mehren, B. *The development of a sheltered care environment scale: A preliminary report*. Paper presented at the Annual Meeting of the Gerontological Society, San Francisco, November, 1977.

Murray, H. A. *Explorations in personality*. New York: Oxford University Press, 1938.

Myers, P. *Neighborhood conservation and the elderly*. Washington, D. C.: The Conservation Foundation, 1978.

National Center for Health Statistics. Inpatient Health Facilities. *Vital and Health Statistics*, 1976, *14*(16), Rockville, Md.: U.S. Department of Health, Education, and Welfare.

National Citizens Coalition for Nursing Home Reform. *Boarding home issues: A resource sheet*. Washington, D. C. May, 1981.

National Citizens Coalition for Nursing Home Reform. *Boarding home abuse: An outgrowth of the deinstitutionalization process*. Washington, D. C., undated.

Newcomer, R. J. An evaluation of neighborhood service convenience for elderly housing project residents. In P. Suefeld & J. A. Russell (Eds.), *The behavioral basis of design* (Vol. 1). Stroudsburg, Pa.: Dowden, Hutchinson & Ross, 1976, pp. 301–307.

Newman, E. S., & Sherman, S. R. Community integration of the elderly in foster care family care. *Journal of Gerontological Social Work*, 1979, *1*, 175–186.

Peterson, J. A., Hamovitch, M., & Larson, A. E. *Housing needs and satisfactions of the elderly*. Los Angeles: Ethel Percy Andrus Gerontology Center, University of Southern California, 1973.

Rausch, K. J. Mobile home movement. *Generations*, 1979, *3*(3), 34.

Rausch, K. J., & Hoover, S. L. *Mobile home elderly: Structural characteristics of their dwellings*. Philadelphia: Philadelphia Geriatric Center, 1980.

Regnier, V. A. Neighborhoods as service systems. In M. P. Lawton, R. J. Newcomer, & T. O. Byerts (Eds.), *Planning for an aging society*. Stroudsburg, Pa.: Dowden , Hutchinson & Ross, 1976, pp. 240–257.

Regnier, V. A., Eribes, R. A., & Hansen, W. *Cognitive mapping as a concept for establishing neighborhood service delivery locations for older people*. Paper presented at Eighth Annual Association for Computing Machinery Symposium, New York City, 1973.

Rosenberg, G. S. *The worker grows old*. San Francisco: Jossey-Bass, 1970.

Rosow, I. *Social integration of the aged*. New York: Free Press, 1967.

Select Committee on Aging, U.S. House of Representatives. *Fires in boarding homes: The tip of the iceberg.* Washington, D. C.: U.S. Government Printing Office, April 25, 1979.

Select Committee on Aging, U.S. House of Representatives. *Condominium conversions.* Comm. Pub. No. 96–246. Washington, D. C.: U.S. Government Printing Office, August 29, 1980. (a)

Select Committee on Aging, U.S. House of Representatives. *Income status of the rural elderly.* Comm. Pub. No. 96–253. Washington, D. C.: U.S. Government Printing Office, August 29, 1980. (b)

Select Committee on Aging, U.S. House of Representatives. *Analysis of the impact of the proposed fiscal year 1982 budget cuts on the elderly.* Comm. Pub. No. 97–273. Washington, D. C.: U.S. Government Printing Office, April 6, 1981. (a)

Select Committee on Aging, U.S. House of Representatives. *Impact of fiscal year 1982 budget cuts on the elderly.* Comm. Pub. No. 97–284. Washington, D. C.: U.S. Government Printing Office, April 6, 1981. (b)

Shapiro, J. Single room occupancy: Community of the alone. *Social Work,* 1966, *11*(4), 24–33.

Shapiro, J. *Communities of the alone: Working with single room occupants in the city.* New York: Association Press, 1971.

Sherman, S. R., & Newman, E. S. Foster-family care for the elderly in New York State. *The Gerontologist,* 1977, *17,* 513–519.

Siegal, H. *Ouposts of the forgotten, New York City's welfare hotels and single room occupancy tenements.* Edison, N.J.: Transaction Books, 1977.

Silverstone, B. The social, physical, and legal implications for adult foster care: A contrast with other models. In N. K. Haygood & R. E. Dunkle (Eds.), *Perspectives on adult foster care.* Cleveland, Ohio: Human Services Design Laboratory, Case Western Reserve University, 1978, pp. 29–37.

Sjoberg, G. Community. In J. Gould & W. L. Kolls (Eds.), *Dictionary of the social sciences.* New York: Free Press, 1964.

Sokolovsky, J., & Cohen, C. The cultural meaning of personal networks for the inner-city elderly. *Urban Anthropology,* 1978, *7,* 323–342.

Stephens, J. *Loners, losers, and lovers.* Seattle: University of Washington Press, 1976.

Streib, G. F. An alternative family form for older persons: Need and social context. *The Family Coordinator,* 1978, *27,* 413–420.

Streib, G. F., & Streib, R. B. Communes and the aging. *American Behavioral Scientist,* 1975, *19,* 176–189.

Struyk, R. The housing situation of the elderly Americans. *The Gerontologist,* 1977, *17,* 130–139.

Sussman, M. B. The family life of older people. *In* R. H. Binstock & E. Shanas (Eds.), *Handbook of aging and the social sciences.* New York: Van Nostrand, 1976, pp. 218–243.

Teski, M. *Living together: An ethnography of a retirement hotel.* Washington, D. C.: University Press of America, 1979.

Tissue, T. Old age, poverty, and the central city. *International Journal of Aging and Human Development,* 1971, *2,* 235–248.

U.S. Department of Housing and Urban Development. Condominium/cooperative study I–7. Washington, D. C., July, 1975.

U.S. Department of Housing and Urban Development. *How well are we housed? 5. Rural.* Washington, D.C.: Office of Policy Development and Research, 1976.

U.S. General Accounting Office. *Report to Congress: Rental Housing: A National Problem that Needs Immediate Attention.* Washington, D. C., November 8, 1979. (a)

U.S. General Accounting Office. *Report to Congress identifying boarding homes housing the needy aged, blind, and disabled: A major step toward resolving a national problem.* November 19, 1979. (b)

Urban Systems Research and Engineering. *Evaluation of the Effectiveness of Congregate Housing for the Elderly.* Washington, D. C.: U.S. Department of Housing and Urban Development, 1976.

Wallin, P. L. Home ownership problems of the elderly. *Clearinghouse Review,* August–September, 1972, Vol. 6, 227–232.

Weitzman, J. Mobile homes: High cost housing in low income market. *Journal of Economic Issues,* 1976, 576–597.

Wood, E. F. Condominium conversion and the elderly. *In* J. A. Weiss, *Law of the elderly.* New York: Practicing Law Institute, 1977, 323–336.

Zorbaugh, H. W. *The gold coast and the slum: A sociological study of Chicago's near north side.* Chicago: University of Chicago Press, 1929.

5

Aging in Rural Environments

GRAHAM D. ROWLES

INTRODUCTION

In 1978 some 8,467,000 persons over 65 years of age (approximately 38% of the noninstitutionalized elderly population) resided outside standard metropolitan statistical areas (U.S. Bureau of the Census, 1979). An increasing proportion of these old people live in small-town and rural environments. During the 1970s the significant numbers of elderly who had "aged in place" in such settings were complemented by a steady stream of return migrants from metropolitan areas (Aday & Miles, 1982; Beale, 1976; Bowles, 1978; Fuguitt & Tordella, 1980; Koebernick & Beegle, 1978). As this transition has occurred, a few pioneering anthologies (Atchley & Byerts, 1975; Youmans, 1967) have been supplemented by a proliferation of research on the rural and small town elderly (Ansello & Cipolla, 1980; Kim & Wilson, 1981; Wilkinson, Rowles, & Maxwell, 1982). Unfortunately, very little of this research has been concerned with the environmental experience, defined as physical, cognitive, and emotional transactions with the physical setting, of rural old people.

A similar, extremely rapid growth has occurred in the field of environmental psychology. However, most work in this domain has been concerned with urban contexts. There is still no environmental psychology of rural aging (Dibner, 1982). This chapter, focusing on the environmental experience of the rural elderly, seeks to lay the groundwork for

GRAHAM D. ROWLES • Department of Geology and Geography, West Virginia University, Morgantown, West Virginia 26506.

the emergence of such a perspective. First, distinctive characteristics of rural environments as locales in which to grow old will be identified. Second, the somewhat fragmented literature on the current characteristics, status, and well-being of the elderly who live in such settings will be reviewed. A third segment of the chapter focuses on an important methodological issue: the need for exploratory ethnographic approaches in seeking to develop an environmental psychology of rural aging. Some characteristics of such an approach are outlined. This material provides a context for the fourth section of the chapter which, focusing on a case study in rural Appalachia, identifies building blocks for understanding the multifaceted environmental experience of the rural elderly. These building blocks include distinctive patterns of physical participation in rural environments, a generic differentiation of the rural setting into a series of annular cognitive zones, and the existence of an array of emotional attachments to particular locations within the rural setting. A fifth section of the chapter argues that specific manifestations of these themes are strongly influenced by the sociocultural milieu that provides the backdrop to life in much of rural America. Finally, the chapter identifies gaps in our understanding and lists potentially fruitful future research directions.

CHARACTERISTICS OF RURAL ENVIRONMENTS

The Problem of Definition

There is considerable ambiguity in definitions of the rural elderly and in characterizing rural environments (Ansello, 1980). Some studies have employed extremely crude definitions, considering the rural aged as comprising elderly persons living in communities of less than 50,000 (Sauer, Seelbach, & Hanson, 1980). Others, employing U.S. Census Bureau definition, have restricted the designation to old people living in communities of less than 2,500 (Taietz, 1975). More refined analyses distinguish between *rural farm* and *rural nonfarm* populations or between rural and small-town elderly. However, even these breakdowns do not adequately reflect the diversity of environmental contexts inhabited by the nonmetropolitan elderly. Within a very small area there may be major variations with critical implications for the lifestyle and well-being of individual old people. Residence in the center of a small town, with perhaps 300 residents in close physical proximity, provides a distinctive milieu. Old people can see their neighbors from their windows and often receive important practical, social, and psychological support from the arena immediately adjacent to their homes (Rowles, 1981a). A short distance away, a major transition may occur in the potential for support. Toward the margins of a settlement, homes become more widely separated spatially. Elderly residents become increasingly isolated. Such settings require old people to evolve lifestyles that differ from their peers in town (Rowles, 1981b). Beyond such local variations, there are considerable regional variations in rural environments. The expanses of rural Kansas, Appalachian hollows, Texas rangelands, and the communities of rural Vermont provide contrasting physical and cultural settings in which to grow old.

CONTRASTS WITH URBAN ENVIRONMENTS

Despite this diversity, it is generally acknowledged that rural environments have many shared characteristics and, in both a physical and a social sense, are very different from urban ones. The vast concrete expanses of the metropolis, where generally 20% of land is devoted to roads and highways, 30% to residences, and 13% to manufacturing or commercial structures, are conspicuously absent (Yeates & Garner, 1980).

Differences in physical context are but one area of contrast. In 1938 Louis Wirth published his classic essay on urbanism, in which he identified large population size, high population density, and population heterogeneity as primary characteristics of the city environment (Wirth, 1938). More recently, Stanley Milgram's well publicized paper has captured subtle psychological features of life in the city that stem from these characteristics (Milgram, 1970). Separation of the self from the physical and social overload of the setting through a variety of defense and screening strategies and a sense of alienation, he argues, are the price of physical and psychological survival.

Many scholars dispute the highly deterministic and somewhat uncharitable view of urban life presented by Wirth, Milgram, and their adherents (see, for example, Fischer, 1976). However, the perspective is useful because in many respects rural environments provide the antithesis of Wirth's and Milgram's scenarios. They are characterized by few people, low population densities and, in most cases, a degree of social homogeneity. Few rural settings provide the alienating social and psychological ambience described by Milgram. It is helpful to codify the differences more thoroughly under the rubric of three sets of contrasts: physical, demographic, and sociocultural.

Physical contrasts with the city are most readily apparent. Rural settings more closely approximate *natural* environments. They possess more plant life, more trees, and greater spaciousness. There is an absence of the high degree of verticality presented by contemporary urban building forms. In addition, as Carson notes: "Horizons appear in nature, but there are few natural places quite as uniformly horizontal as the floors" of urban structures (Carson, 1970, p. 196) or the paved expanses of urban parking lots. Where urban settings provide vistas of whites and reds but predominantly grays, rural environments are characterized by blues, greens, and browns. Rural physical settings tend to present *lower levels of cognitive complexity and stimulus input,* a feature of critical importance in facilitating old people's ability to function in such settings. Finally, the physical context of most rural settings remains fairly *stable through time.* Change in such environments tends to be gradual, making it possible for the vulnerable old person to harness the advantages of familiarity in negotiating the setting.

A second set of considerations is essentially demographic. They pertain to the population structure of an environment. Where urban settings are characterized by large numbers of people and high population densities, rural environments have relatively *few residents,* mostly living at *low densities.* Indeed, they are characterized by a population that is *geographically dispersed.* This feature not only makes service provision more difficult but also requires distinctive modifications of lifestyles that are a direct consequence of spatial isolation. In addition, rural settings tend to possess a higher level of *population stability,* a feature that reinforces the development of supportive relationships over many years.[1]

Third, and somewhat paradoxically, it may be the sociocultural milieu of rural environments that exerts the greatest influence upon old people's transactions with the physical setting. In this context, the sociocultural milieu is defined as the accepted norms of behavior and values that permeate and condition relationships among individuals and social groups. Generally, these characteristics of an environment are grounded in the history of a community, in a traditional way of life that provides the template for present-day lifestyles. Rural settings may be particularly supportive of old people for they tend to provide the type of sociocultural milieu that encourages maintenance of function and ongoing environmental participation. The *slower pace of life* is supportive of individuals who are less than nimble, whose reaction times have slowed, and who have the time and inclination for leisurely rather than rapid fragmented social exchanges (Bornstein, 1979). Rural values placing em-

---

[1]At this juncture it should be pointed out that this stability may be a historical rather than a contemporary phenomenon that may not hold for future generations of more mobile old people who will be living in rural areas.

phasis upon *self-reliance* reinforce the desire for ongoing independence and instill within the community social ethos an acknowledgement of the importance of maintaining such independence. This argument is particularly well expressed in the work of Lozier and Althouse on the community context of the elderly in rural Appalachia (1974, 1975). At the same time, the rural sociocultural milieu has a variety of characteristics with critical supportive potential when competence begins to decline. Most important is the sense of identity, of *being known*, that is an accepted benefit of rural residence. Despite the spatial separation of population, rural domains are characterized by awareness networks in which individuals know the names, lifestyles, state of health and many more intimate details about others in the community (Rowles, 1983a). The existence of an extensive information network reduces the potential for alienation and for the tragedies that sometimes result from anonymity. Being known is intimately linked to the existence of extensive and intensive indigenous *social support networks* in most rural communities that provide assistance to old people as they become progressively more environmentally vulnerable (discussed in detail in Rowles, 1983a).

The importance of these observations is that they provide the basis for suggesting that rural old people's transactions with the physical environment may be qualitatively different from those of their urban counterparts. *A distinctive sociocultural milieu, nurtured by physical and demographic characteristics of rural environments, provides a filter mediating the rural old person's experience of the physical setting.* This filter (a) conditions patterns of physical participation within the environment, (b) generates distinctive cognitions of community space, and (c) fosters an array of emotional attachments to place that provide a sense of identity in old age. These three themes are developed in some depth later in the chapter. At this juncture, it is useful to review what we already know about the lives of the rural elderly.

CHARACTERISTICS OF RURAL ELDERLY PEOPLE

OBJECTIVE CONDITIONS

A variety of research reports and detailed case studies provide a scenario of the rural elderly in the United States living under "objective" conditions far inferior to those of their urban counterparts (Kim & Wilson, 1981; Kivett & Scott, 1979a; Lassey, Lassey, & Lee, 1980; Youmans, 1977). Incomes are lower (Lee & Lassey, 1980a; Kim, 1980; Youmans, 1977). Housing of the rural elderly is older, of lower value, of poorer physical quality and more likely to be lacking in basic facilities such as plumbing than that of the urban elderly (Atchley & Miller, 1979; Bylund, Crawford, & LeRay, 1979). The rural elderly are in poorer health and have inferior access to health services (Konan, Tweed, & Longest, 1979; McCoy & Brown, 1978). Many rural old people have dietary deficiencies (Fisher, Hendricks, & Mahoney, 1978; Glover, 1981; Rawson, Weinberg, Herold, & Holtz, 1978). The rural elderly have less access to transportation (McKelvey, 1979; Orr, 1978, Patton, 1975). Rural areas tend to be lacking services for the elderly (Coward, 1979; Nelson, 1980; Taietz & Milton, 1979). Finally, there is evidence that significant numbers of rural elderly poeple are spatially isolated from their children and other family members (Powers, Keith, & Goudy, 1979; Rowles, 1983b) and that some rural elderly experience problems of loneliness (Kivett, 1978a,b, 1979).

SUBJECTIVE WELL-BEING

Although there is no denying its seriousness, this dismal litany of disadvantage is tempered by an important paradox. The inferior "objective" conditions of the rural elderly are not necessarily paralleled by lower levels of "subjective" well-being. Many studies indicate high morale and life-satisfaction among diverse rural elderly populations (Donnenwerth, Guy, and Norvell, 1978; Grams & Fengler, 1981; Hynson, 1976; Lee & Lassey, 1980a,b; Rowles, 1981b).

EXPLAINING THE PARADOX

There are two possible explanations for the apparent dissonance between objective conditions and subjective well-being. First, it suggests the need for reinterpretation of the data on disadvantages of the rural elderly. One or two illustrations suffice to illustrate how apparent disadvantages are, to some extent, a product of definition and interpretation. The use of dollar income statistics as an index of well-being does not consider the hidden resources of many rural old people: the property they own; their lower food costs—the rural elderly are far more likely than the urban elderly to cultivate gardens and to own freezers (Atchley & Miller, 1979); the degree to which expenses are lower as a result of participation in what is generally more of an exchange economy; and contrasting perceptions of the meaning of income (Grams & Fengler, 1981). While the housing of the rural elderly is of poorer quality than that of the urban elderly, there are compensations that result in high levels of satisfaction with the dwelling (Grams & Fengler, 1981; Montgomery, Stubbs, & Day, 1980). Ninety-one percent of the rural elderly have fulfilled the American dream—they live in single-family dwellings; 82% of all rural elderly housing units are owner-occupied, and 40% of elderly rural nonfarm homeowners and 53% of elderly farm owners have not moved for more than 20 years (Beall, Thompson, Godwin, & Donahue, 1981). Partly because such length of residence makes gradual property deterioration less readily noticeable and partly because they do not view their anticipated lifespan as justifying the outlay, rural older people are often reluctant to contemplate renovation of their dwellings (Atchley & Miller, 1979). It is not merely a question of cost. Moreover, large units, although they may be difficult to maintain, are often viewed as desirable because they provide extra space to encourage the visits of family (Atchley & Miller, 1979). Finally, residential satisfaction is often reinforced by the emotional significance with which the dwelling becomes imbued after many years of residence (Rowles, 1980, 1982b). Similar compensating factors can be identified in the area of transportation, where recent research has documented the degree to which the rural elderly receive rides from family, friends, and neighbors, often preferring these alternatives to reliance on publicly funded transportation programs (Rodeheaver, 1982). Finally, it is possible to question the impact of the spatial dispersion of families. Although many of their children move away, most rural elderly have at least one child living within one half hour's driving distance. These children provide much practical assistance. Moreover, children who have moved away provide forms of support that may be just as significant, including letters, telephone calls, and financial assistance. Spatial separation does not appear to be accompanied by any lessening of emotional commitments or perceived adequacy of interaction (Heltsley & Powers, 1975; Osterreich, 1965; Rowles, 1983a).

A second and in this context more significant explanation for the rural-urban paradox is that it is attributable to the supportive environment afforded by rural settings. Lee and Lassey (1980a) conjecture that many rural environments are distinctive in fostering high levels of social participation and social support, reduced fear of the crime that is so debilitating for the elderly urban dweller, and a sociocultural milieu allowing a more gradual process of retirement and transition to aged status. However, very little research has been undertaken that specifically seeks to isolate the environmental features of rural settings that might impinge on well-being.

WELL-BEING OF THE SMALL TOWN ELDERLY: A CASE STUDY

A significant exception is a large-scale research program initiated by Windley and Scheidt (Scheidt, 1981; Windley, 1981; Windley & Scheidt, 1980a,b, 1982). Using an innovative town panel approach (Windley &

Scheidt, 1980a), an interview survey was undertaken of 990 elderly residents of 18 small rural Kansas communities. One of the objectives of this study was to assess the influence of a variety of demographic, psychosocial, and, more important in this context, ecological-architectural factors upon well-being. Well-being was measured by indices including: housing satisfaction; contact with friends; contact with relatives; mobility; presence of a confidante; feelings of security; frequency and type of activity participation, and several measures of psychological well-being including the Affect Balance Scale (Bradburn, 1969), the Philadelphia Geriatric Center Morale Scale (Lawton, 1975), and the Langner Twenty-Two Item Screening Score (Langner, 1962). Windley and Scheidt also adopted a multidimensional approach to collecting information on architectural-ecological variables within the 18 settings. Their survey protocol included an assessment of respondents' perceptions of: sensory stimulation (degree of orientation to visual, auditory and olfactory stimuli); cognitive legibility of neighborhood and community; residential comfort (measured in terms of temperature, space, and lighting); privacy; adaptability of dwelling for multiple uses; degree of control or jurisdiction over residence; sociality (the degree to which social participation was hindered by physical and social barriers); population density (including both age and population density preferences); meaning or degree of attachment to the setting (house and neighborhood); and aesthetic quality (attractiveness of home and neighborhood) (Windley & Scheidt, 1980b).

In analyzing the mass of data developed from the project, Windley and Scheidt employed factor analysis to yield more parsimonious measures of each domain. Stepwise multiple regression analysis was then employed. An important finding was that seven of the dimensions of well-being were most strongly predicted by ecological-architectural variables (Windley, 1981), which were found to have strong impact upon housing satisfaction, mobility, functional health, two components of morale ("attitude toward own aging" and "agitated depression"), and two factors derived from the Langner Screening Score. Subsequently, two composite dimensions from the ecological-architectural data—dwelling features and a measure of environmental constriction—were employed in a path model of environmental and demographic effects on mental health (Windley & Scheidt, 1982).

From their analyses Windley and Scheidt were able to suggest that "older people most involved in community affairs (experiencing least environmental constriction) are psychologically happier, healthier individuals" (Windley & Scheidt, 1982, p. 241) and that "those who are happier with their dwellings are also more likely to be psychologically happy and healthy" (Windley & Scheidt, 1982, p. 242). They conclude that improved mental health of small town rural elderly will result from interventions that heighten satisfaction with immediate features of the dwelling unit and remove physical and social barriers to environmental participation.

These findings are useful contributions in seeking to identify those aspects of rural environments which contribute to well-being in old age. However, they represent selected components of a far more complex relationship with the physical setting that is mediated by the sociocultural milieu. The need to incorporate an understanding of this theme in exploring the rural old person–environment transaction from a more holistic perspective presents a critical methodological quandary. How can we develop sensitive understanding of the norms of behavior and values permeating rural life that are necessary prerequisites to grounded theory?

METHODOLOGICAL ISSUES IN DEVELOPING AN ENVIRONMENTAL PSYCHOLOGY OF RURAL AGING

THE NEED FOR AN EXPLORATORY INDUCTIVE APPROACH

A basic problem arises because very little is known about the experience of growing old in rural environments. We are still at the exploratory, information-gathering phase that precedes the emergence of a dominant paradigm (Kuhn, 1962). The few commentaries that exist on the experience of rural aging viewed in phenomenological and sociocultural context, suggest that in developing a grounded paradigm it will be necessary to evolve a new lexicon and to incorporate variables that are distinctive to this domain (Ansello, 1980; Gardner, 1981; Pihlblad, 1975). As Ansello has noted:

> The danger exists that we may transfer urban methods and models to rural contexts simply because we have methods and models. (Ansello, 1980, p. 343)

It is clearly necessary to avoid prestructuring and to seek empirically grounded theory through studies employing an exploratory inductive approach (Blumer, 1969; Glaser & Strauss, 1967). Research should focus on deriving categories, concepts, and hypotheses that authentically represent rural older persons' environmental experience because they result from the researcher's immersion in the subjects' lifeworlds (Rowles, 1978; Von Eckartsberg, 1971). This implies ethnographic and case study research. Although such an approach has been advocated (Britton, 1975; Montgomery, Stubbs, & Day, 1980), only a few researchers have pursued this option in studying the rural elderly (Gardner, 1981; Lozier & Althouse, 1974, 1975; Rowles, 1980, 1981a, 1982a, 1983b; Wang, 1979).

ETHNOGRAPHIC AND CASE STUDY RESEARCH

The necessity for ethnographic research is, in part, reinforced by the inappropriateness and practical difficulties of conducting research on the rural elderly within more traditional research paradigms. Beyond logistical problems of deriving statistically meaningful samples from highly dispersed rural elderly populations and the obtrusiveness of conducting observation-oriented research in rural communities (Rowles, 1982a), it is often difficult to gain entry into the worlds of rural elderly people. Barriers to effective communication often mean that, even when responses are obtained to structured surveys, there is some doubt as to the validity of the inferences drawn. Understanding *from within* requires establishing rapport with research participants at a level of intimacy allowing them to reveal customarily taken-for-granted dimensions of their experience. Such understanding also involves viewing their life-styles in personal and historical context (Mills, 1959).

Consequently, at this stage in our understanding, approaches to research that build upon and extend a lengthy tradition of participant observation and ethnographic research may be the most appropriate (see, for example, McCall & Simmons, 1969; Spradley, 1979). An intense form of participant observation defined as "experiential fieldwork" is advocated (Rowles, 1978; Von Eckartsberg, 1971). This approach is premised upon establishing strong interpersonal relationships with study participants. Such relationships make it possible to correct an epistemological deficiency in much rural aging research—the paucity of insight into the phenomenological worlds of rural old people.

Adopting such an approach has a variety of methodological implications (Rowles, 1978). First, in developing authentic interpersonal relationships it is necessary, at least temporarily, to suspend the scientists' pretense of objectivity and to engage in a form of dialogue with participants that is unconstrained by the customary detachment of researcher from respondent. Such dialogue results in insight through a process of mutual discovery as participants become co-researchers feeding back on each others' inputs (Von Eckartsberg, 1971). In this endeavor the researcher becomes the translator, responsible for communicating the "text" of the experience to a larger audience.

Establishing such relationships implies a lengthy time investment in field research in order to develop an appropriate level of rapport with each participant and to develop some immersion within and empathy for the local social and historical context. The intensity of relationships sought means that research samples are necessarily small, comprising a limited number of individuals studied in depth over an extended time period. A series of case studies of individuals or members of a single community with which the researcher has developed a high level of familiarity (generally through an extended period of residence in the field) often becomes the most effective and cost-efficient research strategy.

Adopting such a case study approach also carries important implications with regard to the interpretation of data. The focus of interpretation becomes inductive inference and the *generation* of categories, relationships, and hypotheses directly from the research experience rather than the testing of *a priori* hypotheses. Clearly, in a traditional methodological sense, findings are illustrative and cannot be extended beyond the population studied. Their value lies in the potential for discovery. Finally, an exploratory approach requires alternative modes of presenting findings, using approaches that do minimal violence to the substance of the research experience. This requires description and accurate reporting of the process whereby categories, relationships, and hypotheses were derived—what Becker has termed the "natural history" of the enterprise (Becker, 1958).

To argue for more exploratory ethnographic research is not to reject the important contributions that result from survey research and other more traditional approaches. Indeed, as fieldwork progresses a variety of formal measures, developed in response to emergent themes in the data and attuned to the varying capabilities of the participants, are clearly appropriate. Rather, it is suggested that meshing of information from formal measures and large scale surveys with an understanding of the subtleties of rural life revealed by ethnographic case studies will enrich our perspective and result in a more comprehensive environmental psychology of rural aging. In the next section we turn to the findings of research that has sought to implement such an approach.

ELDERLY PEOPLE IN RURAL ENVIRONMENTS: SOME EMERGENT THEMES

Due to the limited amount of completed exploratory inductive research on the environmental experience of rural aging, much of what follows is based on my own work in a rural Appalachian community (Rowles, 1980, 1981a,b, 1982a,b, 1983b). Where findings from other research are available they are integrated into the discussion. The concepts presented should properly be viewed as hypotheses for several reasons. First, they are heavily weighted toward findings from a relatively secluded community nestled in the hollows of Appalachia that may not represent a normative situation for rural America. Second, they are derived from a residentially stable population with a high proportion of old-old (over 75 years of age) residents who have not lived elsewhere. The growing number of rural elderly who formerly resided in metropolitan areas are not represented. Finally, the insights are based primarily on small numbers of individuals studied in depth rather than on statistical samples.

THE COLTON STUDY

A study was conducted over a four-year period in Colton (a pseudonym), a declining community of 400 persons that had experienced significant outmigration of its younger population. Over three summers' residence in the community and frequent visits during the remainder of each year, a strong relationship was developed with a panel of 15 elderly residents ranging in age from 62 to 91 at the commencement of the study. In addition to participant observation and over 800 hours of unstructured tape-recorded interviews, a variety of more formal procedures including space–time activity diaries, cognitive mapping tasks, social network and life satisfaction measures, and photography (including aerial photography of the area surrounding each person's home) were employed in compiling a detailed dossier on each participant's transaction with the environmental context (Rowles, 1981b). These data were supplemented by information obtained through informal interactions with other old people in Colton during field phases of the study, and by an understanding of the sociocultural milieu of the community that evolved over the four years.

From the mass of data collected, three primary themes emerged as complementary components o the study participants' transactions with their physical environment. The environmental experience of the Colton elderly could be summarized within the rubrics of (a) physical participation in the environment, (b) cognitions of space that formed the backdrop to these patterns of activity, and (c) emotional attachments to particular places within the physical setting.

PHYSICAL PARTICIPATION IN THE ENVIRONMENT

Old people in rural areas, particularly the old-old, generally do not stray far from their home community. Apart from occasional vacation trips and annual extended visits to children living far away (Rowles,

1983b), few trips are taken beyond the nearest large community. Trips to these nearby towns are generally biweekly visits to a supermarket or to services unavailable within the local community (Table 1). Particularly important in this respect are infrequent trips to banks, to the doctor, to a pharmacy, and to other medical facilities. Indeed, the Colton elderly reveal a bimodal pattern of service activity involving reliance on opportunities within the community for everyday services and upon nearby towns for those for which the local population by itself does not provide a sufficient population threshold and for which demand is less frequent (Berry, 1967). This bimodal pattern contrasts with that found in many urban areas where most services are often available within the neighborhood (Cantor, 1979). As they grow older, it becomes progressively more difficult for the Colton elderly to make trips to nearby towns. Increasingly, they become obliged to rely on rides from their children or friends or on scheduled trips on the Senior Center bus. Moreover, such trips gradually become less frequent as, apart from medical trips, the elderly rely on others to make service trips for them.

TABLE 1
SERVICES[a] UTILIZED OVER 12-MONTH PERIOD

	Service obtained from less than 1 mile radius	Service obtained from 2–5 mile radius	Service obtained from 6–15 mile radius	Service obtained from 16–25 mile radius	Service obtained from beyond 25 miles
Physician	2		8	3	
Eye doctor			10	2	
Pharmacy			10	2	
Bank			13		1
Grocery (convenience)	8	2	1		
Grocery (major provisions)	4		9		
Hardware	2		6	1	
Church	9	1	1		
Most visited[b] restaurant			12		
Clothing			2	6	2
Hairdresser	2	7	5	1	

Note. N = 14, as one married couple completed joint response to survey instrument. Data not included if service not utilized in 12 months prior to survey. Table includes only partial data for one participant, Asel, 92 years old, whose daughter obtains his groceries and other services. Asel does not know where these services are obtained.
[a]Refers to *primary* source of service.
[b]Does not include meals at Colton Senior Center.

Most activity takes place within the community and involves regular travel to specific behavior settings such as the post office, general store (for convenience shopping), church, or Senior Center (Barker & Barker, 1961). In Colton it was discovered that several of the old men in the community would travel to the post office (located in a trailer next to the store) at about 10:00 a.m. each morning. After picking up their mail they would congregate on the bench outside the store next to the telephone booth where they would visit for some time before returning home. Later in the morning, just before noon, the women who attended the Title III nutrition program at the Senior Center would arrive. They would visit the post office and the store before walking over to the center for their meal (Rowles, 1982a). Such trips tend to establish a regular rhythm in the older person's daily life. Maintaining a daily routine in the use of space may be supportive to the functioning of the rural old person. Over time the establishment of a regular set of paths results in these routes' becoming ingrained in the individual's subconscious. A "body awareness" of the setting, functioning much like an automatic pilot, may facilitate ongoing participation in an environment that otherwise might be beyond the physiological and cognitive capabilities of the individual (Rowles, 1980; Seamon, 1979). We can posit that such a phenomenon may be directly reinforced by characteristics of rural environments that have been identified earlier in this chapter, specifically, lower levels of cognitive complexity and stimulus overload and the tendency for greater stability of the physical context than is found in most urban environments.

Beyond familiarity, there are secondary advantages to the regular routine of trips around the community established by many elderly. As Gardner notes in discussing a small Kentucky community:

> Middle-aged and younger residents there become attuned to the relatively regularized daily routines of the older ones; should one fail to make the expected daily walk to the post office, for instance, it would be noted and investigated. (Gardner, 1981, p. 6; see also Britton and Britton, 1972)

In spite of such compensations, the activity spaces of the rural elderly become progressively more constricted as they spend more and more time closer to home. Barker and Barker (1961) discovered that such "behavioral regression" resulted in a mean occupancy time in all behavior settings that was equivalent to that of the preschool child. Windley and Scheidt (1982) also discovered significant "environmental constriction" in the use of space in their Kansas sample. While 88% of their respondents said that they got out of the house almost every day, only 30% reported leaving the neighborhood with similar frequency (Windley & Scheidt, 1980a).

COGNITIONS OF SPACE

Emphasis upon the local setting in environmental participation is reflected in cognitions of space. Evidence from Colton suggests that rural elderly people may cognitively differentiate the physical environment into zones of decreasing intensity of involvement away from their homes (Figure 1). Home is the fulcrum of the individual's world, the locus of departure and the focus of return (Bachelard, 1969; Bollnow, 1967; Eliade, 1959; Porteous, 1976; Rakoff, 1977). The length of residence of many rural elderly is such that this space assumes distinctive meaning as an expression of identity and repository for the artifacts and memo-

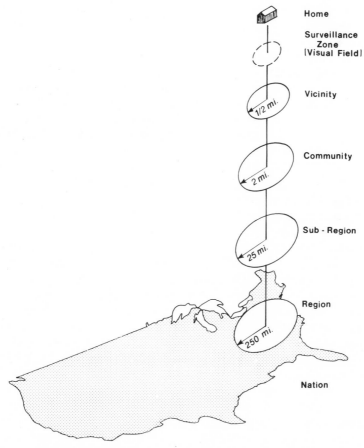

Figure 1.   A hierarchy of environmental spaces. (Reproduced from Rowles & Ohta, 1983c. Reprinted by permission.)

ries that constitute the individual's personal history. This space is thus cognitively differentiated from space "outside" (Rowles, 1980, 1982b).

Outside the home, the "surveillance zone," space within the visual field of the dwelling, assumes special significance for many rural old people (Lozier & Althouse, 1975; Rowles, 1981a; Wang, 1979). In addition to important practical and social reciprocity between old people and their neighbors, the fact that much time is spent on the porch or at the window, watching events within the visual field—the children playing and the passing cars—and being watched, means that this space assumes increasing significance as physical limitations dictate progressively more time spent at home. Lozier and Althouse provide a sensitive interpretation of the significance of this zone as an arena in which the old person is still able to exert important social control as he or she becomes increasingly vulnerable (Lozier & Althouse, 1975). Of course such benefits cannot be fully enjoyed by those rural residents who live "out in the country" beyond the visual field of neighbors or major roads. However, even here, old people may gain an important sense of involvement through monitoring the passing of the seasons and other natural events as they gaze from their windows or muse away summer evenings on the porch swing.

Immediately beyond the visual field, the vicinity, may also be construed as a distinctive space. Within this zone, geographical proximity coupled with considerable shared length of residence may lead to the emergence of an area perceived as a distinctive "social space" (Buttimer, 1969), in which old people know the life history, lifestyles, and more intimate details of the lives of those who live nearby. Intensive telephone networks, particularly among age peers, may develop within this zone (Rowles, 1983a). Within a very small community there may develop a series of such localized social spaces that serve to differentiate the rural community into localities that are perceived as functionally and socially discrete and even have distinctive local folk names. The perception of such spaces is reinforced by patterns of practical support from younger persons who reside in the vicinity, often including middle-aged women who assume the role of "caretakers" within localized "natural care networks." These women may assist the old person with wallpapering or painting a room, may run errands, or provide other forms of support (Gardner, 1981; Rowles, 1983a).

Each old person's vicinity is embedded in a larger arena, the community. Rural communities vary considerably in size depending upon topography, population density, and regional characteristics. In her Missouri study, Wang (1979) found that the community she investigated extended a radius of about two miles from the center of the settlement.

In Colton, the community as perceived by the participants was generally considered to be similar in spatial extent, but there was substantial variation in perception among individuals. This was a reflection, in part, of the spatial dispersion of residences. On the periphery of the study community there tended to be overlap with other communities in terms of the psychological allegiance of rural old people (Rowles, 1983a). In addition, the uniqueness of each individual's geographical location resulted in there being many overlapping perceptions of community. Perceptions of the physical extent of the community are complicated by the existence of social rather than solely spatial definitions of this realm (for elaboration on this theme, see Lee, 1968). Thus, in Colton, community was viewed not only as a distinctive physical space but also as the domain of a network of age peers and their families and was oriented around social relationships focused on institutions such as the church, senior center, and fraternal organizations. The community is perceived in this respect as the zone in which everyday support may be received from those family members who remain within its bounds, from friends accumulated over a lifetime, and from an age-peer-group "society of the old." Due to geographical dispersion, the telephone may become an especially critical medium for such support (Dibner, 1982; Rowles, 1983a). Finally, community may be viewed by rural old people in terms of the array of "perceived community functions," that is, potentials for "maintenance," "recreation," "personal relations," and "personal development," that it fulfills (Blake & Lawton, 1980; Blake, Lawton, & O'Leary, 1981).

Moving farther away from each old person's home, the physical environment becomes even less clearly cognitively differentiated. Several additional zones may be identified from the Appalachian study, but their boundaries are more transitions on a continuum of change in the nature of participation and cognitions than clearly defined break points. The community is located within the subregion, a zone of approximately 25 miles radius in the Appalachian study. This zone not only embraces the spatial extent of services utilized by the rural elderly, but also represents the limit of space known and identified with through personal experience. The range of local newspapers and radio stations within this sphere of interest reinforces vicarious involvement in local political issues, sports activities, and social events. Beyond the subregion, cognition of space within the region (a zone extending up to a distance of 250 miles) becomes a series of fragments of space adjacent to the homes of children who moved away from Colton. These cognitive "islands" are visited on occasion and their local spatial configuration may become known in detail. Space in the nation beyond 250 miles is primarily experienced vicariously through the media and is outside the purview of the Colton elderly's daily lives, although events in this realm are acknowledged to impinge upon the community.

In sum, it is hypothesized that the rural elderly construe the physical environment as a hierarchy of zones, focused on their homes. The existence of such cognitive zones is strongly linked to both the type and frequency of their physical participation in these spaces. Increasing distance from the threshold is associated with less intense psychological involvement. The dimensions of this generic hierarchy are obviously highly variable. Distances in rural Texas and in rural Appalachia have entirely different meaning. More important, several characteristics of rural environments that have been previously identified serve to distinguish this hierarchy of cognitive spaces from comparable differentiations of urban space. The lack of cognitive complexity and low population density of rural environments facilitates a considerable spatial extent of cognitive awareness, not only of the physical setting but also of its inhabitants. Thus many of Colton's elderly were found to be able to describe each house on every street within the community and were able to list the names and genealogy of most of their occupants. It can be hypothesized that the physical and demographic stability of rural settings also facilitates the development and retention of such detailed "cognitive maps."

Emotional Attachments to Place

The isomorphism between physical participation in the rural environment and the differentiation of this space into a series of distinctive cognitive zones is further reinforced by emergent findings from the Appalachian research suggesting that rural old people tend to imbue local space with personal and social meanings that result in strong emotional attachments to particular places within the community. Emotional attachments to place, for the Colton elderly, are closely linked to the concept of *insideness*. This motif distinguishes proximate spaces from the more peripheral zones, identified in the previous section, that are progressively viewed as *outside* (Rowles, 1980, 1983a). The inside-outside continuum involves three distinctive components. First, a sense of physical insideness, of being almost physiologically melded into the environment, results from an intimacy with its physical configuration stemming from the rhythm and routine of using the space over many years (discussed previously). Second, emotional attachment to proximate space is enhanced by a social insideness that evolves not only from everyday social exchanges and relationships but also from a sense of being known well and knowing others. The study participants claimed to know well a median number of 77 of the 142 persons over 60 years of age who lived in the Colton area even though they rarely saw many of these individuals (Rowles, 1983a). Such awareness of the potential for shared concern instills an aura of belonging and integration within the social space of the community that over the years becomes translated into an affinity for the physical setting (Buttimer, 1969, 1972).

Third, and most important, places assume meaning as foci of an autobiographical insideness grounded in personal history. Locations in and around the community evolve into incident places, locales where significant events within the old person's life transpired. This theme has been explored in some detail in another chapter (Rowles, 1980). It is helpful to quote a brief segment of this work in which a journey I took with 87-year-old Bertha, one of the study participants, is described.

> We passed "old Graveney's cabin" which Bertha explained, was known as the place "where the slaves used to stay." Nearby was the "swimming pond" where her "kids" used to go swimming. The cabin was gone and the pond had become clogged with mud and weeds and "all overgrown." We passed the remnants of a tree which, 80 years previously, provided a lofty vantage point from which she was able to sight the dentist as he rode into the valley and, having done so, to make herself scarce before his arrival in Colton. Farther on, she showed me a crevice in a large boulder. "We used to get dirt back in underneath there . . . for our house lawn and for the porch box where the flowers growed so good." We came to the "Green Tree," an imposing oak which served as a childhood rendezvous. "The kids on that end of the country road and us kids would come over here and meet and play." We passed the place where she was born and raised in a family of 21 children. The farmhouse had disappeared. In its place stood a mobile home. But for Bertha the old "home place" still existed. There was the now abandoned farmstead where a daughter died of pneumonia, the family gravesite, indeed, a host of places richly imbued with meaning in terms of events that transpired within them. (Rowles, 1980, pp. 161–162)

Over many years the physical setting inhabited by the rural old person may, as in Bertha's case, accumulate a plethora of such meanings. It may become a scrapbook of the individual's life and an important reinforcement to personal identity. Indeed, place may come to embody so many layers of meaning that it becomes an expression of self—implying the most intense level of reciprocity between person and environment (Ley, 1977; Rowles, 1980, 1982b, 1983a).

In developing the theme of emotional attachment to place the dimension of *time* emerges as a critical consideration. The population stability of traditional rural settings and the fact that many old people, like Bertha, have lived their entire lives within a single locale means that the physical environment may become a repository of cues evoking an array of emotions. During my trip with Bertha, she was in tears for much of the time. Memories evoked by a physical environment that, because of the slow pace of physical and social change in rural settings, is experienced not only as a contemporary setting but also, simultaneously, as the place it was many years previously stimulate particularly strong emotions. Such emotional identification may be incomprehensible to more mobile contemporary generations.

For many of the Colton elderly, emotional attachment to the physical setting was implicit; it was taken for granted and extremely difficult to articulate to an outsider such as myself. Eighty-four-year-old Beatrice, in describing her husband Walter's reluctance to abandon their home reveals the poignancy of such sentiment.

> This spring, my son talked. He says, "Now Mom, you just can't stay in this house forever. You got to get a smaller place and live someplace where you can be on the level." And he took us, just by force almost, to look at mobile homes and trailers. . . . And we almost bought one. They were so beautiful. And I said, "Well, are we going to sign?" And Pop said, "Well, let's think about it till morning." So we came home and he just sit down and started to cry. "I can't do it. I can't do it," he said. He lived in this house 57 or 8 years. And he said, "I just can't do it. We'll stay here."

Clearly, attachment to home and a sense of identification with the physical environment is not the exclusive preserve of the rural elderly. However, it is suggested that certain characteristics of rural environments, physical and demographic stability and a social context conducive to being "known" and to the maintenance among peers of shared memories of past events that transpired in particular locations, do provide particularly strong nurturance to such feelings.

Environmental participation, cognitions of space, and the emotional attachments with which places become imbued are intimately intertwined within the totality of the rural old person–environment transaction. More important, we have argued that the sociocultural milieu constitutes a critical *filter* mediating transactions with the physical environment in all three domains. It is appropriate at this juncture to examine the nature of this filter.

THE SOCIOCULTURAL MILIEU OF RURAL AGING

Rural old people, particularly the old-old, tend to be socialized to a lifestyle and value system that typified rural society in the formative years of their youth (Pihlblad, 1975). In Mead's terms, they represent vestiges of a socially stable postfigurative society in which the actions and lifestyles of parents provided the model of behavior (Ansello, 1980; Mead, 1970). Children were expected to care for their aged parents, often at a great personal sacrifice. Social worlds were of small scale, stable (social change was extremely slow), and intimately tied to the local physical setting. Over the span of the current generation of old people's lives, rural culture has changed. Incursion of mass media, increased mobility, and a variety of other factors have not only begun to blur once clear distinctions between urban and rural but have also led to altered lifestyles and changing value systems. The value systems of elderly long-time rural dwellers, in contrast to the young who are socialized within these more contemporary value systems, have not undergone this transformation. They remain as survivors of a different subculture. As Ansello writes: "Elements of the postfigurative can continue in pockets amidst larger contrary values" (Ansello, 1980, p. 345).

The sociocultural milieu of many rural old people remains very much a highly personalized one, based on a history of face-to-face contact and norms of mutual responsibility among individuals rather than upon formal or purely instrumental relationships (Pihlblad, 1975; Weller, 1965). This ethos not only underlies relationships between individuals but also is at the root of the functioning of the "society of the old" that exists in many rural communities (Rowles, 1980). Within this subculture of age peers, focused on the senior center or local church and an extensive telephone network, status is ascribed on the basis of previous contributions judged within an interpersonal framework.

> Status was gained through a reputation as good cook, strictness in child rearing, leadership in the "ladies aid society" or the missionary circle. Among husbands' status criteria were: reputation as a hard worker, being a "good provider," providing a "nice home," prominence in the church, support of "civic improvements" and progressive local programs such as Chautauqua, the lyceum course in the winter, sponsoring of Boy Scouts, uplift organizations of all types.((Pihlblad, 1975, p. 51)

The society of the old provides a context for supportive relationships among old people who have shared lengthy residence in a common space (Rowles, 1983a). However, this society and the values it represents is not independent of the larger community. Rather, it is a subculture within a larger multicultural social system. Within this larger system, relationships are based in part upon functional associations. More important, as Lozier and Althouse (1974) have eloquently illustrated, they are based on the accumulation of a reservoir of social credit upon which the individual can draw for support in old age. Over a lifetime, each person accumulates social credit from contributions to family and community and the status thus earned. This generates an expectation within the community that those in a position to provide assistance to the old person will furnish needed support as an accepted part of their own accumulation of social credit. As West, cited in Pihlblad (1975, p. 54) remarks, old people become "cares" (see also Gardner, 1981). The sense of social obligation within a community structure that characterizes many rural areas provides reassurance to old people as they grow more vulnerable because it forms the underlying rationale for an elaborate matrix of informal social supports (Rowles, 1983a).

The sense of mutual social obligation within the sociocultural milieu of most rural areas permeates elderly residents' lifestyles and in so doing conditions their transactions with the physical environment. The sociocultural milieu dictates a strong emphasis upon the local setting with regard to old people's physical participation within the environment. When Beatrice walks to the store or to the senior center she knows she can always receive a ride home if she has one of her dizzy spells. Being known as part of a community and acknowledged as a "care" provides an important sense that help is always available if needed. This encourages independence and continued physical participation in the environment using familiar paths. The sociocultural milieu also influences the way the physical setting is cognized by reinforcing the differentiation of space into cognitive zones closely related to different types of social relationships—the intimacy of surveillance zone transactions, the strong interdependency of peers within each other's vicinity, and the coherence of the society of the old on the level of the community. In sum, physical space is differentiated in terms of social meanings with which it is imbued. Finally, the sociocultural milieu of many rural old people is conducive to developing strong emotional attachments to place because it emphasizes stability, localism—even parochialism and a sense of "belonging" to a community.

WHERE FROM HERE?

Clearly, the limited empirical basis and exploratory inductive focus of the preceding observations indicate the need for extensive replication and corroboration. In addition, future research into the environmental experience of the rural elderly might profitably focus on a number of themes.

First, it is necessary to conduct more specific research on the manner in which the sociocultural milieu of rural areas mediates the old person's experience of the physical environment. For example, with regard to physical participation in the environment, to what extent do rural old people accept rides to services in nearby towns from family, friends, and others as part of the community's inherent obligation toward them—part of the system of social credit identified by Lozier and Althouse—rather than as merely the acknowledgement of their increasing frailty? Do such considerations influence the frequency with which they make trips? Does the knowledge that they are "cares" and that their behavior will be watched encourage rural old people to continue to walk along paths they might otherwise be reluctant to traverse? Do lifelong residents participate in the physical setting any differently than their age peers who have only recently migrated to the community and are not fully integrated within its sociocultural milieu?

Second, there is a need to broaden the range of rural environments considered. The desirability of more research on rural-urban comparisons has been well documented (Lee & Lassey, 1980b). At this point, there is also a need for rural-rural comparisons, particularly on a regional basis. How does the environmental experience of the elderly Kansas farmer differ from that of the Vermont retiree? To what extent is the situation reported in rural Appalachia an anomaly? Beyond such broad distinctions, greater emphasis is desirable on microscale distinctions in the characteristics of rural environments. There is a need to discriminate between old people living in small towns (the focus of most research to date) and those who live in more isolated settings in open country. Specific site differences between individual rural old people (for example, between those who have a neighbor within visual range and those who do not) may also account for important variations in lifestyle and environmental experience.

A third need is for consideration of variables that have not been fully incorporated into studies of aging in rural environments. Sex differences in environmental experience may be critical. Strong recent emphasis upon the situation of older women, particularly the large numbers of widows living alone in rural environments (Douglas, 1981; Hooyman, 1980; Kivett, 1978b; Kivett & Scott, 1979b; Lenihan, 1979; Sebastian & Payne, 1981), should be balanced by detailed studies of elderly men (especially widowers) who form an almost unnoticed minority population in these settings (Pihlblad & McNamara, 1965; Rowles, 1981b). It is also appropriate to distinguish different subpopulations of the rural elderly. Given the increasing flow of elderly return migrants to rural areas, length of residence may emerge as a critical variable influencing environmental experience. It will be necessary to distinguish between those who have aged-in-place and their neighbors who have only recently moved into the community after a lifetime in the city and are unaccustomed to the mores of rural life.

Finally, deriving a coherent environmental psychology of rural aging will have critical implications for enhancing the quality or perhaps even changing the nature of service provision to the rural elderly. Deeper understanding of the sociocultural milieu of rural environments is already leading to important modifications in the provision of therapy (Dunckley, Lutes, Wooten, & Kooken, 1980). There is also mounting evidence and intensifying advocacy in support of the efficacy and desirability of service options that build upon indigenous support networks and are more attuned to the characteristics of rural life (Douglas, 1981; Hooyman, 1980; Lohmann & Lohmann, 1977; Rowles, 1983a). Clearer understanding of the environmental psychology of rural aging can only enhance such efforts.

In the quest for deeper insight, it is critical to acknowledge historical change in rural areas and avoid the danger of nostalgic romanticism for a world that in a few years may only survive in the most remote settings. Technological and cultural change is leading to increasing homogenization of both environments (the supermarket in the rural small town, part of a corporate conglomerate, may differ very little from another store in the chain located in a suburban shopping mall or inner city neighborhood) and culture (elderly ladies in both urban and rural settings hurry home from the nutrition site to watch the same soap operas on their color television). Some of the characteristic differences between rural and urban environments, outlined at the beginning of this chapter, may be becoming less significant influences on lifestyle (Britton & Britton, 1971, pp. 143–148). Rural older populations are also changing. The young-old in particular, even those who have aged-in-place, are becoming more mobile, less tied to the immediate physical setting, and less bound by values that pervaded their parents' lives. They, and the generations that follow, will provide another test of the thorny age, cohort, and period effects trilemma that has bedeviled gerontological research (Nydegger, 1981). While bucolic Rockwellian images—of the friendly store and post office and social integration within a supportive society focused on family, neighbors, and church—may grace our fond (although frequently erroneous) perceptions of life in the rural communities of past generations, we should not allow such images to obscure the changing realities of old age in contemporary rural America.

REFERENCES

Aday, R. H., & Miles, L. A. Long term impacts of rural migration of the elderly: Implications for research. *Gerontologist*, 1982, 22, 331–336.

Ansello, E. A. Special considerations in rural aging. *Educational Gerontology*, 1980, *5*, 343–354.

Ansello, E. A., & Cipolla, C. E., (Eds.). Rural aging and education: Issues, methods and models. *Educational Gerontology*, Special Issue, 1980, *5*.

Atchley, R. C., & Byerts, T. L. (Eds.). *Rural environments and aging*. Washington, D. C.: Gerontological Society, 1975.

Atchley, R. C., & Miller, S. J. Housing and households of the rural aged. In T. O. Byerts, S. C. Howell, & L. A. Pastalan (Eds.), *Environmental context of aging: Lifestyles, environmental quality and living arrangements*. New York: Garland STPM Press, 1979, pp. 62–79.

Bachelard, G. *The poetics of space*. Boston: Beacon Press, 1969.

Barker, R. G., & Barker, L. S. The psychological ecology of old people in Midwest, Kansas, and Yoredale, Yorkshire. *Journal of Gerontology*, 1961, *61*, 231–239.

Beale, C. L. A further look at nonmetropolitan population growth since 1970. *American Journal of Agricultural Economics*, 1976, *58*, 953–958.

Beall, G. T., Thompson, M. M., Godwin, F., & Donahue, W. T. *Housing older persons in rural America: A handbook on congregate housing*. Washington, D. C.: International Center for Social Gerontology, 1981.

Becker, H. S. Problems of inference and proof in participant observation. *American Sociological Review*, 1958, *33*, 652–660.

Berry, B. L. *Geography of market centers and retail distribution*. Englewood Cliffs, N.J.: Prentice-Hall, 1967.

Blake, B. F., & Lawton, M. P. Perceived community functions and the rural elderly. *Educational Gerontology*, 1980, *5*, 375–386.

Blake, B. F., Lawton, M. P., & O'Leary, J. *Perceived community functions and services for the elderly* (Station Bulletin No. 292). Department of Agricultural Economics, Agricultural Experiment Station, Purdue University, West LaFayette, Indiana, 1981.

Blumer, H. *Symbolic interactionism: Perspective and method*. Englewood Cliffs, N.J.: Prentice-Hall, 1969.

Bollnow, O. Lived space. In N. Lawrence & D. O'Connor (Eds.), *Readings in existential phenomenology*. Englewood Cliffs, N.J.: Prentice-Hall, 1967, pp. 178–186.

Bornstein, M. H. The pace of life: Revisited. *International Journal of Psychology*, 1979, *14*, 83–90.

Bowles, G. K. Contributions of recent metro/nonmetro migrants to the non-metro population and labor force. *Agriculture Economics Research*, 1978, *30*, 15–21.

Bradburn, N. *The structure of psychological well-being*. Chicago: Aldine, 1969.

Britton, J. H. Reaction to "Family Relationships and Friendships" by Powers, Keith and Goudy. In R. C. Atchley & T. O. Byerts (Eds.), *Rural environments and aging*. Washington, D. C.: Gerontological Society, 1975, pp. 91–94.

Britton, J. H., & Britton, J. O. *Personality changes in aging*. New York: Springer, 1972.

Buttimer, A. Social space in interdisciplinary perspective. *Geographical Review*, 1969, *59*, 417–426.

Buttimer, A. Social space and the planning of residential areas. *Environment and behavior*, 1972, *4*, 279–318.

Bylund, R. A., Crawford, C. O., & LeRay, N. L. Housing quality of the elderly: a rural-urban comparison. *Journal of Minority Aging*, 1979, *4*, 14–24.

Cantor, M. H. Life space and social support. In T. O. Byerts, S. C. Howell, & L. A. Pastalan (Eds.), *Environmental context of aging*. New York: Garland STPM Press, 1979, pp. 33–61.

Carson, D. H. Natural landscape as meaningful space for the aged. In L. A. Pastalan & D.

H. Carson (Eds.), *Spatial behavior of older people.* Ann Arbor: University of Michigan–Wayne State University, Institute of Gerontology, 1970, pp. 194–210.

Coward, R. F. Planning community services for the rural elderly: Implications from research. *Gerontologist,* 1979, *19,* 275–282.

Dibner, A. S. Is there a psychology of the rural aged? In A. W. Childs & G. B. Melton (Eds.), *Rural Psychology.* New York: Plenum Press, 1982, pp. 95–112.

Donnenwerth, G. V., Guy, R., & Norvell, M. J. Life satisfaction among older persons: Rural-urban and racial comparisons. *Social Service Quarterly,* 1978, *59,* 578–583.

Douglas, B. *Relationships among coping styles, personal contact networks, and selected demographics among rural elderly women.* Paper presented at Gerontological Society of America Annual National Meeting, Toronto, Canada, November 1981.

Dunckley, R. A., Lutes, C. J., Wooten, J. N., & Kooken, R. A. Therapy approaches with rural elders. In S. S. Sargent (Eds.), *Nontraditional therapy and counseling with the aging.* New York: Springer, 1980, pp. 74–99.

Eliade, M. *The sacred and the profane.* New York: Harcourt, Brace & World, 1959.

Fischer, C. S. *The urban experience.* New York: Harcourt, Brace, Jovanovich, 1976.

Fisher, S., Hendricks, D. G., & Mahoney, A. W. Nutritional assessment of senior rural Utahns by biochemical and physical measurements. *American Journal of Clinical Nutrition,* 1978, *31,* 667–672.

Fuguitt, G. V., & Tordella, S. J. Elderly net migration: The new trend of nonmetropolitan population change. *Research on Aging,* 1980, *2,* 191–204.

Gardner, M. A. Caring and sharing. *Perspective on Aging,* 1981, *10,* 4–7.

Glaser, B. G., & Strauss, A. L. *The discovery of grounded theory: Strategies for qualitative research.* Chicago: Aldine, 1967.

Glover, E. E. Nutrition and the rural elderly. In P. K. H. Kim & G. P. Wilson (Eds.), *Toward mental health of the rural elderly.* Washington, D. C.: University Press of America, 1981, pp. 97–116.

Grams, A., & Fengler, A. P. Vermont elders: No sense of deprivation. *Perspective on Aging,* 1981, *10,* 12–15.

Heltsley, M. E., & Powers, R. C. Social interaction and perceived adequacy of interaction of the rural aged. *Gerontologist,* 1975, *15,* 533–536.

Hooyman, N. R. Mutual help organizations for rural older women. *Educational Gerontology,* 1980, *5,* 429–447.

Hynson, L. M. Rural-urban differences in satisfaction among the elderly. *Rural Sociology,* 1976, *40,* 269–275.

Kim, P. K. H. The low income rural elderly: Under-served victims of public inequity. In P. K. H. Kim & C. P. Wilson (Eds.), *Toward mental health of the rural elderly.* Washington, D. C.: University Press of America, 1981, pp. 15–27.

Kim, P. K. H., & Wilson, C. P. (Eds.), *Toward mental health of the rural elderly.* Washington, D. C.: University Press of America, 1981.

Kivett, V. R. Loneliness and the rural black elderly: Perspectives on intervention. *Black Aging,* 1978, *3,* 160–166. (a)

Kivett, V. R. Loneliness and the rural widow. *Family Coordinator,* 1978, *17,* 389–394. (b)

Kivett, V. R. Discriminators of loneliness among the rural elderly: Implications for intervention. *Gerontologist,* 1979, *19,* 108–115.

Kivett, V. R., & Scott, J. P. *The rural by-passed elderly: Perspectives on status and needs (the Caswell study)* (Technical Bulletin, No. 260). Greensboro, North Carolina: North Carolina Agricultural Research Service and School of Home Economics, University of North Carolina, 1979. (a)

Kivett, V. R., & Scott, J. P. Rural frail older women: Implications for policy and planning. *Journal of Minority Aging,* 1979, *4,* 113–122. (b)

Koebernick, T., & Beegle, J. A. *Migration of the elderly in rural areas: A case study in Michigan.* Research Reports, Michigan State University Agricultural Experiment Station, East Lansing, No. 344, 1978, 86–104.

Konan, M., Tweed, D., & Longest, J. Poverty and the distribution of mental health resources: Rural-urban comparisons. *Rural America*, 1979, *4*, 283–284.

Kuhn, T. S. *The structure of scientific revolutions.* Chicago: University of Chicago Press, 1962.

Langner, T. A 22-item screening score of psychiatric symptoms indicating impairment. *Journal of Health and Human Behavior*, 1962, *3*, 269–276.

Lassey, M. L., Lassey, W. R., & Lee, G. R. Elderly people in rural America. In W. R. Lassey, M. L. Lassey, G. R. Lee & N. Lee (Eds.), *Research and public service with the rural elderly.* Corvallis: Oregon State University, Western Rural Development Center, Publication No. 4, 1980, pp. 21–38.

Lawton, M. P. The Philadelphia Geriatric Center Morale Scale: A revision. *Journal of Gerontology*, 1975, *30*, 85–89.

Lee, G. R., & Lassey, M. L. Rural-urban differences among the elderly: Economic, social and subjective factors. *Journal of Social Issues*, 1980, *36*, 62–74. (a)

Lee, G. R., & Lassey, M. L. Rural-urban residence and aging: Directions for future research. In W. R. Lassey, M. L. Lassey, G. R. Lee, & N. Lee (Eds.), *Research and public service with the rural elderly.* Corvallis: Oregon State University, Western Rural Development Center, Publication No. 4, 1980, pp. 77–87. (b)

Lee, T. R. Urban neighborhood as a socio-spatial schema. *Human Relations*, 1968, *21*, 241–267.

Lenihan, A. A. H. *A profile of rural elderly women: An assessment of human functioning and available resources.* Unpublished doctoral dissertation, University of Maryland, 1979.

Ley, D. Social geography and the taken-for-granted world. *Transactions of the Institute of British Geographers*, 1977, *2*, 499–512.

Lohmann, N., & Lohmann, R. Urban designed programs for the rural elderly: Are they exportable? In R. K. Green & S. A. Webster (Eds.), *Social work in rural areas: Preparation and practice.* Knoxville, Tenn.: Department of Social Work, Continuing Education, 1977, pp. 284–297.

Lozier, J., & Althouse, R. Social enforcement of behavior toward elders in an Appalachian mountain settlement. *Gerontologist*, 1974, *14*, 69–80.

Lozier, J., & Althouse, R. Retirement to the porch in rural Appalachia. *International Journal of Aging and Human Development*, 1975, *6*, 7–15.

McCall, G. J., & Simmons, J. L. *Issues in participant observation: A text and reader.* Reading, Mass.: Addison-Wesley, 1969.

McCoy, J. L., & Brown, D. L. Health status among low income elderly persons: Rural-urban differences. *Social Security Bulletin*, 1978, *41*, 14–26.

McKelvey, D. J. Transportation issues and problems of the rural elderly. In S. M. Golant (Ed.), *Location and environment of elderly population.* Washington, D. C.: V. H. Winston, 1979, pp. 135–140.

Mead, M. *Culture and commitment: A study of the generation gap.* Garden City, N.Y.: Natural History Press/Doubleday, 1970.

Milgram, S. The experience of living in cities. *Science*, 1970, *167*, 1461–1468.

Mills, C. W. *The sociological imagination,* New York: Oxford University Press, 1959.

Montgomery, J. E., Stubbs, A. C., & Day, S. S. The housing environment of the rural elderly. *Gerontologist*, 1980, *20*, 444–451.

Nelson, G. Social services to the urban and rural aged: The experience of Area Agencies on Aging. *Gerontologist*, 1980, *20*, 200–207.

Nydegger, C. N. On being caught up in time. *Human Development*, 1981, *24*, 67–76.

Orr, R. H. *The need for transportation services among rural elderly.* Tennessee Farm and Home

Science Progress Report, No. 105, Tennessee Agricultural Experiment Station, Knoxville, 1978, 16–18.

Osterreich, H. Geographical mobility and kinship: A Canadian example. In R. Piddington (Ed.), *Kinship and geographical mobility.* Leiden: E. J. Brill, 1965, pp. 131–144.

Patton, C. V. Age groupings and travel in a rural area. *Rural Sociology,* 1975, *40,* 55–63.

Pihlblad, C. T. Culture, life style and social environment of the small town. In R. C. Atchley & T. O. Byerts (Eds.), *Rural environments and aging.* Washington, D. C.: Gerontological Society, 1975, pp. 47–62.

Pihlblad, C. T. & McNamara, R. L. Social adjustment of elderly people in three small towns. In A. M. Rose & W. A. Peterson (Eds.), *Older people and their social world.* Philadelphia: F. A. Davis, 1965, pp. 49–73.

Porteous, J. D. Home: The territorial core. *Geographical Review,* 1976, *66,* 383–390.

Powers, E. A., Keith, P., & Goudy, W. J. Family relationships and friendships among the rural aged. In T. O. Byerts, S. C. Howell, & L. A. Pastalan (Eds.), *Environmental context of aging: Lifestyles, environmental quality and living arrangements.* New York: Garland-STPM Press, 1979, pp. 80–101.

Rakoff, R. M. Ideology in everyday life: The meaning of the house. *Politics and Society,* 1977, *7,* 85–104.

Rawson, I. G., Weinberg, E. J., Herold, J. A., & Holtz, J. Nutrition of rural elderly in southwestern Pennsylvania. *Gerontologist,* 1978, *18,* 24–29.

Rodeheaver, D. *Going my way? The social environment of elderly travelers.* Morgantown, W.V.: Office of Research and Development, West Virginia University, 1982.

Rowles, G. D. Reflections on experiential fieldwork. In D. Ley & M. Samuels (Eds.), *Humanistic geography: Prospects and problems.* Chicago: Maaroufa Press, 1978, pp. 173–193.

Rowles, G. D. Growing old "inside": Aging and attachment to place in an Appalachian community. In N. Datan & N. Lohmann (Eds.), *Transitions of aging.* New York: Academic Press, 1980, pp. 153–170.

Rowles, G. D. The surveillance zone as meaningful space for the aged. *Gerontologist,* 1981, *21,* 304–311. (a)

Rowles, G. D. *The geographical experience of the elderly.* Washington, D. C.: Final Progress Report, National Institute on Aging, Grant AGOO862, August 1981. (b)

Rowles, G. D. *Observing the rural elderly.* Paper presented at 35th Annual Scientific Meeting of The Gerontological Society of America, November 1982. (a)

Rowles, G. D. *The meaning of place in old age: Examples from Appalachia.* Paper presented at 13th Annual National Meeting of the Environmental Design Research Association, April, 1982 (b)

Rowles, G. D. Geographical dimensions of social support in rural Appalachia. In G. D. Rowles & R. J. Ohta (Eds.), *Aging and milieu: Environmental perspectives on growing old.* New York: Academic Press, 1983, pp. 111–130. (a)

Rowles, G. D. Between worlds: A relocation dilemma for the Appalachian elderly. *International Journal of Aging and Human Development,* 1983, *17*(4), 301–314. (b)

Rowles, G. D., & Ohta, R. J. (Eds.). *Aging and milieu: Environmental perspectives on growing old.* New York: Academic Press, 1983. (c)

Sauer, W., Seelbach, W., & Hanson, S. Rural-urban and cohort differences in filial responsibility norms. *Journal of Minority Aging,* 1980, *5,* 299–305.

Scheidt, R. J. Psychosocial environmental predictors of the mental health of the small town rural elderly. In P. K. H. Kim & C. P. Wilson (Eds.), *Toward mental health of the rural elderly.* Washington, D. C.: University Press of America, 1981, pp. 53–80.

Seamon, D. *A geography of the lifeworld: Movement, rest and encounter.* New York: St. Martin's Press, 1979.

Sebastian, M., & Payne, E. Health care for rural older women: Attitudes toward nurse practitioners. In P. K. H. Kim & C. P. Wilson (Eds.), *Toward mental health of the rural elderly*. Washington, D. C.: University Press of America, 1971, pp. 195–203.

Spradley, J. P. *The ethnographic interview*. New York: Holt, Rinehart & Winston, 1979.

Taietz, P. Community facilities and social services. In R. C. Atchley & T. O. Byerts (Eds.), *Rural environments and aging*, Washington, D. C.: Gerontological Society, 1975, pp. 145–156.

Taietz, P., & Milton, S. Rural-urban differences in structure of services for the elderly in upstate New York counties. *Journal of Gerontology*, 1979, 34, 429–437.

U.S. Bureau of the Census. *Social and economic characteristics of the older population: 1978* (Current Population Reports, Series P–23, No. 85). Washington, D. C.: U.S. Government Printing Office, 1979.

Von Eckartsberg, R. On experiential methodology. In A. Georgi, W. F. Fischer, & R. Von Eckartsberg (Eds.), *Duquesne studies in phenomenological psychology* (Vol. 1). Pittsburgh, Pa.: Duquesne University Press/Humanities Press, 1971, pp. 66–79.

Wang, Y. *Natural support systems and the rural elderly: A Missouri case*. Unpublished doctoral dissertation, University of Missouri, Columbia, 1979.

Weller, J. E. *Yesterday's people: Life in contemporary Appalachia*. Lexington: University Press of Kentucky, 1965.

Wilkinson, C. W., Rowles, G. D., & Maxwell, B. *Comprehensive annotated bibliography on the rural aged* (1975–1981). Morgantown: West Virginia University Gerontology Center, 1982.

Windley, P. G. The effects of ecological/architectural dimensions of small rural towns on the well-being of older people. In P. K. H. Kim & C. P. Wilson (Eds.) *Toward mental health of the rural elderly*. Washington, D. C.: University Press of America, 1981, pp. 81–96.

Windley, P. G., & Scheidt, R. J. The well-being of older persons in small rural towns: A town panel approach. *Educational Gerontology*, 1980, 5, 355–373. (a)

Windley, P. G., & Scheidt, R. J. Person–environment dialectics: Implications for competent functioning in old age. In L. Poon (Ed.), *Aging in the 1980s*. Washington, D. C.: American Psychological Association, 1980, pp. 407–423. (b)

Windley, P. G., & Scheidt, R. J. An ecological model of mental health among small-town rural elderly. *Journal of Gerontology*, 1982, 37, 235–242.

Wirth, L. Urbanism as a way of life. *American Journal of Sociology*, 1938, 44, 1–24.

Yeates, M., & Garner, B. *The North American city* (3rd ed.). New York: Harper & Row, 1980.

Youmans, E. G. (Ed.). *Older rural Americans*. Lexington: University of Kentucky Press, 1967.

Youmans, E. G. The rural aged. *Annals of the American Academy of Political and Social Science*, 1977, 429, 81–91.

6

Supportive Residential Settings for Older People

RUDOLF H. MOOS AND SONNE LEMKE

INTRODUCTION

It is difficult to obtain accurate figures, but it is estimated that about 10% of the 24 million Americans over the age of 65 reside in specialized residential settings (Lawton, 1979; National Center for Health Statistics, 1979). These settings include nursing homes, which house about 1.1 million older poeple, and foster family and board and care homes, residential care facilities, congregate apartment housing, and some single room occupancy (SRO) hotels, which together house over one million older people. Some of these settings provide a full range of medical and personal care (skilled nursing facilities), some provide a moderate level of supportive services (residential care settings), and others offer only limited services, such as a meal plan (most congregate apartment houses and selected SRO hotels).

These forms of specialized housing are the end product of a number of historical trends. First, there has been increasing segregation of care for the elderly from that of other age groups. Even the mentally ill older person is more likely to be cared for in a nursing home than in an age-

RUDOLF H. MOOS and SONNE LEMKE • Social Ecology Laboratory and the Geriatric Research, Education, and Clinical Center, Veterans Administration and Stanford University Medical Center, Palo Alto, California 94304. Preparation of the chapter was supported by NIMH Grant MH28177 and by Veterans Administration Health Services Research and Development funds.

mixed ward in a mental hospital. A second and related trend is that settings have become more specialized in their functions. Thus federally assisted housing and direct financial assistance are available to the elderly poor. Personal care homes offer assistance in activities of daily living for those whose functioning is impaired but who do not require continuing medical supervision. Nursing homes provide medical attention for those with chronic conditions that do not call for hospital treatment. A current issue is whether care should be further segregated on the basis of the degree of mental impairment. Accompanying the increased differentiation of various types of specialized housing has been some emphasis on integration of these different types within a larger setting, as in life care homes.

The growth and differentiation of group housing for older people is related in part to changes in life expectancy and the population distribution. Since 1900 the proportion of the population that is over 65 has more than doubled to 11%, and the proportion over 75 has increased at an even faster rate. Aside from greater age, such factors as low socio-economic status, widowhood, and lack of surviving children are related to the likelihood that an individual will utilize specialized housing in old age. Longitudinal studies have shown that up to 40% of the elderly may find themselves in a nursing home at least once before their death. In one study of an urban sample, a full 15% had stays of six months or more in a nursing home (Vicente, Wiley, & Carrington, 1979). Additional numbers will use the alternatives of personal care homes or age-segregated apartment housing at some point in old age. Moreover, current demographic and social factors will probably accelerate the demand for group living among older people (Dunlop, 1979).

As the number and variety of residential programs for older people increase, the need for comprehensive evaluations of these programs becomes more acute. Information is needed on the characteristics of different housing, the impact of group housing on survival and quality of life of older people, and the needs and preferences of older people. Some longitudinal evaluations of supportive housing have been conducted (for a review, see Moos & Lemke, 1984), while other efforts have focused on conceptualizing and measuring environmental attributes. Such studies can contribute to improving currently existing facilities and planning future options.

Like students in dormitories, employees in work places, or patients in psychiatric wards, older people in congregate housing share a common environment which may contribute to their life quality, health, and functioning. Thus, this field offers an excellent opportunity to apply a social-ecological approach to issues of practical significance. Using our work in other settings as a foundation, we have developed a research program to evaluate congregate housing for the elderly. This program has been guided by a conceptual model of the interaction between the older person and the residential environment. This framework helps identify domains where improved measures are needed and suggests relationships to examine in light of the resulting data. In particular, the model highlights the need for better measures of environmental factors, a primary objective of our research program.

CONCEPTUAL PERSPECTIVES

To organize our program evaluation efforts, we have found it help- ful to formulate explicitly a conceptual framework. The model shown in Figure 1 considers the link between an environmental system (panel I) and a personal system (panel II) and subsequent adaptation (panel V) to be mediated by cognitive appraisal (panel III) and coping responses (panel IV). The model specifies domains that should be included in a comprehensive evaluation. The model can also help guide more limited evaluations in which only a few of these domains and their relationships are investigated. And it can serve as an integrative framework for the results of prior research.

The environmental system includes such factors as the physical design and organizational structure of the setting, the aggregate charac- teristics of the individuals involved, and the quality of their interper- sonal relationships. Theorists have identified numerous relevant dimen- sions of the residential environment. For example, architects and designers have focused on the structure and quality of the physical features of a setting, such as location, accessibility for the handicapped, and safety. Goffman's (1961) description of the total institution sug- gested salient issues in evaluating the organization of group residential settings which have been incorporated in more recent work. On the whole, however, the task of describing and measuring the environmen- tal system has been neglected.

Measures of the personal system are more fully developed and include an individual's sociodemographic characteristics and such per- sonal resources as health status, functional ability, and self-esteem. A number of classification schemes have been proposed to order this vast array of measures. For instance, Lawton (1975) described a system for ordering behaviors according to their complexity within and across do-

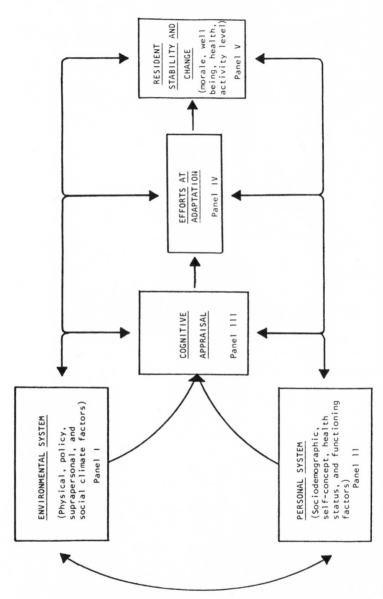

Figure 1.   A model of the relationships among environmental and personal factors and resident stability and change.

mains. The domains range from life maintenance behaviors, through such activities as perception and cognition, to effectance behavior and social interaction.

The direct influences occurring between individuals and settings result primarily from selection of settings by individuals and of residents by settings. An individual's attitudes, life experience, and present support systems help to determine the housing options actually considered. A socially active older person may be more likely to choose a residence with many formal activities. A variety of criteria, such as economic status, functional health, and personality, may enter the decision by a facility administrator to accept a particular resident. Continual feedback occurs between these selection processes. Lawton, Greenbaum, & Liebowitz (1980) suggested, for instance, that as the residents within a congregate apartment age and experience declining functional health, the pool of applicants also changes. This change may contribute to altering further the suprapersonal environment of the setting.

Cognitive appraisal processes mediate some person–environment transactions, and they influence efforts to adapt (coping) and the results of such efforts (outcome). An individual's appraisal is affected to varying degrees by both personal and environmental characteristics. For example, various aspects of the environmental system may contribute to the perception that residents are active and involved with each other, including such physical features as the availability of special activity areas and such policies as offering many organized social activities. Such personal characteristics as age, functional health, socioeconomic status, and present activity level may also influence the appraisal of activity level and group cohesiveness in a setting.

The next step in the model represents the individual's efforts to adapt to the environment by using a preferred set of coping responses. These responses are again determined by both the personal system and the environmental system. For example, an individual who is in poor health may handle diminished opportunities for outside social activity by trying to establish substitute informal interactions with fellow residents. The environmental system can also influence how individuals cope with reduced outside contacts. A setting in which residents have more influence may encourage them to take responsibility for planning and conducting activities. An individual's use of a coping skill can in turn effect a change in either system. Residents who make more social contacts or who participate in planning activities may experience improved self-esteem (a change in the personal system). Residents who express dissatisfaction with the lack of activities may help effect a change in the environmental system, such as the hiring of a director to plan activities.

Efforts at adaptation ultimately influence such outcome indices as the resident's health, well-being, and level of functioning. These outcome criteria also are more directly affected by personal factors. For example, individuals whose health is better when they enter a facility are more likely to be in better health a year later. Environments may have more direct effects, as well, as when an individual experiences better health due to good health care provided in a setting. Finally, the model acknowledges the continuing, reciprocal interplay between individuals and their environment. Outcomes at a given point in time are inputs to future adaptation in the form of aspects of the personal system. Individual outcomes also contribute to defining the environmental system. For example, when the health outcomes for individuals in a setting are considered together, they constitute one aspect of the suprapersonal environment.

Although most program evaluators would endorse the idea that behavior is determined by both personal and environmental influences, the typical paradigm used in evaluation research systematically minimizes the role of environmental factors. The residential program (Panel I in our model) is generally treated as a "black box" between resident inputs and resident outcomes. The housing environment is usually assessed in terms of gross categories, such as whether it is specialized housing, and other environmental determinants of resident functioning are omitted. Better methods of measuring environmental factors will enable us to identify specific aspects of housing programs that are related to various outcome criteria, as well as to identify contextual factors that alter the connections between environmental and outcome indices (Finney & Moos, 1982).

ELABORATING THE ENVIRONMENTAL SYSTEM

The development of measures of environmental factors is an initial step in implementing our social-ecological perspective. Here we illustrate our approach by discussing the development of a new procedure designed to assess the environmental resources of supportive residential settings, the Multiphasic Environmental Assessment Procedure (MEAP). The MEAP builds on earlier work identifying salient features of residential settings for older people and represents an attempt to create a comprehensive, conceptually based environmental assessment procedure.

Development of the MEAP

From a thorough review of the literature and discussions with older people, administrators, and licensing personnel, we generated an initial version of the MEAP that contained more than 800 items that describe the environment of congregate residential settings. Questions covered a broad range of content, including "Is the front entrance sheltered from sun and rain?" "Is dinner served each day?" and "How many residents can dress themselves without assistance?" Also included were items tapping qualitative judgments: "Is this place very well organized?" "Can residents change things here if they really try?" and ratings of the facility's cleanliness, attractiveness, and the quality of staff–resident interactions. In terms of content, these items were combined into four major domains: physical and architectural resources, policy and program resources, suprapersonal resources, and social-environmental resources. Although not exhaustive of possible perspectives from which to view residential environments, these four domains have proven useful in characterizing social settings and exploring their impacts (Moos, 1976, 1979).

The initial version of the MEAP was completed in a representative sample of 93 residential settings drawn from five counties in California. Facilities were identified from directories of licensed skilled nursing, intermediate care, and community care facilities, from telephone directories and from listings of HUD-funded apartments for the elderly. They were selected to represent the range of ownership types, size, and location. Within this sample, three facility subtypes were defined: skilled nursing facilities (SNFs), independent apartments (APTs), and an intermediate category that we have termed residential care facilities (RCs). In order to ensure that facilities were relevant to the study's purposes, three general criteria were set: each facility had to have a minimum of ten residents, these residents had to be predominantly elderly, and each facility had to offer at least a meal plan.

On the basis of data from this sample, the MEAP was revised using both conceptual and empirical criteria. Items were first grouped into dimensions unified by a common functional implication for residents. Items on a dimension represent opportunities or environmental "resources" for a given area of functioning. For example, the existence of a lounge near the entry that is furnished for resting and casual conversation offers residents an opportunity to engage in "people-watching," to interact with others, and to experience a sense of cohesion, as do other items on the dimension of social-recreational aids. Such a design feature commonly reflects an underlying philosophy toward older persons and their housing needs, which also manifests itself in other ways.

Some items were dropped from the MEAP because they failed to apply to the full range of facility types or to discriminate among facilities. The conceptual grouping was adjusted and confirmed by calculating internal consistencies for dimensions. Finally, an effort was made to minimize the overlap between dimensions by combining dimensions with high intercorrelations. The revised MEAP consists of four main instruments which can be used either separately or in conjunction with one another by a facility staff member or outside evaluator to obtain a comprehensive picture of a supportive residential setting. In general, the content of the instruments follows the conceptual organization of the four environmental domains.[1] Further information on the sample, as well as on the psychometric and normative characteristics of the dimensions, is presented elsewhere (Moos & Lemke, 1979).

Physical and Architectural Features

A growing body of literature indicates that the physical design of group housing can affect the behavior and functioning of older people. Some demonstrations of this linkage deal with the general hypothesis that better physical environments have beneficial impacts on residents, while others test more specific hypotheses about the interrelations of behavior and the physical environment. At the global level, for example, Carp (1976a) has noted that positive physical qualities of the housing environment can influence an elderly person's activity level, social contacts, well-being, and general life style. Moreover, the physical attractiveness of housing has been related to tenant satisfaction (Carp, 1976b), and better physical facilities have been associated with enhanced resident functioning (Lawton, 1975, 1977; Linn, Gurel, & Linn, 1977).

The first part of the MEAP, the Physical and Architectural Features Checklist (PAF), operationalizes the relevant design factors in terms of nine dimensions (see Table 1); information is obtained through direct observation (Moos & Lemke, 1980). Two dimensions focus on the presence of physical features that add convenience and special comfort and foster social and recreational activities (physical amenities, social-recreational aids). Three dimensions assess physical features that aid residents in activities of daily living and in negotiating the facility environment

---

[1] In addition to the four parts described here, the MEAP includes a Rating Scale which covers evaluative judgments by outside observers on four dimensions: two tap physical and architectural resources and two tap resident and staff resources.

TABLE 1
DIMENSIONS OF THE MULTIPHASIC ENVIRONMENTAL ASSESSMENT PROCEDURE
(MEAP)

Physical and architectural features	Policy and program features	Suprapersonal factors	Social climate factors
Physical amenities	Selectivity	Residents' social resources	Cohesion
Social-recreational aids	Expectations for functioning	Resident heterogeneity	Conflict
Prosthetic aids	Tolerance for deviance	Resident functional abilities	Independence
Orientational aids	Policy clarity	Resident activity level	Self-exploration
Safety features	Policy choice	Resident community integration	Organization
Architectural choice	Resident control	Staff richness	Resident influence
Space availability	Provisions for privacy		Physical comfort
Staff facilities	Availability of health services	(Utilization of health services)	
Community accessibility	Availability of daily living assistance	(Utilization of daily living assistance)	
	Availability of social-recreational activities	(Utilization of social-recreational activities)	

(prosthetic aids, orientational aids, safety features). Two dimensions assess the extent to which the physical setting provides residents with potential flexibility in their activities (architectural choice, space availability). The PAF also measures the presence of features that make the setting more pleasant for staff (staff facilities) and the degree of physical integration between the facility and the surrounding community (community accessibility).

Policy and Program Factors

Characteristics sometimes observed among the elderly in group residential settings, such as depression, helplessness, and accelerated physical decline, have been attributed to the restrictive policies and overabundance of services in these settings. Residents are more alienated in settings that offer less freedom of choice, and they report less life satisfaction and self-esteem in high- than in low-constraint settings.

Moreover, Lieberman (1974) found that the outcome of relocation of elderly people was more positive in "facilitative" environments, that is, those that fostered autonomy, gave residents control, and treated residents in an individualized manner.

We operationalized these factors by constructing the Policy and Program Information Form (POLIF), a part of the MEAP that assesses ten dimensions of the policy and programmatic resources of a setting (see Table 1) as reported by the administrator or other responsible staff members (Lemke & Moos, 1980). The first three dimensions reflect how selective the facility is in admitting residents and the degree to which behavioral requirements are imposed on residents once they are in the facility. The second set of dimensions taps the balance that exists between individual freedom and institutional order and continuity (policy clarity, policy choice, resident control, and provisions for privacy), while the third set measures the provision of services and activities in the facility (health services, daily living assistance, and social-recreational activities).

Suprapersonal Factors

The use of average background and personal characteristics as measures of environmental factors is based on the belief that the character of an environment depends in part on the typical characteristics of its members (the suprapersonal environment). The work in residential settings for older people has focused primarily on the relative degree of age homogeneity. For instance, in comparison to those in age-integrated housing, elderly tenants in age-segregated housing tend to have more new friends and visit more with neighbors and age-peer friends. However, they have fewer younger friends and interact less with their children and other relatives (Sherman, 1975a; Teaff, Lawton, Nahemow, & Carlson, 1978). Other suprapersonal factors include the average functional ability and activity level of residents.

We focused on these factors in the MEAP by developing the Resident and Staff Information Form (RESIF) to tap six dimensions that characterize the residents and staff in a facility (see Table 1). Information is obtained from records, from knowledgeable staff members, or from the residents themselves (Lemke & Moos, 1981). Two dimensions are based on the sociodemographic characteristics of residents: one (resident social resources) measures indicators of social competence, such as high educational and occupational levels; the other (resident heterogeneity) measures the diversity of residents in terms of such factors as age, ethnicity, and religion. Three dimensions measure aspects of residents' current functioning. These are the ability to perform various daily functions independently (functional abilities), involvement in leisure time activities (activity level), and participation in activities outside of the facility (integration in the community). Three additional dimensions measure the extent to which the residents utilize facility services and organized activities (utilization of health services, daily living assistance, and social-recreational activities).[2] For staff resources, the RESIF considers staffing levels and includes a measure of the diversity, training, and turnover of staff and the contribution of volunteers (staff richness).

Social Climate

The social climate perspective assumes that apparently discrete events possess an underlying continuity and consistency that can be conceptualized in terms of environmental "press." For example, if older people in a residential setting have a say in making the rules, if their suggestions are acted upon and if they can try out new and different ideas, then it is likely that the program emphasizes resident influence and the development of assertive responses on the part of residents. These conditions help to establish the climate or atmosphere of a setting. The Sheltered Care Environment Scale (SCES), which comprises another part of the MEAP, assesses residents' and staff members' perceptions of seven characteristics of the social environment of a setting (see Table 1). The subscales cover the quality of interpersonal relationships (cohesion, conflict), the opportunities for personal growth (independence, self-exploration), and the mechanisms for system maintenance and change (organization, resident influence, physical comfort) (Moos, Gauvain, Lemke, Max, & Mehren, 1979).

DESCRIBING SUPPORTIVE RESIDENTIAL SETTINGS

Environmental assessment procedures can be used to characterize and compare existing facilities. To illustrate the type of summary information that is obtained by these methods, we present the PAF and POLIF profiles of a congregate apartment facility. The scores are expressed as the percentage of the characteristics tapped by a dimension that were actually present in the facility. Thus, for example, just over 90% of the social-recreational aids included in our measure were present in Eden Apartments (Figure 2). The averages for a normative sample of

---

[2]For ease of administration, the items are included on the POLIF data collection form in conjunction with questions about their availability.

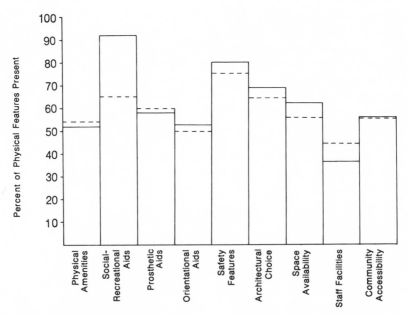

Figure 2.   Physical and architectural resources for Eden Apartments. Dashed lines represent averages for apartments.

other apartment facilities are shown by the dotted lines. The PAF and POLIF scores of a facility can also be profiled as standard scores based on norms from a sample of similar types of settings (for examples, see Lemke & Moos, 1980, Moos & Lemke, 1980).

Eden Apartments, currently housing just over 200 residents, was constructed in the mid-1970s under the sponsorship of a local church group. Because it was constructed under Section 231 of the Housing Act, it is less austere than most public housing projects. However, rents remain moderate for the area, and in addition, over half its residents receive federal rent assistance. Though their current economic circumstances may be somewhat limited, the residents are largely middle class in background. Most completed high school and worked in clerical, managerial, or professional occupations. Nearly 90% are women, of whom only 6% are currently married. In contrast, nearly half the men are currently married. As in other apartments in the normative sample, the average age of residents is about 77 years of age, though their functional abilities are somewhat lower than in the comparison group.

The PAF results for Eden Apartments reveal a setting that is rich in social-recreational aids and that is more flexible and spacious than the average apartment facility (architectural choice and space availability). Although the residents are slightly more impaired than those typically found in congregate apartment settings, the facility includes just an average number of physical features to meet the needs of more impaired residents (average prosthetic aids and orientational aids). Also typical is the number of features designed to ensure the security and safety of residents (safety features). Eden Apartments' suburban location is within easy walking distance of a moderate number of community resources. The one area of comparative deficiency at Eden Apartments occurs for the provision of physical resources for the staff. It has a staff–resident ratio typical for apartment settings; however, there is less office space than in the average apartment facility and no provision for a staff lounge or conference room.

Turning to the policies in the facility (see Figure 3), we see that they reflect a greater acceptance of physical disability (low expectations for functioning), which is consistent with residents' lower-than-average functional abilities. However, this attitude of tolerance does not extend to deviant behavior (low tolerance for deviance). The residents are ex-

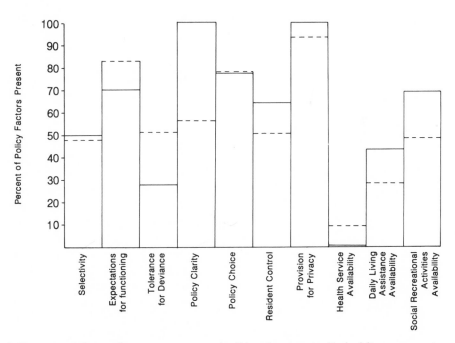

Figure 3.   Policy and program resources for Eden Apartments. Dashed lines represent averages for apartments.

pected to conform to high standards of socially accepted behavior, and these norms are communicated to residents and staff in a clear and systematic manner (high policy clarity). As is typical of most congregate apartments, the program at Eden Apartments offers no health services, but it does provide a reasonably rich array of personal care services and programmed social and recreational activities. Residents have private apartments and enjoy a fair amount of freedom in the use of their own rooms and in structuring their daily routine (high provision for privacy and average policy choice). In addition, there are formal avenues by which residents can influence the operation of the setting (above-average resident control).

The MEAP thus permits us to characterize a facility on a number of dimensions and to make systematic comparisons with existing facilities. It can help organize perceptions of a facility into a more clearly differentiated picture. For example, a visit to Eden Apartments generally results in a global impression of plushness. But the profile reveals that resources are concentrated in the form of social-recreational aids, not as physical amenities or prosthetic aids. In addition, relatively more space at Eden Apartments is devoted to public and private areas for residents and less to staff areas. Standards are demanding in some respects (social conformity) and lenient in others (physical disability). Such comprehensive and detailed information about facility environments can contribute to program planning and to evaluation research.

EXPLORING ENVIRONMENTAL DOMAINS AND THEIR IMPACTS

Building upon information about the setting, it becomes possible to examine the interrelationships within the environmental system (Panel I in our model). Along with information about individual characteristics (Panel II) and appraisal and coping (Panels III and IV), systematic assessment of the environmental system can help clarify the impact of residential settings on their inhabitants. Our research program has begun to explore these broader applications, three of which we illustrate here.

PERSON–SETTING SELECTION AND ALLOCATION

The first step in the model is the process of mutual selection between persons and settings (the connection between Panels I and II). Through acquaintances, contacts with professionals, and attitudes based on previous life experiences, prospective residents and their families come to consider only a few of the many group residential options actually available. Facilities also limit the range of applicants through requirements concerning functioning, financial resources, or group affiliation. Administrators and staff often conduct interviews to select "desirable" residents from among the applicants to their facility. Moreover, federal and state reimbursement procedures and placement decisions by social work and other paramedical personnel can further influence the allocation of individuals to particular settings.

These processes can be studied by following individuals as they make placement decisions. They can also be examined indirectly by looking at their product: the distinctive characteristics of the resident populations of different facilities. Does the distribution of residents give evidence of nonrandom assortment? To what extent do older people create homogeneous environments by selecting settings composed of residents with whom they share personal and social attributes? Do selection and social allocation tend to perpetuate or to break down differences in privilege?

To address these issues, we used the MEAP to describe the personal and social characteristics of residents in skilled nursing, residential care, and congregate apartment settings. We then related these factors to the architectural, policy, and social climate resources of these settings. As would be expected, selection into the three types of settings was related largely to residents' functional abilities rather than sociodemographic factors. Residents' functional capacities, activity level, and participation in community activities were highest in apartments, intermediate in residential care settings, and lowest in skilled nursing facilities. On the other hand, resident characteristics such as gender, age, marital status, and race were similar for each of the three types of facilities.

Within each of the three kinds of settings, however, selection occurred on the basis of both social background and functional ability. Residents who were well educated, married, and of higher socioeconomic status were likely to be in homogeneous settings with others of similar background. These settings were more selective and provided more physical amenities, social-recreational aids, privacy, and space and were seen as more physically comfortable. On the average, these residents were more active in both the facility and the community. They enjoyed greater flexibility in scheduling their daily activities and had more input into decision making. Residents also reported more friendly interaction, better organization, and greater influence over facility operation (Lemke & Moos, 1981).

If older people are rationally matched to settings, there should be a positive relationship between their need for services (as measured by their current health and functioning) and the services provided them, even beyond the gross differences among types of facilities. Settings in which residents had more disabilities did have more prosthetic aids, but staffing level and staff richness were no higher. Contrary to expectations, facilities provided more health services and daily living assistance where residents' functional abilities were higher and where residents were more active (controlling for facility type). Similarly, residents who initiated more activities on their own were also likely to have more activities provided by the facility.

These results indicate that there are relatively strong mechanisms of selection and social allocation that determine where a person is likely to live. The population in a facility is not simply a random sample of the available group of older people in sheltered housing. In general, older people with more personal and social resources enjoy residential settings with more physical resources, less restrictive policies, and a group of homogeneous, congenial peers (see also Kart & Manard, 1976). The fact that these settings are also more expensive indicates that individuals of higher socioeconomic status retain their privileged position in old age. It highlights the need for social policies to help equalize the environmental resources available to people in their later years.

Opportunities for Environmental Choice and Control

There is considerable controversy about the amount of choice and control that should be provided for elderly residents of group living settings. Some investigators have suggested that an optimal milieu should maximize independence and individual choice (Fozard & Popkin, 1978), while others have noted the value of a stable, structured setting (Coleman, 1975). In this regard, recent studies have shown that experimentally induced increases in choice and control in residential settings may have beneficial short-term effects on the morale and adaptation of residents, but that long-term effects occur only when such increases are due to stable factors that persist over time (Rodin, 1980). To complicate the issue further, policies that are thought to enhance flexibility and independence may not be perceived as such by residents, and the effects of such policies may depend in part on residents' characteristics. For example, less functionally able residents may find a high degree of choice and control stressful and may benefit from a more structured setting.

Personal control in group living settings can be fostered in two major ways: by providing options from which residents can select individual patterns of daily living (policy choice) and by providing formal institutional structures that give residents a voice in running the facility (resident control). We used the measures of these factors included in the POLIF to describe the variations among settings in resident choice and control and to explore their potential impacts in conjunction with resident characteristics. In terms of the conceptual framework, this work is an initial attempt to describe the environmental system (Panel I) and to relate policy and suprapersonal factors to aggregate indices of resident morale and functioning (Panel V).

We found considerable variability in the opportunities for choice and control available in group living settings (see Table 2). Overall, the

TABLE 2

PERCENTAGE OF FACILITIES RESPONDING IN THE SCORED DIRECTION ON SELECTED POLICY CHOICE AND RESIDENT CONTROL ITEMS[a]

	Percentage in scored direction		
	Skilled nursing facilities (N = 41)	Residential care facilities (N = 28)	Apartment facilities (N = 24)
Choice in daily living			
1. Can residents choose when to get up?	43.9	42.9	95.8
2. Can residents choose when to take baths or showers?	17.1	57.1	100.0
3. Can residents choose when to eat dinner?	14.0	28.6	87.5
4. Are residents allowed to keep a fish or bird in their room?	9.8	35.7	33.3
Participation in facility operation			
5. Do any of the residents perform chores or duties in the facility?	19.5	67.9	54.2
6. Are any residents hired and paid for jobs in the facility?	7.3	17.9	66.7
7. Do residents help plan welcoming or orientation activities?	0.0	17.9	45.8
8. Do residents plan educational activities?	7.3	25.0	50.0
Participation in setting policies			
9. Are there committees which include residents as members?	7.3	32.1	54.2
10. Do residents help to set meal times?	12.2	28.6	50.0
11. Do residents help select new residents?	2.4	21.4	25.0
12. Are residents involved in hiring or firing staff?	7.3	14.3	12.5

[a]All items are scored in the "yes" direction and discriminate significantly among the three types of facilities.

93 settings in our California sample (see above) scored positively on only 52% of the 20 policy choice items and 36% of the 29 resident control items. There were sharp differences between types of settings, with skilled nursing facilities (SNFs) obtaining average scores of 37% and and 24% on the two dimensions, residential care settings (RCs) obtaining average scores of 53% and 42%, and congregate apartment houses (APTs) obtaining average scores of 78% and 51%.

More specifically, only 14% of SNFs and 29% of RCs gave residents a choice of time during which they could have dinner (this was also the case for breakfast and lunch). Less than half the SNFs allowed residents a choice about when to get up or when to take baths or showers, while less than 10% permitted them to keep a fish or bird. Residents in SNFs and RCs had very little input in planning social and recreational activities or in making decisions about facility policies. For instance, less than 30% of these facilities allowed residents to help plan orientational or educational activities, set meal times, or help select new residents or staff.

To explore the concomitants of variations in choice and control, we attempted to predict the quality of social environment and resident functioning from information about these two policy factors, in combination with selected suprapersonal factors (residents' social resources and functional abilities and the proportion of women in the setting).[3] As expected from our findings on selection and allocation, women residents and residents with more social and functional resources were more likely to live in facilities high in choice and control. These suprapersonal and policy factors were associated with more cohesive, organized, independence-oriented social environments that had relatively little conflict. These factors also enhanced residents' activity level and may have helped reduce turnover rates by contributing to resident cohesion.

There was some evidence that residents with more personal resources were better able to take advantage of environmental opportunities. A combination of high choice and control in a facility that had residents with greater functional resources enhanced cohesion, organization, and observer-rated pleasantness beyond what would be expected from the relevant policy and suprapersonal factors alone. We also found that women were more affected by a relative lack of environmental choice than were men. Apparently these older women were used to organizing their own pattern of everyday activities and found the absence of such choices as when to get up, go to bed, bathe, and eat especially irksome. In most settings in which a large proportion of resi-

---

[3]The effects of type of facility or level of care were statistically controlled.

dents were men, residents were also veterans and may have been accustomed to more structured group-living arrangements (Moos, 1981).

It is important to note that these sets of factors can mutually influence each other. For example, a cohesive resident population is more likely to be perceived as a social entity by the administrator and as such to be given a greater voice in running the facility. The turnover rate may be increased by resident dissatisfaction, but a higher turnover rate may also diminish the perceived need for resident input. Such reciprocal influences highlight the need to use comprehensive environmental assessments in evaluating the impact of specific setting features. One implication of these findings is that studies that attempt to increase choice and control in residential settings must examine not only the existing opportunities for residents to exercise control, but the levels of other environmental and personal resources as well. As the conceptual framework suggests, the impact of any one set of environmental resources is related to the types of individuals for which it is provided, as well as the general context in which these individuals function.

Environmental Change Accompanying Relocation

A considerable body of research has examined the influence of relocation on the patterns of activity, morale, and health status among older people. Some studies have identified pervasive negative effects of relocation, including increased morbidity and mortality rates, whereas other have not only failed to show such effects but have noted some positive impacts. These variations in results are thought to be a function of three main factors: (1) the degree of similarity between the premove and postmove environments, (2) the amount of choice and control provided for residents in the two settings, and (3) the quality of the two settings (Coffman, 1981; Kasl & Rosenfield, 1980; Schulz & Brenner, 1977). Although investigators have invoked these factors to account for variations in outcomes following relocation, systematic measures of the similarity and quality of environments before and after a move have been notably lacking. Environmental assessment procedures can help to document the extent and type of change involved in different moves.

For example, we used the MEAP and a behavior mapping procedure to compare the premove and postmove settings in an intra-institutional relocation (David, Moos, & Postle, 1981; Lemke & Moos, 1983). Oakview Nursing Home,[4] located in a building not originally designed to accommodate older or disabled residents, was relocated to a

---

[4]MEAP profiles of this facility obtained about two years prior to the move have been presented elsewhere (Moos, Lemke, & Clayton, 1983).

modern, architect-designed building. The old building was a two-story, H-shaped structure with a long central corridor connecting two shorter wing corridors. Each floor had a nurses' station, some staff offices, and its own dining room and lounge space, all of which were located on the central corridor. Some multiple occupancy resident rooms were also on the central corridor, and the wing corridors contained resident bedrooms and a large lavatory–shower room.

The new building into which Oakview moved is a single-story structure with three distinct 50-bed units. One section of the building contains staff offices and areas for residents such as a single large dining room, a central lounge, and rooms for occupational and physical therapy. The three units are essentially identical in plan, with each containing an open nurses' station and some limited office and lounge space. Bedrooms are located on the outer side of the units along short hallways (wing halls); most are shared by two residents and all have their own bathrooms (sink and toilet). The nurses' stations are located at the point where the wing halls and the corridors to the other units (main halls) meet.

The MEAP indicated that the postmove setting represented an improvement over the premove setting in both environmental quality and controllability. Oakview offered a spacious, flexible physical environment before the move, but it lacked prosthetic aids. Once the new building was furnished, all PAF dimensions were as high as or higher than they had been in the old building, with one exception. The new building was slightly lower on orientational aids (a more complex floor plan, no large clock in the lobby). The new building had more prosthetic aids (wider hallways, automatic doors, volume controls on telephones), as well as slightly more physical amenities (a sheltered entrance, decorated hallways, air conditioning). It also provided more office and lounge space for staff.

Throughout the first year in the new building, policies changed to allow a gradual increase in opportunities for individual resident choice. The facility also offered a greater variety of activities and a wider range of daily living services to supplement the already high level of health services. Prior to the move, residents were given more privacy and opportunities to participate in facility governance than in the average nursing home, but few channels existed for aiding open communication of policies (low policy clarity). Although the move initially disrupted communication still further, the facility eventually developed a handbook for residents and an orientation program for new staff. These changes improved the clarity of policies and the predictability of the environment for residents.

The new building had a 50% greater capacity, and new staff and residents were gradually added following the move. New staff were brought in first. Consequently, the staffing level was higher after the move, as was the level of volunteers. New residents continued to have about average social resources, but they came from more varied backgrounds and had higher functional abilities than did the residents from the old building.

These MEAP results help to clarify some of the changes observed using the behavior mapping procedure. Residents spent more time in organized facility activities, consistent with increases in the number of available activities. More staff were available, and observations showed increased interactions between residents and staff members. The higher level of resident functional ability was reflected in the observation of more resident self-care activity.

The larger scale and altered layout of the new building resulted in substantial changes in spatial location patterns. Specifically, residents spent more time in their bedrooms and the main hall by the nurses' station in the new building and less time in the communal dining room, lounge, and lobby areas. This change involved altering the use of space in order to maintain contiguity between staff and residents. In the old building, the dining rooms and lounges were located near the nurses' stations and the main locus of activity and traffic. These areas served as convenient locations for staff to monitor immobile residents and for residents engaging in mainly passive behavior to maintain contact with staff-generated activity, obtain cigarettes and medications, and observe the activity of other residents.

The design of communal areas in the new building was not sensitive to the staff's need for visual surveillance and ease of access to residents nor to residents' need for proximity to staff. The main hallways near the nurses' stations absorbed many of the functions previously occurring in the lounges and dining rooms, both because they were spacious enough to accommodate this use and because other areas were not so attractive as before for these purposes. The dining room and main lounge were distant from staff locations, and the lounge on the unit was small and isolated from activities. Moreover, staff did not manage communal areas in a way that fostered design intentions. As a case in point, most of the furniture in the main lounge was arranged in a classic "sociofugal" configuration around the periphery of the room, replicating the inactive milieu of the lounges in the old building on a much larger, more impersonal scale. Perceiving the need for a "lounge" area near the nurses' station, chairs and ashtrays were placed along one side of the main hallways. Staff thereby encouraged residents to remain on the units rather than to go to the distant communal social areas.

In a similar way, the shifts in staff behavior reveal limitations in the design of the new building. The proportion of time staff spent in the nurses' stations declined after the move, while that spent in offices, the conference room, and staff lounges and in staff meetings increased. This change in staff behavior was probably due to the more open design of the nurses' station in the new building, as well as to the fact that the development of new programs made it necessary for staff to spend more time in meetings. The new building provided a large conference room, which was heavily used, as well as staff lounges that served multiple functions as meeting areas, work areas, and lunch rooms for unit staff. Ironically, the attractiveness of these areas may have contributed to the change in location of staff from the nurses' stations to staff areas, where they were less accessible to residents.

As in this example, environmental assessment procedures can help in monitoring a complex social system. Not only did the physical environment change when Oakview Nursing Home relocated, but policies, services, and characteristics of residents changes as well. The new physical setting appeared to facilitate some uses and impede others. For example, more generous provision of staff areas was accompanied by increased utilization. In contrast, the large lounge area was less heavily utilized, in part because of its location and the arrangement of furnishings. In spite of architectural intentions, staff and residents used the space in the new building according to their established pattern by designating halls as lounge areas. In this respect, the response of staff and residents to the new lounge arrangement illustrates the inertia of large social systems.

IDENTIFYING DESIGN AND PROGRAM PREFERENCES

Information about older people's preferences concerning housing features (Panel II in the model) can help clarify their choice of and reactions to different group living options. Accordingly, we constructed a method for tapping personal preferences about physical design and program factors in group housing by rephrasing PAF and POLIF items. Thus, for instance, the PAF item, "Are there handrails in the halls?" (a prosthetic feature), was reworded as, "Should there be handrails in the halls?" The majority of the items were answered on four point scales varying from "not important" to "desirable," "very important," and "essential." POLIF items that might be viewed as undesirable were answered on scales ranging from "definitely not" to "preferably not," "preferably yes," and "definitely yes."

The Ideal Forms of the PAF and POLIF were administered to several groups of respondents, including 371 older people drawn from eight supportive residential settings (current residents) and 205 older people living in their own homes and apartments (prospective residents). Overall, the respondents were of moderate to high socioeconomic status and relatively well educated, with almost two thirds of both groups having completed at least some education beyond high school (for further details, see Moos, Lemke, & David, in press).

We envision several applications of such a procedure. It can be used to compare the preferences of different groups of respondents, for example, current and prospective residents or staff and residents. Person–environment congruence can be measured by contrasting the preferences of current or prospective residents with the actual features of a setting. Finally, individual variations in preferences for design and program features can be explored. Designers need to consider such variations as they plan residential settings for heterogeneous groups of older people.

PREFERENCES FOR PHYSICAL DESIGN FEATURES

Based on the average ratings of items, the eight PAF dimensions can be ranked in order of their relative importance to residents.[5] Safety features received the highest overall rating, followed by prosthetic aids, community accessibility, and orientational aids. Physical amenities, architectural choice, staff facilities, and social-recreational aids received slightly lower overall ratings but were still viewed as important. This ranking depends in part on the specific items included but nevertheless gives a sense of the relative priority accorded a variety of features thought to be important in facility design.

Older people have strong preferences for physical features that support secure and effective use of the facility environment and that compensate for physical impairment. Not surprisingly, residents had close to unanimous preferences for such safety features as adequate lighting in outside areas and on steps, nonslip surfaces in appropriate places, strategically located smoke detectors, and call buttons in living areas and bathrooms. More than half of the residents of group living settings considered such prosthetic features as a bell or call system outside, parking reserved for handicapped people, handrails in the hallways and bathrooms, lift bars next to the toilet, and wheelchair access as very important or essential. Residents also strongly preferred such orienta-

[5]We have not yet been able to develop an acceptable item format to tap preferences for space availability.

tional aids as a reception area or desk, posted instructions that explain how to get in if the door is locked, a posted list of rules, and a conveniently located bulletin board. Prospective residents generally agreed with current residents in their preferences, although they had even stronger preferences for the prosthetic and safety features.

Social-recreational aids emerged as somewhat less important, though a sizeable group of respondents endorsed physical features in communal social areas to facilitate social interaction and recreational activities. In fact, more than 50% of the respondents in residential settings strongly desired seating in the lobby, a lounge or community room near the entrance that was comfortably furnished for visiting, small tables around which several people could sit and talk or play games, and a library from which books could be borrowed. Underlining their desire to maintain contacts with the outside community, about two thirds of the respondents rated adequate parking for visitors as very important.

Preferences for Program Features

A critical part of the planning of a supportive residential setting is determining the mix of services and activities that will be offered as a part of the facility's program. When current and prospective residents are asked to evaluate the importance of these program features, they rate health services as most important overall, followed by social and recreational activities and assistance with tasks of daily living. Among the health services, residents felt most strongly about having scheduled doctor's and nurse's hours, having a doctor on call, and being able to obtain assistance in the use of prescribed medications. Meal preparation was the most frequently desired form of assistance in daily living. A transportation service, which could link residents to a variety of services in the community, was also viewed as very important. Other services valued by substantial minorities included a barber or beauty service and assistance with housekeeping and cleaning, laundry, shopping, and financial matters. The social and recreational activities that were most often preferred included exercise or physical fitness groups, arts and crafts, religious services, organized games such as bingo, and classes and discussion groups.

In contrast to physical features and program services, facility policies could be rated as either desirable or undesirable. Considerable consensus of opinion emerged on the dimensions of policy choice and resident control (see Table 3 for examples). Not surprisingly, a large majority of older people wanted to regulate their own daily routines. A high proportion wanted to be able to skip breakfast to sleep late, to have

TABLE 3
PREFERENCES FOR SELECTED ASPECTS OF POLICY CHOICE AND RESIDENT CONTROL
(% PREFERABLY OR DEFINITELY YES)

	Current residents	Prospective residents
Choice in daily living		
1. Choosing time to get up	90.0	88.8
2. Choosing bath time	80.6	92.7
3. Choosing dinner time	88.4	92.2
4. Having a fish or bird in room	46.4	61.0
Participating in facility operation		
5. Helping with chores	84.6	87.8
6. Performing jobs in the facility	60.6	75.1
7. Planning orientation	69.8	84.3
8. Planning educational activities	66.3	79.0
Participation in setting policies		
9. Serving on resident committees	85.7	87.8
10. Setting meal times	56.9	71.2
11. Selecting new residents	28.3	36.1
12. Hiring or firing staff	31.5	48.3

access to alcoholic beverages, to do some laundry in the bathroom, to stay out in the evening as late as they wished, and to have unrestricted visitors' hours. Most of the older individuals also stressed the importance of being involved in planning orientation, entertainment, and educational programs as well as of having regular residents' council and house meetings.

Data such as these concerning preferences allow one to examine the match between older people's preferences and existing conditions in various types of facilities. For selected policy choice and resident control items, the information in Tables 2 and 3 provides a basis for such a comparison. More specifically, comparisons can be made between the ideals expressed by current and prospective residents and the policies and programs offered by a particular facility. Eden Apartments, for example, has most of the physical amenities, social-recreational aids, and safety features desired by its residents. There are no health services available at Eden Apartments, but only between 10% and 25% of the residents rated these services as very important. Eden Apartments provides transportation, assistance with banking and finances and with shopping, and dinner five days a week; these are the personal care services rated most important by the residents. Residents' preferences are also well met by the provisions for privacy at Eden Apartments and by the mechanisms for communicating policies and expectations (policy clarity). However, Eden Apartments lacks prosthetic and orientational aids and staff facilities that residents view as very important, including reserved parking for the handicapped, a call system by the entrance, a public phone at wheelchair height, color coding, and ample office space.

Together, these results illustrate several important points. First, they indicate that older people can respond in a meaningful way to questions about their preferences with respect to the design and programming of supportive residential settings. Second, the results show that their preferences for some factors are stronger than for others. Thus, for example, prosthetic and orientational aids and program flexibility are rated very important, whereas physical amenities, social-recreational aids, and daily living assistance are rated as somewhat less important. Third, we found that in some areas of preferences a consensus exists among individuals and between various groups of respondents. Features that impact on safety, such as well-lighted steps and a safe neighborhood, or policies that discourage deviant behavior elicit a high level of agreement from respondents. Opinions are more divided concerning the need for accessibility for wheelchairs, policies on alcohol use, whether meals should be served, and what medical services should be offered. Finally, we have illustrated how such information on preferences can be compared to descriptions of an existing facility to enrich our understanding of its environment. For example, since Eden Apartments appears to be well suited to the preferences of its residents, it is not surprising that residents report it to be a highly cohesive, well organized, and pleasant setting in which they are encouraged to be independent and to affect policies.

PRACTICAL APPLICATIONS

Information about the environmental resources of residential settings has various uses, such as in designing and comparing settings and in monitoring and improving them. For example, the PAF can be used as a checklist to help planners develop a specific and comprehensive guide to the design of a new facility. Assessment of a facility's social climate can alert evaluators that a program fails to accomplish desired objectives, as when residents report that they have little influence in a setting with many resident committees and a residents' council and in which the administrator reports high resident participation in decision making.

Highlighting Design Choices

Program designers can use information about preferences and design–behavior relationships to help inform design choices and guidelines. For instance, several issues arise in planning the therapeutic facet of supportive residential settings, which consists of the physical features designed for those with functional impairments (prosthetic and orientational aids) and the services incorporated into the program (including health services and assistance with daily living). One concern is that a service-rich, prosthetic environment could maximize satisfaction and comfort among impaired older people but undermine residents' independence. Lawton suggests, for example, that "protected," service-rich congregate settings may encourage "passive contentment" (decreased activity and enhanced satisfaction) and lead to a decline in health, whereas traditional housing is associated with "active strain" and continued independent behavior (Lawton, 1976). Results from a survey of tenants of senior housing sites, showing that they have higher morale and are more involved in social activities but have poorer health and less involvement in off-site activities than community residents, are used to support this contention (Lawton & Cohen, 1974). On the other hand, Gutman (1978) found no evidence of differential decline in health status, activity level, or level of interaction with family and friends for older people moving into multilevel facilities as compared to those in housing with fewer services. Sherman (1975b) reached similar conclusions.

A related concern is that prosthetic features, orientational aids, and on-site services may label the older person as different and less competent. For example, the administrator at Eden Apartments has purposely decided to do without certain of these features in order to keep it as much like a "normal" apartment complex as possible. On the other hand, older people, particularly those with some impairment, show a strong desire for many of these features. It should be noted that the absence of certain features may also lead to negative self-labeling. For example, a floor finish that makes walking difficult or seats that make standing up a strain may lead older persons to view themselves as frail or sick. One way of balancing these divergent points of view is to make prosthetic features as unobtrusive as possible while still fulfilling their function.

Most designers try to provide an environment that includes many of the prosthetic and orientational aids and services residents prefer. Such a design is oriented toward the development of an accommodating environment (Lawton et al., 1980), since residents tend to show an increase in their need and preference for prosthetic features as their functional abilities decline. Other important design issues involve the provision of safety features, the inclusion of architectural and programming elements to facilitate resident activity, and the development of ways to enhance residents' control over their daily lives. By influencing the choices made by program designers, information about facility practices and residents' preferences can have an important effect on the quality of life in residential settings (for a discussion of these issues, see Moos, Lemke, & David, in press).

MONITORING AND IMPROVING RESIDENTIAL SETTINGS

Information from environmental assessment procedures can be used to monitor and improve a facility during all phases of its existence. For instance, data on older people's preferences can be used to develop alternative blueprints for new settings, to attempt to match resident preferences with facility practices, and to facilitate the process of orientation and adaptation among new residents. In the postoccupancy phase, assessment can document the stability and change in a facility over time, provide ongoing information to program managers about how the setting is functioning, and guide the formulation and evaluation of design modifications. Moreover, program evaluators can assess changes in preferences and sources of satisfaction over time, as well as problems in adaptation to specific design features (for an example, see Carp, 1976b).

Knowledge of the determinants of social-environmental factors can identify directions in which change is likely to occur and indicate the types of settings that are most amenable to change. For example, we have found that a climate of cohesion and independence is more likely to emerge in facilities with certain physical and policy features: more physical amenities, better social–recreational aids, more available personal space and architectural flexibility, personal choice for residents in their daily routines, an opportunity to participate in making decisions about how the setting should be run, and a richer array of social and recreational activities (Moos & Igra, 1980). Such findings provide facility administrators and staff with guidelines for understanding and changing the social milieu.

In one such effort, Dean (1978) asked the residents and staff of a nursing home to evaluate the facility on a number of dimensions, including those tapped by the SCES. Interventions based on the resulting data included changes in the physical environment, establishment of a resident government and a resident newsletter, and development of role-playing sessions for residents, which were designed to increase their cohesion, independence, and self-exploration. The interventions had the desired effect; there were increases in residents' space utilization and significant positive changes in the social climate. Residents saw more independence, self-exploration, and resident influence, and staff saw more cohesion and better organization following the interventions (see also Waters, 1980).

EDUCATING GERONTOLOGICAL PRACTITIONERS

Gerontological practitioners can be taught to use environmental assessment procedures to understand some of the factors involved in the adaptation of older people to residential settings. For example, the SCES has been employed as an instructional aid to help train social gerontologists. Students completed the SCES on the basis of their observations during an extended visit to a long-term care setting, and comparisons were made between students' perceptions and the perceptions of the residents and staff in the facility. Waters (1981) reported that this exercise enhanced students' understanding of long-term care settings. Information about the work stresses faced by staff in such settings may also provide a useful perspective for training purposes (Koran, Moos, Moos, & Zasslow, 1983; Waters, 1978).

Feedback about program characteristics may help to increase communication among staff and between staff and residents in residential settings and may motivate them to seek to change their facility. An important benefit derived from this process is the exposure of staff to a differentiated framework for thinking about their programs and policies. Instead of locating their program in a one-dimensional space defined by "high quality" and "low quality," staff are encouraged to think about it in terms of several dimensions (for example, the MEAP subscales). The assessment process may prepare a facility for later modifications by clarifying the conceptual framework of the administrators and staff, giving staff members a common language for discussing their setting and encouraging staff to adopt the role of program designer and planner. Finally, after first-hand experience with the application of program assessment techniques, staff may be more receptive to subsequent research efforts, including an evaluation of the program's impact on resident adaptation.

FUTURE DIRECTIONS

We hold that better concepts and measures of environmental factors are needed in order to explore how residential settings influence health and adaptation. We also see the need to place more emphasis on the processes intervening between personal and environmental factors and resident outcomes. To understand the influence of group living settings more fully, it is necessary to examine the social and coping resources people use to adapt to such stressful circumstances as relocation or living in inadequate housing facilities. An expanded framework should encompass the cognitive appraisal and coping resources that moderate the impact of environmental conditions on adaptation. In such a framework, housing choice is an outcome of the adaptive search for a congruent residential setting as well as an input predictive of resident functioning (Lawton, 1981). Although the complexity of person–environment transactions has been recognized, empirical work has not adequately reflected the multicausal, interrelated nature of the process.

Supportive residential settings provide a context in which both group and individual processes operate to affect resident adaptation. Residents in a congregate living situation are part of a social entity; they share common experiences and are exposed to common environmental factors. At the same time, individual residents perceive and respond differently to the environmental features of their setting. Different processes operate at the group and individual levels; both levels can be incorporated into conceptualization and analyses.

By helping to identify the general processes by which contextual factors affect individuals, environmental assessment procedures can broaden our understanding of the ways in which social settings influence the individuals who reside in them. These procedures can help program evaluators and managers to conduct formative evaluations of residential programs, to monitor their stability and change, to evaluate the impact of program factors, and to improve programs by providing feedback on evaluation results. Such applications may enable psychologists and behavioral scientists to promote residential contexts and adaptive strategies that are conducive to well-being among older people.

Acknowledgment

We wish to thank Diane Denzler for her valuable comments on an earlier version of the manuscript.

REFERENCES

Carp, F. M. Housing and living environments of older people. In R. H. Binstock & E. Shanas (Eds.), *Handbook of aging and the social sciences.* New York: Van Nostrand Reinhold, 1976, pp. 244–271. (a)

Carp, F. M. User evaluation of housing for the elderly. *Gerontologist,* 1976, *16,* 102–111. (b)

Coffman, T. L. Relocation and survival of institutionalized aged: A reexamination of the evidence. *Gerontologist*, 1981, *21*, 483–500.

Coleman, P. G. Social gerontology in England, Scotland, and Wales: A review of recent and current research. *Gerontologist*, 1975, *15*, 219–309.

David, T., Moos, R., & Postle, E. *Adaptation of elderly residents to a new nursing home environment.* Presented at the American Psychological Association Convention, Los Angeles, August 1981.

Dean, L. *The effects of environmental and social climate changes in a nursing home.* Unpublished doctoral dissertation, Department of Psychology, University of Missouri, Kansas City, 1978.

Dunlop, B. D. *The growth of nursing home care.* Lexington, Mass.: Lexington Books, 1979.

Finney, J., & Moos, R. H. *Environmental assessment and evaluation research: Examples from mental health and substance abuse programs.* Unpublished manuscript, Social Ecology Laboratory, Department of Psychiatry and Behavioral Science, Stanford University and Veterans Administration Medical Center, Palo Alto, Calif., 1983.

Fozard, J., & Popkin, S. Optimizing adult development: Ends and means of an applied psychology of aging. *American Psychologist*, 1978, *33*, 975–989.

Goffman, E. *Asylums: Essays on the social situation of mental patients and other inmates.* Garden City, N.Y.: Doubleday, 1961.

Gutman, G. Issues and findings relating to multi-level accommodation for seniors. *Journal of Gerontology*, 1978, *33*, 592–600.

Kart, C. S., & Manard, B. B. Quality of care in old age institutions. *Gerontologist*, 1976, *16*, 250–256.

Kasl, S. V., & Rosenfield, S. The residential environment and its impact on the mental health of the aged. In J. E. Birren & R. B. Sloane (Eds.), *Handbook of mental health and aging.* Englewood Cliffs, N.J.: Prentice Hall, 1980, pp. 468–498.

Koran, L., Moos, R. H., Moos, B., & Zasslow, M. Changing hospital work environments: An example of a burn unit. *General Hospital Psychiatry*, 1983, *5*, 7–13.

Lawton, M. P. *Planning and managing housing for the elderly.* New York: Wiley, 1975.

Lawton, M. P. The relative impact of congregate and traditional housing on elderly tenants. *Gerontologist*, 1976, *16*, 237–242.

Lawton, M. P. The impact of the environment on aging and behavior. In J. E. Birren & K. W. Schaie (Eds.), *Handbook of the psychology of aging.* New York: Van Nostrand Reinhold, 1977, pp. 276–301.

Lawton, M. P. How the elderly live. In T. O. Byerts, S. C. Howell, & L. A. Pastalan (Eds.), *Environmental context of aging.* New York: Garland, 1979, pp. 7–15.

Lawton, M. P. Community supports for the aged. *Journal of Social Issues*, 1981, *37* (3), 102–115.

Lawton, M. P., & Cohen, J. The generality of housing impact on the well-being of older people. *Journal of Gerontology*, 1974, *29*, 194–204.

Lawton, M. P., Greenbaum, M., & Liebowitz, B. The lifespan of housing environments for the aging. *Gerontologist*, 1980, *20*, 56–64.

Lemke, S., & Moos, R. H. Assessing the institutional policies of sheltered care settings. *Journal of Gerontology*, 1980, *35*, 96–107.

Lemke, S., & Moos, R. H. The suprapersonal environments of sheltered care settings. *Journal of Gerontology*, 1981, *36*, 233–243.

Lemke, S., & Moos, R. H. *Coping with an intrainstitutional relocation: Behavioral change as a function of residents' personal resources.* Palo Alto, Calif: Social Ecology Laboratory, Stanford University, and VA Medical Center, 1983.

Lieberman, M. A. Relocation research and social policy. *Gerontologist*, 1974, *14*, 494–501.

Linn, M. W., Gurel, L., & Linn, B. S. Patient outcome as a measure of quality of nursing home care. *American Journal of Public Health*, 1977, *67*, 337–344.

Moos, R. H. *The human context: Environmental determinants of behavior.* New York: Wiley, 1976.

Moos, R. H. Social-ecological perspectives on health. In G. Stone, F. Cohen, & N. Adler (Eds.), *Health psychology: A handbook.* San Francisco: Jossey-Bass, 1979, pp. 523–547.

Moos, R. H. Environmental choice and control in community care settings for older people. *Journal of Applied Social Psychology*, 1981, *11*, 23–43.

Moos, R. H., & Igra, A. Determinants of the social environments of sheltered care settings. *Journal of Health and Social Behavior*, 1980, *21*, 88–98.

Moos, R. H., & Lemke, S. *Multiphasic Environmental Assessment Procedure (MEAP): Preliminary Manual.* Palo Alto, Calif.: Social Ecology Laboratory, Stanford University and VA Medical Center, 1979.

Moos, R. H., & Lemke, S. Assessing the physical and architectural features of sheltered care settings. *Journal of Gerontology*, 1980, *35*, 571–583.

Moos, R. H., & Lemke, S. Designing and evaluating specialized living environments for older people. In J. E. Birren & K. W. Schaie (Eds.), *Handbook of the psychology of aging* (2nd ed.) New York: Van Nostrand Reinhold, 1984.

Moos, R. H., Gauvain, M., Lemke, S., Max, W., & Mehren, B. Assessing the social environments of sheltered care settings. *Gerontologist*, 1979, *19*, 74–82.

Moos, R. H., Lemke, S., & Clayton, J. Comprehensive assessment of residential programs: A means of facilitating evaluation and change. *Interdisciplinary Topics in Gerontology*, 1983, *17*, 69–83.

Moos, R. H., Lemke, S., & David, T. G. Environmental design and programming in residential settings for the elderly: Practices and preferences. In V. Regnier & J. Pynoos (Eds.), *Housing for the elderly: Satisfactions and preferences.* New York: Garland, in press.

National Center for Health Statistics. *The national nursing home survey: 1977 summary for the United States.* Washington, D. C.: U.S. Government Printing Office, 1979.

Rodin, J. Managing the stress of aging: The role of control and coping. In S. Levine & H. Ursin (Eds.), *Coping and health.* New York: Plenum Press, 1980, pp. 171–202.

Schulz, R., & Brenner, G. Relocation of the aged: A review and theoretical analysis. *Journal of Gerontology*, 1977, *32*, 323–333.

Sherman, S. R. Patterns of contacts for residents of age-segregated and age-integrated housing. *Journal of Gerontology*, 1975, *30*, 103–107. (a)

Sherman, S. R. Provision of on-site services in retirement housing. *International Journal of Aging and Human Development*, 1975, *6*, 229–247. (b)

Teaff, J. D., Lawton, M. P., Nahemow, L., & Carlson, D. Impact of age integration on the well-being of elderly tenants in public housing. *Journal of Gerontology*, 1978, *33*, 130–133.

Vicente, L., Wiley, J. A., & Carrington, R. A. The risk of institutionalization before death. *Gerontologist*, 1979, *19*, 361–367.

Waters, J. E. Assessing the work environment of long-term health care facilities. *Long-Term Care and Health Services Administration Quarterly*, 1978, *2*, 300–307.

Waters, J. E. The social ecology of long-term care facilities for the aged: A case example. *Journal of Gerontological Nursing*, 1980, *6*, 155–160.

Waters, J. E. Enriching the teaching of social gerontology through use of a social climate scale. *Gerontology and Geriatrics Education*, 1981, *2*, 65–68.

7

Human Factors Research and Functional Environments for the Aged

MARTIN V. FALETTI

OVERVIEW

It is generally recognized that physical and psychological changes which occur with age do affect the ability of the older person to continue functioning independently in community environments. Specifically, the ability to carry out activities of daily living such as shopping, meal preparation, bathing, and cleaning is a major dimension in the assessment of an older person's degree of impairment. Results from such assessments play a role in recommendations regarding the older person's continued independence versus placement in a more sheltered setting.

Many authors have suggested that the older person's inability to function in various settings can be traced to disparities between the demands for action implicit in the design and structure of a particular environment and the capacity of the older person to meet these demands (e.g., Gelwicks & Newcomer, 1974; Lawton, 1977; Lawton & Nahemow, 1973). The extensive work in barrier-free design (e.g., Bednar, 1977) and other approaches to supportive environments for the elderly (e.g., Parsons, 1981; Rashko, 1974) flows from the view that

MARTIN V. FALETTI • Stein Gerontological Institute, Miami Jewish Home and Hospital for the Aged, Miami, Florida 33137.
 This research was supported by NIA (NIH) grant R01 AG 2727.

levels of functioning or adaptation might be improved through changes in environmental features which better recognize the reduced capacities for action often associated with advanced age. Human factors engineering, with its focus on the analysis and design of physical spaces and objects which best match human capabilities, needs, and limitations, has direct conceptual and methodological relevance to the study of problems involving the older person and the physical environment (Chapanis, 1974a; Fozard, 1981; Olshan, 1977).

This chapter reviews work in gerontology and human factors research which is relevant to the person–environment view of functional ability as a basis for considering applications of human factors research methods and techniques to the analysis of problems of daily living experienced by older persons. The chapter focuses on development and use of task taxonomies as a means of developing and linking detailed data regarding personal capabilities and environment demands in analyses of performance problems in daily activities. One prototype daily activity, meal preparation, is used to illustrate how daily living might be viewed in human performance terms. The information developed by a human factors approach is related to understanding changes in aging as they affect functional aspects of daily living and to developing applications of technology and design engineering which can extend and enhance the independent functioning of older persons in community residence environments.

FUNCTIONAL ABILITY: A PERSON–ENVIRONMENT PROBLEM

Within the past decade, work in the field of aging has focused increased attention on functional changes in aging and the design of systems to accomodate these changes. While it is recognized that changes in physical and psychological capabilities are often associated with advancing age (see Saxon & Etten, 1978, for a recent review), the changes are of greatest concern when they begin to influence the older person's ability to live and function independently. The extension of independence and autonomy for older persons in community settings has been a major concern of researchers and practitioners in aging. Much work emerging from this concern suggests that the physical environment is a major factor affecting the extent to which an older person can continue to live independently.

FUNCTIONAL ABILITY IN ACTIVITIES OF DAILY LIVING

The growth and use of multidimensional approaches to functional assessment of older adults is in part a response to the fact that there is little data which systematically relate specific physical or psychological changes to corresponding changes in the ability to function independently in community environments. Specifically, one of the more widely cited examples of a multidimensional approach to assessment, the Older Americans Resources and Services project (OARS; Pfeiffer, 1975), establishes several dimensions relevant to functional ability, including physical health, mental health, social resources, economic resources, and activities of daily living. It is significant that the ability to function in activities of daily living is assessed independently of physical and mental health. Perhaps the major reason for this separation is that, although physical and mental health problems can, and often do, affect the ability to carry out daily activities, the absence of health problems does not necessarily mean that one is then functional with respect to daily tasks and activities.

The fact that physical and mental status information does not provide specific and reliable *predictions* of functional ability in daily tasks suggests that our understanding is, at best, incomplete. Part of this knowledge gap can be attributed to the fact that there are significant numbers of older persons who, although not ill, are considered frail, a distinction which recognizes that normal changes in aging operate to reduce physical strength, manual dexterity, sensory acuity, and other capabilities. Because these reductions in capabilities affect the extent to which the person can meet demands for action implicit in the design of standard environments, it is possible for functioning to be impaired for reasons other than specific physical or mental health problems.

DAILY ACTIVITIES AS PERSON–ENVIRONMENT TRANSACTIONS

At least two major bodies of literature in gerontology support a view of the elderly individual's functioning in activities of daily living as a person–environment problem. The first has concentrated on development of person–environment models of adaptive behavior of elderly people (e.g., Lawton, 1977). Whether emphasizing fit (Kahana, 1975), competence (Gelwicks & Newcomer, 1974), or adaptation (Lawton, 1977), these person–environment models have emphasized an interactional or transactional (cf. Schwartz & Proppe, 1970) view of the older person and the environment. *Transaction,* as used here, denotes active or purposeful behavior, within an environment that is designed to accomplish a given task or activity. The performance of the task or activity, that is, the transaction outcome, is a joint product of the person and the environment. For example, Gelwicks and Newcomer (1974) have drawn on the work of Lawton and Nahemow (1973) to suggest a model in which "the ability of the individual to function within any environmental setting depends on his capabilities and the characteristics of that setting" (p. 39). The model takes into account an individual's competence to cope with environments and views the problem of functioning as one of matching individuals with the most appropriate setting. The model suggests that adaptive behaviors (i.e., competences in functioning) are the result of interactions between person capabilities (e.g., physical health) and environmental supports (e.g., resources and incentives in the environment for use of services). Matches of individual capabilities with an environment of a particular structure are associated with a zone, or range of adaptability. Mismatches which create oversupport lead to dependency, whereas those which create undersupport (i.e., demand) can result in diminished levels of functioning and increased levels of stress.

A second body of literature has sought to reflect this person-environment perspective in the design of housing and environment for older persons. The major emphasis has been on applications of research to development of standards and/or guidelines which recognize the changing capacities of many older people by tailoring or modifying environments to make them more supportive, or at least less demanding and barrier-free (e.g., Byerts, 1977; Green, Fedewa, Deardorff, Johnston, & Jackson, 1974; Knocelik, 1976). Although the majority of authors have focused on the structure and features of residential environments for older persons (e.g., Gelwicks & Newcomer, 1975; Grandjean, 1976; Green et al., 1974; Lang, 1978; Zeisel, Welch, & Demos, 1977), suggestions have also included design for institutional (Koncelik, 1976; McClannahan, 1973) and semi-independent living facilities, (e.g., Gutman, 1978; Heumann, 1978). Some authors have focused extensively on the design process itself, providing suggestions for approaching definition of user needs, design requirements, and solution strategies (e.g., Byerts, 1977). This focus on the needs of older persons as a basis for development of more supportive environments has contributed to the expanding array of alterations to, and designs for, residential environments for the aged.

PERSON–ENVIRONMENT TRANSACTIONS AND FUNCTIONING:
UNRESOLVED ISSUES

Person–environment research in aging and the design-oriented translation of this perspective into specifications for supportive environments for the aged have served to establish the importance of the environment to functional ability in older persons. However, the current state of the art reflects gaps in empirical knowledge about the dynamics of person–environment transaction and the relationship between these dynamics and functional ability. These gaps have in turn limited the specific application of results to the design of more functional environments for older persons.

First, there is a lack of systematic data on the characteristics and capabilities of older adults. While existing research is available which addressed anthropometric characteristics (e.g., body dimensions) of older adults (e.g., Stoudt, 1981) and in some cases, the implications of these data for design of environments (e.g., Grandjean, 1976), studies vary in the selection of parameters measured and in the older populations studied. For example, Grandjean's work considers data from British and Scandanavian research as part of a discussion of the extent to which older adults differ from more general populations and the types of design changes which might respond to these differences. Although this work does illustrate how capability data can be related to specific implications for design, applications of these data cross-culturally (e.g., European to United States populations) is problematic and should be approached with caution (Chapanis, 1974b). Further, results often focus more on what older people *can not* do relative to more general populations than on what they *can* do relative to environmental demands. This latter tendency is most evident in data on body measurements and capabilities which aggregate the elderly and the handicapped. For example, the presentation of anthropometric data in *Humanscale 1/2/3* (Diffrient, Tilley, & Bardagjy, 1974) includes sections on wheelchair dimensions and postures reflecting the elderly and handicapped. While the problems faced by these two groups of people might be similar in particular instances, the wisdom of consistently aggregating an 80-year-old wheelchair patient with a 28-year-old wheelchair patient must be questioned. Major differences in terms of strength in upper arms (for use of grab bars), stamina to negotiate vertical inclines, and ability to travel distances may be expected. Most often, however, handbooks and articles on development, planning, and design of housing for the older users reference only general information on the human factors of older populations (Brody, Kleban, & Liebowitz, 1973; Green, *et al.*, 1974; Rashko, 1974).

Second, person–environment research has focused primarily on general outcomes of transactions such as satisfaction, morale, and anxiety. Lawton (1977) has suggested the need for better operational definitions of the transactions and of factors associated with the physical environment. There is a need to attain closer comparability in empirical characterizations of person and environment factors to support development of more precise and more dynamic person-environment models of functioning.

Third, the tendency toward development of discrete environments (e.g., congregate, semi-independent) with each environment oriented to general level or type of need on the part of the potential users does not effectively address the continuous and often subtle changes in functional capacities in nonpathological aging. People do not age in the sense of experiencing diminished capacities in a homogeneous fashion, nor do similar physical or mental changes necessarily reflect the same levels of reduced functional behavior. Discrete environments designed for a given level of functioning are likely to be appropriate for a finite period of time because both the levels and types of needs are ever changing. Because of individual differences in levels of functioning and associated rates of change (Fozard, 1981), some proportion of residents in any particular setting are likely to be underserved or overserved.

Fourth, assuming that environments and user characteristics could be fine-tuned for better matches, the employment of discrete environments as a response to changing needs implies an increased number of relocations by older people to new environments. While relocation itself may not be a problem, forced relocations can have adverse psychological (and sometimes physical) effects on older people (see, e.g., Schulz & Brenner, 1977). These changes may be an additional stress and may minimize any advantage offered by the new environment. (The suggestion by Green and his colleagues (1974) that design should consider the *elder's residence unit as a home, not as transient housing*, is at odds with the strategy of relocation to increasingly supportive housing environments as a means of addressing functional problems.

Finally, there is the question as to whether existing work in environmental design for older people provides the requisite information to develop a range of responses to problems in independent daily living. For the most part, suggested design interventions are based on generalized attributions about the needs and capabilities of the elderly consumer and are usually of the form appropriate to housing that is being newly constructed (e.g., Lang, 1978). From the pragmatic point of view, we must begin to consider the current housing supply already inhabited by older persons. It is unlikely that development of newly constructed, responsive environments will be available to meet growing needs and numbers. In fact, the cost-efficiency of this approach is marginal at best. Reconfigurations of existing environments, as well as identification of alternative product designs and technologies which are adaptable to and supportive of the elder's activities of daily living, must be explored.

The person–environment approach to human performance and functioning has characterized much of the work in human factors engineering and ergonomics. The methods and techniques from these disciplines provide a variety of tools with which to improve operational definitions of person–environment transactions and specify person and environment factors which effect outcomes of these transactions.

HUMAN FACTORS RESEARCH: A PERSON–ENVIRONMENT PARADIGM

Human factors engineering and ergonomics focus on the study of *man* (person)–*machine* (environment) relationships and their effects on human performance. The central proposition in human factors engineering is that "human use of virtually any man-made thing can be enhanced, or, conversely, degraded by its design (McCormick, 1970, p. 3). The basic aim of ergonomics is to "measure the capabilities of the man and then to arrange the environment to fit such abilities" (Oborne, 1982, p. 3). While each has focused on particular problem areas or dimensions of performance, both emphasize research and application of data to the design of environments, including facilities and physical objects, which best match human capabilities, needs, and limitations. Both have developed a wide array of specific methods and techniques for assessing characteristics of persons and environments and their relationship to human performance. The elements of these human factors approaches to functioning have direct and potentially powerful applicability to issues in person–environment research and can provide the basis for development of more functional environments for older persons.

HUMAN FACTORS RESEARCH: CHARACTERISTIC PROBLEMS AND METHODS

Human factors research is primarily concerned with human performance or functioning with respect to particular tasks or activities. The starting point for most investigations is a task or activity which the human operator must perform to achieve a particular objective or purpose. In many applications, these are defined *de novo* because a new system or environment (e.g., new aircraft, new machine) requires tasks not previously accomplished. However, a task approach may be applied to everyday environments (e.g., work settings, automobiles). Specifically, existing activities may be subjected to a task analysis which specifies particular behaviors or behavior sequences required for the accomplishment of the desired activity. The essential goal of task analysis is systematically to define the relevant points of transaction between the human operator and the environment in ways which specify what is being accomplished and what purpose it serves. Although such analyses most often involve observation and classification of behavior in terms of some schema, there is no single universal approach used for task analysis (Companion & Corso, 1977; Fleishman, 1982).

This functional approach to relationships between persons and environments narrows the definition of *transaction* since it presents a situation in which there is less concern with person–environment interactions where the major outcome is aesthetic satisfaction or some affective response. Instead, transactions are purposeful, and environments are *used* by the person rather than simply being perceived or reacted to in some way. This approach, however, does facilitate operational specification of transactions between persons and environments and, in turn, identification and examination of specific person and environment characteristics which affect these transactions.

The level of behavior examined is largely a function of the specificity of the transaction definition. For example, one might consider each activity of daily living (e.g., shopping, meal preparation, bathing) as constituting a task. However, each of these activities actually involves a number of more specific and distinct transactions between the older person and the environment. For example, meal preparation might include retrieval of objects from storage and manipulation of appliance controls or utensils. These transactions involve different person and environment characteristics. These transactions are more properly the tasks which must be defined in terms which recognize and specify these differences. While one can readily define and measure a large number of person or environment characteristics (e.g., the lifting force of a person, the weight of an object), all characteristics are not relevant to all transactions. The human-factors approach uses the task as a means to specify which of the many aspects of person and environment play roles in a transaction, and this serves to facilitate selection and use of measures which can yield comparable data for each.

HUMAN FACTORS RESEARCH AND AGING: APPLICATION ISSUES

The conceptual and methodological relevance of human factors research to functional environments for the aged has been widely articulated by authors within the field (e.g., Chapanis, 1974; Olshan, 1977), as well as by those involved in person–environment research in aging (e.g., Lawton, 1976, 1977) and those seeking optimal designs of supportive environments for the elderly (e.g., Grandjean, 1976; Parsons, 1981). Some recent work does reflect an attention to human performance characteristics of older populations in the context of tasks and activities in daily living. This work has encompassed definition of residence activities (Rohles, 1978) as well as more specific considerations of performance capabilities of older persons as they relate to functional aspects of residence design (e.g., Grandjean, 1976; Lang, 1978; Parsons, 1981) and safety requirements (e.g., Browning & Saran, 1978).

However, much human factors research done with older populations has not focused on environment design issues. Rather, it has been more concerned with the effects of age on characteristics relevant to human performance such as anthropometric stature (Stoudt, 1981) perceptual-motor capability (Levinson, 1981), or signal perception (Welford, 1981) without specifically relating these data to designs for task environments. Whether these studies seek to describe characteristics of an older population, or contrast younger and older populations, the overall objective has been to establish age-relevant values for accepted or standard human performance characteristics (Fozard, 1981). Results generally suggest that task performance and physical capabilities show age-related differences. Areas of reduced capability include anthropometric stature (Stoudt, 1981) and, to some extent, biomechanical motions (Grandjean, 1976). While results have also indicated reduced performance on perceptual-motor and sensory discrimination tasks, a number of other factors appear to be involved besides chronological age (Fozard, 1981). Recent work has suggested reviewing these changes in terms of more comprehensive and developmentally oriented models (e.g., Fozard, 1981; Welford, 1981).

Not withstanding this growth in human factors research which addresses older populations, Fozard (1981) suggests that little direct attention has been given to assessing systematically age differences in performance with a focus toward the types of compensatory factors which must exist in a standard situation involving people of different ages in order to achieve a designated outcome. For example, he suggests that much data on psychological changes in aging do not address concerns in human factors engineering because it is difficult to relate such changes to design requirements. Related to this is the need to develop data on age-related differences in performance across a spectrum of tasks and task conditions in order to improve applicability of results as well as better to examine interactions between task factors (e.g., task complexity, information load) and age change factors (e.g., memory function, perceptual acuity).

Work in rehabilitation engineering (e.g., Gilad, 1982) and occupational therapy for handicapped and impaired populations (Klinger, 1978) has better addressed some of the concerns raised by Fozard. For example, Klinger provides a wealth of task-related observations on capability changes associated with specific handicaps (e.g., loss of limbs or the loss of limb use) and specific tools, objects, and other environmental changes which can enhance the ability to accomplish specific tasks or classes of tasks. While this work often considers the elderly and the handicapped as analogous populations, it reflects an attention to performance of specific activities in daily living situations and develops results and interpretations which address design changes or environmental modifications to compensate for performance limitations.

While human factors research and ergonomics, especially as practiced in Europe, reflect a wealth of new approaches as well as data on performance capabilities of general populations relevant to daily activities, there is a need to develop and replicate this work in designs which focus on aging populations, or at least age-related differences, as a basis for addressing Fozard's concerns. Most importantly, there remains the need to develop research approaches which are capable of providing the types of human performance data which can yield applications in the form of design engineering and technological options which can improve the functional aspects of environments for older people. The potential utility of human factors research as a means of addressing these concerns is illustrated by the parallel which may be drawn between the role of human factors research in applications of technology to life support systems in the manned space program and its potential for supporting applications of design and technology to what one may certainly call life support systems in the residence environment of the older person.

Beginning with the concept of *functional level* as a way of describing the *result* of a person–environment transaction, impairment or ability is a function of the disparity between the demands of the environment and the capability of the individual to meet those demands. The situation of person as a crew member facing the demands of a mission in space and as an elder facing the demands of daily activities in the standard residence environment are conceptually analogous. In both cases, the structure of the environment demands actions which exceed the *unassisted* capabilities of the individual. For example, the crew member in an early space mission requiring protective suits and small crew station could be fairly characterized as having (relatively) limited manual dexterity, limited torso movement, difficulty with natural consumption of nutrients and elimination of wastes, and limited information-processing skills relative to mission requirements. This list of impairments is not dissimilar to that often associated with the situation of the older person whose capabilities have diminished in the face of stable levels of environmental demand. Many older persons with diminished physical and psychophysical capabilities can be characterized in terms similar to those used to describe the crew member, especially in the context of the demands of normative residence environments. In each situation, limitations on person capabilities *relative* to environmental demands can cause a loss of control over the environment and the transactions within the environment.

Given this similarity of problem structure, the disparity in solution approaches is both significant and provocative. The crew member was not labelled as impaired and was largely unable to benefit from human service assistance. Problems were addressed by using a human factors approach to generate design engineering and technology which enhanced the impact of the limited capabilities to a level congruent with environmental demands. Solutions varied from the redesign of simple food packages (reducing environmental demands) to the use of computer technology as an aid with certain memory tasks (extending the impact of cognitive capabilities). Regardless of the complexity, technology was used to provide the necessary links between person and environment for effective transactions. With older adults, capacities are often made secondary by use of a human service provider who assists with or accomplishes necessary transactions, (e.g., meals-on-wheels, homemaker assistance).

The structural similarity of the two situations reinforces the view of *impairment* and *functioning* as relative terms describing person–environment transactions rather than *person per se*. Thus the application of a human factors approach offers not only the means of addressing the design relevance of performance data but also an improved approach to person–environment research in aging.

HUMAN FACTORS MODELS OF PERSON–ENVIRONMENT TRANSACTIONS

Figure 1 presents one approach to operationalizing a person–environment model of functional behavior in human factors terms.

This analytic model begins a systematic decomposition of an activity (e.g., meal preparation) by identifying a k number of component tasks (1). Each task k is a transaction defined in terms which specify an i number of person characteristics and a j number of environment characteristics which operate respectively as person capabilities and environment demands (2) relevant to task performance. Comparability in measurement of characteristics provides the means to examine the equivalence or disparity between capability (k,i) and demand (k,j) pairs (3). The aggregation of equivalences and disparities can be related to the

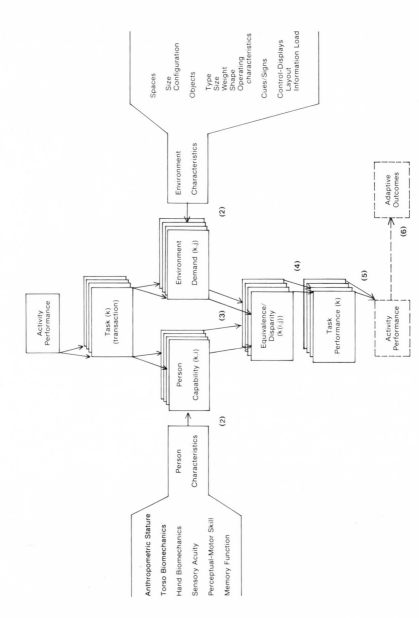

Figure 1. Components of a human factors approach to person–environment transactions.

performance of the particular k task (4) and to the performance of the overall activity through recomposition data of all k tasks relevant to the activity (5). The model also considers potential adaptive outcomes (6) such as stress or satisfaction associated with activity performance (c.f. Gelwicks & Newcomer, 1974).

This approach appears to provide specificity with respect to person–environment factors affecting task transactions and yet also allows flexibility with respect to use of task or person as the unit of analysis. Specifically, the most important features of this approach are that person and environment characteristics are defined in terms of relevance to the task and that comparable indices of these characteristics are selected and examined for equivalence or disparity (i.e., the person–environment *fit*). This approach makes no assumptions about capabilities of persons (e.g., the aged, the handicapped, the adolescent), but rather defines relevant capabilities required so that persons may be assessed empirically to determine the extent to which differences (or changes) in capabilities might affect performance under a given set of environmental conditions. For example, if a task involves physical motions and actions, then stature and body dimensions (anthropometrics) as well as ranges of motion or applications of force (biomechanics) are assessed. This is done in order to establish congruity between the physical movements *required* by the task and the *capacities* of the human operator. If the task involves perceiving cues in one or more of the sensory modalities (visual, auditory, tactile), then perceptual acuity, vigilance, and other aspects of human information processing must be assessed. The environment is also described in terms which are both relevant to the task and comparable to those used to describe the human operator. Controls, for example, may be characterized in terms of dimensions such as circumference and size, parameters also relevant in describing a comparable capability of the human operator (e.g., hand size and grip circumference). While much work in human engineering has focused on measurement of physical aspects of the environment such as spatial dimensions, weights of objects, or shapes of controls, many tasks require sensory and perceptual processing of specific information in an environment for the purpose of making decisions about particular behavior choices. These types of tasks would require that attention be given to conceptualizing and operationally defining *informational* properties of environments (e.g., cue salience, signal to noise in communications) and *information-processing* capabilities of human operations (e.g., memory, decision speed, vigilence).

Although the approach fosters specificity in defining person and environment characteristics relevant to task performance, it does not, *per se*, require that performance be measured along a single dimension nor does it require that analysis be accomplished using group data. It is both possible and desirable to consider several dimensions of performance (e.g., speed, reliability, efficiency). This set of model steps might be replicated to relate components to each of several measures of performance or used with some overall index which aggregates several dimensions of performance. It is important to reemphasize that this approach can be applied to a single individual accomplishing a particular task or task set in a given environment, or to groups of individuals accomplishing the same task(s), each in their own environment. Group level data could be developed here through aggregations of data from individual cases involving performance of the same task or tasks from the same set. The specific application of this approach to a specific problem in meal preparation by older persons is considered in subsequent sections. This application did provide for development of performance data at the level of the individual case for each of a range of tasks even though initial analyses focused on group level aggregations of these data. As noted in previous sections, much work in human factors is focused not only on developing general standards based upon population level data, but also on expressing relationships between person characteristics and environmental characteristics in ways which can be used to assess likely performance of an individual of given capabilities (see, e.g., Thompson & Booth, 1982, analysis of standards for work surface heights).

HUMAN FACTORS ANALYSIS OF FUNCTIONAL ABILITY

The sections to follow consider specific procedures and instrumentation designed to operationalize a human factors approach to the study of functional abilities of older persons in daily activities. Although the procedures for task analysis and measurement of person and environment characteristics were developed from work focused on only one daily activity (i.e., meal preparation), this application is presented here as an exemplar which will, we hope, stimulate more varied and refined applications of human factors methods and techniques to the study of older populations. In keeping with this objective, discussions include relevant research drawn from human factors studies on the aged (e.g., Stoudt, 1981) and on general populations (e.g., Thompson & Booth, 1982) as well as work from rehabilitation engineering (e.g., Dryden, Leslie, & Norris, 1982; Gilad, 1982) and rehabilitation and occupation therapy oriented toward home settings (e.g., Hale, 1979, Klinger, 1978). The specific approach developed here represents only one possible selection and synthesis of methods and techniques from these diverse but relevant areas of work.

ELDER–ENVIRONMENT TRANSACTIONS: SAMPLING ACTIVITIES AND PERFORMANCE

Fozard (1981) has commented on the need to represent adequate ranges of both task-related and performance-related variation in human factors research with older populations. Perhaps the most formidable aspect of trying to approach daily activities systematically is their tremendous variability. No two individuals are likely to accomplish activities in the same way and each individual is likely to vary from day to day in terms of both the type and level of activity performance. While there has not been a single national inventory of activities which are part of daily living, existing sources (Lawton, 1977; Rohles, 1978) have suggested sets of activities which individuals accomplish in the residence environment on a daily, or at least weekly, basis (e.g., preparing meals, cleaning, personal care).

Meal preparation is consistently included in taxonomies of daily activities and is used here as an exemplar for several reasons. First, the author's research has focused on this area and thus specific examples of instruments and procedures are available to illustrate the general approach. Second, meal preparation was a heuristic prototype because it involves a range of task transactions between the older person and the physical environment, and a range of environment variation in terms of spaces, utensils, machines, and physical objects. Finally, the fact that many older people trying to maintain their independence in the community have difficulty with this activity is manifested in the range of programs designed to provide graded support with respect to meal preparation (e.g., homemaker service, meal services, congregate housing). This suggested that a range of person capabilities and task performance levels would be represented in samples of older persons from various living arrangements. Therefore, the approach developed here sought to utilize sampling as a means of representing variation in task profiles associated with meal preparation activity and variation in the older operator's performance of particular tasks. It should be noted that availability of techniques for use in field settings (e.g., behavior observation) was a factor in the decision to sample from actual activities performed by older persons in their own environments. While laboratory approaches have been more widely used in human factors research, the difficulty in fully simulating the work settings and residence environments has given rise to variations in recognition of the need for field-based approaches to human factors research (Johnson & Baker, 1974).

Sampling Activities

Once meal preparation was selected as a target activity, the immediate objective was to sample a range of cases representing persons and conditions under which actual instances of the activity occured. The meal preparation research focused initially on older women (aged 60 years and older) who were accomplishing the meal preparation activity without assistance in community residence environments. While the sampling plan focused on older women because of potential problems in developing a gender-balanced group of cases, it did recognize and address variation in type and frequency of meals prepared as a function of living alone as opposed to living with others (e.g., a spouse), preparation activity, use of appliances, and other factors affecting how preparation was accomplished. This was achieved by developing a relatively large pool of participants who completed (1) meal logs for ten days and (2) a questionnaire concerning appliance use, special diet restrictions, and other information concerning meal preparation activities. The meal log was a one-page checklist designed to get basic information on types of food used (e.g., fresh, frozen) and activities involved in preparation for the major or largest meal each day. This type of information allowed the selection of a varied and representative sample of independent cases of unassisted meal preparation by healthy, unimpaired older persons in community residence settings.

Sampling Performance

This sample of older women preparing meals independently in community settings may be viewed as relatively homogeneous with respect to overall activity performance and yet potentially heterogeneous when examined in terms of specific, measured performance on the activity or specific tasks. For example, whereas persons in this sample are all accomplishing meal preparation tasks at a level which meets or exceeds that required for autonomy, they might differ on task performance, which is scaled in terms of safety (e.g., frequency of accidents), or efficiency (e.g., energy expenditure). While refinement and application of these types of scales to studies of daily tasks are needed to specify ways of enhancing performance, an equally important concern is the objective of supporting an autonomous or safe level of task performance by the older operators with reduced capabilities who have difficulty meeting demands of standard performance environments. This latter concern has been reflected in application of human factors research to rehabilitation engineering (e.g., Gilad, 1982). These approaches examine the patterns in impaired and compensatory person capabilities in the context of required tasks in order to fashion environments which the person can utilize to perform those tasks which are not possible when demands of more standard or normal environments are encountered. For example, Klinger's (1978) manual characterizes homemakers in terms of specific debilities or characteristics (i.e., "works with one hand . . . weakness in upper extremities") and discusses specific environmental aids and prostheses which can foster autonomy in task performance by each type of operator. Hale's (1979) source book for disabled populations uses a similar approach but extends beyond meal preparation to include the complete range of daily activities and the total residence environment.

The enhancement and rehabilitation approaches to task performance are both important to the development of more functional environment for the aged discussed above. The meal preparation research seeks to examine directly those limitations in the older person's capability which, in the standard environment, impact on autonomous levels of task performance. The sample of independent older persons provides the basis for development and test of protocol of task-related person capabilities (e.g., grip strength, limb motion, postural change, hand dexterity) which can in turn be utilized to assess capabilities of dependent samples whose performance is marginal (prepares meals with assistance) or nonexistent (no meal preparation). Rather than focus solely on scaling performance of the independent sample, analysis of disparities between capabilities of marginal performers and demands of standard environments can provide specific data on person and environment factors which underlie observed performance differences and specify environmental changes which might elevate performance levels of these operators. Therefore, in addition to the independent sample discussed above, the meal preparation research has also focused on sampling older women from each of several dependent living arrangements associated with varying degrees of autonomy in meal preparation. These samples include persons receiving homemaker services and residents of congregate housing (limited or marginal performance) as well as some receiving meals in institutional environments (nonperformance). This set of samples provides the means to examine both performance enhancement, (independent samples already performing tasks) as well as performance rehabilitation (dependent samples with marginal performance).

The potential utility of this sampling approach to performance and capability variation is best considered in the context of illustrative relationships between person capability, environment demand, and task performance. Figure 2 presents an idealized illustration which relates task performance to environment demand for each of several hypotheti-

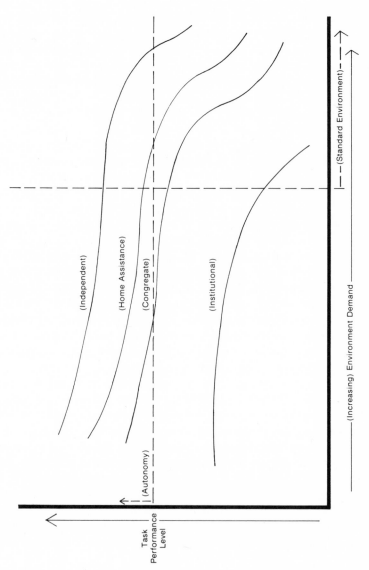

Figure 2.   Conceptual model relating task performance and environment demand for levels of person capability.

cal levels of capability which could reflect individual or group data (e.g., operator types). The curves are labeled to show levels of capability, which might potentially characterize the average or typical operators from each of the samples previously described. Independent sample cases would be characterized by a relatively high person capability, whereas congregate and homemaker and meal service groups are characterized by decreasing capability levels. The relative values on the curves at the vertical dashed line labeled "standard environment" shows the absolute differences in daily activity performance associated with these groups by virtue of the amount of assistance they require to cope with demands of that environment.

Further, the level of performance under conditions of increasing environment demand differs across the four levels of person capability. At lower levels of environmental demand, absolute differences among independent and marginal performance groups may be small relative to those associated with higher levels of demand. However, demand can become so great that even performance for those with higher levels of capability is affected. The horizontal dashed line defining a hypothetical autonomous performance level suggests that levels of performance under conditions of increased environment demand can fall below a level consistent with autonomy or be so close to it that performance may be unreliable or potentially unsafe (e.g., congregate or home assistance groups at standard environment demand levels). While the absence of continuous data on performance of the meal preparation tasks in this research limits the ability to develop this type of relational function, the development and analysis of empirical data on task-related capabilities and demand levels of standard environments can begin to specify at least one set of comparable points on these curves. Future work will, one hopes, examine capability–performance relationships across greater possible ranges of environment demand through manipulation of actual environments or in modeling studies which can incorporate more continuous performance measurement through scales or indices. The meal preparation approach sampled only for major differences in the range of overall performance in order to begin development and testing approaches to specifying sets of person capability–environment demand variables which could be directly related to specific tasks required for the activity.

Human Factors Data in Field Settings

Although it is usual to discuss variables and measures for research prior to specific procedures or instrumentation, an inversion of the sequence is necessary here. The depth and precision of the task analysis procedures are functions of the data available. Laboratory settings allow use of film records and/or direct observation by multiple judges to track and characterize ongoing behavior sequences and assess reliability of protocols through replicated ratings. It is, however, difficult to envision the requisite numbers of judges converging on an apartment to watch an older person make a meal or clean a room. Moreover, with direct observation, behaviors are not strictly replicable and thus rerating the same subject on the same behavior according to revised schemes is not possible.

The research on meal preparation drew on experience with movie film in human factors research and videotape in nonverbal communications studies to apply a field-portable videotape unit to development of a visual record of the performance of the activity. The unit is capable of multiplexing images from each of two cameras synchronously onto a video cassette. Two cameras are used to capture, as closely as practicable, views of the subject from frontal-lateral and dorsal-lateral planes. Although full frontal and lateral views would be preferable, they are only achievable in a laboratory kitchen arranged to provide such access for filming. The compromise to off-angles for views in field settings did not reduce the richness of the behavior captured or the level of reproduction consistent with its use as a tool for task analysis. The videotape equipment used was of a standard brand marketed for home use, with cameras and recorder modified to accept synchronization signals from a specially designed multiplexer unit. The unit also demultiplexes the signal to reproduce one track of images on one video monitor and the second on a second monitor—not unlike stereo separation. Since the images are synchronized, two views of any activity are available. The technical details of the system are described in Wellens, Revert, & Faletti (1982).

The advantages of the videotape approach to field data collection have become rather dramatic over the past year of use. First, it is a minimally reactive approach to developing data in field settings which is rich in its ability to capture related detail. There has been little problem adapting participants to the presence of the cameras. Second, the twin views allow effective reconstruction of entire behavior sequences for purposes of rating and analysis. Observational ratings are all made using the same "behavior stream" and thus the reliability of task analysis and classification schemas can be readily tested via multiple judges. Third, when reliability assessment necessitated a revision of a task analysis system following trial runs on a pilot sample, the same tapes could be rerated using new procedures with new judges. Finally, this approach supports development of detailed person and environment data when combined with a second visit to collect anthropometric and environmental data relevant to the meal preparation activity captured on the videotape record.

TASK ANALYSIS OF DAILY ACTIVITIES

The sample development and collection of complete visual records of the activity provide the requisite base for the development of the task taxonomy to be used in specifying and measuring relevant person and environment characteristics. Task categorizations for some daily activities, including kitchen and meal preparation activity can be found in some design handbooks. For example, Woodson (1981) provides a list of tasks broken down in terms of specific features of kitchen environment involved in the task. Entries take the form of "tasks performed at the . . . sink . . . range . . . counters," together with the proportions of activity accounted for by each type of task (p. 344). While this taxonomy does specify points of transaction between the person and specific features of the environment, there is little to suggest what types of behaviors are involved (i.e., motions, postural changes, manipulative activity). Also, the features addressed are mostly architectural (i.e., space and furnishing) and do not specify objects or utensils involved in the task. The meal preparation research protocol required a more refined system for analysis and characterization of tasks which could still be used with the videotape record of the entire activity and assessed for its utility and its reliability.

Bennett (1971) has summarized arguments relating to task analysis as an empirical process and as a rational or judgmental process. As an *empirical process,* task analysis is the development of task taxonomies based on hard data which demonstrate that the taxonomy contains only those categories required to explain the observable variations in performance. The most usual way in which this goal has been accomplished has been through factor analysis (e.g., the work of Fleischman, 1964, 1967). As a *judgmental process,* task analysis is conceptual, heuristic, and based upon the investigator's perspectives and criteria. In considering both, Bennett offers a third alternative of consensus judgment in which taxonomies are empirically derived from data gathered from a number of judges. Specifically, he examined a semantic approach using verbs and verb phrases on primary descriptors of tasks. Judges were presented with descriptions of tasks in paragraph form and asked to judge the applicability of selected descriptive verbs to each task. Resulting ratings by all judges were collapsed over tasks and examined in a factor analysis of the intercorrelated ratings between all possible pairs of verbs. Results yielded several major dimensions for task descriptors (cognitive, social, physical, and procedural) and loading of specific task descriptors on each. This illustrates a reasonable attempt to compromise the wider applicability of rational methods with the greater precision of empirical approaches to derive schemes for classifying tasks and developing taxonomies.

Companion and Corso (1977) offer a useful discussion of issues in task analysis and suggest criteria for judging the effectiveness of a task taxonomy, however it might be derived. According to them, task taxonomies should

1. simplify the description of tasks in the system;
2. be generalizable and not system-specific;
3. be compatible with terms used by others;
4. be complete and internally consistent;
5. be compatible with the theory or system to which it is being applied;
6. help to predict operator performance;
7. have some utility vis-à-vis understanding the phenomena examined;
8. be cost-effective; and
9. provide a framework around which all relevant data can be integrated.

The operational approach to task analysis of meal preparation sought to implement suggestions by Bennett and Companion and Corso. Specifically, the task analysis schema was developed as a judgmental process and was then empirically tested with a pilot set of videotapes of meal preparations. Task analysis using the videotape sequences involved two distinct components: (1) *defining* a specific task behavior such that it is distinguished from behavior occurring immediately before or after it and (2) *characterizing* the behavior in human performance terms. The first discriminates the task while the second describes it.

There are at least two advantages to this phased approach to task analysis. First, the definition phase is the only phase in which terms specific to meal preparation are used. The phase-two characterization uses descriptors which could be applied to other daily activities and tasks. Second, separate assessments of interjudge reliabilities could be accomplished for the identification phase of the task analysis procedure and the characterization phase. Thus analysis and refinement of procedures for each phase could be based upon interjudge reliabilities for the phase being considered. This was extremely important since it turned out that there were more problems in procedures for identification of discrete task behaviors than there were in procedures for characterization of the task behavior once it was identified.

Task Definition

Utilizing Bennett's conceptualization of language as the vehicle for defining and characterizing tasks, the operator (elder) is, in grammatical terms, the subject and the principal analysis work involves the development of a system using verbs and objects to describe what the subject does. Task descriptors developed in this research viewed an activity in terms of subject or operator (person), verb (transaction), and object (environment). The verb describes what the subject is doing and the object describes the component(s) of the environment involved in the subject's action. This approach uses the structure and rules of language as a system for creation and use of task descriptors. Table 1 presents the verb and object pairs from the application of this approach to development of a schema for the definition phase of the meal preparation task analysis. The proportions of occurrences based upon preliminary data from five pilot cases are presented simply to illustrate the range of activity in meal preparation. Two major classes of tasks are identified: transports, in which the sole purpose of the activity was to move some object from one point to another, and manipulations, which involve object manipulation.

The transport task list distinguishes retrieval versus replacement (from storage). Although it would appear that one is the obverse of the other, the objective here was a taxonomy of tasks and thus both were assessed independently. While many items which are replaced were at one point retrieved, some, most notably food items, are retrieved but not replaced. Thus the relative occurrences of these tasks are not always totally interdependent. Transport task descriptors specify the extent to which postural changes to access storage and move items of given weight from one place to another must be made. As such, the difference in frequency suggested that the distinction was useful and more descriptive of actual activity. Repositioning recognizes that items are often moved which do not involve access to a storage location. Manipulation tasks are, as might be expected, more variable. The manipulation task list illustrates how classes of objects can suggest differences in usage of the verb portion of the task descriptor. For example, *rinse* usually involves running water from a sink tap (following actuation of a control device), but *cleaning*, often semantically similar to *washing*, was used to describe removal of parts of food items from the whole item.

The central purpose of this schema was to develop a reliable system

TABLE 1
DESCRIPTIVE SCHEMA FOR TASK DEFINITION

Transport tasks (41%)[a]

Action (verb)		Environment (object)
Retrieve	8	(Object)
Replace	4	(Object)
Reposition	27	(Object)
Dispose	2	(Object)

Manipulation tasks (59%)[b]

Action (verb)		Environment (object)
Open/close	10	(Container/spatial location)
Turn on/off	16	(Device)
Rinse	9	(Object)
Clean/remove	3	(Part of object from whole)
Pour/run	8	(Liquid/solid from container)
Shake	3	(Liquid/solid—in or from container)
Cut/chop	2	(Object)
Draw/pull out	2	(Object from container)
Mix/stir	4	(Liquid or semi-solid object)
Cover/apply	NS	(Semi-solid to solid object)
Scoop/ladle	2	(Solid to liquid object)
Peel/grate	NS	(Object)

Note: Table reflects preliminary data from 750 characterized tasks. All scores are in percentages.
[a] $n = 308$.
[b] $n = 442$.

for categorizing meal preparation into component tasks. This taxonomy can then be used to develop frequency distributions indicating the number of times in a meal preparation the person accomplished a discrete task. This stage of the system admittedly violated Companion and Corso's (1977) point regarding generalizability of descriptors. However, activity-specific content in descriptors was needed to help judges define the tasks as a precursor to second phase characterization of them in more generalizable terms. Judges blind to each other's ratings achieved an overall 65% agreement on task definitions for the pilot sample. Most disagreement appears to involve defining the discrete points where the task behavior starts and ends. Where judges agreed as to the start and end of a task, agreement on the specific type of transport task was 92% and agreement on the specific type of manipulation task was 84%. Current work is focusing on improved criteria for viewing tapes, use of training tapes, and experience for judges as a means of improving single-judge reliability.

Task Characterization

The differences in transport versus manipulation tasks suggested the need to develop distinct but comparable approaches to a more detailed characterization of the activity involved in each. The second phase of the task analysis aimed at a task characterization which was (1) expressed in descriptors generalizable beyond meal preparation activity and (2) specified relevant person and environment components in the transaction. The task characterization protocols were developed using the verb–object concept but sought to refine actions and objects in ways which better specified the person actions and environment components involved in the task transition.

Figure 3 presents the components used in characterization of manipulation and transport tasks together with descriptors used with each component. Illustrative proportions are from preliminary data on 750 tasks characterized using the schema. Three of the components, action, grip type, and object, are used with schemas for both classes of tasks while other components are selectively relevant to either transports or manipulations. Action descriptors, as shown, characterize a generic vector of movement accomplished as part of the task. These movements usually involve imparting some motion to an object. While oscillations may be viewed as being series of other actions in rapid sequence, it was most useful to characterize them separately rather than attempt a decomposition of component motions. Although the assignment of descriptors to the various force vectors is admittedly judgmental, judges found this set easiest to use. Grip descriptors reflect three major grip types defined by Drury and Coury (1982): (1) the power grip (fully closed hand), (2) the hook grip (use of palm and fingers without gripping by the thumb), and (3) the precision grip (fingers and thumb pinching the object). The cradle grip was added to address those cases where the object is supported from the bottom and not grasped but rather loosely contained within the hand. The object descriptors reflect a first level of characterization which distinguishes the objects as classes. This class designation, together with the specific frame, are used to complete a detailed characterization of the object as part of the person–environment data set. The use of this general typology for objects

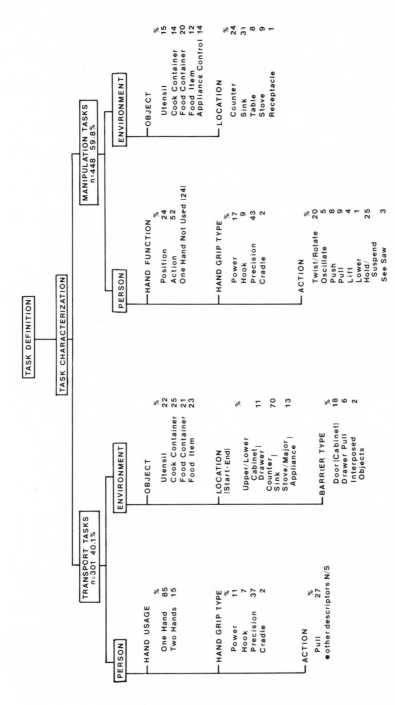

Figure 3. Task characterization schema and illustrative proportions (in parentheses) of occurrence.

facilitated task characterization and yet still provided sufficient information to allow development of detailed data describing attributes of the object which are relevant to its use in accomplishing the task.

Transport Tasks. Each transport task identified in the definition phase is characterized in terms of (1) the types of barriers to retrieval (e.g., cabinet door), (2) the actions required to negotiate the barriers (e.g., pulling a cabinet door open), (3) the object transported, (4) the grip used to hold it, and (5) the starting and ending points of the transport motion. The schema here is designed to recognize that a postural change is likely to occur unless the start and end points are on the same horizontal plane (as in repositioning) and that one or both hands will be used to grip the object in one of the ways specified. As will be shown, the information developed in this characterization defines a total person–environment data record which includes (1) a description of the biomechanics of the grip and posture change made to accomplish the motion, (2) the operator's grip strength, (3) the height and location of the start and end points in the environment, and (4) the weight and handling configuration (e.g., size, shape) of the object. This approach to task characterization does focus on the task as a transaction and allows the use of the task as a means of specifying relevant person and environment characteristics.

Manipulation Tasks. Manipulation tasks proved to be more problematic and required a greater number of descriptor types. As shown in Figure 3, the schema provides for the use of a system of descriptors to describe the actions of both hands. The same sets of descriptors for action and grip are used for both hands as in transport task characterizations. The characterization reflects the fact that a hand may be engaged in positioning an object as well as actually doing something to the object (i.e., action). Unless the hand is not engaged in either position or action, the object, grip, and action are specified. The descriptors are applicable to either positioning (e.g., hold or suspend) or action (e.g., pull, seesaw, twist).

The entire data set for manipulation tasks specifies the general role played by each hand (i.e., position, action, or no role) and, for each hand, (1) the grip used to hold the object, (2) the action involved in the use of the object, (3) the specific object involved, and (4) the location of the object during the task. The location provides a link to the position of the entire torso during the task. This position is coded even though in most cases the posture essentially involves standing at the main counter. As with transports, the relational data set includes specific person actions and positions as these involve specific objects and work areas in the environment. However, the manipulation data sets become rather

more involved because of the need to specify more details such as operating requirements of appliances or utensils which are not normally
relevant in transport of the item.

Task Analysis Reliability and Utility

While final conclusions regarding the reliability of the above protocol await analyses using kappa statistics (Fleiss, Cohen, & Everitt,
1969), the proportions of agreement among the judges suggest that the
system does result in acceptable levels of interjudge agreement. However, while statistical reliability will likely support the use of single judges
as the primary data source, the current procedures for task analysis in
meal preparation reflect a decision to use consensus judgment of two
judges in all phases as the source of final task data. Because the development of observation data is always a judgmental process no matter how
specific, refined, and presumably reliable the criteria, two judges working together on a particular tape can produce more reliable characterizations.

The utility of the system in providing detailed characterizations of
specific aspects of task performance is evident when considering the
array of specific combinations possible with the descriptor set. Preliminary results illustrate, for example, the prevalence of the precision grip.
It is possible to select for those tasks involving this grip and begin to
examine and categorize the various actions of object types involved.
Moreover, the system can be used to develop aggregates of task descriptors comparable to other systems. For example, Table 2 presents task
data from Woodson (1981) together with data from the characterization
phase (Figure 3) compiled in terms of Woodson's task descriptors. As
may be seen, there are some similarities in overall proportions (e.g., task
performed at the sink), but many more differences, at least in this set of
preliminary data (e.g., our subject's greater proportional use of the
counter). However, the refinement in the task set is perhaps the most
salient feature, even when very simple distinctions between transport
and manipulation task are made. For example, manipulative tasks at the
counter are likely to involve different capabilities relative to transport
tasks which simply involve getting an object to the counter. While
Woodson's schema aggregates these tasks, they probably differ in terms
of the demands placed on the person and thus the height of the main
counter is not the only portion of the environment which affects task
performance.

It should be emphasized here that the taxonomy developed above
did not address tasks which involved information processing in the

TABLE 2
RELATIVE FREQUENCIES FOR TASKS CHARACTERIZED BY
LOCATION OF OCCURRENCE

Task type	Woodson (1982) (percent ranges)	Faletti (proportions)[a]
At sink	43–50	48.6
At counters	12–15	26.5
At range (stove)	14–20	7.2
At refrigerator	7–8	6.4
To/from dining area	7–8	[b]
Storing dishes	5–8	9.5

[a]Preliminary data from 750 characterized tasks.
[b]The meal preparation task protocol did not include this type of postmeal preparation activity.

absence of some instrumental response. The meal preparation research, because it is a prototype application, admittedly narrowed its focus at the expense of this more difficult area. It is quite likely that searches of stimulus arrays and discrimination tasks are precursors to, as well as components of, the types of activities characterized in the task analysis presented above. As Fozard has suggested, there is a need to develop information on sensory and perceptual functions as they relate to designed environments. It remains for future application to attempt to address sensory and information-processing task profiles for daily activities in ways which relate measures of sensory and perceptual-cognitive function to the informational characteristics of environments such as signal-to-noise ratios for various cues, embeddedness of information in an array, rate of information presentation, and other factors which might affect task performance and which could be modified through design changes.

Although the research using this task schema is still in progress, the overall approach is viable and can be empirically assessed for reliability. The phased procedure produced a characterization system which serves to specify the transaction—the point of contact—between person and environment in the problem setting chosen here. One might create separate sets of phase-one task descriptors for tasks in other activities (e.g., cleaning tasks such as sweeping a floor, washing a vertical wall surface). However, the phase-two characterization of any task set could be accomplished using some modified version of the characterization system developed here. It is hoped that this approach will stimulate replication, review, and, above all, other conceptual and operational approaches to define transactions in person–environment terms as a means of studying their dynamics.

Person Capabilities

The variables and procedures for measurement used in the meal preparation research to assess person capabilities are selected subsets of the total array used in human factors research. While the selections are a useful exemplar, discussions of the following sets of variables used in the meal preparation research are selectively expanded to include human factors research illustrative of other variables and measurement procedures which could have utility in other applications: (1) the anthropometric and biomechanical capabilities of the whole body or torso, (2) the special anthropometry and biomechanics of the hand, and (3) sensory-perceptual information-processing abilities. Assessment of body stature (anthropometry) and movement and strength (biomechanics) reflect a focus on capabilities relevant to instrumental behaviors required for meal preparation. While the distinction between the torso and the hand is admittedly arbitrary, it is used here to highlight the special problems and considerations involved in assessment of the manipulative capabilities of the human hand. While sensory and perceptual information processing is clearly relevant to instrumental behavior, the discussion here is more conceptual since, as will be shown, precise assessments of these capabilities could not be accomplished in the field-based prototype approach used in the meal preparation research.

Torso Anthropometry

The stature of the human body and the dimensions of the various limbs are relevant to performance on most instrumental tasks because they affect the types and ranges of actions which the operator can perform. The human body is often modeled as a machine (Reynolds, 1982) consisting of a framework with various fixed and moving parts. Anthropometric measures focus on the framework; the lengths of limbs and torso and the interconnections between the various components. The link operator models often used in presenting anthropometric data reflect this abstraction by representing the body as a stick figure composed of straight line sections and joints. Available research in anthropometry provides a wide range of parameters relevant to human performance and specific techniques and instrumentation to measure these parameters (e.g., Diffrient et al., 1974; Woodson, 1981). While anthropometric research usually involves very large samples and standard sets of parameters (Jurgens, 1982), the meal preparation research involved a relatively small sample and thus parameters were limited to those relevant to specifying the scale (i.e., size) of the operator relative to the scale of structure in the environment. The measures taken of the lengths of all the body components (i.e., limbs) needed to construct a link operator type model of older persons are presented in Figure 4. Sophisticated computerized approaches to assessment of anthropometric dimensions are often used in studies where detailed data on large samples is the prime focus of research (Snyder, 1982). However, the field-based approach used with meal preparation employed calipers and anthropometric tape measures to allow manual collection of data in a participant's residence. While the measurement error is likely to be larger using a field-based manual approach, the data thus far developed show fairly close agreement with available results from other studies of older adults.

Torso Biomechanics

Postural Change and Motion.   Body movement has been described in the human factors literature with varying degrees of sophistication. Studies have used statistical treatments of data (e.g., Lane, 1982) as well as more complex computer modeling of motions (e.g., Ayoub, Ayoub & Ramsey, 1970; Gallenstein & Huston, 1973; Ignazi, Mollard, & Coblentz, 1982; McDaniel, 1982) and somotography, which integrates a range of anthropometric and biomechanical parameters in dynamic simulations (e.g., Jenik & North, 1982). Regardless of the measurement sophistication, most treatments describe human motion in terms of deviation from a standing-resting state using a three-axis system for describing vectors and ranges of limb displacement. Actual motion is expressed as degrees of arc subtended in one or more reference planes by the body parts involved in the motion. The combination of these data with anthropometric dimensions allows specification of an operator's range of performance and the examination of how this range affects task performance in an environment of given dimensions with controls or objects located at particular distances (e.g., Kennedy, 1982; Rosier, 1977). Thus a person's "performance envelope" (i.e., the range of possible movements) can be assessed against an environment's "demand envelope" (i.e., the range of motions required, to ascertain the presence or absence of complementary relationships.

In the meal preparation application, the multiplexed views of body motions associated with specific tasks provided a means of quantifying the posture when used with a link operator simulator. Specifically, the

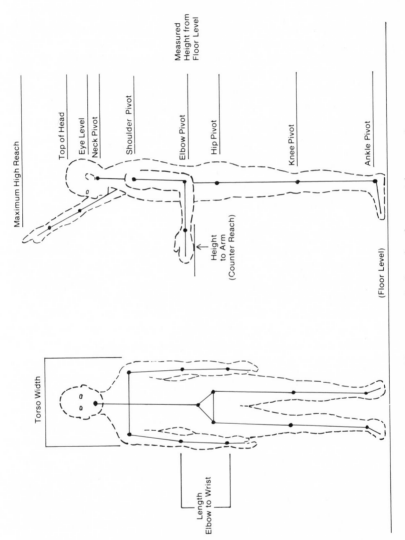

Figure 4.   Field measures of selected anthropometric parameters.

procedure extrapolates experience with drawing board manikins (cf., Kennedy, 1982) to use an adjustable doll with limbs and torso components which can be (1) calibrated to the anthropometric dimensions of the operator being studied and (2) conformed to the posture reflected in the multiplexed videotape view. Biomechanical angles can then be measured directly from the doll. Known measures obtained on the height and position of points in the environment accessed by the postural change provided a second check on the posture represented using the simulator. A posturegram developed by Priel (1974) provides a coding system for posture which can be used to describe a motion by coding the maximum deviation of the postural change during the motion relative to an at-rest position (standing erect, hands and arms at sides). Priel's system for quantifying descriptions of posture can be used with either observational ratings or instrumented measures. The variables assessed in this system are the location of limbs and torso components relative to standard reference planes and the degree and direction of arc subtended by limbs or torso components from the reference positions. Priel defined reference planes and positions (i.e., standing person with arms in a resting position) from which changes in the displacement of one or more parts of the body can be quantitatively represented and which thus can systematically describe virtually any posture. Motions can be described in terms of the deviation from the resting position or, if one chooses, from the posture at some time (T1) to a posture at some other time (T2).

While one might just as well say *bend* or *reach* and get around the problem of quantifying posture, data thus far have suggested that a variety of postural changes are used for more generic motions. For example, bending down to reach lower storage areas can involve leaning forward with one hand on the edge of the counter for support or a simple deep knee bend. While both achieve the same result, the biomechanics involved are quite different. The posturegram approach also has the capability to handle ranges of motions which in other daily activities (e.g., shopping, cleaning) might go well beyond simple, in-place bending down or reaching up.

Force Applications and Lifting. Current literature provides approaches to assessment of strength (e.g., Freivalds, 1982; Herrin, 1982) as well as to more dynamic modeling of various types of exertions of force such as lifting an object (e.g., Konz, Dey, & Bennett, 1973). Specific and reliable assessment of muscle strength and the ability to exert particular levels of force in particular tasks requires sophisticated instrumentation and measures which are best implemented in laboratories or other controlled settings. For example, Konz et al. (1973) employed a six-axis platform which, with subjects standing on it and lifting a weight in a given manner, resolved the action into six components: vertical, lateral, and frontal forces; and twist, somersault, and cartwheel torques; and yielded three classes of factors affecting lifting forces: task (e.g., weight), individual (e.g., stature, muscle mass), and technique (e.g., type of lift). Since older persons are most often characterized as having reduced muscle mass and hence reduced physical strength, biomechanical variables must clearly include those which can index how much their capability to grip, lift, or carry is reduced *relative* to requirements of the meal preparation tasks considered here. Replication of the above approach with older adults using tasks and objects with weights and configurations characteristic of daily activities could support more direct applications of capability data to design and engineering for independent functioning.

The meal preparation application began this effort by developing data on the weights and configurations of objects which older people must manipulate in order to accomplish meal preparation tasks. In activities of daily living such as those considered here, one is initially interested in these factors as they affect dynamic task performance which, Kroemer (1970) suggests, is not effectively estimated by more static force measurements. Thus specific data developed in field visits focused on description of all physical objects handled during task performance in terms of weight, dimensions, and, where relevant, operating characteristics in addition to the type of motion or action associated with the exertion of force to move or lift the object.

Hand Antropometry and Biomechanics

Instrumental tasks in work and residence environments often involve significant amounts of manual and/or manipulative activity. Literature in human factors research reflects attention to describing not only the basic dimensions of the hand and fingers (e.g., Garrett, 1971) but also models of grip and manipulative strength and dexterity (e.g., Armstrong, 1982; Drury & Coury, 1982). Garrett's work is valuable because of the number and range of hand parameters for which data are developed and presented. His work includes not only anthropometric dimensions of the hand and fingers but also relevant biomechanical parameters such as flexion in finger joints, palm, and wrist used in various grips as well as assessments of grip strength. More recent work has focused on models which seek to relate parameters of hand function to specific types of tasks involving particular grips or manual actions. For example, Drury and Coury consider data from previous studies on hand size, grip type, and grip strengths in the context of developing recommendations regarding optimal size for containers and handles. Armstrong's work reflects attention to more general mathematical formulations designed to describe forces exerted by, and on, the hand in various types of grip tasks.

The meal preparation research adapted a number of measures defined by Garrett to develop data on the lengths of finger sections (joint to joint), palms, and the whole hand as well as flexion in finger joints and in the palm. Finger flexion was assessed using a finger goniometer designed to measure angles of displacement from a straight plane when the hand was fully closed. Strength measurement was confirmed to assessment of compression force associated with a power grip applied to a hand dynamometer in each of five handle size conditions.

These parameters admittedly address description of a basic set of hand parameters and represent only a beginning in this area. There is a clear need to expand assessment of hand capability in older populations to address more directly dynamic and task-relevant parameters of hand function. While the distinct types of grips identified in task analysis are reasonably adequate for purposes of defining general levels of hand-related motion, telephoto pictures of hand motions used in meal preparation tasks reflect extremely complex series of motions involved in many supposedly ordinary tasks such as peeling a potato or opening a food container. The predominance of manipulation tasks seen thus far suggests that it may be at the level of the hands that the battle for independence in daily activities in standard environments is won or lost. While design engineering relevant to the hands would involve food packages, utensils and tools, and controls, this area of applications remains relatively unaddressed in the literature on supportive environments for the aged. Replications of Garrett's (1972) work on the hand using older persons reflecting the spectrum of frailty and/or with specific types of problems such as arthritis could be of tremendous value in establishing basic parameters of hand function in older populations. These data could then be applied in more dynamic and interactive formulations aimed at design of objects and tools and utensils which are optimally suited to the manipulative capabilities of older persons.

Sensory and Perceptual Information Processing

Task performance in daily living clearly requires a range of mental functioning. Since biomechanical aspects of task performance are in essence psychophysical, a person's physical capabilities can, and often are, equal to the task demands and yet the total task capability is often first reduced by the changes in sensory or perceptual capabilities. Literature on specific sensory and perceptual handicaps is replete with design engineering which utilizes the capability of an intact sensory-perceptual system to compensate for limitations in other systems. The use of tactile stimulation as a means of transmitting information usually provided in a visual mode (e.g., a touch-coded control) is but one example. However, many changes in sensory and perceptual capabilities which occur with aging are more complex and gradual than is often the case with specific handicaps. Recent reviews of age-related performance changes in areas such as vision (Hughes & McNeer, 1981) and signal detection (Welford, 1981) amply illustrate the complexity involved in basic assessment and characterization of these changes. Fozard (1981) has also suggested that many studies of psychological capabilities do not include all relevant task conditions and often utilize performance parameters (e.g., speed) which may not be relevant to actual situations. Finally, the problem of capability assessment is further compounded by the lack of reliable and valid assessments of cognitive deficits in aging which have the precision required to specify effects of particular deficits on task performance.

Because the assessment of psychological capabilities is best accomplished with laboratory-based, manipulative designs which can vary task complexity and other performance conditions, the use of a field-study approach in the meal preparation research precluded any attempt at such assessment. The meal preparation research has focused more on trying to develop a basic taxonomy of the types of information processing involved in task performance and the information-processing "demands" of the environment. For example, transport tasks are examined to specify the extent to which visual search of the environment, discrimination of relevant cues to locate the object, and hand–eye coordination are required to accomplish the task. Manipulative tasks are similarly examined to estimate the extent to which learned or habituated actions, memory for task sequences, and hand–eye coordination are involved in accomplishing specific action sequences. These taxonomies developed in the meal preparation research can serve only as a first tentative step toward assessing informational demands of environments for daily living and the types of capabilities required to meet these demands. Although discussion of the psychological human factors involved in daily living is incomplete unless motivation is considered, motivation remains one of the most difficult and intractable areas of human behavior from the standpoint of scientific and systematic assessment. The ability of an operator to adapt to and work with a task environment is often affected by the extent to which the operator makes the effort to adapt or use the environment. While no attempt was made to examine possible "motivational" factors in the meal preparation research, future efforts aimed at developing functional environments for the aged must take into account those factors which affect the motivation of older operators to use these environments effectively.

ENVIRONMENTAL DEMANDS

The concept of an environment as demanding particular actions or behaviors is not new, but it is rarely employed in discussions of everyday environments. However, once one accepts the proposition that independent daily living requires that certain person–environment transactions by accomplished at a given level of effectiveness and that the characteristics of the environment affect the level of these transactions, it is possible to conceptualize the everyday environment in terms of demands. As a specific example, consider canned foods in meal preparation. There are usually two equipment options available to obtain the food in the can, a manual opener or an electric opener. If canned food is to be used, then the preparer must use one or the other type of opener. While the electric opener might be theoretically easier to use, if one does not have the resources to purchase it, the choice is narrowed to the manual opener. If the operator is unable to use either, then he or she must get someone who can use the opener or give up canned food in favor of alternative food-packaging options which might include plastic or boxes. These may, however, limit nutritional aspects of the diet since some foods may not be well preserved by these types of packages. This chain of reasoning illustrates the means by which choices of designs and configurations for these objects clearly result in levels of demand for operator actions and consequences if those demands are not met. Work with meal preparation has thus far focused on four general clusters of environmental features: (1) spaces and furnishings, (2) packages and containers, (3) tools and utensils, and (4) control-displays.

The arrangement and size of spaces in the residential environment has been a primary focus of concern in design of housing for older adults. The meal preparation research has been primarily concerned with the height and location of storage and work areas and the use of various spaces for storage of particular types of items. While many approaches have used scale plans and elevations to develop data on this aspect of the environment, measurement of these variables in the meal preparation research has been facilitated by forms and checklists which abstract specific spatial features for measurement such as the heights of horizontal work surfaces and shelves and drawers, their position in the environment relative to major appliances, and the barriers to accessing them (e.g., doors on cabinets, protruding counters).

The protocol for objects and utensils encompasses a range of variations relevant to the use and handling of objects in task performance. Basic information common to most items includes the type of object, its location, shape and linear size dimensions, and weight. The protocol then distinguishes between objects with specifically designed grasping points (i.e., handles) and those without such features. Objects with handles are assessed in terms of handle configuration and handle size (girth and length) while objects without a specific handle or grip are assessed only in terms of the overall dimensions. Operating characteristics of utensils and packages are noted in terms of actions required (e.g., twist, push).

Controls (e.g., light switches, oven and stove controls) and, to a lesser extent, displays of control-related information (e.g., on-off lights, control setting cues) present a wide range of configurations and operating characteristics. Since this is an area of environment which, like sensory and perceptual capabilities of persons, is best addressed in more manipulative paradigms, the meal preparation research has again focused on developing taxonomies which describe the range of configurations and operating characteristics of various types of controls and the frequency of their use in meal preparation tasks. This will, we hope, provide the basis for development of task-relevant simulations to determine the efficacy of various designs given the physical and psychophysical capabilities of older populations (e.g., Koncelik, 1976).

ELDER–ENVIRONMENT TRANSACTIONS: ANALYSES AND RESULTS

Previous sections have considered variables and measures designed to specify tasks performed in meal preparation by older persons as well as comparable data on person capabilities and environment demands relevant to performance of these tasks. This section addresses the utilization of these data in analyses of capability–demand relationships involved in performance of tasks using preliminary data from the meal preparation research to illustrate various options. The sequence of options presented is that adopted for the particular design employed in the meal preparation research and, as such, discussions are expanded to consider analyses which would be relevant to research on functional environments for the aged not specifically included in this research.

The initial set of analyses in the meal preparation research focused on data from the independent sample of older women. The first stage involved analysis of task data to develop the taxonomies of tasks involved in meal preparation and the components of persons (i.e., actions, hand grips) and environments (i.e., objects, locations) involved in these tasks. The second stage of analysis focused on person capability data related to the person components of the tasks to examine the levels of capability currently associated with task performance in standard environments. The third stage drew in corresponding data on environment components to model capability–demand relationships involved in a particular task. Results from these analyses provided the basis for refinement of the person capability protocol used with persons in the dependent samples who no longer prepare meals independently to accomplish (1) contrasts of absolute levels of capabilities between independent and dependent samples and (2) examine data from all samples using capability–demand contrast models.

Figure 5 presents some preliminary data (i.e., a subset of 20 cases from the independent and dependent, congregate samples) to illustrate the above approach to person capability–environment demand analysis. The tasks of concern in these data are those transport and manipulation tasks which involve a power grip (illustrated in the drawing in the righthand graph). For both samples, the person parameter examined is grip strength as measured by a dynamometer at each of five different handle-size positions and selected dimensions of the (right) hand which index grip size. The figure presents graphs of data from both samples to illustrate (1) the absolute grip force levels (left graph) and (2) a crude but illustrative example of a performance model involving person (hand size) and environment (handle size) data linked by task. The lefthand figure presents median values for absolute levels of grip force (Kg) attained at each of five handle positions on the dynamameter by both samples plotted as a function of the size (e.g., midline circumference) of the dynamometer handle at that position. Two features of these data are noteworthy. First, results indicate that within each sample grip force was greatest at the midrange handle positions. While many objects with handles do have circumferences similar in size to the dynamometer positions, many utensils have handles much smaller in size than even the smallest dynamometer position. More importantly, many objects without handles (e.g., packages, containers) have a much larger grip surface to be covered by the hand than was represented in even the largest dynamometer handle setting. Second, the differences in absolute grip strength between independent and congregate samples indicate reduced adaptation ranges in power grip strength for persons in the congregate sample. These lower absolute values suggest even less ability to adapt to outsize object configurations in tasks involving power grips.

The righthand figure presents median values for a fit index which relates inside hand circumference (calculated from hand measurements

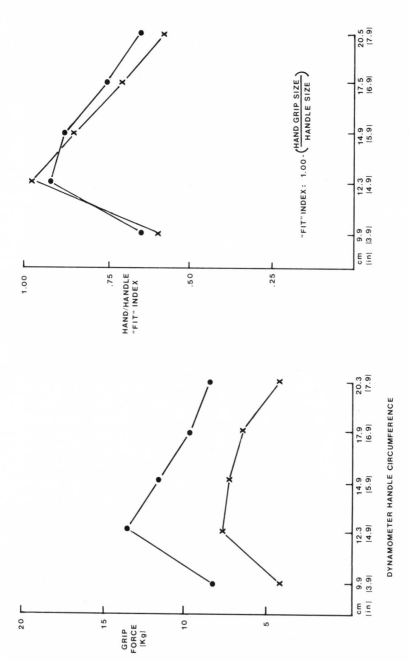

Figure 5. Grip force (left) and person–environment fit index (right) for hand grip task (preliminary independent and congregate samples $n = 20$). Dots represent independent and x's represent congregate.

taken in the field) to each of the five handle sizes on the dynamometer. Although there are not yet enough data to support use of regression analysis to see if in fact the handle-size to hand-size ratio predicts level of force exerted, there is, at this early stage, the suggestion that object sizes disproportionate to the hand (i.e., a small fit index) are associated with less force application. Further, the fit functions for both samples are similar even though absolute force levels are quite different. This function does suggest that the fit between hand and handle does relate to the maximum force which an operator can exert. Specifically, the more closely the two fit, the greater the efficiency in bringing the optimal force to bear. However, the similarity in fit functions between these two pilot level samples suggests that a refined analysis should use a model which includes some assessment of joint flexion and muscle mass or other index of strength in order to account for absolute differences between samples. The model as shown explains only relative differences within samples as affected by object size. However, the model does illustrate how the strength of the operator, as assessed by a dynamometer, can be modeled using comparable person and environment variables. Refined analyses will include compilation of all objects actually handled and assessment of proportions which fall into moderate as opposed to outsize categories to examine the extent to which the older operators in the sample are confronting objects which facilitate or inhibit applications of optimal levels of grip strength. The assessment of grip strength with other samples of dependent older women no longer preparing meals is in progress.

Both absolute difference and capability–demand analyses are viewed as important. Nonperformer samples (as illustrated above) might show the same relationship in terms of optimal force at median levels of object (i.e., handle) size and yet have reductions in absolute values below the independent group, such that handling any but the most ideal sizes of objects is not possible. This approach can better specify how changes in object design parameters (i.e., size) might facilitate task performance by these persons. Although the real situation is clearly more complex than this single illustration, systematic use of task as a relational element can serve to provide more meaningful contrasts of person capability and environmental demand and identify areas of environment design which, if changed, might elevate performance.

HUMAN FACTORS RESEARCH IN AGING: A POSSIBLE AGENDA

Fozard's (1981) review of both the state of the art and future agendas for human factors research in aging addresses the relevance of much research to both the extension of knowledge about the effects of the aging process on human physical and psychological capabilities and the development of data to support more functionally oriented design and engineering of environments for the aged. This chapter has admittedly focused on operational approaches to systematic application of methods and techniques from human factors engineering to problems in daily living experienced by older persons in order to create functionally oriented environments which are more adaptive to changing capabilities. This focus on the second of two areas developed by Fozard does not suggest that human factors research oriented to design and engineering is of greater salience or importance relative to human factors research oriented to more basic questions regarding the effects of aging on humans. Rather, it is likely that both must develop similar types of information to realize specific objectives. First, the development and application of techniques and methods with which to assess more precisely human performance capabilities is equally important to both. Similarly, the improved specification of the role of environment in performance of adaptive behaviors has utility for those seeking improved approaches to person–environment models of behavior.

However, there are a number of areas in which the expanded information provided by human factors research can significantly further progress toward functional environments which can enhance the autonomy of the older person. Major knowledge objectives include (1) analyses of products and equipment in terms of demand levels and suitability for particular ranges of older operator capabilities and (2) development of task-related capability profiles to support applications of design engineering and technology to improve the prosthetic aspects of environments and thereby enhance and extend functional autonomy of older persons. The research agenda required to realize these objectives across the spectrum of "life support" daily activities of the older person appears truly massive. Figure 6 attempts to present a task-by-capabilities matrix of research efforts needed simply to specify transactions which currently involve the older person and the standard residence environment. The column entires list one synthesis of the set of life support tasks required in daily living which, in standard environments, become difficult for many older persons. The row entires present a hypothesized list of possible areas of person capabilities relevant to meeting demands of standard environments in performance of daily activities. The shaded area represents the modest beginning attempted in the meal preparation research. The expansion and refinement of human factors research oriented toward the aged and the aging process can provide more accurate representations of "our future selves" and, if knowledge is indeed

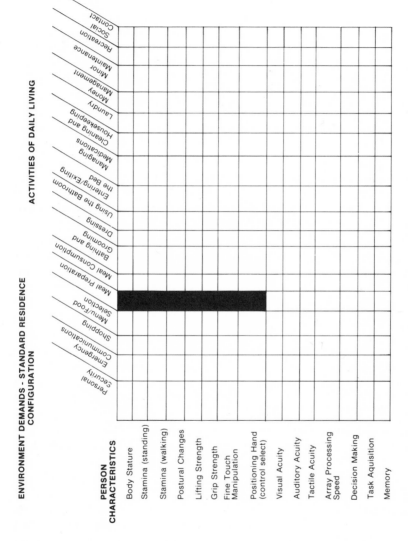

Figure 6.   A research agenda: tasks by capabilities analyses for daily activities in standard environments.

power, provide a greater range of means with which to enhance our functioning and autonomy in later years.

REFERENCES

Armstrong, T. J. Development of a biomechanical hand model for study of manual activities. In R. Easterby, K. Kroemer, & D. Chaffin (Eds.), *Anthropometry and biomechanics: Theory and application.* New York: Plenum Press, 1982, pp. 183–192.

Ayoub, M. A., Ayoub, M. M., & Ramsey, J. A stereometric system for measuring human motion. *Human Factors,* 1970, *12,* 523–536.

Bednar, M. J. *Barrier-free environments.* Stroudsburg, Pa.: Dowden, Hutchinson & Ross, 1977.

Bennett, C. Toward empirical, practicable, comprehensive task taxonomy. *Human Factors,* 1971, *13,* 229–236.

Birren, J. E., & Schaie, K. W. (Eds.). *Handbook of the psychology of aging.* New York: Van Nostrand Reinhold, 1977.

Brody, E., Kleban, M. & Liebowitz, B. Living arrangements for older people. *AIA Journal,* 1973, *59,* 35–40.

Browning, H., & Saran, C. A proposed plan of home safety for the older adult. *Proceedings of the 22nd Annual Meeting of the Human Factors Society,* 1978, pp. 592–596.

Byerts, T. (Ed.) Environments and aging. *Journal of Architectural Education.* 1977, *31,* 1–48.

Chapanis, A. Human engineering environments for the aged. *Gerontologist,* 1974, *14,* 228–235. (a)

Chapanis, A. National and cultural variables in ergonomics. *Ergonomics,* 1974, *17,* 153–175. (b)

Companion, M., & Corso, C. Task taxonomy: Two ignored issues. *Proceedings of the 21st Annual Meeting of the Human Factors Society, 1977,* pp. 358–361.

Diffrient, N., Tilley, A., & Bardagjy, J. *Humanscale 1/2/3/.* Cambridge, Mass.: MIT Press, 1974.

Drury, C., & Coury, B. *Container and handle design for manual handling. In R. Easterby, K. Kroemer, & D. Chaffin (Eds.), Anthropometry and biomechanics: Theory and application.* New York: Plenum Press, 1982, pp. 259–268.

Dryden, R., Leslie, J., & Norris, R. Anthropometric and biomechanical data acquisition and application to rehabilitation engineering. In R. Easterby, K. Kroemer, & D. Chaffin (Eds.), *Anthropometry and biomechanics: Theory and application.* New York: Plenum Press, 1982, pp. 55–66.

Fleishman, E. A. *The structure and movement of physical fitness.* Englewood Cliffs, N.J.: Prentice-Hall, 1964.

Fleishman, E. A. Performance assessment based on an empirically derived task taxonomy. *Human Factors,* 1967, *9,* 349–366.

Fleishman, E. A. Systems for describing human tasks. *American Psychologist,* 1982, *37,* 821–834.

Fleiss, J., Cohen, J., & Everitt, B. Large sample standard errors of kappa and weighted kappa. *Psychological Bulletin,* 1969, *72,* 323–327.

Fozard, J. L. Person–environment relationships in adulthood: Implications for human factors engineering. *Human Factors,* 1981, *23,* 7–27.

Freivalds, A. The development and use of biomechanical strength models. In R. Easterby,

K. Kroemer, & D. Chaffin (Eds.), *Anthropometry and biomechanics: Theory and application.* New York: Plenum Press, 1982, pp. 173–178.

Gallenstein, J. J., & Huston, R. Analysis of swimming motions. *Human Factors*, 1973, *15*, 91–98.

Garrett, J. The adult human hand: Some anthropometric and biomechanical considerations. *Human Factors*, 1971, *13*, 117–132.

Gelwicks, L., & Newcomer, R. *Planning housing environments for the elderly.* Washington, D.C.: National Council on Aging, 1974.

Gilad, I. Biomechanical and engineering anthropometry considerations for the assessment of amputees' work performance. In R. Easterby, K. Kroemer, & O. Chaffin (Eds.), *Anthropometry and biomechanics: Theory and application.* New York: Plenum Press, 1982, pp. 241–251.

Grandjean, E. Ergonomic aspects of aging and the built environment. *Proceedings of the Sixth International Congress, International Ergonomics Society*, 1976.

Green, I., Fedewa, B. E., Deardorff, H. L., Johnston, C. A., & Jackson, W. M. *Housing for the elderly: The development and design process.* New York: Van Nostrand, 1974.

Gutman, G. Issues and findings relating to multi-level accommodations for seniors. *Journal of Gerontology*, 1978, *33*, 592–600.

Hale, G. *The source book for the disabled.* London: Imprint Books, 1979.

Herrin, G. Standardized strength testing methods for population descriptions. In R. Easterby, K. Kroemer, & D. Chaffin, (Eds.), *Anthropometry and biomechanics: Theory and application.* New York: Plenum Press, 1982, pp. 145–150.

Heumann, L. Planning assisted independent living programs for the semi-independent elderly. *Gerontologist*, 1978, *18*, 145–158.

Hughes, P., & McNeer, R. Lighting for the elderly: A psychobiological approach to lighting. *Human Factors*, 1981, *23*, 65–86.

Ignazi, G., Mollard, R., & Coblentz, A. Progress and prospects in human biometry; Evolution of the measurement techniques and data handling methods. In R. Easterby, K. Kroemer, & D. Chaffin (Eds.) *Anthropometry and biomechanics: Theory and application.* New York: Plenum Press, 1982, pp. 71–89.

Jenik, P., & North, K. Somatography in workspace design. In R. Easterby, K. Kroemer, & D. Chaffin (Eds.), *Anthropometry and biomechanics: Theory and application.* New York: Plenum Press, 1982, pp. 215–224.

Johnson, E., & Baker, J. Field testing: The delicate compromise. *Human Factors.* 1974, *16*, 203–214.

Jurgens, H. W. Results of large-scale anthropometric surveys. In R. Easterby, K. Kroemer, & D. Chaffin (Eds.), *Anthropometry and biomechanics: Theory and application.* New York: Plenum Press, 1982, pp. 17–24.

Kahana, E. A congruence model of person–environment interaction. In P. G. Windley, G. Ernst, & T. O. Byerts (Eds.), *Theory development in environment and aging.* Washington, D.C.: The Gerontological Society, 1975, pp. 181–214.

Kennedy, K. Workspace evaluation and design: USAF drawing board manikins and the development of cockpit geometry design guides. In R. Easterby, K. Kroemer, & D. Chaffin (Eds.), *Anthropometry and biomechanics: Theory and application.* New York: Plenum Press, 1982, pp. 205–213.

Klinger, J. *Mealtime manual for people with disabilities and the aging.* Camden, N.J.: Campbell Soup Co., 1978.

Koncelik, J. A. *Designing the open nursing home.* Stroudsburg, Pa.: Dowden, Hutchinson & Ross, 1976.

Konz, S., Dey, S., & Bennett, C. Forces and torques in lifting. *Human Factors*, 1973, *15*, 237–246.

Kroemer, K. H. E. Human strength: Terminology, measurement and interpretation of data. *Human Factors*, 1970, *12*, 297–314.

Lane, N. E. Issues in the statistical modeling of anthropometric data for workplace design. In R. Easterby, K. Kroemer, & D. Chaffin (Eds.), *Anthropometry and biomechanics: Theory and application*. New York: Plenum Press, 1982, pp. 115–123.

Lang, C. Seniors plan senior housing. *Proceedings of the 22nd Annual Meeting of the Human Factors Society*, 1978, 545–549.

Lawton, M. P. Research in environments and aging. In *Housing and environment project 1971–1975* (Final report to the Administration on Aging—USDHEW). Washington, D.C.: Gerontological Society, 1976, pp. 1–17.

Lawton, M. P. The impact of environment on aging and behavior. In J. E. Birren & K. W. Schaie (Eds.), *Handbook of the psychology of aging*. New York: Van Nostrand Reinhold, 1977, pp. 276–301.

Lawton, M. P., & Nahemow, L. Ecology and the aging process. In C. Eisdorfer & M. P. Lawton (Eds.), *Psychology of adult development and aging*. Washington, D.C.: American Psychological Association, 1973, pp. 619–674.

Levinson, W. H. A methodology for quantifying the effects of aging on perceptual-motor capability. *Human Factors*, 1981, *23*, 87–96.

McClannahan, L. Therapeutic and prosthetic living environments for nursing home residents. *Gerontologist*, 1973, *13*, 424–429.

McCormick, E. J. *Human factors engineering*. New York: McGraw-Hill, 1970.

McDaniel, J. W. Biomechanical computer modeling for the design and evaluation of work stations. In R. Easterby, K. Kroemer, & D. Chaffin (Eds.) *Anthropometry and biomechanics: Theory and application*. New York: Plenum Press, 1982, pp. 91–96.

Oborne, D. J. *Ergonomics at work*. New York: Wiley, 1982.

Parsons, H. M. Residential design for the aging (for example, the bedroom). *Human Factors*, 1981, *23*, 39–58.

Pfeiffer, E. (Ed.). *Multidimensional functional assessment: The OARS methodology*. Durham, N.C.: Duke University Center for the Aging and Human Development, 1975.

Priel, V. A numerical definition of posture. *Human Factors*, 1974, *16*, 576–584.

Rashko, B. Physiological and behavioral characteristics of the elderly: A basis for design criteria for interior space and furnishings. *Rehabilitation Literature*, 1974, *35*, 10–31.

Reynolds, H. The human machine in three dimensions: Implications for measurement and analysis. In R. Easterby, K. Kroemer, & D. Chaffin (Eds.), *Anthropometry and biomechanics: Theory and application*. New York: Plenum Press, 1982, pp. 25–34.

Rohles, F. Preference for thermal environment by the elderly. *Human Factors*, 1969, *11*, 37–41.

Rohles, F. Habitability of elderly in public housing. *Proceedings of the 22nd Annual Meeting of the Human Factors Society*, 1978, pp. 693–697.

Rozier, C. Three-dimensional workspace of the amputee. *Human Factors*, 1977, *19*, 525–533.

Saxon, S. & Etten, M. *Physical change and aging*. New York: Tiresias Press, New York, 1978.

Schulz, R., & Brenner, G. Relocation of the aged: A review and theoretical analysis. *Journal of Gerontology*, 1977, *32*, 323–333.

Schwartz, A., & Proppe, H. Toward person/environment transaction research in aging. *Gerontologist*, 1970, *10*, 228–232.

Snyder, R. G. Fundamentals of anthropometric survey measurement techniques. In R. Easterby, K. Kroemer, & D. Chaffin (Eds.), *Anthropometry and biomechanics: Theory and application*. New York: Plenum Press, 1982, pp. 9–14.

Stoudt, H. W. The anthropometry of the elderly. *Human Factors*, 1981, *23*, 29–37.

Thompson, D., & Booth, R. The collection and application of anthropometric data for domestic and industrial standards. *In* R. Easterby, K. Kroemer, & D. Chaffin (Eds.), *Anthropometry and biomechanics: Theory and application.* New York: Plenum Press, 1982, 241–251.

Welford, A. T. Signal, noise, performance and age. *Human Factors*, 1981, *23*, 97–109.

Wellens, A. R., Revert, R., & Faletti, M. V. *A videotape field observation system for behavioral research.* Unpublished manuscript, University of Miami, 1982.

Woodson, W. E. *Human factors design handbook.* New York: McGraw-Hill, 1981.

Zeisel, J., Welch, P., and Demos, S. *Low-rise housing for older people:* Behavioral Criteria for design. U. S. Department of Housing and Urban Development, HUD-483 (TQ)-76, 1977.

8

The Effects of Residential and Activity Behaviors on Old People's Environmental Experiences

STEPHEN M. GOLANT

INTRODUCTION

The quality of life in a community is often judged from the perspective of its residents. Their subjective accounts reveal the *contents* of the environment with which they transact,[1] defining "all the actual things or ongoing events" (Leff, 1978, p. 112) that provide them with information about their place's "people, activities, buildings, vegetation, weather conditions, media messages, and so on." Their reported awareness of the services and facilities in their communities, the boundaries of their neighborhoods, the people and stores that leave their community, and the architectural forms of their houses are examples. Their accounts further reveal how they evaluate the *outcomes* or *consequences* of their environmental transactions. Reports by residents of their dwelling or community satisfaction, difficulties in walking on sidewalks, fear of

---

[1]Transactions are defined broadly here and refer to individual–environment information exchanges variously accomplished by the behavioral, affective, or cognitive functioning of the individual. Informational exchanges can result from concrete (or material) and face-to-face contact or operations or by less direct, vicarious cognitive learning processes (see Downs & Stea, 1970, p. 23; Stokols, 1978, p. 259).

STEPHEN M. GOLANT • Department of Geography, University of Florida, Gainesville, Florida 32601.

driving at night, and postponing plans because of bad weather are examples. Together, these responses, describing an environment's subjectively interpreted content and consequences, are referred to in this chapter as people's *environmental experiences* or *experiential environment*. Such a conceptualization of the environment has many precedents in the psychological literature. Environments defined by perceiving and thinking individuals are exemplified by Koffka's (1935) "behavioral environment," Murray's (1938) "beta environmental press," Rogers's (1951) "phenomenal field," Gibson's (1960) "effective stimulus," and Ittelson's (1973) "perceptual information."

During the 1970s an increased concern with how the qualities of the residential setting influenced the mental and physical well-being of people as they became old (Lawton, 1977) resulted in several empirical investigations of the environmental experiences of the noninstitutionalized elderly population (Lawton, 1978). These studies produced three findings: (a) the housing environment is not similarly experienced by all old persons; for instance, old people are not equally satisfied with their communities, neighborhoods, and dwellings; (b) the environmental experiences reported by the older population differ systematically from those reported by the younger population; for example, older people are found to be more satisfied with their housing than younger populations; and (c) the environmental experiences reported by the elderly often appear inconsistent with the quality of their housing environments as judged by objective indicators; for instance, subjective reports are often more favorable than would be expected in light of the noxious aspects of the objective environment or situation.

This chapter outlines a theoretical perspective to account for the occurrence of these three typical findings. Certain individual behaviors—identified as *behavioral relationships*—are found to differ systematically among members of the older population and between those of older and younger populations. These behaviors are proposed as antecedents of the variable content and consequences of older people's environmental experiences, the dissimilar environmental experiences of older and younger populations, and the apparent discrepancy between old people's environmental experiences and objective indicators of their residential quality of life.

DEFINITION OF BEHAVIORAL RELATIONSHIPS

Two distinctive categories of behavioral relationships are theorized as antecedents of an individual's environmental experiences: residential and activity behaviors. The individual's residential behavior refers to the act of moving into or out of a place and the length of time a place (room, dwelling, neighborhood, community) is occupied. Residential behaviors are initiated relatively infrequently, at intervals of years and decades rather than weeks or months. Such behavior also occurs irregularly; constant intervals of time seldom separate a person's moves. Activity behavior refers to the everyday actions or pursuits of individuals by which they temporarily occupy, utilize, and manipulate distinguishable parts and properties of their environment (its contents) in order to attain their needs and goals. The designation of activity as *behavior* emphasizes that to engage in such concrete or direct environmental transactions requires the individual to *select* locations or places with appropriate contents. This necessarily implies that individuals either remain in some currently occupied location or alternatively travel elsewhere (that is, initiate locomotor behavior). In this chapter three specific aspects of this activity behavior are differentiated: (1) the frequency with which individuals leave their permanent dwelling (e.g., house or apartment) to engage in outside environmental transactions (i.e., level of activity), (2) the change over time in the frequency of this individual activity, and (3) the usual spatial or locational context of the behavior. A suitable operationalization of this last aspect would consist of asking persons where they usually carry out a representative set of activities (Chapin, 1974): in their dwellings, in their neighborhood, in their community, or outside their community.[2] In contrast to residential behavior, activity behavior is initiated more frequently and occurs at more regular intervals. Most activity behavior is routinized and habitual in terms of the time of day it takes place, its duration, purposes, and destinations.

MECHANISMS BY WHICH BEHAVIORAL RELATIONSHIPS INFLUENCE ENVIRONMENTAL EXPERIENCES

The following sections identify the basic mechanisms by which behavioral relationships influence an individual's environmental experiences. Initially, it is necessary to define the existence of an objectively defined environment.

OBJECTIVELY DEFINED ENVIRONMENT

As objectively defined environment is recognized that has an empirical reality independent of thinking and perceiving human beings.

---

[2]Activity behavior need not be conceptualized as narrowly or specifically as above. For instance, it can be distinguished by its purpose, its origin–destination links, its behavior mechanisms (Barker, 1968), and obligatory or discretionary status (Chapin, 1974).

This environment is identified as being *functionally relevant* to emphasize that its contents have the *potential* of evoking, reinforcing, or modifying the individual's or population's behaviors and experiences (Pervin, 1978). It is assumed that different parts and properties of the environment do not have the same informational exchange potentials. That is, they offer individuals different opportunities to satisfy (or not to satisfy) their purposes, needs, and goals (Bloom, 1964; Ittelson, 1973). For example, some sections of the city offer a greater potential for the individual to have new, different, and novel experiences; other sections of the city offer a greater potential for the individual to have anxious, stressful, or unpleasant experiences; and yet other sections are more likely to reinforce the individual's prior—and status quo—environmental experiences. In practice, the functionally relevant environment—henceforth referred to simply as the *environment*—will coincide with the spatial and temporal boundaries of the research investigation's site.

DIRECT AND TANGIBLE ENVIRONMENTAL CONTACT RESULTING FROM INDIVIDUAL'S BEHAVIORAL RELATIONSHIPS

People, old and young alike, display variable residential and activity behaviors in their environment. For example, many people have lived almost all their lives in the same community; others have lived in the same place for only a short time. Some people regularly and frequently travel to numerous locations in their city to satisfy their entertainment needs; others seldom leave their dwellings. Some people frequently shop in nearby stores; others regularly shop in more distant regional centers. The important result is that people differ as to the spatial and temporal contexts in which they conduct their everyday environmental transactions. This implies that residents living in the *same* environment do not similarly occupy or utilize its contents nor initiate environmental transactions having the same potential consequences. In more abstract terms, individuals are not availing themselves directly of the same sensory information about their environment's objects and events. They are engaging in behavioral relationships that are observably and tangibly linking them—both spatially and temporally—to only selective parts and properties of their environment (Norberg-Schulz, 1971; Wheatley, 1976).

COGNITIVE AND MOTIVATIONAL STRATEGIES ASSOCIATED WITH INDIVIDUAL'S BEHAVIORAL RELATIONSHIPS

These behavioral relationships do not only reveal differences in people's tangible or concrete links with their environment; they also are an overt expression of the differing attempts by individuals to satisfy their everyday demands and needs—purposively, adaptively, and rationally.

Various psychologists have conceptualized human organisms as *purposively behaving* or *goal-oriented*, who actively initiate transactions with their environments in a unique way that is consistent with their own cognitive and motivational contexts (Cantril, 1965; Leff, 1978; Wapner, Kaplan, & Cohen, 1973). Purposively behaving individuals are not merely goal-oriented, however; they are *goal-directed*, that is, *adaptively-behaving* (Buckley, 1967). Activity and residential behaviors may constitute corrective responses designed to eliminate, weaken, or avoid the unfavorable outcomes that resulted from earlier environmental transactions (Shibutani, 1968). Thus individuals "ideally strive to achieve 'optimal environments,' or those that maximize the fulfillment of their needs and the accomplishments of their goals and plans" (Stokols, 1978, p. 259). Although rationally seeking these ends, individuals are "bounded" by a world view that inevitably is simplified, limited, and erroneous (Simon, 1957). Moreover, as Stokols (1978, p. 258) emphasizes, "people are often forced by situational constraints to accept undesirable environmental conditions, or at best to 'satisfice' (Simon, 1957)."

The net result is that activity and residential behaviors are initiated by individuals who are operating by variable cognitive and motivational strategies. For example, the residential and activity behaviors of some elderly persons will be intended to maintain status quo environmental experiences; the same behaviors carried out by other elderly persons will be intended to create novel, different experiences. For some elderly persons their long duration in the same dwelling is a reflection of their financial inability to move and their dwelling may be associated with constraining experiences; for others who voluntarily seek and welcome residential stability, the dwelling may be linked to feelings of mastery or control. Thus elderly people's behaviors, even when conducted in identical spatial and temporal contexts, may produce very different experiences if they are motivated for different reasons and the environmental information generated by the behaviors is processed and interpreted in different ways.

PRECEDENTS FOR PROPOSING RESIDENTIAL AND ACTIVITY BEHAVIORS AS ANTECEDENTS OF ENVIRONMENTAL EXPERIENCES

The proposing of activity and residential behaviors as influences of environmental experiences obviously constitutes a major departure from prior research. The literature has usually treated these behaviors as output or performance variables, as something to be explained, rather than something to do the explaining. Past studies have investigated why attitudes and personality traits lead to certain behaviors; how perceived environmental barriers (for example, large distances, poor transportation facilities) restrict travel behavior; and how social, psychological, and economic factors influence people's moves from their residences. Environment–behavior analyses of the elderly population have also failed to evaluate the impact of these behavioral relationships. Although researchers have studied the moving, transportation, and activity patterns of the elderly (Golant, 1979; Lawton & Nahemow, 1973) and have noted their potential effects on environmental interactions (Lawton, 1977, pp. 280–281), these behaviors have not been formally integrated as *explanatory* factors in current theoretical models (Howell, 1980; Parr, 1980; Windley & Scheidt, 1980).

However, the literature does contain epistemological, theoretical, and empirical precedents for this direction of causation. Most generally, the proposed theoretical perspective is compatible with an interactionist model of person–environment relationships (Endler & Magnusson, 1976).

Interactionists identify two senses in which the environment is a function of the person, expressed symbolically as $E = f(I)$. First, because individuals differently interpret and perceive their environment, it is "impossible to completely separate the environment from the person observing it" (Bowers, 1973, p. 328). Second, individuals by their overt behaviors create, select, and maintain environments with properties congenial to their own cognitive, motivational, and behavioral states (see Altman, 1975). As a consequence, the environment transacted with is instilled with qualities that are consistent in some respects to the individual's purposes and intentions.

Proposing the behavioral relationships of individuals as antecedents of their environmental experiences is a conceptual and operational articulation of the second sense in which $E = f(I)$. By their residential behaviors, individuals select, modify, or maintain their everyday environment by moving into or out of a place and by remaining shorter or longer periods in a place. By their activity behaviors, individuals select, modify, or maintain their everyday environment by the extent to which they differently occupy (temporarily) and utilize its varied contents.

The literature contains several examples in which these individual behaviors are interpreted as playing comparable antecedent roles. For example, Barker (1968), as one explanation for the behavior–environment congruence found in "behavior settings" (physical settings with predictable and uniform patterns of behavior), theorized that people actively select and occupy behavior settings consistent with their goals, abilities, and values. Wachtel's (1973) research suggested that compatible and predictable social environments are created by individuals who seek out supportive interpersonal relationships. The "drift hypothesis" (Faris & Dunham, 1939) implied that individuals, because of a decline in competence, move from their present residential settings to others that are more consistent with their weakened state and vulnerable behaviors. Gans (1967) described how former central-city residents deliberately relocated to a low-density suburb in order to engage in an anticipated and desired suburban life-style. Fischer and Jackson (1976) have similarly stressed the importance of this self-selection process for understanding the population characteristics of the suburbs.

It is important to emphasize that proposing these individual behaviors as antecedents of environmental experiences does not rule out their usual conceptualization as consequences of a person's experiences. Of course, it can be correctly questioned whether the analytical separation—theoretically or operationally—of the components of such reciprocal relationships is ever possible without "destroying the subject we are setting out to study" (Ittelson, Franck, & O'Hanlon, 1976, p. 193). Although this is an important issue, it is not addressed in this chapter.

ALTERNATIVE CONCEPTUALIZATIONS OF INDIVIDUAL DIFFERENCES AS ANTECEDENTS OF ENVIRONMENTAL EXPERIENCES

The proposed behavioral relationships constitute but one category of individual factors underlying the environmental experiences of individuals, and the question of whether these are more important sources of explanation than others is not examined in this chapter. Wohlwill (1976, pp. 75–76) distinguished four other approaches that have been used to conceptualize differences among individuals for the purpose of explaining their variable evaluative and affective responses to their environments. These included the measurement of (a) "personality types" as illustrated by applications of personal construct theory to environmental cognition; (b) "environmental dispositions," "that have particular reference to environmental response, in contrast to the personal-construct approach"; (c) "complexity and adaptation level" distinguished from the others because they have "specific reference to the processing of environmental stimulation"; and (d) demographic characteristics, such as age, sex, and occupation.

Two of these approaches, exemplified by the measurement of people's environmental dispositions, adaptation levels, and capabilities of processing information (complexity dimension), conceptualize individual differences such that they are relatable to objective properties of the environment. Individuals are differentiated along dimensions that can be compared with commensurate dimensions of objective indicators. For example, the complex individual can be examined in environments that vary from high to low complexity, or the individual disposed to an urban way of life can be examined in environments that vary from urban to rural.

The conceptualization of individual differences in this chapter's theoretical model distinguishes itself in an important way from the above approaches. The proposed individual behaviors do not describe something *about* individuals (like their demographic characteristics and environmental processing abilities) or *in* individuals (like their dispositions). Rather, they describe observable tangible relationships *between* persons and their objective environment. In this sense, these individual behaviors more correctly denote individual-environmental differences since they explicitly incorporate concrete environmental referents. For instance, one moves to *someplace*, remains *somewhere*, or travels to or remains in some *location*. It is for this reason that activity and residential behaviors are labeled behavioral *relationships*. They literally have no meaning independent of the objective environment to which they are spatially and temporally linked.

INFLUENCE OF RESIDENTIAL BEHAVIOR ON OLD PEOPLE'S ENVIRONMENTAL EXPERIENCES

So far the chapter has treated in relatively abstract terms the influence of people's behavioral relationships on their environmental experiences. Attention now focuses on more concrete and factual evidence that links regularities in the properties of residential and activity behaviors to the content and consequences of older and younger people's environmental experiences.

The effects of residential behavior are considered first. An initial section describes the variable lengths of dwelling occupancy of older and younger populations. This is followed by six sections that attempt to impose order on what are now fragmented insights in the literature concerning the impact of residential behavior on environmental experiences. Although these sections contain some overlapping arguments, they are organized according to issues that are currently differentiated in the literature.

Within *each* of the six sections, the discussion will be organized in the following way. Theoretical and empirical evidence is first presented as to how the length of residential occupancy in a place impinges on people's environmental experiences. When this evidence is combined with the knowledge that the length of dwelling occupancy varies systematically *among* elderly persons and varies systematically *between* older and younger persons, predictions are possible as to why the experiences of elderly persons differ and why elderly persons have experiences that differ from those of younger persons. Each of the six sections then speculates on whether the objective properties of the environment are likely to influence the form of the above relationships. One need not stress that many other individual and contextual factors will influence the form of these predicted relationships. These may constitute more important determinants than residential duration or counteract its influences. However, the primary task of the following sections is to clarify the causal role of residential duration alone.

Patterns of Residential Behavior in Old Age

There is considerable variability in how long older people have lived in their present dwellings (Golant, 1977–1978). In 1970, about 27% of elderly-headed (aged 65 and older) households had lived in their present dwelling 5 years or less; 15% between 5 and 10 years; 21% between 10 and 20 years; and 38% for over 20 years (U.S. Bureau of the Census, 1973). On the average, however, old people are less likely than younger people to have lived a short period in the same dwelling. In 1980, 21% of the United States population aged 65 and older had moved in the previous five years, in contrast to 45% of the total population (aged 5 and older). The lower the chronological age of persons, the more likely it was that they had moved in the previous five years (U.S. Bureau of the Census, 1981).

Amount of Unchanging, Continuous Exposure

Evidence of the Impact of Residential Duration

In contrast to the person who has relocated one or more times in his or her recent past, the person who has lived a long time in the same dwelling or community is more likely to have been exposed to an environment that has changed relatively little and slowly over time. Obviously, exceptions to this generalization exist, as when neighborhoods undergo rapid and dramatic changes in their land uses and population compositions.

Certain experiential outcomes are more likely than others as a result of the longtime, continuous exposure to the same environment. It is probable that the longtime resident has more stable, continuous, and predictable experiences than does the person who moves more frequently. The very constancy of the environment should make its reinforcement potential stronger (Bloom, 1964). It is reasonable to expect that such environmental stability facilitates the recalling of long-term memories of pleasant environmental transactions. Zajonc (1980), reviewing his own and others experimental research, also finds that the "mere repeated exposure" (p. 160) to objects leads to individuals' expressing increasing preference for them.

However, there is reason to be uncertain as to whether the longtime exposure to a relatively unchanged environment actually produces good as opposed to bad environmental experiences for the old person. On the one hand, unchanged environmental experiences may be interpreted in positive terms because of their predictability, certainty, unambiguity, and order. Such general outcomes may enable elderly persons to maintain strong continuity with their pasts. Their own sense of competence and control may be enhanced because of environmental transactions that result in such outcomes. In a society that often appears to be changing rapidly and unsympathetically, objects and events to which such constant, long-term meanings are associated can be of considerable comfort to elderly people (Cantril, 1965). Together, such continuity and feelings of control contribute to the environment's being perceived as more harmonious with the person's needs and goals. In turn, a more positive self-image may result. On the other hand, the very constancy and certainty of the environmental experiences that accompany longterm occupancy may yield undesirable outcomes. They may contribute to the individual's feelings of boredom, monotony, and apathy because they deprive the individual of needed environmental variation or diversity (Wohlwill, 1976). A constant environment may be inappropriate also if it is interpreted by the old person as an indicator of an inflexible or insensitive environment. This may result if the individual's needs or competence have changed such that the resources of the present environment are perceived as inadequate. Such circumstances may apply to the longtime elderly dweller of the auto-oriented suburb who is no longer able to drive and requires nonexistent public transportation.

Adaptation-level or comparison-level theory (Helson, 1964; Thibaut & Kelley, 1959) also suggests certain consequences of longtime occupancy in a relatively unchanging environment. An increasing number of environmental transactions should generate affectively neutral responses from the individual. However great the interpreted environmental diversity is on initial residential occupancy, over time the elderly person is likely to adapt or accommodate to its earlier effects. Consequently, for the longtime resident, it is less likely that environmental transactions result in either extremely positive or extremely negative feelings.

Predictions

Two interacting factors suggest that in contrast to younger people the older population will have more positive and satisfying experiences, and certainly those will less extreme negative outcomes. These include the longer average length of residence of older people coupled with the probability that older people are less likely than younger populations to have stimulus-seeking dispositions. Exceptions to this prediction will occur when older people have witnessed a sharp decline in their competence and subsequently view the unchanged environmental setting as inflexible and unresponsive, or when they have strong stimulus-seeking personalities and thus view the status quo environment as boring or monotonous.

By similar reasoning it is predicted that old people who have lived longer in their place of residence and who have weaker dispositions toward novel environments—and whose competence has not declined—are more likely than other old people to have favorable and satisfying environmental experiences.

These relationships are predicted to persist in environments with diverse (objective) qualities of life provided that historically their contents have not changed dramatically.

ADJUSTMENT PROBLEMS OF THE RECENT ELDERLY MOVER

Evidence of the Impact of Residential Duration

Old persons who have recently moved are more likely to experience various unpleasant consequences because they have difficulties adjusting to or coping with a new and different environment. The nature of these experiences can be better understood by examining their antecedents.

First, recent occupants may have moved initially for reasons that would predispose them to certain types of environmental adjustment problems. For example, moves by old people are sometimes initiated because of poor health, lowered income, or recent social role losses. Thus, these old people enter a new environment in a somewhat weakened state and with less ability to satisfy demands and cope with the consequences of unfavorable environmental transactions. Second, the stress generated by the physical relocation itself may contribute to old people's negative evaluations of their new environment (Kasl, 1972; Lawton, 1977; Schulz & Brenner, 1977). For example, such events as dealing with the movers, packing possessions, paying out large relocation expenses, saying goodbye to friends and neighbors, and traveling to the new place of residence all are potential sources of physical and emotional stress. Such vulnerabilities can be aggravated by a move that was imposed on the old person and resulted in "a loss of decisional control" (Schulz & Brenner, 1977, p. 329). The mere *anticipation* of these and related moving events may be another basis for stress. Third, the old person may have left a familiar and predictable environment that generated a lifetime of positive experiences to enter a new environment devoid of such memories and certainty. Consequently, all new environmental transactions may be tempered with negative emotions. Fourth, the information used to select the new environment may have been erroneous or incomplete. The old person may be confronted with unexpected unpleasant experiences. Fifth, however desirable the interpreted attributes of the new environment might be, negative experiential outcomes can arise for elderly people who find that the differences between their old and new environments are not easily reconciled. On the one hand, the new residence may be perceived as having features that are less attractive than those found in the previous residence (for example, smaller and fewer rooms in dwelling, less friendly neighbors). Alternatively, confronted with an environment perceived overall as more attractive than the previous residence, the old person may not easily adjust to the "new" (and unfamiliar) kitchen appliances, the large shopping centers (in contrast to the corner grocery store of the previous location), or the modern building (in contrast to the "ancient charm" of the previous one). Sixth, the failure of some old people to adjust successfully to a new environment may be due to their inability to disassociate now inappropriate meanings that were attributed to objects in their past environment (Mischel, 1973). This "living in the past" may prevent individuals from dealing effectively with the realities of their new situation (Cumming & Cumming, 1963).

Predictions

In contrast to elderly persons who move more frequently, elderly persons who have lived a longtime in the same place are less likely to confront these stressful and unpleasant experiences. Moreover, as length of occupancy increases, accommodation to a place's problems is more likely (see subsequent section on residential satisfaction).

Because younger people move more often than elderly people, they will probably experience (over the same time period) these unpleasant consequences more frequently. (This prediction assumes that younger movers experience coping and adjustment problems comparable to those experienced by older movers.) On the other hand, a comparison of recent elderly movers with recent younger movers would probably reveal that the former group—more emotionally and physically vulnerable to the stresses of moving—is more likely to have these unpleasant experiences.

The above relationships are predicted to persist in environments that vary widely in quality. All antecedent conditions but the fifth, which is a function of the actual qualities of the prior and present residences, result in adjustment problems linked more closely with the mover's cognitive, motivational, and behavioral states than with the properties of an objective environment. In contrast, the fifth antecedent condition results in adjustment problems that are often due to the noxious aspects of a new environment.

STRENGTH OF COMMUNITY SOCIAL BONDS

Evidence of the Impact of Residential Duration

A considerable sociological literature documents a strong positive relationship between the length of residence of individuals and the strength of their community social bonds (Lansing & Mueller, 1967, pp. 143–144; Speare, 1970; Taylor & Townsend, 1976; Zimmer, 1955). It is theorized that as length of residence increases a greater likelihood exists that persons will become assimilated into the social fabric of the community. Thus extensive friendship and kinship bonds and widespread associational ties are more likely to occur in the absence of residential mobility of a place's occupants. More positive social experiences follow that in turn lead to more favorable overall community experiences (Kasarda & Janowitz, 1974). Relevant empirical evidence comes from a study of a stratified random sample of people in 100 English local authority areas (Berry & Kasarda, 1977). After controlling for class, age, density, and size, the investigators found that "length of residence was the key exogenous factor influencing local community attachment" (p. 65). Indirect evidence comes from research on the rural elderly who are more likely to be longtime residents than the urban elderly. Lee and

Lassey's (1980) review of various studies indicated that "friendship relations and neighborhood sociability [of the elderly] may be stronger in rural areas" (p. 68). Similarly, Arling's (1976) study of urban and rural widows concluded that "elderly widows in small towns and rural areas saw their children more often and had more neighbors than they felt they could visit" (p. 83). Bultena's (1969) research concluded that rural and urban respondents did not differ in the frequency with which they interacted with children *living nearby* and that the majority of the rural aged had at least one child remaining nearby who was seen frequently.

Predictions

In light of the longer average length of residence of older people, they are predicted to have stronger community social bonds and in turn greater community satisfaction than younger populations. Furthermore, because social ties are more likely to be disrupted in old age (because of the death of friends, loss of employment, and loss of contact with friends and relatives), the personal significance of maintaining permanent, stable community social bonds should also be greater.

By similar reasoning it is predicted that old people who have lived longer than other elderly in the same place are more likely to have these strong social linkages and favorable community experiences. This was found by Windley and Scheidt (1982) in their study of old people living in 18 small Kansas towns.

A social climate (Moos, 1976) in the community (for example, the age-segregated status of the population) can potentially weaken this relationship if it is evaluated as incompatible with an occupant's lifestyle. Similarly, community social bonds may be weakened when the population composition of a neighborhood changes due to renewal, racial change, gentrification, and so on. Thus the objective properties of the environment may dampen or prevent the positive relationship predicted between environmental experiences and length of residential occupancy.

DEVELOPMENT OF PSYCHOLOGICAL ATTACHMENT

Evidence of the Impact of Residential Duration

Evidence exists that length of residence is positively associated with individuals' psychological attachment to a place, that is, their strong affective involvement with and sense of belonging to their longtime residence (Taylor & Townsend, 1976).

Literature produced primarily by psychologists specifically considered the meanings of attachment behavior. Its major emphasis was on attachments between mother and infant and how these subsequently influence attachment to peers and nonfamily persons in early childhood (Hartup & Lempers, 1973). More recently, however, literature emphasizing a life-span approach to old age interprets the concept of attachment more broadly (Antonucci, 1976; Lerner & Ryff, 1978). Kalish and Knudtson (1976), for example, proposed an attachment model in which types of attachment included not only people and social groups but also "things and places." In this framework, a person's attachment, of whatever type, is distinguished by its "strong affective involvement with the attachment object" (Kalish & Knudtson, 1976, p. 172) and its "self-produced feedback" (that is, some form of sensory, affective, or cognitive stimulus received from the attachment object). Such attachment (and resulting feedback) serves two functions, according to Kalish and Knudtson (1976, p. 1973). First, it contributes to the sense of mastery felt by individuals because their relationships with the attachment object are anticipated and predictable. Second, it increases the feelings of security of individuals and thereby enables them to explore other aspects of their environment with greater creativity and abandonment.

Predictions

Because older people are more likely than younger people to have lived longer in the same place, they are predicted to be more strongly attached to their environment and in turn more likely to enjoy the accompanying positive feelings of belonging and mastery. Furthermore, there is reason to predict that such feelings achieved through attachment behavior become especially important in old age. Because of developmental and cohort effects, old persons may perform less competently—physically or socially—than younger persons in several domains of their life, and they may feel less in control or less independent. Consequently, there is a theoretical basis for the prediction that attachment behaviors toward the dwelling, neighborhood, or community and their concomitant experiential outcomes (e.g., the feeling of security) are likely to be of greater significance to older than younger people. This will be especially true when earlier objects of old people's attachment—a career, a spouse, or a longtime friend—no longer exist.

By similar reasoning, it is predicted that old people who have lived longer in the same place than other elderly will be more attached psychologically to their residences and will be more likely to enjoy the accompanying positive feelings of belonging and mastery.

It can be predicted that certain characteristics of the environment, such as its smallness of population, lower population density, or homogeneous population, will strengthen the elderly individual's sense of place attachment, but supportive empirical evidence is unavailable.

DEGREE OF FAMILIARITY WITH ENVIRONMENT'S CONTENTS

Evidence of the Impact of Residential Duration

Various studies report that people living longer in the same place are more familiar with their environment. Representative of the elderly literature, Lawton, Kleban, and Carlson's (1973, p. 447) study suggested that older people's "preference for the familiar (knowledge of how to get about, or which routes to take when going to visit, or which shops to patronize)" may underlie the motivation of longtime older occupants to remain in a neighborhood that is otherwise very unattractive because of physical deterioration and decline. In a very different setting, Rowles (1979) argued that older people, when they first enter a nursing home, experience adjustment problems because the new environment offers little in the way of familiar objects or spatial cues. Thus these older people find themselves in a state of geographical disorientation.

In their national survey of the American population, Campbell, Converse, and Rodgers (1976, p. 164) similarly pointed to the significance of the longtime occupied residential setting to old people. In their words, "the new learning required to achieve a comparable familiarization with another environment may appear particularly forbidding to the elderly, long past the period when exploration of the new is an intriguing challenge."

The positive relationship between length of residence and environmental familiarity is supported by analyses of the psychological or cognitive representations that individuals have of their city (Milgram, 1970; Moore, 1979). Golledge (1978, p. 81) argued that greater familiarity with a city's physical environment contributes to an individual's having a more coherent and cohesive cognitive representation of its nodes, paths, and areas. A greater likelihood exists that the individual has learned (through direct, instructional, and observational processes) to discriminate efficiently an environment's physical objects that are personally more salient (Golledge & Zannaras, 1973). Such a cognitively represented environment should contribute to environmental transactions that more predictably and effortlessly yield positive outcomes for the individual. However, Downs and Stea (1973, p. 25) suggested that over time or with individual maturation people forget some of the information that once was included in their cognitive representations. Milgram (1970) argued that such diminution is adaptive and enables the resident to cope with the information overload of everyday life and to focus selectively on the most important environmental information.

Predictions

In light of the longer average length of residential occupancy of elderly persons, it is predicted that older people are more (or at least equally) familiar with the contents of their physical environment than are younger people. A more familiar environment is also likely to result in their having more satisfying experiences and feeling more in control of their environmental transactions. If, on the other hand, longtime older occupants have cognitive representations of their environment less complete than those of younger people, these are still predicted to be more accurate and to contain more salient features.

By similar reasoning, it is predicted that old people who have lived longer in the same place of residence than other elderly, will be more familiar with the contents of their environment and have more accurate and salient cognitive representations.

It is unclear whether the physical arrangement and properties of the environment will influence these predicted relationships. It is possible that the above relationships would be weaker in a smaller community that has a less complex physical layout. Here, for instance, persons could become familiar with an environment's contents in a much shorter period, but supportive empirical evidence is unavailable.

AMOUNT OF RESIDENTIAL SATISFACTION

Evidence of the Impact of Residential Duration

A persistently positive relationship is reported between place (dwelling, neighborhood, or community) satisfaction and a population's length of occupancy. Findings from a national study (Campbell *et al.*, 1976, p. 163) indicated that, for a short period immediately following occupancy in a new environment, reported satisfaction levels are much higher than in later periods. It is suggested that because individuals make a major emotional and financial commitment to a new place— often with the anticipation of long-term occupancy—they initially block out or repress any negative evaluations of their new residences. In effect, this denial by individuals may be essential in the beginning (the first year) when they are confronted with a variety of adjustment problems and must assure themselves that they have made a correct choice. After this initial "momentary phase of dissonance reduction" and period of self-congratulation and pleasure, individuals once more become rational observers and evaluate the faults of their residences less emotionally. After about five years, however, satisfaction levels of individuals increase, in part because of their progressive accommodation to their situation and in part because of a "decline in the salience of competing alternatives" (p. 164). It is argued that this accommodation is a result of individuals' maintaining or lowering their aspiration levels after occupying their new residences such that alternative residential environments are either not considered or viewed less favorably than the individual's present residence.

For a relatively small percentage of elderly, however, their continued longtime residential occupancy will be accompanied by a decline in satisfaction levels in response to a variety of dwelling and neighborhood problems (Newman & Duncan, 1979; Varady, 1980). Declines in health, income, and other personal resources may "lead to a mismatch between the elderly householder's housing needs and his housing situation" (Varady, 1980, p. 307).

Predictions

In light of the longer average length of residential occupancy of older persons, they are predicted to be more satisfied with their physical settings than younger populations. Several researchers have confirmed this empirical relationship (see Campbell *et al.*, 1976; Lawton, 1978).

By similar reasoning, it is predicted that old people who have lived longer in the same place of residence are more likely than other old people to be satisfied with their residences.

It is unclear whether the strength of the above relationships is influenced by the objective qualities of the environment. For instance, there is no empirical evidence confirming or denying that the positive relationship observed between people's residential satisfaction and their length of residence will be as strong in good quality environments as it is in noxious environments.

CONCLUSIONS

The evidence reviewed in the previous sections, although not always in agreement, does allow the following tentative conclusions to be made about the influence of residential behavior.

Older people, because of their longer average length of residence in a place, (1) are more or as likely than younger populations to be aware of the salient features of their environment's contents and to enjoy the associated benefits (e.g., feelings of security); and (2) are more likely than younger populations to have favorable or positive environmental experiences. These include more predictable and controllable environmental outcomes, less frequent moving adjustment problems, more enjoyable social experiences, stronger psychological attachment to their place of residence accompanied by stronger feelings of security, and greater residential satisfaction. The first generalization must be tempered by the virtual lack of empirical studies systematically comparing people's cognitive representations of their everyday environments as they age or systematically comparing the cognitive representations of older and younger populations living in the same residential situation. The second generalization must be qualified by the observation that members of older and younger populations do not always attribute consistent or predictable meanings to their residential behaviors and their outcomes. For instance, longtime elderly occupants of an unchanged community may evaluate this constant environment either positively or negatively—because of either its predictable or its monotonous qualities. Longtime residents also may be motivated to remain in their present settings for different reasons and consequently evaluate and perceive their environments in highly personal ways not always consistent with the above predictions.

Comparable generalizations (and qualifications) can be made about the impact that length of residential occupancy differences have on the environmental experiences of old people. The elderly who have lived longer in their places of residence than other elderly people are expected to be more or as familiar with their environment's contents and to have more favorable environmental experiences.

The above conclusions have been supported by a wide range of arguments. Although many of these explanations do not directly involve the objective qualities of an individual's environment, it is clear that such properties have the potential of either strengthening or weakening the predicted relationships. Although the impact of the environment was speculated on in the previous sections, firm conclusions were not possible because of the absence of empirical evidence.

INFLUENCE OF ACTIVITY BEHAVIOR ON OLD PEOPLE'S ENVIRONMENTAL EXPERIENCES

The examination of how activity behavior influences the environmental experiences of people—old or young—is made more difficult for two reasons.

First, whereas residential behavior is conceptualized and measured fairly uniformly in the literature, this is not the case for activity behavior. As defined here, its interpretation is close to what Chapin (1974) referred to as "out-of-home" activities. The psychologist's concepts of act, action (social), behavior, response, and adaptive behavior share some similarities with activity behavior but also differ substantially in other ways (Wolman, 1973). The sociologist's concept of social activity can variously refer to individuals' locomotor activities for social purposes, their interpersonal contacts and relationships, and the content and complexity of their social role set. These inconsistent definitions become an issue when interpreting the research literature. Inevitably, it becomes necessary to draw on theoretical and empirical literature that does not define activity behavior in a desired fashion but nonetheless offers sufficiently important insights and interpretations.

Second, in contrast to the residential behavior literature, there is almost a complete absence of either conceptual or empirical treatments of activity behavior as an antecedent of everyday environmental experiences. What insights are found in the literature are in response to research issues very different from those presented in this chapter. One exception, however, is the theoretical insights found in a literature reviewed by Kelman (1974), who was concerned with how the acts or behaviors of individuals are reciprocally related to their attitudes. (Attitudes represent one type of self-reported response encompassed within the concept of environmental experiences.) In the cognitive dissonance and self-perception literature discussed by Kelman, attitude change is conceptualized as a cognitive adjustment; individuals attribute to themselves and to others an attitude that is more consistent with the particular way they have acted toward an object. Attitude, in this sense, is viewed as a "post hoc adjustment to action" (Kelman, 1974, p. 315). However, Kelman (p. 317) argues that attitude change should be interpreted more broadly as "an outcome of various motivational and informational processes that are generated by the action." Earlier in this chapter, comparable processes were identified as constituting one basic mechanism by which behavioral relationships influence people's variable environmental experiences.

The issues addressed in the following sections are similar to those considered in reference to residential behavior. These focus on how activity behavior differences among the elderly contribute to their variable environmental experiences; how the contrasting activity behaviors of the older and younger populations lead to differences in their environmental experiences; and why the objective properties of the environment may be poor indicators of old people's environmental experiences. The sections are organized in the following way: First, there is a brief summary of the change in activity behavior patterns of people as they reach old age and of the varied activity behavior patterns among the elderly. The next sections propose that the environmental content known or perceived by older and younger populations is a result of their variable activity behavior patterns. The following sections argue that these variable activity behavior patterns can account for the different outcomes of old people's experiences and for the different outcomes of older and younger people's experiences. The final sections discuss how the different meanings and interpretations that old people ascribe to their activity behaviors lead to their having different experiential outcomes.

PATTERNS OF ACTIVITY BEHAVIOR IN OLD AGE

Various studies confirm that as persons age chronologically, their levels of both interpersonal and noninterpersonal activity are expected to decrease (Botwinick, 1973; Golant, 1972, 1976; Havighurst, Neugarten & Tobin, 1968; Maddox, 1963).[3] Other research found that the frequency of vehicular trip behavior (that is, all locomotor behavior that involves auto, public transit, or taxis as modes of transportation) is lower for older people (over age 65) than for younger populations (Golant, 1972; Markovitz, 1971; Wynn & Levinson, 1967). Also, with increased age, such vehicular activity becomes increasingly oriented to nonwork trips and disproportionately occurs during the daytime hours (Golant, 1972, 1976). According to Havighurst (1961, p. 341) the tempo of activity also slows down in old age and "older people fill their time with less action than younger people do." The locational context of activity behavior also becomes more restricted in old age, with dwelling-centered activities becoming more likely (Chapin & Brail, 1969; De Grazia, 1961; Gordon & Gaitz, 1976). Findings from the National Center for Health Statistics (1974) also point to the more limited activity space of older people. Higher percentages of noninstitutionalized older people are housebound, have difficulty getting around, and are disabled more days of the year. The more restricted activity space of old people is also suggested by studies by Neibanck (1965) and Newcomer (1976). They find that facilities intended for use by the elderly should be within certain critical walking distances of their residence; otherwise dissatisfaction is ex-

---

[3]In these and related studies, *activity* is conceptualized in different ways even within the same measurement instrument.

pressed. More generally, Carp (1971) has emphasized the considerable importance of walking as a mode of transportation for elderly people.

The findings of other studies emphasized the need for caution when making the above generalizations. Maddox (1968), reporting on findings from the Duke Longitudinal Study of older people, concluded that a very high proportion of older people (close to 80%), although displaying changes in their activity behavior over time, persistently maintained their own characteristically high or low levels of activity as they grew older.

Several of the above studies also concluded that among elderly people there is considerable variation in activity behavior patterns. Moreover, this interindividual diversity is often a product of factors unrelated to chronological age, such as race, sex, education, and income. In short, the basis for elderly people's varied travel patterns has often been established well before old age (Chapin, 1974; Golant, 1972, 1976).

ACTIVITY BEHAVIOR'S INFLUENCE ON THE CONTENT OF PEOPLE'S ENVIRONMENTAL EXPERIENCES

The best documented evidence of activity behavior's influence on the contents of the environment that is known and perceived by the individual is found in the cognitive or psychological mapping literature (Downs & Stea, 1973; Moore, 1979). This literature is concerned with describing and understanding people's variable awareness (completeness, schematization, accuracy, and augmentation) of the physical phenomena and properties found in the everyday environment. Geographers have specifically focused on the relative location (attributes) of these phenomena (that is, where they are, how far away, and in what direction). This literature has demonstrated that people's knowledge of their city's contents is at least partially influenced by the extensiveness, organization, and efficiency of their everyday travel behavior. These movements result in individuals' accumulating information about alternative places and routes in their environment and acquiring increasingly complete, accurate, and structurally integrated images of its contents (Golledge & Zannaras, 1973). A comparable investigation of these relationships as they specifically apply to old people is represented by Regnier's (1981) research that demonstrated the close relationship between old people's use of neighborhood facilities and resources and the configuration of their cognitive maps.

The conclusions of this literature, along with scattered findings and inferences from a large environment–behavior literature, led to the construction of the following propositions that relate the content of the individual's environmental experiences to his or her *usual space–time locus of activity behavior*. *Locus* here refers to the *set* of all points (or locations) in time and space defined by the individual's activity behavior. Thus a *usual* space–time locus of activity refers to an individual's average or customary activity regime, implying the usual frequency with which activities occur and their usual spatial or locational extent. These propositions should be viewed as preliminary formulations that are subject to empirical validation.

1. Environmental transactions purposively initiated by people are more likely to occur within the usual space–time locus of their activity behavior.
2. Environmental transactions purposively avoided by people are more likely to be with objects and events found outside the usual space–time locus of their activity behavior.
3. People are more aware of and familiar with environmental objects that are found within the usual space–time locus of their activity behavior.
4. The contents of people's environmental experiences are more likely to coincide with the environmental objects and events found within, rather than outside, their usual space–time locus of activity behavior.

Propositions 1 and 2 argue that people are more likely to perceive and interpret information from those parts of the environment that are enclosed within the boundaries of their usual activity regime. It follows that individuals are more aware of and familiar with these parts of the environment (proposition 3), and that the contents of people's environmental experiences are more likely to coincide with its actual objects and events (proposition 4). Together, the four propositions imply that certain parts of an individual's environment have greater functional relevance than others. That is, the properties of the environment contained within the usual space–time locus of a population's activity behavior are more likely to have the potential of influencing (reinforcing, modifying, evoking) its members' environmental experiences than the environmental properties outside of this activity regime.

Propositions 1 to 4: Different Implications for Younger and Older Populations

It is relevant to inquire whether the direct and tangible environmental links generated by these activity behaviors are more important as information sources to older or younger populations. There is some evidence to suggest that two alternative sources of information are more important to older people: first, communication media (letters, telephone, newspapers, television, mail advertising, etc.) producing environmental content potentially unavailable from that found in the individual's presently circumscribed environment (Atkin, 1976; Graney & Graney, 1974); and second, the memories recalled of past environmental experiences whose contents have been acquired by the individual in a different place and/or an earlier time of life (LoGerfo, 1980).

Situational Proximity versus Activity Behavior as Antecedents of Experiential Content

Propositions 1 to 4 present relationships that together explain why the objective properties attributed to an environment can be very different from those perceived and known by its occupants. This results when the parts of the environment directly or materially transacted with by the individual contain properties that are not consistent with or representative of those typifying the whole environment. (In practice, *whole* and *part* environmental referents will depend entirely on operational decisions made by a particular researcher.) This discrepancy is predicted to increase as the space–time locus of the individual's activity behavior diverges from the boundaries and contents of the whole environment. In the extreme case, the objective attributes of the whole environment will bear no resemblance to the contents of the old person's environment *qua* experienced.

Yet an assumption is often made that the smaller the distances between individuals and parts of their environment, the more likely it is that their behavior and experiences are influenced by its attributes. Thus the individual occupying or living *in* or *near* a particular environment is predicted to have experiences more congruent with its objective attributes than individuals living outside of or farther from such an environment. This assumption can be referred to as the *situational proximity argument*. However, if propositions 1 to 4 are valid, this argument obviously will not be generalizable to all situations. Several examples may help to demonstrate this point. An older woman living in an age-segregated apartment building may carry out most of her socializing with *younger* persons living in a distant suburb. She may rarely see her neighbors if she spends most of her time away from her apartment. A building's homebound elderly residents may never use the grocery store only one block away; neither may elderly residents who do most of their shopping in a distant regional shopping center.

Researchers engaged in situation–behavior analyses may never critically examine this assumption because of the very nature of their research settings. Within a laboratory or a small-scale environment such as a school, a hospital, or an old-age institution, the whole environment is often assumed to be under investigation. To use Barker's terminology (1968, p. 19), the environment is considered circumjacent to the individual: "it is enclosing, environing, encompassing." The situational proximity argument is not raised as an issue because environmental proximity and environmental occupancy (or utilization) are identical referents. This is not the case in a large-scale, natural setting, such as a community located within a larger metropolitan region in which individuals do not live in a temporally or spatially closed system. Here, individuals who live in a particular part of an environment may have little contact with it and be little influenced by its qualities. Nor do large geographic distances between individuals and particular places necessarily imply the absence of environmental transactions or impact.

In total, this discussion argues for the validity of the following proposition:

5. The likelihood of transactions by individuals with objects and events in their environment depends not only on their proximity to them, but, as importantly, on the nature of their activity behavior relationships with them.

This proposition, if valid, has two important implications. First, the properties of the proximate environment (the nearby residential setting, such as the dwelling and neighborhood, and perhaps the small community) will less reliably predict the experiential content of those old people whose activity behaviors occur over a larger locational (environmental) context. Second, the properties of the proximate environment will better predict the experiential content of older than younger people. This is because older people's activity behavior is more likely to be spatially restricted and thereby contained within the boundaries of the proximate environment.

ACTIVITY BEHAVIOR'S INFLUENCE ON THE CONSEQUENCES OF PEOPLE'S ENVIRONMENTAL EXPERIENCES

Although researchers have shown little interest in how activities influence the outcomes of people's experiences, numerous isolated empirical insights can be found in the gerontological literature. For instance, it is noted that bus trips are important for their own sake because they provide some old people with pleasurable, spontaneous, and unplanned personal contacts with other elderly passengers. Similarly,

Rowles (1979) points out the importance of the dwelling window as a source of environmental stimulation for inactive old people. However, at present no conceptual tree exists on which to hang these unconnected observations.

The following propositions—deduced in part from propositions 1 to 5—relate the activity behavior patterns of a population—old or young—to the outcomes of their environmental experiences. These relationships should be treated as preliminary formulations that require empirical verification. Reference to *smaller* space-time locus of activity implies either less frequent travel outside the dwelling (home) and/or travel that is more restricted to locations near the dwelling.

6. The smaller the space-time locus of activity behavior, the more personally salient are the demands people make of objects and events in their proximate environment.

7. The smaller the space–time locus of activity behavior, the more likely that people's environmental demands and goals are satisfied or rewarded by transactions with objects and events in their proximate environment.

8. The smaller the space–time locus of activity behavior, the more likely that people adapt successfully to less desirable experiential outcomes involving objects and events in their proximate environment.

9. The smaller the space–time locus of activity behavior, the less temporally diverse or variable are the outcomes of people's environmental transactions.

10. The smaller the space–time locus of activity behavior, the more likely that people experience predictable, expected, or customary outcomes from their environmental transactions.

11. The smaller the space–time locus of activity behavior, the more likely that people's environmental experiences derive from memories and fantasies of earlier environmental transactions.

Propositions 6 and 7 argue that people—older and younger—who are less active and whose travel is more spatially restricted are more likely to have their most salient (environmental) needs and demands satisfied from transactions in their nearby residential setting. Concomitantly, the more distant (from the dwelling) parts of the environment will be less relevant to these people's needs and goals and probably less attended to as potential sources of pleasure and rewards. There is no shortage of evidence in the gerontological literature demonstrating that old people assign important material and symbolic significance to their proximate environments—such as their dwellings and neighborhoods

(Lawton, 1980, pp. 38-42); however, the relevant analyses have not controlled for the effects of activity behavior.

Proposition 8 is deduced from propositions 6 and 7. It argues that if the proximate environment is satisfying the most salient or central of people's demands and goals, then these people are strongly motivated to ignore, deny the presence of, or constructively deal with the less desirable outcomes experienced in their proximate environment. Without such coping processes, intolerable stress and anxiety is predicted (Lazarus, 1966), given the implicit assumption that an enlarged space–time locus of activity behavior is not a viable coping strategy to counter these unpleasant experiences. Again, there is no shortage of evidence in the gerontological literature indicating that old people often deemphasize the unpleasant aspects of their living quarters—but again the intervening effects of activity behavior are not specified.

Proposition 9 is inspired by methodological insights from the literature on neighborhood racial segregation (Bogue & Bogue, 1976). Probabilistically, smaller blocks or neighborhoods are likely to contain homogeneous (that is, segregated) populations. Similarly, when transactions by individuals occur consistently in a small (and probably homogeneous) part (e.g., neighborhood) of their whole (e.g., community) environment, less diverse and variable experiential outcomes are predicted. In turn, it can be deduced that the experiential outcomes of these transactions are probably more predictable or expected (proposition 10). However, it remains unclear whether such status quo outcomes will be interpreted positively (the virtues of certainty) or negatively (the offensiveness of monotony).

Proposition 11, while relevant to both older and younger populations was derived from gerontological findings showing that less active elderly individuals are also more likely to be psychologically disengaged, which in turn is accompanied by a greater probability of introspection and reminiscing (Havighurst & Glasser, 1972). The implication is that as individuals reduce their material links with the outside world, they become more inner-directed and introspective.

Variability of Environmental Outcomes among Old Population and between Older and Younger Populations

Propositions 6 and 7 account for why old persons differ as to the outcomes they experience in the proximate parts of their environment. Old people with small rather than large space–time loci of activity behavior are predicted to evaluate these places as more salient or central to their needs and to consider them a greater source of environmental satisfaction and rewards. Old people who have activity patterns centered around their proximate environment are also predicted to adapt more successfully to any problems they confront in these places (proposition 8). Several of these relationships have been tested in empirical research by the author (Golant, 1982, 1984). A random sample of relatively independent and healthy elderly persons (aged 60 and older) were interviewed in an older, middle-class, urban, midwestern community. Those old people more satisfied with and proud of their dwellings, neighborhoods, and community had consistently lower activity levels (they travelled less frequently from their dwellings to places within their metropolitan region) and had smaller activity spaces (they displayed more locationally restricted travel behaviors).

Propositions 9 and 10 suggest that old people with small rather than large space–time loci of activity behavior will experience more predictable and expected environmental outcomes. Finally, proposition 11 predicts that old people with small rather than large space–time loci of activity behavior will experience outcomes that depend more on the content and consequences of their environmental memories.

Propositions 6 to 11 also account for why older people experience certain environmental outcomes that differ from those of younger populations. Because older people have smaller (on the average) space–time loci of activity behavior, they are more likely than younger populations to evaluate positively the proximate places in their environment. In contrast to younger populations, older people are also predicted to consider these places as more salient to their needs and goals and to adapt more successfully to any of their unpleasant aspects (propositions 6 to 8). Similarly, older populations are more likely than younger populations to have less temporally diverse or variable environmental experiences (proposition 9), to have predictable experiences (proposition 10), and to derive their experiences from environmental memories (proposition 11).

Experiences of Old People Inconsistent with the Objective Properties of Their Environment

Propositions 6 to 11 provide one explanation for why old people often report high levels of satisfaction even though they occupy physically run-down or deficient dwellings and neighborhoods. Old people whose lives revolve around their proximate environment are predicted to depend heavily on its contents to satisfy their everyday material (shopping, services, and so on) and social needs (friendships, neighbor relationships) (propositions 6 and 7). Furthermore, on the assumption that they do not have easy access to other parts of their community, they are predicted to overlook the deficiencies of their proximate environment (proposition 8). This environment has the added favorable feature (for some elderly) of yielding relatively predictable outcomes (proposition 9 and 10). Beyond this environment's concrete properties, it may also be associated with a lifetime of happy memories (proposition 11).

EXPERIENTIAL IMPACT OF COGNITIVE AND MOTIVATIONAL STRATEGIES ASSOCIATED WITH OLD PEOPLE'S ACTIVITY BEHAVIOR

The gerontological literature contains insights into the varied meanings and interpretations that old people assign to their activity behavior. These, in turn, lead to predictions of why old people experience dissimilar environmental outcomes. Generalizations must be made cautiously, however, because the literature offers contradictory evidence. A summary of the relevant evidence follows, which considers whether higher or lower activity levels are believed to be more adaptive to old people and whether old people's activity behavior is voluntarily initiated.

The Theoretical Basis for Causal Links

Many insights emerged from the debate in the gerontological literature concerning whether high or low activity contributed to higher morale in old age. These were often discussed in the context of the disengagement and activity theories of aging (Hochschild, 1975). On the one hand, *higher* activity levels are suggested to be associated with successful aging or adaptation. That is, higher activity levels:

- Are a sign of strength and dominance, consistent with the American ethic of rugged individualism. Therefore, a failure to maintain the activity patterns of middle age or old age is a sign of personal weakness and submissiveness (Havighurst & Albrecht, 1953; Kuypers & Bengston, 1973).
- Enable old people to ignore or deny the physical frailty of their bodies so as to appear intact or active (Cath, 1975).
- Enable old people to confirm their own competence and to demonstrate that they have not succumbed to the physical frailties and dependence of old age (Kuhlen, 1968).
- Confirm that old age is little different from middle age. Achieving such continuity between middle age and old age is a salient goal for many old people.
- Enable old people unexpectedly and spontaneously to "find out-

lets for [their] feelings," uncover "hidden personal resources," or develop "meaningful relationships with others" (Kutner, 1956, p. 104).

On the other hand, *lower* activity levels are suggested to be associated with successful aging or adaptation. That is, lower activity levels:

- Are consistent with society's values and edicts that condone and support a less active and socially involved aging population and that withholds reinforcements (for example, pleasure, status, or prestige) for the maintenance of many middle-aged roles and activities (Cumming & Henry, 1961).
- Enable individuals to become more emotionally involved with themselves and less involved with the people and material world around them. Thus older people engage freely and guiltlessly in increased introspection, reminiscing, and fantasizing.
- Enable old people whose physical and mental competence has declined to avoid public exposure that would lead to social criticism, ridicule, or embarrassment (Cath, 1975).

A second set of insights emerges from a concurrent debate concerning whether the observed activity behavior patterns in old age are voluntarily or involuntarily initiated.

One group of proponents argue that lower activity, smaller activity spaces, and declining activity levels are *voluntarily* initiated. They contend that old people are desirous of decreased environmental involvement, in part due to inner, developmentally related psychological forces, in part due to a society that condones and welcomes such disengagement (Cumming & Henry, 1961). In contrast are those who argue that lower activity, smaller activity spaces, and declining activity levels are *involuntarily* initiated. They point to the impact of uncontrollable cognitive and physical impairments suffered by old people and an unsympathetic society that erects and tolerates institutional and environmental constraints and barriers to activity and involvement (Cath, 1975; Dowd, 1975; Kuhlen, 1968; Thomae, 1979).

Two Contradictory Sets of Propositions

To represent these opposing perspectives in the gerontological literature, are the following two sets (12a, 13a, 14a and 12b, 13b, 14b) of propositions:

12a. The smaller the space–time locus of activity behavior, the more likely old people feel they have unsuccessfully adapted to old age.

13a. The smaller the space–time locus of activity behavior, the more likely old people's activities are uncontrollable and involuntary.

14a. The smaller the space–time locus of activity behavior, the more likely old people have stressful, unpleasant, or embarrassing environmental experiences.

12b. The smaller the space–time locus of activity behavior, the more likely old people feel they have successfully adapted to old age.

13b. The smaller the space–time locus of activity behavior, the more likely old people's activities are controllable and voluntary.

14b. The smaller the space–time locus of activity behavior, the more likely old people have happy, pleasant, or enjoyable environmental experiences.

The gerontological literature has made clear that high or low activity levels can be adaptive to elderly people (12a versus 12b) and that low activity levels may or may not have been voluntarily sought by elderly persons (13a versus 13b). From these opposing interpretations are deduced the alternative propositions 14a and 14b. Proposition 14a implies that those old people who more closely associate their low activity levels with personal meanings such as vulnerability, lifetime discontinuities, constraints, and involuntariness will have the evaluative outcomes of their transactions dominated by negative affects (emotions). In direct contrast, proposition 14b implies that those old people who more closely associate their lower activity levels with personal meanings such as socially acceptable behavior, greater opportunities for introspection and reminiscing, stress avoidance, and greater personal control will have the evaluative outcomes of their transactions dominated by positive affects (emotions).

Although the presenting of these contradictory propositions is scientifically disagreeable, the issues cannot be obfuscated by the arbitrary selection of one position over another. It is very likely that there are different groups of elderly people whose respective activity-experience relationships are indicative of *both* positions. That is, on the one hand, there are old people who are homebound and evaluate their dwelling-restricted life style and all its environmental referents in very negative terms. On the other hand, there are old people who have voluntarily chosen a home-centered life style (despite having the competence to do otherwise) and enjoy the sedentary experiences connected with their dwellings. Research attempting to verify which of the activity or disengagement theories of aging was the more valid has demonstrated that various personal factors (e.g., life style continuity between middle and old age, personality makeup, timing of life events, role losses, mental and physical competence) interact with activity levels to produce both high and low morale levels (Larson, 1978). It is therefore reasonable to predict that different mental and behavioral states and societal influences will interact with activity levels to produce both enjoyable and unenjoyable environmental experiences. In this regard, the resolution of the following two issues would increase one's confidence of prediction.

The first concerns the temporal constancy of the proposed relationships. There is the question of how long the size of the space–time locus of activity behavior results in environmental experiences with the proposed affect. For instance, from propositions 13a and 14a it is predicted that unpleasant dwelling experiences occur in conjunction with the uncontrollable activity behavior of old people. Left ambiguous, however, is the time period over which this restricted activity continues to lead to unpleasant experiences. A corollary to this proposition may be that over time old people adapt successfully to their changed mobility patterns with the result that restriction ceases to be a factor influencing their environmental experiences. This is a matter for empirical research.

A second and more complex issue is whether propositions 14a and 14b are describing the main or secondary effects of activity behavior. Propositions 6 to 8 earlier predicted that old people with smaller space–time loci of activity behavior will be more satisfied with their dwellings than other old people. To what extent, then, is this relationship weakened if the smaller space–time loci of behavior are involuntary, perhaps due to the old person's physical incompetence? The present view is that the meanings ascribed to activity will, on the average, only *amplify* or *dampen* the evaluative outcomes predicted by propositions 6 to 8. That is to say, the meanings and interpretations ascribed to activity constitute the secondary rather than the dominant or primary effects on a population's environmental experiences. They contribute, for example, to old people feeling *somewhat* less satisfied or *somewhat* more satisfied.

FUTURE DIRECTIONS

A new theoretical approach has been outlined to explain why old people do not similarly experience their everyday residential environment, why old people's experiences differ from those of younger populations, and why the experiences of both young and old populations may be inconsistent with objectively measured conditions of their environment. Such an effort, designed to improve understanding of some phenomena, offers two general directions for subsequent analysis and research. First, the concepts and relationships constituting the foundation of the approach can be subjected to careful scrutiny and criticism; and second, empirical investigations are demanded when propositional statements are insufficiently verified. Many of the conceptual issues requiring clarification and the empirical questions requiring investigation (the majority of the propositions) have been identified in the body of the chapter. However, three as yet unaddressed issues deserve analytical attention.

The first issue concerns an implicit assumption of the theoretical approach, namely, that the impact of people's activity behavior is independent of the impact of their residential behaviors. There was no consideration of the simultaneous effects of these two sets of behavioral relationships. In fact, it is highly probable that the effects of residential and activity behaviors on people's environmental experiences will either reinforce or counteract each other. For example, longtime residential occupancy and lower levels of activity both are theorized as contributing to old people's having more favorable environmental experiences and to their knowing more accurately the most salient features and properties of their proximate environments. In this unambiguous case, it would be predicted that old persons who have lived a long time in their current residences and whose activity behaviors have revolved around their dwellings and neighborhoods will be subjected to reinforcing forces that lead to similarly perceived environmental content and similarly evaluated consequences. More complicated and ambiguous relationships result when old people display counteracting individual behaviors, such as when they are longtime residents but have high activity levels that usually take them outside of their neighborhoods. Whereas longtime residential occupancy is theorized as producing predictable, status quo experiences, more frequent and locationally extensive activity behavior is theorized as increasing the opportunities for new and different environmental experiences. Lacking is any theoretical or empirical basis for predicting which of these individual behaviors will have the stronger or dominant influence. Along with empirical research to resolve this question, it would be informative to inquire whether old people living different lengths of time in the same place have modified or changed their activity behavior patterns for the purpose of obtaining different types of environmental experiences.

A second issue concerns the inability of this theoretical approach to predict unambiguously the impact of the cognitive and motivational states associated with people's initiation and interpretation of their activity and residential behaviors. Although it was proposed that on the average these states have secondary rather than dominant effects on old people's experiences, this was probably an oversimplified generalization. Clear documentation exists that involuntary behavior patterns, whether residential or activity, can produce negative emotional and physiological outcomes for old people (Brail, Hughes, & Arthur, 1976; Byerts, 1975; Cutler, 1975; Schulz & Brenner, 1977). In these circumstances, the outcomes of most environmental transactions are likely to be dominated by negative feelings and evaluations. A profitable empirical inquiry would be to identify how a representative set of personal states act in conjunction with particular activity and residential behaviors to influence old people's experiential outcomes.

A third unresolved issue concerns the range of values of activity and residential behaviors (that is, length of time, frequency, locational extent) that are most likely to "produce" the theorized outcomes. The convenience of analytical discourse dictated that monotonic relationships be implied between the proposed individual behaviors and environmental experiences. These probably oversimplify the true relationships. It is more reasonable to expect that once a particular threshold of activity frequency or residential occupancy length of time has been surpassed, then the marginal effects of more years or more travel will be small. For example, the impact of a residential occupancy period of 10 years may differ little from that of 25 years. Empirical research is necessary to establish these threshold levels.

Proposing activity and residential behaviors as individual differences that influence old people's environmental experiences raises a research issue that has been given considerable attention in the behavioral sciences. This concerns the debate as to whether individual or environmental (situational) factors explain more variation in human behavior. One conclusion from this debate was that the most critical research was not being carried out. This was to identify the environmental conditions (or situations) in which individual variables tended to be better or worse predictors of human behavior (for example, see Mischel, 1973).

This question can be raised in reference to this chapter's theoretical approach. That is, in what types of environments will activity and residential behaviors have a stronger impact on an elderly population's environmental experiences? In part, this question was addressed earlier when it was argued that research taking place in laboratories or other small-scale environments did not have to consider a population's activity behavior because there were in effect no distances to overcome in these settings—environmental occupancy implied environmental contact and utilization. Additionally, more general environmental conditions can be theorized as influencing the impact of a population's variable activity and residential behaviors. Expressed in proposition form:

- The more heterogeneous, complex, unpredictable, unextreme, and unrestrictive the properties of the environment, the more likely that variation in the content and consequences of environmental experiences will be explained by a population's activity and residential behaviors.

Since it is an important research issue, it is helpful to give some of the reasoning behind this proposed relationship.

When an environment's contents are homogeneous (or uniform) and simple (that is, few components, designated by few properties), people's variable activity behaviors are predicted to make less of an impact on their environmental experiences, because similar opportunities for experiences will exist in almost all spatial and temporal contexts. Additionally, the greater environmental familiarity that is theorized as accompanying longer length of occupancy will have little significance, because accurate and complete cognitive representations of these homogeneous and simple environmental conditions will be achievable in a much shorter time period.

In an environment distinguished by its predictability and certainty, human activities are less likely to have the potential of yielding spontaneous experiences, simply because the relevant opportunities will be fewer. Furthermore, in a predictable environment, the greater environmental familiarity and feelings of security that would be derived from a longer duration in residence would be much less significant.

When an environment has properties consistently aligned along the extreme end of certain dimensions of attributes (for example, extremely noisy, very high crime rate, or very hot temperatures), then an individual's residential and activity behaviors will less effectively modify or change the impact of these qualities. In effect, it is less likely that the activity and residential behaviors of individuals can "create" any satisfactory environmental contents.

Finally, and most obviously, when the qualities of the environment continually restrict activity or residential behaviors, then, by definition, these behaviors cease to become mechanisms by which individuals can select, modify, or change the contents of their environment.

At some risk of oversimplification, the presence and absence of these above conditions can be associated with certain archetype environments. At one extreme are the large cosmopolitan urban centers of Paris,

New York, London; at the other extreme are the small rural towns and villages located at considerable distance from other large centers. In the former environments, distinguished by their heterogeneous, complex, unpredictable, and unrestrictive contents (by virtue of their large number of accessible resources), activity and residential behaviors are more likely to influence a population's environmental experiences. (For instance, one can escape from the perceived monotony of the suburbs by travelling to the excitement and lights of the city.) In the latter environments, distinguished by opposite environmental conditions, these behaviors are likely to have much less impact.

The empirical testing of the above proposition in such archetype environments should provide evidence of the strengths and the weaknesses of the theoretical approach presented in this chapter.

REFERENCES

Altman, I. *The environment and social behavior*. Monterey, Calif.: Brooks/Cole, 1975.

Antonucci, T. Attachment: A life-span concept. *Human Development*, 1976, *19*, 135–142.

Arling, G. The elderly widow and her family, neighbors and friends. *Journal of Marriage and the Family*, 1976, *38*, 757–768.

Atkin, C. K. Mass media and the aging. In H. J. Oyer & E. J. Oyer (Eds.), *Aging and Communication*. Baltimore: University Park Press, 1976, pp. 99–118.

Barker, R. G. *Ecological psychology*. Stanford, Calif.: Stanford University Press, 1968.

Berry, B. J. L., & Kasarda, J. D. *Contempory urban ecology*. New York: Macmillan, 1977.

Bloom, B. S. *Stability and change in human characteristics*. New York: Wiley, 1964.

Bogue, D. J., & Bogue, E. J. *Essays in human ecology*. Chicago: Community and Family Study Center, University of Chicago, 1976.

Botwinick, J. *Aging and behavior*. New York: Springer, 1973.

Bowers, D. S. Situationism in psychology: An analysis and a critique. *Psychological Review*, 1973, *5*, 307–337.

Brail, R. K., Hughes, J. W., & Arthur, C. A. *Transportation services for the disabled and elderly*. New Brunswick, N. J.: Center for Urban Policy Research, Rutgers University, 1976.

Buckley, W. *Sociology and modern systems theory*. Englewood Cliffs, N. J.: Prentice-Hall, 1967.

Bultena, G. Rural-urban differences in the familial interaction of the aged. *Rural Sociology*, 1969, *39*, 5–15.

Byerts, T. O. (Ed.). Symposium—The city: A viable environment for the elderly? Phase 1. *The Gerontologist*, 1975, *15*, 13–46.

Campbell, A., Converse, P. E., & Rodgers, W. L. *The quality of American life*. New York: Russell Sage Foundation, 1976.

Cantril, H. *The pattern of human concerns*. New Brunswick, N. J.: Rutgers University Press, 1965.

Carp, F. Walking as a means of transportation for retired people. *Gerontologist*, 1971, *11*, 104–111.

Cath, S. H. The orchestration of disengagement. *International Journal of Aging and Human Development*, 1975, *6*, 199–213.

Chapin, F. S., Jr. *Human activity patterns in the city.* New York: Wiley, 1974.

Chapin, F. S. Jr., & Brail, R. K. Human activity systems in the metropolitan United States. *Environment and Behavior*, 1969, *1*, 107–130.

Cumming, J., & Cumming, E. *Ego and milieu.* New York: Atherton, 1963.

Cumming, E., & Henry, W. *Growing old: The process of disengagement.* New York: Basic Books, 1961.

Cutler, S. Transportation and changes in life satisfaction. *The Gerontologist*, 1975, *15*, 155–159.

DeGrazia, S. The uses of time. In R. W. Kleemeier (Ed.), *Aging and leisure.* New York: Oxford University Press, 1961, pp. 113–153.

Dowd, J. J. Aging as exchange: A preface to theory. *Journal of Gerontology*, 1975, *30*, 584–594.

Downs, R. M., & Stea, D. Cognitive maps and spatial behavior: Process and products. In R. M. Downs & D. Stea (Eds.), *Image and environment: Cognitive mapping and spatial behavior.* Chicago: Aldine, 1973, pp. 8–26.

Endler, N. S., & Magnusson, D. (Eds.). *Interactional psychology and personality.* New York: Wiley, 1976.

Faris, R. E. L., & Dunham, H. W. *Mental disorders in urban areas.* Chicago: University of Chicago Press, 1939.

Fischer, C. S., & Jackson, R. M. Suburbs, networks, and attitudes. In B. Schwartz (Ed.), *The changing face of the suburbs.* Chicago: University of Chicago Press, 1976, pp. 279–307.

Gans, H. *The Levittowners: Ways of life and politics in a new suburban community.* New York: Random House, 1967.

Gibson, J. J. The concept of the stimulus in psychology. *American Psychologist*, 1960, *15*, 694–703.

Golant, S. *The residential location and spatial behavior of the elderly: A Canadian example* (Department of Geography Research Paper No. 143). Chicago: Department of Geography, University of Chicago, 1972.

Golant, S. Intraurban transportation needs and problems of the elderly. In M. P. Lawton, R. J. Newcomer, & T. O. Byerts (Eds.), *Community planning for an aging society.* Stroudsburg, Pa.: Dowden, Hutchinson & Ross, 1976, pp. 282–308.

Golant, S. Spatial context of residential moves by elderly persons. *International Journal of Aging and Human Development*, 1977–1978, *8*, 279–289.

Golant, S. (Ed.). *Location and environment of elderly population.* New York: Wiley, 1979.

Golant, S. Individual differences underlying the dwelling satisfaction of the elderly. *Journal of Social Issues*, 1982, *38*, 121–133.

Golant, S. *A place to grow old: The meaning of environment in old age.* New York: Columbia University Press, 1984.

Golledge, R. G. Learning about urban environments. In T. Carlstein, D. Parkes, & N. Thrift (Eds.), *Timing space and spacing time* (Vol. 1). London: Edward Arnold, 1978, pp. 76–98.

Golledge, R. G., & Zannaras, G. Cognitive approaches to the analysis of human spatial behavior. In W. H. Ittelson (Ed.), *Environmental cognition.* New York: Seminar Press, 1973, pp. 59–94.

Gordon, C., & Gaitz, C. M. Leisure and lives: Expressivity across the life span. In R. H. Binstock & E. Shanas (Eds.), *Handbook of aging and the social sciences.* New York: Van Nostrand Reinhold, 1976, pp. 310–341.

Graney, M. J., & Graney, E. E. Communications activity substitutions in aging. *Journal of Communication*, 1974, *24*, 88–96.

Hartup, W. W., & Lempers, J. A problem in life-span development: The interactional analysis of family attachments. In P. B. Baltes & K. W. Schaie (Eds.), *Life-span developmental psychology: Personality and socialization*. New York: Academic Press, 1973, pp. 235–252.

Havighurst, R. J. The nature and values of meaningful free-time activity. In R. W. Kleemeier (Ed.), *Aging and leisure*. New York: Oxford University Press, 1961, pp. 309–344.

Havighurst, R. J., & Albrecht, R. *Older people*. New York: Longmans Green, 1953.

Havighurst, R. J., & Glassen, R. An exploratory study of reminiscence. *Journal of Gerontology*, 1972, 27, 245–253.

Havighurst, R. J., Neugarten, B. L., & Tobin, S. Disengagement and patterns of aging. In B. L. Neugarten (Ed.), *Middle age and aging: A reader in social psychology*. Chicago: University of Chicago Press, 1968, pp. 161–172.

Helson, H. *Adaptation-level theory*. New York: Harper & Row, 1964.

Hochschild, A. R. Disengagement theory: A critique and proposal. *American Sociological Review*, 1975, 40, 553–569.

Howell, S. D. Environments as hypotheses in human aging reserach. In L. W. Poon (Ed.), *Aging in the 1980s*. Washington, D. C.: American Psychological Association, 1980, pp. 424–432.

Ittelson, W. H. Environment perception and contemporary perceptual theory. In W. H. Ittelson (Ed.), *Environment. and cognition*. New York: Seminar Press, 1973, pp. 1–19.

Ittelson, W. H., Franck, K. A., & O'Hanlon, T. J. The nature of environmental experience. In S. Wapner, S. B. Cohen, & B. Kaplan (Eds.), *Experiencing the environment*. New York: Plenum Press, 1976, pp. 187–206.

Kalish, R. A., & Knutson, F. W. Attachment versus disengagement: A life-span concept. *Human Development*, 1976, 19, 171–181.

Kasarda, J. D., & Janowitz, M. Community attachments in mass society. *American Sociological Review*, 1974, 39, 328–339.

Kasl, S. V. Physical and mental health effects of involuntary relocation and institutionalization—A review. *American Journal of Public Health*, 1972, 62, 379–384.

Kelman, H. C. Attitudes are alive and well and gainfully employed in the sphere of action. *American Psychologist*, 1974, 9, 310–324.

Koffka, K. *Principles of gestalt psychology*. New York: Harcourt Brace, 1935.

Kuhlen, R. G. Developmental changes in motivation during the adult years. In B. L. Neugarten (Ed.), *Middle age and aging*. Chicago: University of Chicago Press, 1968, pp. 115–136.

Kutner, B. *Five hundred over sixty*. New York: Russell Sage Foundation, 1956.

Kuypers, J. A., & Bengston, V. L. Competence and social breakdown: A socio-psychological view of aging. *Human Development*, 1973, 16, 37–49.

Lansing, J. B., & Mueller, E. *The geographic mobility of labor*. Ann Arbor, Mich: Institute for Social Research, University of Michigan, 1967.

Larson, R. Thirty years of research on the subjective well-being of older Americans. *Journal of Gerontology*, 1978, 33, 109–129.

Lawton, M. P. The impact of the environment on aging and behavior. In J. E. Birren & K. Warner Schaie (Eds.), *Handbook of the psychology of aging*. New York: Van Nostrand Reinhold, 1977, pp. 276–301.

Lawton, M. P. The housing problems of community-resident elderly. In R. Boynton (Ed.), *Occasional papers in housing and community affairs* (Vol. 1). Washington, D. C.: U.S. Dept. of Housing and Urban Development, 1978, pp. 39–74.

Lawton, M. P. *Environment and aging*. Belmont, Calif.: Wadsworth, 1980.

Lawton, M. P., & Nahemow, L. Ecology and the aging process. In C. Eisdorfer & M. P. Lawton (Eds.), *Psychology of adult development and aging*. Washington, D. C.: American Psychological Association, 1973, pp. 619–674.

Lawton, M. P., Kleban, M., & Carlson, D. The inner city resident: To move or not to move. *Gerontologist*, 1973, *13*, 443–448.

Lazarus, R. S. *Psychological stress and the coping process*. New York: McGraw-Hill, 1966.

Lee, G. R., & Lassey, M. L. Rural-urban differences among the elderly: Economic, social, and subjective factors. *Journal of Social Issues*, 1980, *36*, 62–74.

Leff, H. *Experience, environment, and human potentials*. New York: Oxford University Press, 1978.

Lerner, R. M., & Ryff, C. D. Implementation of the life-span view of human development: The sample case of attachment. In P. B. Baltes (Ed.), *Life-span development and behavior* (Vol. 1). New York: Academic Press, 1978, pp. 2–44.

LoGerfo, M. Three ways of reminiscence in theory and practice. *International Journal of Aging and Human Development*, 1980–81, *12*, 39–48.

Maddox, G. L. Activity and morale: A longitudinal study of selected elderly subjects. *Social Forces*, 1963, *42*, 195–204.

Maddox, G. Persistence of life style among the elderly: A longitudinal study of patterns of social activity in relation to life satisfaction. In B. L. Neugarten (Ed.), *Middle age and aging*. Chicago: University of Chicago Press, 1968, pp. 181–183.

Markovitz, J. Transportation needs of the elderly. *Traffic Quarterly*, 1971, *25*, 237–253.

Milgram, S. The experience of living in cities. *Science*, 1970, *167*, 1461–1468.

Mischel, W. Toward a cognitive social learning reconceptualization of personality. *Psychological Review*, 1973, *80*, 252–283.

Moore, G. T. Knowing about environmental knowing: The current state of theory and research on environmental cognition. *Environment and Behavior*, 1979, *11*, 33–70.

Moos, R. H. *The human context: Environmental determinants of behavior*. New York: Wiley-Interscience, 1976.

Murray, H. A. *Exploration in personality*. New York: Oxford University Press, 1938.

National Center for Health Statistics. Limitation of activity and mobility due to chronic conditions, United States, 1972. *Vital and Health Statistics* (Series 10, No. 96). Rockville, Md.: U.S. Dept. of Health, Education & Welfare, 1974.

Newcomer, R. J. An evaluation of neighborhood service convenience for elderly housing project residents. In P. Suedfeld & J. A. Russell (Eds.), *The behavioral basis of design* (Vol. 1). Stroudsburg, Pa.: Dowden, Hutchinson & Ross, 1976, pp. 301–307.

Newman, S. J., & Duncan, G. J. Residential problems, dissatisfaction, and mobility. *Journal of the American Planning Association*, 1979, *45*, 154–166.

Niebank, P. *The elderly in older urban areas*. Philadelphia: Institute for Environmental Studies, 1965.

Norbert-Schulz, C. *Existence space, and architecture*. New York: Praeger, 1971.

Parr, J. The interaction of persons and living environments. In L. W. Poon (Ed.), *Aging in the 1980s*. Washington, D. C.: American Psychological Association. 1980, pp. 393–406.

Pervin, L. A. Definitions, measurements, and classifications of stimuli, stimulations, and environments. *Human Ecology*, 1978, *6*, 71–105.

Regnier, V. Neighborhood images and use: A case study. In M. P. Lawton & S. L. Hoover (Eds.), *Community housing choices for older Americans*. New York: Springer, 1981, pp. 180–197.

Rogers, C. R. *Client-centered therapy: Its current practice, implications, and theory*. Boston: Houghton Mifflin, 1951.

Rowles, G. D. The last new home: Facilitating the older person's adjustment to institutional space. In S. Golant (Ed.), *Location and environment of elderly population.* New York: Wiley, 1979.

Schulz, R., & Brenner, G. F. Relocation of the aged: A review and theoretical analysis. *Journal of Gerontology,* 1977, *32,* 323–333.

Shibutani, T. A cybernetic approach to motivation. In W. Buckley (Ed.), *Modern systems research for the behavioral scientist.* Chicago: Aldine, 1968, pp. 330–342.

Simon, H. *Models of man.* New York: Wiley, 1957.

Speare, A. Home ownership, life cycle stage, and residential mobility. *Demography,* 1970, *7,* 449–458.

Stokols, D. Environmental psychology. *Annual Review of Psychology,* 1978, *29,* 253–295.

Taylor, C. C., & Townsend, A. R. The local "sense of place" as evidenced in North-East England. *Urban Studies,* 1976, *13,* 133–146.

Thibaut, J. W., & Kelley, H. H. *The social psychology of groups.* New York: Wiley, 1959.

Thomae, H. The concept of development and life-span developmental psychology. In P. B. Baltes & O. G. Brim, Jr. (Eds.), *Life-span development and behavior* (Vol. 2). New York: Academic Press, 1979, pp. 281–312.

U.S. Bureau of the Census. *Census of housing, 1970: Housing of senior citizens.* Subject Reports. Final Report HC(7)–2. Washington, D. C.: U. S. Government Printing Office, 1973.

U.S. Bureau of the Census. Geographical mobility: March 1975 to March 1980. *Current Population Reports, Series P–20,* No. 368. Washington, D. C.: U.S. Government Printing Office, 1981.

Varady, D. Housing problems and mobility plans among the elderly. *Journal of the American Planning Association,* 1980, *46,* 301–314.

Wachtel, P. L. Psychodynamics, behavior therapy and the implacable experimenter: An inquiry into the consistency of personality. *Journal of Abnormal Psychology,* 1973, *82,* 324–334.

Wapner, S., Kaplan, B., & Cohen, S. B. An organismic-developmental perspective for understanding transactions of men in environments. *Environment and Behavior,* 1973, *5,* 255–289.

Wheatley, P. Levels of space awareness in the traditional Islamic city. *Ekistics,* 1976, *253,* 354–366.

Windley, P. G., & Scheidt, R. J. Person–environment dialectics: Implications for competent functioning in old age. In L. W. Poon (Ed.), *Aging in the 1980s.* Washington, D. C.: American Psychological Association, 1980, pp. 407–423.

Windley, P. G. & Scheidt, R. J. An ecological model of mental health among small-town rural elderly. *Journal of Gerontology,* 1982, *37,* 235–242.

Wohlwill, J. F. Environmental aesthetics: The environment as a source of affect. In I. Altman & J. F. Wohlwill (Eds.), *Human behavior and environment* (Vol. 1). New York: Plenum Press, 1976, pp. 37–86.

Wohlwill, J. F., & Kohn, I. Dimensionalizing the environment manifold. In S. Wapner, S. B. Cohen, & B. Kaplan (Eds.), *Experiencing the environment.* New York: Plenum Press, 1976, pp. 19–53.

Wolman, B. B. (Ed.). *Dictionary of behavioral science.* New York: Van Nostrand Rinhold, 1973.

Wynn, F. H., & Levinson, H. S. Some considerations in appraising bus transit potentials. *Highway Research Record,* 1967, *197,* 1–24.

Zajonc, R. B. Feeling and thinking preferences need no inferences. *American Psychologist,* 1980, *35,* 151–175.

Zimmer, B. G. Participation of migrants in urban structures. *American Sociological Review,* 1955, *20,* 218–224.

9

A Complementary/ Congruence Model of Well-Being or Mental Health for the Community Elderly

FRANCES M. CARP AND ABRAHAM CARP

INTRODUCTION

The scope of this chapter is somewhat unusual. Ordinary treatment of such a topic would be a review and theoretical exposition or a briefer exposition linked to an empirical test of a model. Instead, this chapter comprises a review and theoretical exposition, including the operationalization of cogent variables, but a test of the model is not included. Reference is made to a pilot study, but its results are to follow in later publications. Thus the chapter presents a three-quarter view. The intent is to describe how theory was used to approach a research issue and to grapple with the many problems of measurement. Deviation from a traditional approach hinged on space considerations and the importance of focusing on the processes of trying to bring various perspectives to bear upon a problem. The chapter deals with integration of the literature toward development of a conceptual model and exemplars of the types of measurement strategies that fall within the domain of that model. The

FRANCES M. CARP and ABRAHAM CARP • The Wright Institute, Berkeley, California 94704. Development of the model and instruments with which to make it operational was supported by research grant MH/AG 32668.

first section sketches the model's parentage and special issues that bear upon its development and briefly outlines the model. The next section describes relevant aspects of models which serve as background and resource for subsequent sections describing the attempt to integrate and build upon existing knowledge to provide a framework for studying the effects on older people of personal and environmental characteristics. They deal with model components: person, environment, person–environment congruence, mediators, and outcomes. The final section is traditional in that it points to future work.

OVERVIEW

Development of conceptual models about person–environment transactions for older people has concentrated on special populations, particularly the institutionalized and the frail. This is understandable from a pragmatic point of view, in that conduct of studies is easier; and justifiable on ethical and fiscal grounds, since these are the individuals who are most at risk and who impose the greatest cost on society. However, the large majority live independently in communities. In practical terms, understanding their salient traits, the relevant characteristics of their environments, and the nature of the person–environment transactions in their daily lives can enlighten efforts to improve life quality and reduce institutionalization. In terms of theory building, this triumvirate seems requisite to a conceptual model which will account for the behavior of older adults, generally, the majority as well as the frail.

The need to include "the real world out there" as well as perceptions of it has been stressed (Carp, 1976a; Craik, 1981; French, Rogers & Cobb, 1974; Lawton, 1975a; Moos & Lemke, 1980; Sells, 1963; Wohlwill, 1974). Although the social surround is of great importance, physical aspects of the living environment are also relevant. To avoid confounding in theoretical models, investigators must identify physical and social environmental variables that can be manipulated independently of person traits. For utility to policy and planning, research must deal with aspects of physical and social reality amenable to intervention through design and programs (Byerts, 1973). Ittelson (1960) demonstrated the inevitable circularity of phenomenological theories of perception. Research into person–environment transactions tends to fall into this fallacy, dealing with the environment only in subjective terms. To avoid circularity in theory building and ensure relevance to real-world interventions, the model uses objective measures of the environment of people and things.

Pervin (1974) asserts that Lewin's Field Theory (1951) and Murray's Need–Press Theory (1938) hold the best potential for explicating person–environment transactions, and this is borne out by the selection of bases for recent models. According to Lewin, behavior is a function of person and environment: $B = f(P,E)$. The Ecological Model (Lawton, 1975a; 1982) extends and specifies terms in the Lewinian equation. It focuses on P competence to meet E demand, although recently Lawton (1980a) writes of P as initiator. Our model includes the rationale of Lawton's, as well as that underlying the congruence models of Kahana and her associates (Kahana, 1975; Kahana et al., 1980) and Nehrke and his (Nehrke, Turner, Cohen, Whitbourne, Morganti, & Hulicka, 1981). These models derive from Murray and focus on the fit of E to P needs, a concept noted as important by various investigators (Carp, 1968, 1978; Carp & Carp, 1980; Fishbein & Adjen, 1975; Klinger, 1977; Rokeach, 1973). Our model resembles that of French, Rogers, and Cobb (1974), which is based on both Lewin and Murray and is not age-specific.

Our model is based on Murray's notion that well-being depends on appropriate satisfaction of needs by the environment, and needs are organized according to Maslow' (1954) hierarchy. In our model, the Lewinian equation includes a congruence term: $B = f(P, E, PcE)$.

The model has two parts, differentiated according to the level of need and type of congruence. (1) Part 1 of the model is concerned with lower-order or life-maintenance (LM) needs. Characteristics of P and E are those that facilitate/enable/inhibit lower-order need satisfaction through adequate performance of the activities of daily living ($ADLs$) requisite to continued (independent) living; that is, P competences and E resource/barriers relevant to ADLs. Congruence is the degree of *complementarity* between P competence and E resource/barrier relevant to ADLs. For example, when P competence is poor, prosthetic E may be necessary to achieve a satisfactory level of complementarity. (2) Part 2 of the model is concerned with higher-order (HO) needs and characteristics of E that facilitate/enable/inhibit their satisfaction. The congruence concept, here, is one of *similarity* between strength of need and amount of E supply. To recapitulate: in regard to life-maintenance (LM) needs, congruence is complementarity with or compensation for P competence; in regard to higher-order (HO) needs, congruence is similarity of E resource with P need.

In Part 1 of the model, both P and E variables are posited to affect outcomes directly. That is, some people are able to adapt in almost any E, whereas others are incapable of adapting to almost any E; similarly, some Es facilitate the conduct of $ADLs$ for nearly anyone, whereas others, exert demands or include barriers that can be met or overcome by very few. Both P and E components in Part 1 of the model have positive-negative valences. That is, in general, high or strong competence is favorable from the viewpoint of adaptation and so is positive environmental press (rich resources, low barriers regarding *ADL*), but low competence is unfavorable to adaptation, as is negative environmental press (meager resources, high barriers regarding *ADL*). The *degree of fit* between P competence and E demand will account for additional variance. That is, adaptation depends on P competence and E demand, and on complementarity (e.g., strong, agile P and E with stairs, or poor vision P and well-lighted and well-signed E) or compensation (e.g., wheel-chair P and specially designed kitchen). Here, the complementary or compensation term is represented by a certain statistical interaction as defined in analysis of variance. However, the relationship is not conceived as linear; with regard to (independent) life-maintenance, persons in some low P and low E category are the ones at risk. For those below some threshold of P competence and E demand complementarity, outcomes are likely to be deleterious, whereas, among those above that limen, increasing distance from it may have minimal effect (see Figure 1).

In Part 2 of the model, the degree of fit between higher-order (HO) needs and E resources is considered the major influence. The P and E variables are, in themselves, neither positive nor negative from an adaptational viewpoint; for example, it is no better for a person to have high or low need for privacy, or for an environment to provide much or little. The salient issue is the match between individual and environment. Here, optimal fit does not involve a compensatory or complementary relationship but one of similarity (high P need for privacy and high E provision of privacy) (see Figure 2).

In various studies and models, P has been one or more of a variety

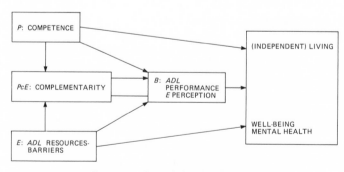

Figure 1.   Partial sketch of Part 1.

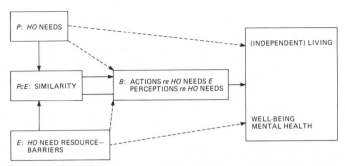

Figure 2.   Partial sketch of Part 2. Solid arrows represent major effect; dashed arrows represent minor effect.

of traits, and E has usually been Murray's "beta press," the environment as perceived and reacted to by the individual. In our model, as in that of French *et al.*, E_o is the factual environment of things and people, Murray's "alpha press," and possibly Lewin's "foreign hull." The perceived environment, French *et al.*'s subjective environment (E_s) and Murray's "beta press," is an intermediate outcome of the P,E_o transaction. In Part 1, P traits predictive of outcomes directly and through complementary or compensatory relationships with E_o characteristics are the traditional coping resources or competences: cognitive, sensory, motor, and health; and E_o characteristics predictive of outcomes directly and through complementary or compensatory relationships with P competences are objective conditions relevant to satisfaction of Maslow's lower-order or life-maintenance (LM) needs through performance of requisite ADLs. In Part 2, P traits predictive of outcomes through similarity with E_o are higher-order needs and personality traits relevant to the living environment; and E_o characteristics are aspects of the physical and human surround, assessed objectively and independently of respondents.

Outcomes may be modified or mediated by (1) other intrapersonal characteristics (sense of personal competence, coping style, and attitude toward current health); (2) extrinsic situations which are the results of previous and current P,E transactions (status resources/deprivations and social supports); and (3) life events.

Intermediate outcomes are perception of and behavior in the environment relevant to each P and E_o combination. Ultimate outcomes are continued (independent) living and overall well-being or mental health. They are affected by the two parts of the model, conjointly: (1) P

competence, E_o demand, and *PcE* complementarity-compensation in regard to *LM* needs; and (2) *PcE* similarity in regard to *HO* needs and personality traits. Death ensues from the failure of the person-in-environment; independent living is a societal goal, and maintenance of autonomous function among the institutionalized seems desirable to gerontologists; and the positive end of whatever is meant by such terms as mental health and overall well-being represents the optimal outcome of the person–environment relationship. Continued (independent) living comprises longevity, noninstitutionalization, and autonomous function within institutions. Mental health or well-being is defined in terms of positive affect, lack of maladaptive behavior, and good morale/life satisfaction as assessed with standard instruments.

Figure 3 shows the full model in simplified form. It sketches only the major elements and indicates their relationships in only one direction. For example, it is obvious that behavior in *E* may affect that factual environment and its congruence with *P* traits. This is but one phase of an ongoing, reciprocal interaction among components. Such simplification is necessary for explanatory purposes.

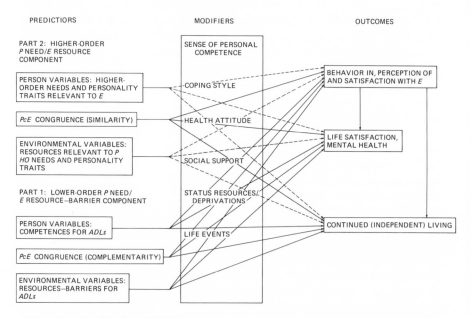

Figure 3.   Simplified model. Solid arrows represent major effect; dashed arrows represent minor effect.

RELEVANT CONTEMPORARY MODELS

THE ECOLOGICAL MODEL

This model (Lawton, 1975a; Lawton & Nahemow, 1973; Nahemow & Lawton, 1973) expands the Lewinian equation to make explicit the interactional term: $B = f(P,E,PxE)$. P traits comprise "competence": "the theoretical upper limit of capacity in biological health, sensation-perception, motor behavior, and cognition" (Lawton, 1982, p. 38). Ego strength is thought relevant but omitted because of measurement problems, and "explicitly excluded are needs and personality traits" (Lawton, 1977, p. 296). E is "demand quality" upon P competence, has physical and suprapersonal (characteristics of persons in the environment) components, and should be measured at both alpha (objective) and beta press (perceived) levels. Excessive E demand in relation to P competence leads to stress and negative consequences; inadequate E demand, to loss of competence through disuse; the ideal E demands full use of residual competence (the "zone of maximum performance potential"). According to the "environmental docility hypothesis" (Lawton & Simon, 1968), the lower P competence, the greater the participation of E demand in accounting for variance in B. This model has had great influence on the field, and aspects of it, particularly the docility hypothesis, have been supported by data. The model as a whole remains to be tested empirically. Part 1 of the present model is essentially the ecological model, operationalized in somewhat different measures.

MOOS' MULTIPHASIC ENVIRONMENTAL ASSESSMENT PROCEDURE (MEAP)

The MEAP, which is based on the conceptualization of Moos and his associates of the ecology of sheltered-care facilities for the elderly, measures four resource domains: physical and architectural, policy and program, resident and staff, and perceived social climate (Moos & Lemke, 1980; Moos, Lemke & Clayton, 1981). After controlling for type of facility, both E attributes (policy choice and resident control) and characteristics of the resident population (social resources, functional ability, and proportion female) explained significant variance in residents' perceptions of the social climate and/or observer ratings of the pleasantness of the facility. The interaction between amount of resident control exercised by the facility and functional ability of residents explained additional variance in three of the six outcome scales. An interaction between degree of policy choice allowed and proportion of female residents also made a significant contribution to pleasantness. These findings support this team's conception of the ecology as comprising effects of environmental and resident population characteristics, and interactions between them, upon outcomes.

WINDLEY'S AND SCHEIDT'S MODEL

This path model (Windley & Scheidt, 1980, 1982) includes five exogenous variables: two ecological-architectural (perceived environmental constriction and satisfaction with dwelling features) and three demographic (age, education, and length of residence); and three endogenous psychosocial variables adapted from Moos (community satisfaction, community involvement, and isolation–withdrawal) which mediate the effects of the exogenous variables on well-being (mental health, activity, security, contact with friends, and contact with relatives). The model accounted for significant though modest variance in mental health for elderly residents of small towns. The best predictors were perceived environmental constriction, satisfaction with dwelling features, and satisfaction with the community. The predictive efficiency of the model was less satisfactory regarding the other four dimensions of well-being.

CONGRUENCE APPROACHES

The degree of fit of the individual's competences, needs, and personality or life style with the environment of things and people is an alternative explanatory concept. Congruence between a person's needs and the environment, which serves as a barrier or resource to meet them, may be relevant to continued (independent) living and to life quality, well-being, or mental health. To clarify the roles of activity (Havighurst, Neugarten, & Tobin, 1968) and disengagement (Cumming & Henry, 1961) in relation to well-being, Carp (1968) studied the effects of congruence between personal proclivities for three kinds of engagement: informal socializing, volunteer (unpaid) activity, and (paid) work, and opportunities to satisfy them. Results support the relevance of congruence between proclivity and opportunity for all three outcomes: respondent happiness, peer sociometric nominations, and adjustment as rated by observers. Carp also demonstrated the influence of congruence between individuals' needs and environmental resources with regard to activity rates (1978) and sociability (Carp & Carp, 1980).

French et al. (1974) developed the congruence concept in a general theory, not specific to aging, based on the Lewinian paradigm and including Murray's attention to E resources relative to P needs. It differentiates objective and subjective environmental characteristics (E_o and E_s) and personal traits (P_o and P_s), making possible measures of objective and subjective fit: $F_o = f(E_o - P_o)$ and $F_s = f(E_s - P_s)$. Adjustment is a function of the summation of congruences. Lack of fit produces stress which can be evaluated behaviorally (e.g., coping response) or biologically (e.g., blood cholesterol). In secondary analyses of data to test the model, results for both types of outcome were in the expected direction: for example, poor fit on pertinent variables was associated with leaving the environment (high school) in one case and higher cholesterol levels in the other (NASA workers).

Kahana (1975), basing her work on that of French *et al.*, proposed that the optimal E is person-specific and that its characteristics are defined by the degree to which it meets the individual's needs. In view of the docility hypothesis, she selected the population for development of her model on the basis of vulnerability to E (relatively intact nursing-home residents). Needs are measured in terms of resident preferences and E supply in terms of staff ratings, using comparable scales on dimensions salient to such settings. The hypothesis that congruence between resident preferences and E opportunities to exercise those preferences is associated with high morale was upheld in two of three nursing homes. Congruence was most important where options were limited by personal vulnerability, environmental restrictions, or the residents' perception of a high degree of external control. Congruence was particularly important for privacy, impulse control, stimulation, continuity with the past, and change versus sameness. Kahana *et al.* (1980) found $P-E$ fit important to morale in the arenas of congregation (i.e., closeness of individuals and degree of privacy), impulse control, and segregationn. P and/or E characteristics were more important than congruence for affective expression and institutional control.

Kiyak (1978) modified Kahana's model with regard to privacy, isolation, and social solitude, using resident perceptions rather than staff ratings for E measures. Dependent variables were satisfaction, morale, and the wish to remain in the nursing home. For physical privacy and isolation, congruence was a better predictor of outcomes than were P and E alone; for solitude, preference was more important than congruence.

Nehrke and his associates (1981) used a variant of Kahana's methodology in long-term care facilities, VA domiciliary and other. As in Kiyak's work, resident perceptions represent E. In neither type of setting did Nehrke's respondents view E along Kahana's dimensions. Using dimensions based on expanded item pools and empirical clustering, data support the role of congruence, the environmental docility hypothesis, and Kahana's finding that prediction is better in restrictive or highly institutional settings.

FURTHER MODEL DEVELOPMENT

The work of Kahana, Nehrke, and their associates indicates that the concepts of personal need, environmental resource/barrier, and congruence between P and E hold promise as a basis for an explanatory model. Lawton's is not explicitly a congruence model, but it includes the interaction term which is one way of expressing the concept and, in discussing the large amount of unpredictability in housing and neighborhood satisfactions, he states:

> The most important missing element . . . is the inability of existing data to allow the analysis of joint effects of environmental deficits and personal deficits/deprivations, i.e., to what extent is there congruence between the capacities of the individual and the environment with which people must cope. (1978, p. 52)

The goal is a conceptual model applicable to the general population of elderly persons. The present model assumes that well-being is influenced by the extent to which P competence meets E demands necessary to continued (independent) living plus the extent to which E resources meet P need, not only for existence but also for higher-order needs such as affiliation, privacy, and esthetic experience. Previous work suggests that for some domains E characteristics or P traits are determinative while in others congruence plays a role. The patterns of P, E and PcE contributions are yet to be determined. With regard to congruence, the issue is whether and, if so, to what extent and in regard to what outcomes it accounts for variance *additional* to that accounted for by P and E. This requires, in analyses, that P and E be entered into the equation prior to entry of the congruence term. In measurement, it requires that scales to measure E and P be developed independently. Making operational these terms has proved difficult for the frail and is more so for the community resident.

In describing the model and its operationalization, reference will be made to a pilot study under way to provide a preliminary and partial test of the model. Respondents are 90 women 60 years and older, living independently and alone in a wide variety of environments in Oakland, California. This population was selected because of its size relative to the older population generally, its unusual vulnerability (Brotman, 1976), and to simplify the pilot by eliminating variance in gender and household composition (relevant to suprapersonal E and the informal support system).

GEOGRAPHICAL UNITS

Prior to selection of P and E variables and their measures, it is necessary to specify the geographic domain of interest. Possible levels of scale are almost endless. "We begin with personal space and room geography and go on to architectural space, neighborhoods, cities, larger conceptual regions, countries and the world" (Saarinen, 1976, p. 3). With the exception of the the work by Windley and Scheidt (1980, 1982), gerontological model building has been based largely on institutional data. We focus on the living unit and local residential area as the most salient for most people.

Living Unit (LU)

With age and retirement, an increasing proportion of time is spent in the living unit (LU). People 65 and older spend more time at home than any other age group beyond five. "Aside from his spouse, housing is probably the single most important element in the life of an older person" (Proceedings of the 1971 White House Conference on Aging, 1973, p. 30). The variable definition of *housing* and its confusion with *living environment* limits specification of causal relationships. *Housing* is sometimes LU and sometimes the entire environment, including not only all space but also the support systems. (For a discussion of this literature see Carp, 1976a) The present model separates LU from the surrounding local area. This is an arbitrary demarcation, but it makes for clarity in describing characteristics of E_o, physical and surprapersonal, and in taking their measures, and it is useful for policy and planning. Physical E_o at the LU level includes the residential structure and surrounding land parcel, exclusive of the interiors of other units in multifamily buildings. Suprapersonal E_o at the LU level comprises the number and characteristics of other household members. (To simplify the pilot study, this important element is omitted.)

Local Area (LA)

A special committee of the Gerontological Society, after review of the literature, suggested that the immediate neighborhood may be more important to well-being than the residence (Havighurst, 1969). "For some older people, economic, physical, and social limitations may restrict movement to a point where their neighborhoods are the only salient supraperson environments" (Lawton, 1977, p. 284). To avoid the subjectivity of *neighborhood*, in obtaining E_o data distances to facilities are measured and counts of facilities within specified distances are taken. (Respondents also draw their own neighborhoods on maps, which allows development of indices of E_o characteristics within the perceived neighborhood.)

PERSON COMPONENTS (*P*)

PART 1 OF THE MODEL

Part 1 is concerned with the universal, physiological, life-maintenance (*LM*) needs of hunger, thirst, and homeostasis. Individual differences are not relevant. For example, concern is not with differences in amount of sleep required or taken, but in the need for sleep as a universal one and in the environmental provision for sleeping and resting as essential. Satisfaction of the *LM* needs is necessary to survival and depends upon satisfactory performance of the basic *ADLs*. In this part of the model, *P* variables are competences for performing *ADLs*, and *E* variables are resources/barriers in relation to *ADLs*. *ADL* categories for *LU* are: nutrition, sleep/rest, medication, medical care, hygiene, phoning, handling money, and housecleaning; for *LA*: nutrition, medication, other shopping, medical care, and banking; for *LU* and *LA*: laundry. Each category is amplified by breaking down each task into components (e.g., for *LU* nutrition: stove-top cooking; baking; cutting, mixing, preparing; keeping food cold; other food and kitchen storage; disposal of wet garbage; disposal of trash; and dishwashing). These *ADLs* are the core around which Part 1 is organized.

P Competence

P variables relevant to *ADLs* are competences. Lawton has paid the most careful attention to them. Part 1 of our model follows his, though we are more concerned with current functioning than with "theoretical upper limits" and suggest different measures.

Physical Health. According to Lawton, health is the absence of disease, as contrasted to functional health, which is an outcome of the interaction of *P* and *E* factors; health is commonly measured by laboratory tests of biological functions, signs, symptoms, and medical diagnoses. We make a similar distinction: objective health is a *P* variable, while perceived health or attitude toward health is a mediating variable. Medical examinations are often impossible due to cost and privacy intrusion. A proxy measure of objective health status is self-report on a checklist of specific diseases and symptoms. It is based on the instrument used by Carp (1966, 1977), the OARS (Duke University, 1977), and the Multilevel Assessment Instrument of the Philadelphia Geriatric Center (Lawton, Moss, Fulcomer, & Kleban, 1982). Only specific ailments and disorders are scored. Neurotic symptoms are scored separately and used to index mental health, an outcome.

Sensation-Perception. In Lawton's model sensation and perception include the primary processes of vision, audition, olfaction, gustation, somesthesis, and kinesthesis, and the more clearly differentiated aspects of these senses such as depth perception, flicker fusion, and pain perception. In terms of adaptation to *LU* and *LA*, various aspects of vision seem of utmost importance, and touch and muscle sense seem relevant. Olfaction, while important to safety and enjoyment, is difficult to measure. It does not seem appropriate to deal with pain thresholds. *Vision* measures include Snellen Charts (distant visual acuity), Graham–Field Cards (near-vision acuity), and Ishihara Plates (color vision). For *tactile sensitivity*, two-point limens are taken (repeated measures in randomly ascending and descending orders) at forearm, wrist, palm, and finger tip and averaged to produce limen scores, which proved scalable into one composite in the pilot data. For ability to *estimate weights*, we use weights of 100, 200, and 500 grams, in identical containers; and standard psychometric procedures for paired-comparison presentation. For *hearing*, an audiometer should be used. The pilot study lacked funds for reliable, valid, portable equipment, so we used the average of ratings made by the interviewer and the psychometrician on every visit (minimum $N = 6$). This is the only subjective item in the P set for the pilot.

Motor Functions. Lawton points out that motor skills are closely related to biological health and sensory-motor capacity and are not usually measured separately, though muscular strength can be measured with a dynamometer and coordination with apparatus such as a pursuit rotor. Fleishman (e.g., 1958) has conducted the most extensive factorial research on motor functions. Among the 11 factors he identified, five seem most relevant to P,E transactions in the living environment: *multi-limb coordination*: ability to coordinate gross movements requiring the simultaneous use of more than one limb in any combination; *manual dexterity*: ability to make skillful, self-controlled arm–hand movements in manipulating fairly large objects under speed conditions; *finger dexterity*: ability to make skillful, controlled manipulations of small objects, involving primarily finger movements; *wrist–finger speed*: ability to tap an object (pencil) rapidly within a relatively large area; and *aiming*: ability rapidly and accurately to place a dot in each of a series of small circles.

The first two are measured using the Minnesota Rate of Manipulation Test (Ziegler, 1946) which has reliabilities in the nineties. It is relatively unaffected by practice, and since practice effect on motor tasks is associated with the contribution of intellectual factors, this test is also a more nearly pure measure of motor function than are many (Anastasi, 1961). The third can be measured with the Finger Dexterity Board in the General Aptitude Test Battery used by the U.S. Employment Service (e.g., Cronbach, 1970) and which has been used with older adults (Nuttall & Fozzard, 1970). Because we were unable to obtain permission to use it, we substituted the number of kindergarten beads strung on a shoelace during a set time period. The fourth and fifth factors are measured by the tests which define those factors: a paper-and-pencil task requiring rapid tapping of a pencil in relatively large areas, and a paper-and-pencil task which requires placing a dot accurately and rapidly in each of a series of small circles. To measure *grip strength* we used a dynamometer.

We worked with physical therapists to develop a reliable *range-of-motion* evaluation. It provides objective standards for observation and numerical scoring of: *sitting:* upper extremeties (shoulder flexion, abduction, external rotation, internal rotation, elbow flexion, and forearm pronation/supination, wrist flexion, wrist extension, finger extension, finger opposition); lower extremeties (hip flexion, knee extension, knee flexion); neck (lateral flexion, rotation, flexion/extension); *standing:* hip abduction, toe/heel flexion; *walking,* and *posture.*

Using scores on all of the motor measures for the pilot sample, we extracted three principal components, which are the motor predictors.

Cognition.   Lawton suggests use of a standardized vocabulary test to approximate the "theoretical upper limit." We are more concerned with current level. A considerable amount of research into the cognitive abilities of the elderly has been carried out using psychometric tests and laboratory tasks, but little has been done to relate performance on cognitive tasks to performance in real life.

One exception is the work of Storandt, Wittels, and Botwinick (1975), who used the Bender–Gestalt, Hooper, Trailmaking, WAIS Comprehension, WAIS Digit Symbol, and Cross Off tests as measures of current function to predict well-being 11–19 months after testing (at or soon after admission to housing for the elderly). Criteria were averages of two independent ratings on five-point scales (e.g., played out, senile vs. vital, alert). Results were interpreted as supporting the role of cognition in making a new adaptation. However, it is not clear to what extent criterion ratings were based on cognitive cues. "Senile" and "alert" are common descriptors of cognitive status. In another study, WAIS IQs correlated substantially with a composite of interviewer ratings on confusion–clarity in regard to time, place, and person ($r = .62, p < .001$) but showed no relationship with one adjustment criterion, respondents' happiness, and modest associations with the other two, administrators' ratings of adjustment ($r = .19, p < .01$) and other residents' ($r = .21, p < .01$) over an 18-month period (and about one year after respondents moved to public housing) (Carp, 1966); and findings were similar at a nine-year interval (Carp, 1974).

Our battery comprises: MSQT, Cross Off, Trailmaking, WAIS Digit Symbol, Hooper Visual Organization, WAIS Comprehension, WAIS Information, WAIS Digit Span, and Primary Mental Abilities (PMA) Spatial Relations. Included are the Storandt *et al.* tests that best predicted their indices of well-being, measures of long-and short-term memory, and measures sensitive to organic brain damage. Testing begins with WAIS Comprehension, and there is a decision rule about whether to drop back to MSQT or continue with other parts of the battery. Use of MSQT was not required for any pilot respondent but would be with a frailer sample. Principal components analysis of the cognitive tests for the pilot data produced three components which are the cognitive predictors.

Limitations of Competences as Descriptors of Persons. Restriction of P characteristics to competences seems inappropriate for a model to accommodate independent-living as well as frail persons, and when concern is with life quality and well-being as well as with performance of ADLs. Biological health, sensation–perception, motor behavior, and cognition may be the salient P traits in accounting for the behavior of the frail elderly (the present model allows test of this hypothesis). Within normal ranges of P competence and E demand, other P traits may be more important to outcomes. In one study of community-resident elderly, personality variables (e.g., extraversion) accounted for more of the variance in well-being than did competence or social-status variables, and for criterion variance over and above that accounted for by competences and social status combined (Carp & Carp, 1983a).

The slopes of the lines or shapes of the curves representing relationships of the competences of older people with outcomes are not yet known throughout the score ranges. The situation may be as it is with cognitive abilities in educational research: applicants with scores below a cutting-point are likely to fail but, above that cutting-point, other factors such as motivation and study habits become more important in predicting academic success (e.g., Krech, Crutchfield & Livson, 1969). Competences may be powerful in determining outcomes of P,E transactions for elderly persons with scores or score profiles below some threshold value, but of limited utility in predicting outcomes for those within an adequate range of competences. In our model, P traits include but are not limited to competences; and the hypothesis regarding threshold values can be tested.

PART 2 OF THE MODEL

The second part of the model proposes that the fit, in terms of similarity, of higher-order needs and personality traits with relevant E resources will affect outcomes. P variables, like their E_o counterparts, have no positive-negative valences relative to adjustment, in and of themselves. That is, it is neither better nor worse, from an adaptation viewpoint, to have high or low need for affiliation; similarly, neither congregate nor solitary E_o is, in itself, "better." However, the P with high affiliative need will remain unsatisfied in that regard in an E_o with meager affiliation resources; and the P with low need will similarly be a misfit in an E_o rich in affiliation resources which, to that person, may represent unwelcome demands. The important issue, in the second part of the model, is that strength of need or personality trait be matched with that of the resources in E_o.

Higher-Order Needs

The Kahana and Nehrke groups propose needs as P predictors. There are problems in making that concept operational. Lawton (1975a) pointed out in respect to Kahana's model that expressed preference may not be an adequate measure of psychological need. The criticism is as germane to the models of Kiyak and Nehrke, and they involve additional statistical problems of nonindependence between P and E components of congruence, due to a common source (McNemar, 1962). In long-term care facilities such as those in which all of these investigators are working, expressed preference may partly reflect accommodation to institutional norms (which constitute Kahana's E measures), tendency to acquiesce (e.g., Messick & Jackson, 1961), and time since admission (Firestone, Lichtman, & Evans, 1977; Kiyak, 1978; Lawton & Bader, 1970). When community-resident elderly are "stuck" in a negative situation, their levels of aspiration accommodate to the situation, that is, aspirations lower (Campbell, Converse, & Rogers, 1976). This suggests that expressed preference (P) would also accommodate to the situation and therefore become more like perceptions of it (E), so that $P-E$ fit would improve. However, this may not be beneficial. Compbell *et al.* found that although stated satisfaction with the specific situation improved in such cases, overall happiness diminished. This accommodation process may involve a defensive psychological adaptation that is not without cost (Carp & Carp, 1981a). Measuring psychological need through stated preference seems questionable in predicting well-being for older people generally. It is even more questionable for the outcomes of satisfaction, morale, and the wish to remain in the institution, among frail and captive populations. The fact that Kahana's and Nehrke's models work best for residents for whom options are most limited is further evidence that these models may have little power in accounting for the behavior of noninstitutionalized people.

Also, their variables are institution-specific. A model to accommodate the full range of elderly people requires needs of general relevance. The lower-order (LM) needs provide the basis for Part 1 of the present model. Part 2 includes higher-order (HO) needs as defined in the psychological literature which seem relevant to measureable E_o variables: n Harmavoidance, n Noxavoidance, n Order, n Affiliation, n Similarity, n Privacy, and n Esthetic Experience. Most are familiar to readers, as discussed primarily in the work of Murray (1938) and his followers. One, n Similarity, although rooted in Murray's work, requires some explanation.

Need for Similarity. Given a choice, people seem to opt for homogeneity. Blacks and whites in planned housing tend to choose friends of their own color; German-born Jews tend to choose each other rather than other Jews (Simon & Lawton, 1966). In one development, the more a resident perceived other residents to be similar to oneself, the higher the satisfaction with other residents and with living there (Francescato, Weidemann, Anderson, & Cenoweth, 1979). In another, those who perceived their neighbors as being in the same social groups as themselves were the most satisfied with the project (Cooper, 1975). Similarity in age, gender, and race lessens effects of distance upon friendships (Nahemow & Lawton, 1975). These findings may obscure individual differences in need for similarity.

Several studies suggest that attitude toward age-segregated versus age-integrated setting may depend upon the strength of the individual's need for age-homogeneity. Sherman (1975) concluded that either situation can be satisfactory if the resident made the choice according to his or her own needs. People tend to select environments to maximize $P-E$ fit, and those who prefer or choose age-segregated and age-integrated environments have different opinions about which is better. Hamovitch and Peterson (1969) found the majority of older persons in high-density, age-peer situations negative to having families with children living nearby, whereas those in low-density, age-peer situations were about evenly split. After one year, tenants of age-specific public housing were "overwhelmingly" favorable about such a facility's being restricted to one age group; eight and a half years later, 56% were favorable (Carp, 1976b). People in age-segregated settings "overwhelmingly" approved of that life-style, and 37% of people in ordinary community settings would prefer it in the hypothetical situation of making a move (Lawton, 1980b). A secondary analysis of the Harris (1975) national-sample data showed that 52% of those 65 and older prefered living with "people your own age" (Lawton, personal communication). From a review of the literature, Lawton (1980c) concludes: "those already living in age-segregated environments approve heartily of that mode of living, but a minority of those still living in the community showed this preference" (p. 93).

Various studies show that residents of age-homogeneous settings differ from their age peers in desire to be among their own kind in ways additional to age. Others demonstrate status, life-style, and motivational differences between people who do and do not prefer age-segregated situations. Rosow (1967) and Rosenberg (1970) found that effects of age-density of elderly neighbors were modified by socio-economic status. Hamovitch and Peterson (1969) reported that preference for age-density was related to characteristics of present housing (quality and single-family rather than apartment) and to personal and social characteristics (marital status, social class, and distance from children). Sherman, Mangum, Dodds, Walkley, and Wilner (1968) reported that many retirement community residents had no children nearby and would like to see their children more often. Winiecke (1973) found that those who prefer or move to housing for the elderly tend to be habitual apartment renters, nondrivers, lonely and bored, and would like to live where everyone is "pretty much like themselves."

Clearly the need for age-homogeneity is not homogeneous across the elderly population. The same individual differences are posited with regard to P-Suprapersonal E_o similarity in other dimensions. People may vary in general desire for or tolerance of "the other." The long line of research on ethnocentrism (e.g., Adorno, Frenkel-Brunswick, Levinson, & Sanford, 1950; Allport, 1954) supports this view. Although in general interaction is facilitated by having something in common, and well-being is enhanced by the perception that one is "among one's own," the effects may depend upon individual differences in what might be called "need for similarity," which resembles Tolerance (Megargee, 1972) and n Rejection (Murray, 1938). In our model, n Similarity is a higher-order need, and one E_o variable is the factual similarity between P and su-prapersonal E. With respect to measurement, the Ethnocentrism, Conservation, and Fascism Scales (Adorno et al., 1950) have items rooted in the time of World War II. A derivative, the CPI Tolerance Scale (Megargee, 1972) is a very broad-band instrument and items are mostly of a neurotic type. Although it has proved valid in studies of prejudice and discrimination, our need was for a measure sharply focused on the issue of need for similarity with those in one's living environment. Therefore a 16-item scale was developed with alpha $= 0.85$ in pilot data.

Personality Traits

In addition to the higher-order needs, Part 2 includes two personality traits, extraversion and nosiness/gossip. The first is a traditional psychological variable with a good track record, and relevant E_o resources can be identified. The second proved important in congregate setting for the elderly (Carp, 1966, 1974; Carp & Carp, 1983b), and it has both physical and suprapersonal E_o counterparts.

Measures

Our approach, throughout, was to depend as heavily as possible upon the literature for instruments. Existing scales were used whenever possible, after pretesting as seemed necessary with community-resident elderly. Modifications or new instruments were developed only when necessary. With respect to the P traits in Part 2, in view of the problematic nature of preference as stand-in for psychological need, several years were spent in scale preparation. The first step was to specify a definition of each need and personality trait from the psychological literature. The second was to screen existing instruments which seem to measure what the definition describes or which include apparently relevant items. An earlier instrument by the authors was used. In predicting adjustment to Victoria Plaza and a replication at Villa Tranchese (Carp, 1966, Carp & Carp, 1983b), several of the components had proved important: extraversion, n Affiliation, n Order, n Esthetic Experience, and nosiness/gossip. Initial results were based on observer ratings, but efforts were immediately launched to provide self-report scales. In eight pretests using ad hoc samples, candidate scales and items for all sources were assessed for item variance and consistency within item pools, as well as score correlations with observer ratings. Table 1 shows the descriptive statistics for seven scales (n Similarity was not included in this pretest) for one sample ($N = 367$) who took these items, scrambled

TABLE 1
DESCRIPTORS OF NEED SCALES FOR ONE PRETEST

Scale	N of items	M	SD	T1 alpha	T2 alpha	Test–retest r	r with Crown-Marlowe
Harmavoidance	6	11.91	3.48	.69	.74	.81	−.16
Noxavoidance	5	15.23	3.28	.48	.36	.80	.00
Order	8	26.14	6.44	.78	.79	.80	.33
Affiliation	10	38.39	.35	.71	.74	.80	−.08
Extraversion–introversion	9	36.51	5.41	.76	.79	.76	.02
Privacy	13	47.56	9.94	.85	.86	.84	.10
Esthetic–cultural	16	36.79	9.25	.81	.83	.78	−.27

(N = 367)

TABLE 2
ALPHA COEFFICIENTS OF HIGHER-ORDER NEED SCALES IN
PILOT STUDY DATA

Need	Number of items	Alpha
Harmavoidance	25	.94
Noxavoidance	13	.82
Order	27	.94
Affiliation	30	.91
Similarity	13	.89
Extraversion	23	.88
Privacy	25	.89
Esthetic	26	87

$(N = 90)$

among several hundred, twice with a two-week interval. Social-desirability bias is indicated by correlations with the Crowne-Marlow Scale (1964). Pilot data are in Table 2.

OBJECTIVE ENVIRONMENTAL COMPONENTS (E_o)

Inclusion of the objective environment is easier recommended than accomplished. The problem surfaced early. Although Lewin's (1951) concept of "life space" implies an external referent, and Lewin coined a phrase ("foreign hull") for the objective environment, he treated E phenomenologically. Murray (1938) postulated both "alpha press" and "beta press," but studied only the latter in relation to behavior. The difficulty persists. Although French et al. (1974) specify E_o as well as E_s in their model, their tests of it are based largely on the latter. In one analysis of data on high-school boys, E_o was the intelligence required by the school as rated by teachers, and E_s was students' ratings of the school on how much it allowed and required them to use their intelligence. The other analysis dealt with affiliation. E_s was the students' ratings of how much the school provided opportunity to spend time with friends, and there was no E_o. In the second test, using responses from male NASA employees to parallel questions about current and desired job environments, perception of current job environment measured E_s, and again there was no E_o.

Lawton insists on the importance of objective measures of E and has made strenuous efforts toward making the ecological model operational along these lines. In one study Lawton and Kleban (1971) collected data on various aspects of the environment and used factor analysis to produce six *E* variables: central location (near transportation, park, amenities); distance from shopping facilities; independent household (own TV, stove, toilet, refrigerator); busy block (traffic and people); well-kept block and buildings; and nonresidential block (commercial, vacant houses, or lots). Measurement techniques are not described. In another (Lawton, Nahemow, and Teaff, 1975), physical characteristics of planned housing environments and their neighborhoods were sponsorship, community size, building size, and building height. The first is not a physical characteristic. In a later study (Lawton, Brody, & Turner-Massey, 1978), *E* was assessed by counts of the steps to climb to the entrance, and of steps from entrance to the tenant's bedroom; and by researcher ratings on size of dwelling unit, preponderance of dwelling-unit type on the block (single or multi-family), amount of commercial land use in the neighborhood, and 12 other neighborhood characteristics (e.g., apparent economic conditions, cleanliness, vacancy rate, age composition) plus 10 dwelling-unit characteristics (e.g., lighting, upkeep). *Neighborhood* was not defined. Principal components analysis produced two neighborhood factors: general quality and status similarity of neighbors to self, and two dwelling-unit factors: positive versus negative ambience and quality of maintenance. *E* variables used in analyses were the four factor scores and five single items: ratings on single versus multiple units, commerical versus residential land use, and dwelling size; and count of steps to entrance and to bedroom.

In yet another study (Lawton, 1980d), using Annual Housing Survey data, measures of "objective housing characteristics" were age of structure, number of units, number of floors, and length of occupancy. Does long or short tenancy by the present occupant describe superior *housing?* A more recent study (Lawton, 1981) also uses items from the Annual Housing Survey. Some are objective (e.g., single-family structure, hotel, rooming-house, one-room dwelling) and can be observed or obtained from the respondent without concern for bias. Others are necessarily dependent upon respondents to provide data (e.g., income, property value, repairs in last year, rent and housing costs exceed 25% of income) and objectivity is less secure. Some are questionable as *housing* descriptors. Even if income is *correlated* with housing quality, is it a *descriptor* of objective housing quality? Some applicants with incomes low enough to qualify them for public housing lived in standard or excellent physical housing but were eligible because of seriously adverse interpersonal situations (Carp, 1966). Do repairs in the past year indicate better or worse housing? Is the fact that rent or total housing costs exceed 25% of income a *housing* characteristic?

In Kahana's model, E variables are staff ratings on aspects of a nursing-home milieu, and P variables are resident preferences with regard to the same issues. In Kiyak's work and that of Nehrke and his associates, resident perceptions of the setting are the E variables and resident preferences the P variables. Kiyak and Nehrke's group hold that staff perceptions may not represent environmental reality for residents; Kahana's view is that independence must be maintained between P and E. Both views are defensible. However, in all these models E measures are taken of representations in someone's head.

In the MEAP of Moos and his associates, instruments for the physical and architectural resource domain are observer ratings, and those for policy and program, resident and staff, and perceived social climate are questionnaires for staff and residents. In the Windley and Scheidt model, the ecological and architectural variables are resident *satisfactions* with privacy, space, and so forth, and the degree to which they perceive that physical and social barriers hinder their participation in activities.

It is hardly surprising that people who like privacy and say their environments provide them with privacy are satisfied with the privacy they have. It is similarly unstartling that people who like privacy, and whose staff thinks the environment provides privacy, are satisfied about privacy. Boys who believe their school does not make appropriate academic demands upon their abilities or provide for their affiliation needs would quite likely think about dropping out of school. Satisfaction by residents with the architectural and physical aspects of their small towns, quite unsurprisingly, correlate with their general satisfaction with the towns.

Although it is reassuring to find relationships among different response formats and sources, attribution of causality remains a problem. Potential school dropouts may rationalize the decision in terms of academic demands and/or affiliation resources. Would changing the NASA job environment lower blood cholesterol? Satisfaction with physical and architectural attributes of small towns is perhaps more appropriately considered an aspect of the *outcome* of the P,E transaction. In long-term care facilities, E as measured by resident perceptions may tap accommodation to institutional norms, acquiescence set, and time since admission, all of which may also influence residents' stated satisfaction (outcome). If E is measured by staff ratings, institutional norms (which would be reflected in those ratings) may influence outcomes.

The debate regarding pros and cons of the various rating approaches continues. They share the common limitation of being restricted to a subjective interpretation of E, whether that of respondent, staff, or outside observer. Wohlwill (1974) points out that recent theories of environmental cognition may more greatly retard progress toward understanding the P,E transaction than do theories which simply ignore external reality, because them *seem* to deal with the issue of environmental input whereas actually they are concerned only with E as it is represented inside someone's head. He argues that unless "the environment out there" is used as a standard, there is no basis for interpreting individual differences in cognition of E. Inclusion of the real world is equally cogent when the purpose is improvement of people's living situations. Brunswik (1955) and Barker and his colleagues (1963) included aspects of E that are, at least in part, physical (the behavior setting). Moos increasingly emphasizes objective E measures. Nehrke's goals lie in that direction. One of the great strengths of Lawton's approach is the emphasis on truly environmental variables.

In making causal inferences or devising interventions, it is essential to know whether the independent variable is an objective fact or a perception of it. For example, if restriction of activity due to fear of mugging is caused by real street danger, money is appropriately spent on escort service and/or reducing street crime. However, older people may not always be particularly subject to victimization (Antunes, Cook, Cook, & Skogan, 1977) and in some cases fear and activity restriction are out of proportion to actualities of the situation. In the latter case, the need is to invest in altering perceptions (of older people and others, including the news media). The choice of an appropriate intervention or causal inference depends upon separation of objective and subjective environments. In addition, if improvement of E is a desired end, it is necessary to specify environmental elements that can be manipulated. Planners, designers, and program staffs are not much helped by research that finds privacy or convenience important. How can they translate the results into ways to improve the real world?

DEFINITION OF "OBJECTIVE"

Objective indices have had two different bases or some combination of them: observer judgments and direct measures. The former are criticized as actually "subjective" (Payne & Pugh, 1976) or "perceptual" (Pervin, 1978). Craik (1981) finds these terminological opinions unsatisfactory, since observers can produce composite measures with adequate reproducibility and generalizability. However, observer-based measures may be influenced by characteristics of the panel (Canter, 1969; Craik & Zube, 1976; Gifford, 1980; Hershberger, 1970), which questions their validity as descriptors of external reality. Observations by experts do not agree with those of nonexperts (Daniel & Boster, 1976; Fines, 1968; Kaplan, 1973; Milbrath & Sahr, 1975; Zube, 1974). Those of managers and planners do not coincide with those of users (Carp,

1976b, 1983; Kaiser, Weiss, Burby, & Donnelly, 1970; Lansing & Marans, 1969; Lucas, 1970; Michelson, 1966; Mitchell, 1971; Peterson, Bishop, & Michaels, 1974; Troy, 1971). Therefore, when interest lies in environmental impacts on residents, indicators based on observer data may not be appropriate. According to Craik (1981), "the value of observational assessment derives from its ability to tap differentiations among places that can be made only by human judges and that embody meaning within a socio-cultural framework" (p. 40). This implies that some E variables may be measurable only by human observers but does not deny that some may be measured directly.

Objective E and the Support Systems

There has been confounding of physical E_o, suprapersonal E_o, and the social support systems. In the Carp housing study (1966, 1974), the generally positive effects of the new E cannot be attributed to any one, since there was change in physical housing, characteristics of neighbors, and opportunities for social support. Although residents emphasized physical features in assessing the situation (Carp, 1976b), this is no guarantee that these were indeed more potent than the social; and results do not distinguish between suprapersonal E_o and the social support systems.

Several other studies fail to provide clear distinctions regarding whether impacts are determined by physical, suprapersonal, or social-support aspects, or how these influences interact to determine outcomes. Lawton (1976) looked at differences in outcome following entrance into a housing situation with supportive services or one requiring independent living. Persons in independent situations were more active and involved outside the facility while those in projects with more services showed greater improvement in morale and housing satisfaction and more loner status as rated by interviewers. No effect related to housing type was seen in breadth of activities, orientation to children, or satisfaction with the status quo categories. Both situations fell within acceptable ranges of E demand for competence of Ps in them (zone of maximum performance potential).

Gutman (1978) studied older persons in various housing situations. Among those who moved into even the most supportive residence, no evidence of differential decline was seen in self-reported health, activity level, or social interaction; benefits were seen in improved morale and increased interaction with neighbors. Kahana's, Kiyak's, Moos's, and Nehrke's environmental dimensions reflect staff attitudes, organizational structure, and administrative practices. These models do not attempt to measure parallel physical and situational aspects.

Both because of its nature and in terms of measurement, the informal support system cannot be assigned to either P or E_o but must be classified as an interactive variable which is influenced by both and mediates the effects of both upon outcomes. In measurement, there is no way to elicit the membership or quality of the informal support system except from the respondent. The amount and nature of contact are clearly P,E interactions. Such items as number of children or other relatives are objective in that they are factual, but they are the results of earlier P,E transactions which may have been influenced by enduring traits of the respondent. Frequency and quality of contact with friends and acquaintances are even more patently current P,E functions.

With regard to the formal support system of organizations and institutions, it is possible to collect data independently of the respondent. This part of the system can be defined in terms of what is "out there" in the community, apart from whether the respondent uses or is aware of it. Taietz (1975) made this distinction between services available in the community and those known to its elderly residents. We include the former in E_o. With regard to the functional support system, particular assistance can be provided by either the informal or formal systems, or both; and the salient issue is whether it is provided at all. Moreover, both informal and formal support systems serve mediating functions between the individual and external resources for meeting needs. Therefore we place the functional social support system at an intermediate level in the model and make it operational in terms of relevant needs.

Physical E_o

If a study is to have policy relevance, that is, produce results useful in improving environments, and to clarify theory regarding P,E transactions, one set of independent variables must be attributes of the physical world which can be measured independently of the respondent. Inclusion of physical E variables in behavioral science has been more apparent than real. Environment has been applied to the physical surround, the social surround, the organizational surround, and various combinations. Developmental and personality theorists such as Freud and Allport often meant interpersonal relationships when they said environment. Organizational theorists and sociologists refer to group processes, milieux, norms, and cultural pressures as environment without specifying to what extent these concepts are composed of physical and of multiindividual influences. Psychologists who give important place to the environment often make little attempt to differentiate its social from its physical aspects.

Taxonomies of E are largely social. The classification by Sells (1963) has nearly 250 items in social stimulus categories but only four under "natural environment" (gravity, weather, terrain, and natural resources). Among over 300 items regarding "environments for organizations," Indik (1963) includes only four physical E items, the same as those specified by Sells. A number of investigators have attempted to dimensionalize the domain but, as Lawton (1975a) points out, the resulting dimensions vary widely in terms of whether external physical data are sufficient bases for scoring. Most are subjective and depend heavily on the rater.

Suprapersonal E_o

Characteristics of other persons in the environment are highly relevant. According to Sells (1963), an environment is partially defined by characteristics of individuals in it, such as age, ability level, socioeconomic background, and educational attainment. Moos (1974) suggests that the character or climate of an environment depends on the typical characteristics of its occupants. According to Wohlwill (1974), the broadly social (which would include suprapersonal E_o and the support system), as contrasted with the physical environment is an aspect of the situation in which the individual behaves, and its stimulus value is influenced by physical aspects.

In the present model, suprapersonal E_o comprises characteristics of people and services in the setting. The respondent is irrelevant to its definition. Clean separation in measurement is obtained between objective reality and respondents' perceptions by using census and other independent sources. Since the places in which people live are to some extent dependent upon their own choices, the independence is not total; but we feel it is permissible to include suprapersonal E under E_o as long as independence from P is maintained in definition and measurement.

Direct Measurement of Objective Environmental Quality

Many studies have used measures of physical and social-institutional environments based largely or wholly on observer data. Direct E_o measurement is sparser. The development of one set of E_o scales is relevant because it served as a base for preparation of scales to operationalize the present model. A secondary analysis of data collected to provide a baseline for assessment of the Bay Area Rapid Transit System (BART) upon residential environmental qualities (Appleyard & Carp, 1974) tested the hypothesis that objective features of the environment, measured and scaled independently of anyone's impressions, account for significant and meaningful amounts of variance in residents' response about that environment and in their overall well-being (Carp & Carp, 1982a).

The central point was to restrict E_o items to those measureable objectively and independently of respondents. For physical E_o, one set of descriptors has to do with transportation systems in view of their pervasive effects on noise, esthetics, safety, and convenience in urban areas (Appleyard & Lintell, 1972; Feldman & Brandt, 1971; Goodchild, 1974; Grier, 1970; Manheim, 1970; Orleans & Schmidt, 1972; Peterson & Worrall, 1970). Intensity of auditory and visual effects is influenced by the number of units, distance from home, and barriers between stimulus source and residence. Visual and auditory stimuli follow similar rules: a land barrier is the most effective in reducing intensity of stimulation (Schultz & McMahon, 1971). With BART, an additional consideration is its diverse construction types: subterranean tunnel, subterranean cut-and-cover (trench dug, trackway tunnel built and covered over), on grade, on berm (earth mound), and aerial (elevated on concrete supports). Impact should increase in the order listed: the higher the track or station, the greater the distance it can be seen and heard, and the more of the visual and auditory fields of residents of nearby houses it covers.

A second set of descriptors has to do with land use and value. Most are traditional census items: primarily residential, some commercial, some industrial, some urban-vacant, some recreational or open vegetation or water. An index of variety was included since the mixture in a residential area affects interaction among residents (Jacobs, 1961; Whyte, 1956).

Two items deal with housing quality: average dollar value and percent lacking some or all plumbing. Housing density is represented by the percentage of units in structures of 10 or more units. Characteristics of the structure influence the degree to which external stimuli (e.g., noise, weather) impinge upon residents. Construction type (e.g., wood, reinforced concrete) is one consideration (Schultz & McMahon, 1971). Type of dwelling (e.g., apartment house, single-family) may be relevant (Hendricks, 1970). Elevation relative to sea level is positively related to housing value and quality in the Bay Area.

Physical E_o data were taken from U.S. Geological Survey Topological (USGST) maps scaled at one-half inch to 1,000 feet, to which other information was added. The USGST maps included elevation as well as locations of railroads, highways, freeways, and arterials. Information on BART was obtained from the Metropolitan Transportation Commission and land-use data from the census, and both were coded onto the USGST maps. Each respondent's residence was marked on the map.

Distances from it were measured with engineering rulers scaled at one-half inch to 1,000 feet. To count the number of items within a given distance of a home, plastic overlays were used. Coding reliabilities were high (Carp, Appleyard, Shokrkon, & Zawadski, 1973). The only judgmental items were the interviewer's recordings of dwelling type and construction type.

Variables were: (1) distance from home to nearest freeway; (2) distance from home to nearest arterial; (3) distance from home to nearest BART channel; (4) absence or presence of land contour (barrier) between home and BART track higher than a straight line between the two; (5) BART track construction type at the point nearest home; (6) distance from home to nearest BART station; (7) construction type of nearest BART station; (8) absence or presence of a land contour between home and nearest BART station higher than a straight line between the two; (9) distance from home to nearest railroad; (10) number of transportation elements (BART + freeways + arterials + railroads) within one mile of home; (11) industrial land-use within one-quarter mile of home; (12) urban-vacant land within one-quarter mile of home; (13) recreational, open vegetation, or water land-use within one-quarter mile of home; (14) number of different land uses within one-quarter mile of home; (15) average dollar value of owner-occupied units in the census block; (16) percentage of units in the census block without complete plumbing; (17) percentage of units in the census block in one-unit structures; (18) percentage of units in the census block in structures of 10 or more units; (19) home construction (wood-frame vs. all other); (20) elevation of home above sea level; (21) type of unit (single-family versus all other).

Suprapersonal E_o data were figures for the census block in which the respondent lived: percentage of population (1) 62 and older, (2) under age 18, (3) black; (4) percentage of one-person households; and (5) percentage of households with female heads. Indices of crowding were: (6) ratio of population to living units and (7) percentage of units with more than one person per room. Because home-owners were expected to take better care of property, (8) percentage of owner-occupied units was included.

Nine factors were obtained with one sample ($N = 1513$) and replicated with another ($N = 1006$). These scales account for significant and meaningful amounts of variance in 13 factorially based scales of interview data from residents for whom E_o data were collected (Carp & Carp, 1982b). However, people seek environments congruent with their competences and needs, and socioeconomic forces concentrate certain groups into certain types of environment (e.g., poor maintenance, unsafe). In other words, environments are not randomly applied to residents nor are residents randomly assigned to environments; rather, the two are linked. Furthermore, for those with options, dissonance reduction (Aronson, 1968) or personalized perception (Bem, 1970) following choice of a residence may affect outcomes such as stated satisfaction. For those without options, inability to extricate oneself may accentuate the influences of such psychological processes. Therefore, a critical test of E_o scales is whether they account for criterion variance, over and above that accounted for by characteristics of respondents. The E_o scales account for significant and sizeable amounts of variance in outcomes, even when nine factorially-based scales of person traits, plus age and gender, are partialed out (Carp & Carp, 1982a).

These findings lent encouragement to pursuit of direct measures of E_o. In making operational the concept of objective physical and suprapersonal environment, our model builds on the scales from this study for direct measures of the local area and takes a similar approach to scale development for the living unit.

E_o Scales for the Model

Using the *ADL* (Part 1) and higher-order need and personality trait definitions (which served also as criteria for selection, modification, and development of *P* measures) as categories, items were collected. In view of what seem to be major environmental concerns, the E_o component paired with *n* Harmavoidance was broken down into four parts: Crime, Accidents, Health, and Fire; and that paired with *n* Noxavoidance, into: Inconvenience/Discomfort, Noise, and Air Quality. The literature provided items; others were developed in preliminary field surveys. An environmental assessment protocol was developed and revised in several field tests to provide instructions for taking objective measures which yield reliable data (as indexed by interobserver agreement). Data were collected by trained environmental observers who inspected the *LUs* and *LAs* of participants and recorded measurements using the precoded protocol. Environmental observers had no contact with interviewers of psychometricians. *LU* data include such items as areal measurements of rooms and activity spaces, volumes of various types of storage spaces, instrumental readings of light and of noise levels at prespecified locations (e.g., relevant to *ADLs*), inventories and structured evaluations of appliances and fixtures, and visibility of specified conditions outside *LU* from prespecified locations within *LU*. Outside *LU*, the environmental assessment records attributes of the premises and those of adjacent properties visible from the street. Noise levels and vehicular traffic volumes and speeds are measured at peak hour and off-peak periods for the street outside the respondent's home, and traffic volumes are measured on the closest nonlocal street. A windshield survey records on maps the locations of specified facilities and land uses (relevant to *ADLs* and *HO* needs and personality traits) within specified distances of home.

A variety of secondary-source E_o data are also collected and mapped for measurement. The census provides block and tract data on population characteristics and housing conditions (e.g., crowding and lack of plumbing). The data were coded on maps to enable scoring for various radii around each respondent's house, as more accurate than direct use of census block or tract data, since any individual may be at the edge of one census unit and be more influenced by another. In addition, because proximity to home may affect perceived environmental impacts (Carp & Carp, 1982b), various radii were used. Tract-level mortality and cancer morbidity information was obtained from local health agencies, and subarea crime incidences were obtained from the Oakland Police Department. Both were coded on maps in order to compute incidences within the specified radii.

In scaling the E_o items, relationships with intermediate outcome scales (i.e., perception of and behavior in the environment, in respect to each *ADL, HO* need, and personality trait) might have been used (Craik & Zube, 1976). However, use of outcome measures as criteria for developing E_o predictor scales would nullify any attempt to assess the separate roles of *P,E,* and *PcE* (congruence), since the structures of E_o measures would maximize their correlations with outcomes. Throughout the entire effort, our strategy was to keep total separation among *P, E,* and intermediate outcome scales. They had in common only the definitions of *ADLs, HO* needs, and personality traits which served as categories for collection of item pools. To scale E_o items, those which had been collected under each *ADL* (Part 1) and *HO* need and personality trait (Part 2), for *LU* and *LA* separately, the criterion was internal consistency (Cronbach, 1951).

Prior to alpha scaling, modifications were made in view of apparent differences in importance, range, and skew among items. Some items (e.g., presence of a kitchen stove) seem more important than others (e.g., exhaust-fan above cooktop). Values ranged from presence or absence dichotomies to continuous variables with values in the thousands (e.g., sound recordings). Some had highly skewed distributions and might drop out during alpha scaling due to constricted variance rather than lack of consistency with other items in the pool. To take into account differences in importance, items were categorized on an *a priori* basis into major and minor, and the former were weighted double. For some pools with two or more highly skewed (10%–90% or worse) items, it was possible to define a composite with satisfactory skewness. The heterogeneity of item ranges was handled in two steps. First, all items were recoded as either dichotomous or five-value. Then the average weight of items was approximately equalized by multiplying dichotomous items by the grand mean for five-value items and multiplying five-value items by the dichotomous-item grand mean. Table 2 gives the descriptive statistics for the E_o scales using pilot study data. Figure 4 shows one scale, as an example.[1] Scale descriptors for the pilot are in Tables 3 and 4.

OBSERVER-BASED MEASURES

The model does not discard observer ratings. While it seems important to maintain a clear distinction between direct and observer measures to the greatest extent possible, it is likely that both will prove valuable. The intent is not to avoid ratings, but to determine the relative merits of direct and observer ratings and to learn how to use them in complementary fashion. As Craik (1981) points out, some environmental qualities may be so deeply imbedded in the sociocultural milieu that they can be measured only by human observers. Observer judgments based on intensive and extensive direct measures may prove more useful than the direct measures themselves. Therefore the environmental

TABLE 3
ALPHA COEFFICIENTS OF SCALES OF OBJECTIVE
ENVIRONMENT FOR LIFE-MAINTENANCE TASKS

Tasks in LU	Number of items	Alpha
Nutrition	42	.78
Sleeping and resting	13	.79
Personal hygiene	19	.64
Housecleaning	12	.67
Task in LA		
Nutrition	10	.81
Task in LU or LA		
Laundry	13	.82
$(N = 90)$		

[1]The environmental assessment protocol and procedures for development of E_o scales are available, at cost, from the senior author.

Major issues, dichotomous:
   Private off-street parking presence/absence
   Lockable private garage presence/absence
   Nonresidential uses on premises absence/presence
   Fast-food restaurant within ⅛ mile absence/presence
   Liquor store presence/absence within ⅛ mile
   Cocktail lounge presence/absence within ⅛ mile
   Adult entertainment presence/absence within ⅛ mile

Major issues, five value:
   Number of dwelling units in building
   Number of dwelling units on lot
   Number of residents on premises
   Number of arterial streets within ⅛ mile
   Percent decline in Caucasian population in census block
   Percent vacant units in census block
   Percent population in poverty in census block
   Percent single-family units within ¼ mile
   Percent units with 1.01 persons per room within ¼ mile
   Robbery rate within ¼ mile
   Purse-snatching incidence within ¼ mile
   Total criminal offenses rate within ¼ mile

Minor issues, dichotomous:
   Presence/absence of fast-food restaurants within ⅛–¼ mile
   Presence/absence of liquor store within ⅛–¼ mile
   Presence/absence of cocktail lounge within ⅛–¼ mile
   Presence/absence of adult entertainment within ⅛–¼ mile
   Presence/absence of park within ⅜ mile

Minor issues, five value:
   Number of convenience/grocery shops within ¼ mile
   Number of arterial streets within ⅛–¼ mile
   Number of collector streets within ⅜ mile
   Percent population Causasian in census tract
   Percent owner-occupied units in census tract
   Percent change in single-family unit value within ¼ mile
   Median number of years of school completed for population in census tract
   Percent decline in Caucasian population in census tract
   Median income for census tract
   Percent units in 10+ unit structures in census block
   Percent owner-occupied units in census block
   Percent population Caucasian in census block
   Percent units in 10+ unit structures within ¼ mile
   Percent owner-occupied units within ¼ mile
   Percent population Caucasian within ¼ mile

Skewed composites: none
Mean = 84.98; *SD* = 28.38; alpha = .95.

Figure 4.   Scale for objective environment regarding crime in local area.

TABLE 4
ALPHA COEFFICIENTS OF SCALES OF OBJECTIVE
ENVIRONMENTAL QUALITY RELEVANT TO HIGHER-ORDER
NEEDS

LU scales	Number of items	Alpha
Harmfulness		
Crime	11	.64
Health	8	.69
Accidents	17	.59
Fire	13	.75
Noxiousness		
Inconvenience	52	.88
Noise	11	.73
Air quality	8	.71
Order	10	.89
Affiliation	23	.82
Privacy	28	.89
Esthetics	22	.86
LA Scales		
Harmfulness		
Crime	44	.95
Health	15	.82
Accidents	33	.82
Fire	9	.79
Noxiousness		
Inconvenience	35	.91
Noise	16	.83
Air quality	17	.76
Order	28	.76
Affiliation	25	.89
Similarity	23	.85
Privacy	44	.92
Esthetics	22	.79

($N = 90$)

observers who take the direct measures also rate the environment on components of the model, immediately following completion of the measurement step, except for the following E_o component.

CONSONANCE AND DISSONANCE OF SUPRAPERSONAL E_o WITH P

In addition to the general impact of suprapersonal E_o, there is the matter of person–surround similarity. According to Byerts, Carp, Gertman, Guillard, Leeds, Lawton, and Rajic (1972), the extent to which one differs from the majority of people around one in characteristics such as age, race, or health is a critical determinant of one's behavior. Because most housing in this country for the elderly has been for old-age tenants, interest in P–suprapersonal E_o similarity has centered on the differential impacts of age-segregation and age-integration. Low-cost housing for the elderly and retirement communities have been largely successful, and there is a tendency to attribute this to the age homogeneity of residents. However, early retirement communities tended not to be so age-segregated as generally believed (Hamovitch, 1968); and today, since many require only that one person in the household be 45 or older, residents include people who could be parents or grandparents of others.

The generally beneficial effects of age-specified housing may not be due solely to the fact that its tenants are older people. A limited, though not small, age range is one of many ways in which housing for the elderly differs from other settings. Winiecke (1973) mentions three advantages: better living conditions, more social contacts, and lower rent. In a community setting, Rosow (1967) documented the advantage to all aspects of socialization of living in apartment houses with a large proportion of older tenants, and the advantage increased with lower status or disadvantage. Similarly at the level of the city block, Rosenberg (1970) found the advantage of a supply of age peers, and again the extent of advantage was related to level of affluence.

With a national sample of public housing, Teaff, Lawton, Nahemow, and Carlson (1978) controlled for the effects of certain physical characteristics (number of units, number of elderly-occupied units, number of units per acre, scatter of project, and building height) and background characteristics of tenant groups (social class, race, religion, and ethnicity). Elderly tenants in age-segregated projects had higher rates of activity participation, better functional health, greater satisfaction with housing, and higher morale. Even this degree of control may not be sufficient to justify age-attribution. The facilities differed in age, and selective factors not revealed by the demographic items may have been present.

In the same settings as those in the study by Teaff et al., Lawton and Yaffee (1979) found higher fear of crime in the age-integrated projects. Crime rates were also higher in projects in which elderly and younger families were indiscriminately mixed. This is one example of how age-mix can be confounded with other factors. Sherman (1975) compared residents of six types of retirement facilities with matched controls in age-integrated housing. The former had less interaction with children and other relatives and fewer friends than did controls, but they had more new friends and visited more with age peers.

These studies indicate that age-homogeneous environments have different impacts upon residents than do age-heterogeneous environments, and it seems possible that similarity between a resident and those around him or her in ways additional to age make a difference. Since our intent was to keep all E_o measures objective, and to collect data independently of respondents so that scores would not reflect their perceptions but factual reality, we developed a measure of P-suprapersonal E_o based on absolute differences between characteristics of each P and characteristics of her suprapersonal E_o taken from census and other secondary sources (e.g., mapping of the locations of religious institutions of various denominations within specified distances of P's residence). The 23-item scale has items dealing with factual similarity– difference in age, gender, household composition, ethnicity and race, educational attainment, housing tenure (rent or own), length of occupancy of unit, religion, income, employment status, marital status, dwelling type (single-family or apartment house), housing value, and housing cost.

CONGRUENCE

The concept of congruence is implicit in Lawton's model and central to those of Kahana, Kiyak, and Nehrke's group. Results of tests of the last three have been summarized. Carp (1974) tested the concept in predicting the adjustment of old people to a new E in validating, over an eight and one-half year interval, prediction equations of personal descriptors (competences, social statuses, and personality traits) developed to account for variance at the end of the first year of residence in a particular facility. Terms in the equation vary according to the criterion (resident's happiness, sociometrics by the peer group, or adjustment in the view of staff), but equations developed with short-run data for each criterion also accounted for significant and meaningful variance in that criterion in the long run. Results suggest that it is possible to identify characteristics of elderly persons which predict their subsequent adjustment in a particular E. However, the study is limited in respect to the role of congruence since E was relatively homogeneous across respondents, and the P traits selected as fitting the new E may be adaptively advantageous in any setting.

Sherman (1975) found either age-segregated or age-integrated situations satisfactory if the selection was based on personal choice. Among public-housing tenants, congruence between facility resources and personal characteristics affected activity rate (Carp, 1978) and social behavior (Carp & Carp, 1980). However, in a study of match and mismatch of housing and resident based on statement of needs, Lawton (1976) found P (health) and E (traditional versus congregate housing) effects, but no additional outcome variance was accounted for by the health $\times$ housing cross-product.

Lack of commensurability between measures of P and E has been cited as the major impediment to a direct approach to congruence (French *et al.*, 1974). P variables are quantified in such terms as IQ and E variables in meters of distance and density of barriers, making direct comparison difficult (Lawton, 1975a). Kahana, Kiyak, and Nehrke's group accept the requirement that P and E must be measured on the same scale. As a consequence, they have no recourse but to use staff or resident evaluations to represent E. Kahana opts for independence between P and E and uses staff ratings for the latter. Kiyak and Nehrke argue that staff perceptions may not represent the reality of the resident's environment and use resident ratings instead. In the latter situations, P and E variables are not independent, because of the common source of data and the likely effect of P characteristics upon environmental perceptions. Due to the requirement of measuring P and E on common scales, neither approach can include objective characteristics of the physical and suprapersonal environments. Therefore, although major goals for both Kahana and Nehrke are interventions to improve environments, neither model can deal directly with objective environmental characteristics that might influence outcomes.

Our assumption is that the necessity is not measurement of P and E on common scales, but empirical test of relationships hypothesized on the basis of a conceptual model, using measures of P and E obtained independently of each other. Direct measures of P and E_o variables are, by nature, necessarily in different terms. To investigate the role of congruence it is not necessary to demonstrate a one-to-one relationship between points on P and E scales, but rather to predict and test the effects of P and E combinations.

The cross-product is one way of expressing congruence. Others feel that the concept is better represented by the difference score. However, the latter is statistically problematic (Cronbach & Furby, 1970; Lord, 1963). A basic problem is that it compounds the unreliabilities of its components. If one had perfectly reliable components, so would the difference between them be perfectly reliable; and, if both components were totally unreliable, so would be the difference score. Some order of reliability between these extremes characterizes real data, and the effects of component reliabilities are complex (Bohrnstedt, 1969; Carp, Carp, & Millsap, 1982). The unreliability is accentuated by collinearity. In the present model, in which data for P and E components are collected and scaled independently, there is not the problem of same-source data which is inherent in the Nehrke and Kiyak models (McNemar, 1962).

Various investigators have used different strategies to reduce difference-score unreliability. French *et al.* (1974) used high-low categorization and simple subtraction. Kiyak (1977) trichotomized variables; cases in the diagonal of a nine-cell matrix were considered optimally congruent. Although dichotomization or trichotomization may reduce unreliability, it also decreases the power of the variable. In view of this, Kahana *et al.* (1980) maintained the full ranges of E and P scores and converted each component into standard z-score form before before taking differences. Standardization insures that difference scores are not dominated by either component due to difference in response distributions, but it does not change the basic unreliability problem or the influence of collinearity, and it may nullify the "same scale" requirement for P and E in the Kahana model.

For all models, the focus of interest is the independent and joint power of P,E and congruence in predicting outcomes. In what instances is P most important, E most important, and PcE most important? Regarding the congruence term, the critical question is: does it add to criterion variance accounted for, over and above that accounted for by P and E? This can be represented in a multivariate regression analysis in which the congruence term is added after P and E. A simple difference score cannot make a contribution additional to P and E, since it is a linear combination of the two. Kahana used nonlinear transformations to examine nondirectional, one-directional, and two-directional models.

Our model does not assume linearity of relationship between predictors and criteria. For example, in Part 1, below some threshold value competence may be of crucial importance in determining outcomes but above that value it may have little effect; and the same may be true for E_o variables relevant to life-maintenance. To the extent that PcE_o complementarity or compensation is insufficient to maintain performance of ADLs and therefore meet life-maintenance needs, outcomes will be correspondingly negative; however, when P competence and E_o are positive, differences in congruence scores may be less important. Similarly, in Part 2, if a HO need or personality trait is strong, PcE_o similarity is highly salient whereas, if a HO need or trait is weak, PcE_o may have little predictive power. As a first step, linearity of regression is tested. If it is not found, the type of regression of criterion on congruence can be approximated by two regression lines which join at some point within the range of the predictor. This point of intersection is defined as that which, when used to dichotomize the response distribution, minimizes the error in predicting the criterion through linear regression in each subsample. Both P and E predictors are entered into the equation before this direct scaling of congruence.

MEDIATING VARIABLES

SITUATIONAL RESOURCES AND DEPRIVATIONS

Social Support System

Suprapersonal E is included in the model as one aspect of E_o, since its character is not dependent upon respondents and can be described independently of them. The social support system comprises individuals or organizations with which the respondent interacts. The informal system consists of relatives, friends, and others who, as part of their personal relationship, do or might provide assistance with $ADLs$ and thereby help meet LM needs and who do or might help to meet HO needs such as that for affiliation. A number of studies have noted the importance of the informal system to the well-being of elderly people, both directly in needs-meeting and through assistance in obtaining services from the formal system (Bell, 1973; Cantor & Daum, 1975; Shanas, Townsend, Wedderburn, Friis, Milhoj, & Stehouwer, 1968; Sussman & Burchinal, 1968). Others have stressed the importance of having a confidant during crisis periods resulting from health decrements (Rosow, 1967), role loss (Lowenthal & Haven, 1968), relocation and environmental change (Schooler, 1975), mental disturbance (Giffen, 1969), and widowhood (Lopata, 1971). Increasingly, the formal system provides the floor of basic services for older people in such crucial areas as income, health, and transportation (Cantor & Mayer, 1976; Litwak, 1965). Both systems play essential and related roles. In the pilot study, participation of members of both formal and informal systems was recorded for each ADL (Part 1) and each HO need and personality trait (Part 2).

Status Resources and Deprivations

Another consideration that facilitates or inhibits one's success in changing E better to meet one's needs or moving to an E which does, involves current statuses that are residues of earlier P,E transactions. The concept is similar to Moos's (1976) "social resources dimension," which assesses current status in five sociodemographic variables related to social competence. His idea is that people who are married, had some education beyond high school, held managerial or professional jobs, speak English fluently, and are not on Medicaid or Supplemental Social Security have greater social resources than their counterparts who lack these attributes.

The importance of the concept in understanding the behavior of older people is suggested by the work of Campbell *et al.* (1976). Their model was much less effective for people 55 and older than for those younger, and they attribute this to age. However, the same response tendencies observed in the old, and on which they based the age-attribution, were also observed among the poorly educated and those with low income, across age. Prevalence of reduced status or deprivation in contextual variables in later life is documented in a variety of areas including income (Kreps, 1977), housing (Carp, 1976a), transportation (Cantilli & Shmelzer, 1971), social roles (Rosow, 1967), health care (Shanas & Maddox, 1975), social networks (Lowenthal & Robinson, 1976), and social services (Beattie, 1976). The differences which Campbell and his colleagues attribute to age may derive in part from age-related differences in important statuses.

Results with four large samples of people 60 and older support the hypothesis (Carp & Carp, 1981b). An index composed of demographic items routinely collected in survey research accounted for significant, meaningful variance in satisfaction with housing, income, health, medical care, and several other domains, as well as in overall well-being; and it accounted for far more variance than did age, and for variance over and above that accounted for by age. For income and housing, in which objective indices of reality were available, the index affected the relationship between reality and satisfaction. Mean scores on a similar index are constant from ages 25 to 65 but rise (greater deprivation) sharply thereafter (Carp & Carp, 1983c). The status resources–deprivation index for the pilot study was based on this work.

Recent Life Events

Many studies document the relationship between environmental stress and disease (for one review see Carp, 1977b). Much of this literature deals with transient response to experimentally induced stimuli, but some studies report persistent changes following significant life events. In both retrospective and prospective studies, recent life experiences have proved relevant to a variety of physical diseases (Dohrenwend & Dohrenwend, 1974) and other outcomes (Lowenthal, Thurnher,

& Chiriboga, 1975) among the elderly. Two of the best known instruments for quantifying life events are the Schedule of Recent Experiences (Holmes & Rahe, 1967) and the Multiple Risk Factor Inventory Trail (MRFIT) of life events (National Heart and Lung Institute, 1974).

INTRAPSYCHIC VARIABLES

Sense of Personal Competence

The need to feel in control of one's environment has long been recognized as basic to well-being. Loss of perceived control may be analogous to the psychological effects of growing old, because of reduced effectance, actual and perceived. With aging, a sense of personal competence may be difficult to sustain, because of societal factors and personal changes. Personal control influences even the most basic biological processes such as blood flow and heart rate (Guttman & Brown, 1971) and may therefore influence physiological as well as psychological processes of aging.

As we noted above, many investigators point to negative environmental changes with aging such as loss of roles, norms, and reference groups; reduced income; and inferior housing. On the personal side, while cognitive declines are not inevitable or uniform across persons or abilities (Botwinick, 1977), sensory-motor decrements occur (Corso, 1977; Engen, 1977; Fozard, Wolfe, Bell, McFarland, & Podolsky, 1977; Kenshalo, 1977; Welford, 1977); and health problems accumulate (Shanas & Maddox, 1976). The ego may become less effective in controlling and channeling impulses (Neugarten, 1972); and, in response to internal changes, the aging individual may see himself or herself in a position of lessened mastery relative to the world.

Seligman (1975) suggests that the belief that one cannot effect positive outcomes is a form of learned helplessness in which attempts to control outcomes are lessened and so outcomes are less likely to be positive. Further, Seligman proposes that learned helplessness leads to reactive depression, which is prevalent among the elderly (Butler & Lewis, 1973). More successful aging may occur when the individual maintains a sense of competence in dealing with the environment. When older people report having control or are given control over their lives, their psychological adjustment is better (Kuypers, 1972; Langner & Rodin, 1976; Palmore & Luikart, 1972; Reid, Haas, & Hawkins, 1977; Schulz, 1976; Shulz, & Brenner, 1977). Both Kahana (1975) and Lawton (1975) stress the importance of mastery in determining the degree to which behavior is adaptive and affect positive.

In sum, there is considerable support for including sense of personal competence as a determinant of adaptation, but where in the model does it belong? It may be related to ego strength, which Lawton would include within P competence, except for measurement problems. Some evidence suggests that it is a personality trait, little affected by E factors. Maas and Kuypers (1974) report Locus of Control scores to be relatively unaffected by stressful events or age. Other investigators found age differences; however, they can be interpreted as due to intrinsic developmental processes or external events. Neugarten (1972) found differences in "interiority" (readiness to experience activity and affect in relation to oneself versus in relation to other persons) between 40-year-olds and 60-year-olds. Reader (1974) found a regular drop in externality of control through middle age, and then a regular increase. In none of four samples of people 60 and older (Carp & Carp, 1981b) or two samples 25–98 (Carp & Carp, 1983c) was Sense of Personal Competence correlated with age.

Locus of Control scores are related to intelligence and education (Kuypers, 1972) and to socioeconomic level (Harrington, 1971), all of which are related to age. These findings are ambiguous but suggest that Locus of Control is affected by E. The young person has, in fact, less control over what happens to her or him; as one gains education, income, and adult status, control over one's own destiny does in fact increase; and as one grows old real control over events and the environment diminishes (Lawton, 1975a; Pastalan, 1975). Some evidence seems more clearcut in suggesting the responsiveness of Locus of Control to E influences. Smith (1970) found that patients shifted toward internality following a crisis resolution period. Aloia (1973) found a relationship between privacy and Locus of Control.

In view of its general perception as important, it seemed necessary to include this variable in the model. Evidence for its placement in the P category is not convincing. Therefore it is classified as a mediator.

Most studies have used Rotter's (1966) measure or some variant of it. Reid et al. (1977) point out that although these studies tend to show consistent results among older people correlations with criteria are rarely larger than in the 0.30s. This is not surprising, since the scale was developed as a broad-gauge instrument to allow for a low degree of prediction across a wide variety of situations rather than to provide close prediction in some specific situation (Rotter, 1973). Reid et al., holding it appropriate to develop measures of more narrowly defined domains and provide a higher level of prediction in them, developed an instrument specific to homes for the aged. The Rotter scale seemed too broad for our purpose, and that of the Reid study is institution-specific. Therefore we developed a 14-item Sense of Personal Competence scale with

satisfactory internal consistency; that is, alphas (Cronbach, 1951) between 0.80 and 0.90 for several *ad hoc* samples. Scores accounted for
significant and meaningful variance in satisfaction with various domains
of life experience and in overall well-being among those 60 and older
(Carp & Carp, 1981b) and those 25–98 (Carp & Carp, 1983c). This scale
was used in the pilot study.

Coping Style: Orientation toward the Negative

Generally, older people tend to give rosy views of themselves and
their circumstances (Campbell *et al.*, 1976; Harris, 1976). Effects of a
question-and-answer format and of frame of reference upon this tendency have been demonstrated among the elderly, as have individual differences (Carp & Carp, 1981a). Persons with a strong tendency to suppress or deny the unpleasant will give more sanguine responses about
their environments and their well-being. That is, given the same E_o and
other P traits, the individual with strong need will express more positive
views. Inclusion of this variable is important, to test the hypothesis
implied above and to observe the effects of this bias on the operation of
the model. A scale has been developed; preliminary work with *ad hoc*
samples demonstrated reliabilities between 0.80 and 0.85 (Cronbach,
1951); in four samples 60 and older the existence of individual difference
was documented, and the score accounted for significant and meaningful variance in satisfaction with various life domains and in overall well-
being, in the direction predicted (Carp & Carp, 1983a). This scale was
used in the pilot.

Attitude toward Own Health

Self-perceived health may be more important to outcomes than is
objective health status (e.g., Carp, 1977b; Shanas & Maddox, 1976).
Objective health status, a P variable in the model, is measured by physical examination or a proxy checklist of specific diagnoses and symptoms;
perception of health is classified as a mediator. In the pilot, the Current
Health Factor of the Ware Health Perception Scale (1976) was used. The
author reports test–retest coefficients over a two-year period significant
beyond the 0.001 level; the proportion of variance which remained stable for the Current Health Factor was 0.62.

Summary of Mediating Variables

For Part 1 of the model, variables expected to influence outcomes,
additional to P competences and E_o characteristics, are: (1) sense of

TABLE 5
ALPHA COEFFICIENTS OF MEDIATING VARIABLES

Variable[a]	Number of items	Alpha
Personal competence	14	.74
Suppress/deny	18	.88
Status resources	18	.85

(N = 90)

[a]Social supports varies by task.

personal competence, (2) tendency to suppress or deny the unpleasant, (3) perception of current health, (4) amount of assistance from the support systems in the performance of *ADLs* (which differs for each *ADL*), and (5) status resources and deprivations. For Part 2, variables expected to influence outcomes, along with P and E_o, are (1) sense of personal competence, (2) tendency to deny or suppress the unpleasant, (3) perception of current health, and (4) status resources and deprivations. For the Harmavoidance domain there is, for each of the four components, also a scale based on amount of assistance given or available (in case of fire, accident, health emergency, and crime), at both *LU* and *LA* levels. Pilot data reliabilities for new scales are given in Table 5.

OUTCOMES

DOMAINS AND SUBDOMAINS

For Part 1, there is a scale based on the respondent's evaluation of her situation in regard to the various aspects of each *ADL*. Reliabilities for those used in the pilot are in Table 6. For each, there is also an indicator of expressed need for (more) assistance with the various aspects of each *ADL*. Some domains have additional outcomes: nutrition (percentage under- or overweight, and a composite of interviewer and psychometrician ratings on nutritional status) and housecleaning (a composite of interviewer and psychometrician ratings on how well the housecleaning is accomplished).

For Part 2, scales have been developed on items reflecting the respondent's perception and evaluation of her situation with regard to harmavoidance (safety), noxiousness, order, affiliation, extraversion, privacy, and esthetics. For each of the four components of harmavoidance and each of the three of noxavoidance, an alpha-based scale was

TABLE 6
ALPHA COEFFICIENTS OF PERCEIVED ENVIRONMENTAL
QUALITY FOR LIFE-MAINTENANCE TASKS

Tasks in LU	Number of items	Alpha
Nutrition	29	.91
Sleep and rest	4	.77
Personal hygiene	17	.81
Housecleaning	35	.92
Task in LA		
Nutrition	5	.73
Task in LU or LA		
Laundry	4	.92

$(N = 90)$

developed on the basis of items reflecting the respondent's evaluation of her situation in the relevant respect (See Table 7). For each domain there is also an activity scale which indexes the number and frequency of activities taken in fulfillment of the need, in LU and LA. For example, the LU esthetic activity scale is based on frequency of activities pre-classified as esthetic which the respondent does at home; and the LA esthetic activity scale, on frequency of esthetic activities outside the home. For affiliation, an additional domain outcome is loneliness (new scale, alpha = 0.96).

SATISFACTION WITH LIVING UNIT AND LOCAL AREA

Both the extent to which P competences are congruent (complementary or compensatory) with E_o resources and demands in regard to $ADLs$ for life-maintenance (along with social supports and the other mediating variables), and the extent to which E_o is congruent (similar) to higher-order needs and personality traits (along with mediators) are expected to influence satisfaction with LU and LA. Criterion scales are based on items reflecting general satisfaction–dissatisfaction (LU alpha = 0.93, LA alpha = 0.88).

ULTIMATE OUTCOMES

Continued (Independent) Living

A real test of the model will require longitudinal data including information on death and institutionalization.

TABLE 7
ALPHA COEFFICIENTS FOR SCALES OF PERCEIVED
ENVIRONMENTAL QUALITY IN REGARD TO HIGHER-ORDER
NEEDS

Need	Number of items	Alpha
Living Unit		
Harmavoidance	4	.87
Crime	7	.81
Accident	15	.86
Health	11	.82
Fire	9	.75
Noxavoidance	13	.97
Inconvenience	30	.97
Noise	9	.97
Air quality	11	.71
Order	8	.93
Affiliation	18	.92
Extraversion	23	.94
Privacy	28	.96
Esthetics	15	.90
Local Area		
Harmavoidance	4	.94
Crime	16	.92
Health	12	.83
Accident	27	.87
Fire	8	.74
Noxavoidance	14	.77
Inconvenience	4	.80
Noise	13	.76
Air quality	7	.75
Order	26	.95
Affiliation	23	.90
Extraversion	31	.94
Similarity	16	.85
Privacy	22	.92
Esthetics	35	.95

$(N = 90)$

Overall Well-Being or Mental Health

Scales which seem to fall within six categories descriptive of this outcome were selected. Those which include items on health were not used, since physical ailments are in the model under P and health perception is a mediator. Only mental health is included in the outcome. Categories and scales are: (1) valence of self-concept; Adjective Checklist Self Score (Carp, 1966), Sentence-Completion Self Score (Carp, 1967), Usefulness (new scale); (2) realism of self-concept: respondent–interviewer similarity on assignment of adjectives to respondent (Carp, 1966); (3) affect: Bradburn Affect (1969) and Cavan, Burgess, & Havighurst, 1949) Happiness; (4) morale and life satisfaction: Philadelphia Geriatric Center (PGC) Morale Scale (Lawton, 1975b) and Campbell *et al.* (1976) Well-Being; (5) maladaptive behavior: Senility Index (Cavan *et al.*, 1949), number of neurotic ailments (Carp, 1966, 1974); Anomia/Alienation (new scale), CES-Depression (Radloff, 1977) Apprehensiveness (new scale); and (6) Attitude toward Aging (new).

Alphas for the pilot data are given in Table 8. The low reliabilities for PGC Morale probably reflect peculiarities of our sample. However, the low level of internal consistency in these data seemed to contraindicate its inclusion, in view of the available scales with better alphas. The remaining scales were subjected to principal components analysis. The two resultant components are the well-being criteria for the pilot (alphas = 0.83 and 0.79).

TABLE 8
ALPHA RELIABILITIES OF WELL-BEING SCALES ($N = 90$)

Scale	Alpha
ACL self	.88
SC self	.85
Uselessness	.71
Bradburn Positive Affect	.63
Bradburn Negative Affect	.77
Cavan *et al.* Happiness	.77
PGC: Factor 1	.49
Factor 2	.54
Factor 3	.22
CC&R Well-being	.77
Senility index	.80
Anomia/alienation	.83
CES-depression	.80
Apprehensiveness	.95
Attitude to aging	.69

($N = 90$)

FUTURE WORK

Thus ends the three-quarter view. A pilot test of the model is underway. Its central assumption is that congruence between individuals' needs and their living environments is basic to continued (independent) living and well-being. The role of lower-order needs is to define the tasks of daily living necessary to life-maintenance, around which Part 1 is designed in terms of complementarity and compensation between P competences and E resources and barriers specific to each ADL. Higher-order needs and personality traits are dealt with in Part 2, in terms of their similarity with relevant E resources and barriers. Other personal traits and situational variables comprise mediators. Outcomes are at several levels: perception of and satisfaction with each ADL and higher-order need, with respect to the living unit and the local area, and when the two are considered together (including behavioral measures where appropriate); perception of and satisfaction with the living unit and local area, in general, based on P,E and mediator aspects of each; and overall well-being or mental health, which is expected to be influenced by Parts 1 and 2 jointly.

The pilot tests a variant of the Lawton P competence–E demand model, since Part 1 has the same general rationale but different measures and statistical approach. It also tests the rationale of the Kahana and Nehrke approaches, but using measures of psychological need based on tradition, and measures of E based on direct measurement of E variables as well as ratings. In addition, it tests the proposition that both competence–demand and need–resource considerations add to predictability of outcomes.

Included is a test of the environmental docility and an additional hypothesis: for the relatively incompetent, competences will be relatively powerful predictors whereas for people within some adequate competence range higher-order needs and personality traits will account for more criterion variance. The pilot data may not provide a definitive answer, since all respondents were living alone in the community. However, several are legally (and one, totally) blind, and some are severely motor-handicapped (confined to wheelchairs and with very limited use of hands, while some still work and are active in the community. Included also is test of a threshold hypothesis with regard to higher-order needs, in that, when need is strong, PcE congruence is more relevant.

Changes in the model regarding LM and HO components may be indicated. Harmavoidance (safety) and perhaps noxavoidance (inconvenience, discomfort) may function more like the lower-order needs. That is, environments that are objectively dangerous probably are negative across persons, regardless of need, although need is expected to bear some influence upon environmental perceptions and other outcomes.

Comparisons are made between objective environmental indices based on direct measures and on observer ratings. Data-collection strategies allow specification of the factual contents and characteristics of perceived neighborhoods as well as the arbitrary areas which define *local areas*. Detailed analyses can be made of the support systems which are functional for these old women alone. Microlevel analyses of congruence between P competences and E_o characteristics are possible. For example, subscores of the range-of-motion instrument can be matched with items from E_o scales. Thus the match between vertical range of arm mobility and height of various types of kitchen work- and storage-spaces can be used to test the effects of fine-scale PcE in regard to aspects of LU nutrition; and P vision scores and E_o light measures can be similarly paired, with regard to various $ADLs$.

The pilot sample is small, and conclusive test of the model will require larger groups, not only to insure adequate score ranges but also to ease limitations on statistical treatment of the large number of variables. One necessity was compression of measures into smaller sets of variables. If one is interested, for example, in depression, combination of that measure into one of two well-being criteria may be frustrating. There is considerable overlap among scales in the area of mental health and well-being (Carp & Carp, 1983d). However, the two components in pilot data may reflect sample characteristics. For those interested in specific aspects of this domain, it is proposed to use as outcomes each of the conventional scales that entered into the component analysis (Carp & Christensen, 1983).

Even with the small sample, the pilot should indicate whether the model holds promise. On a conceptual level, the main thrust was to integrate existing models, and the pilot should indicate whether both competence–demand and need–resource considerations are relevant— that is, whether the approach of Lawton and those of Kahana, Nehrke, and others are complementary rather than alternative. At the level of operationalization, efforts have centered on mining the literature to select, adapt, and develop traditional measures of P traits (competences, higher-order needs, and personality traits), mediating variables, and outcomes; and to include scales of objective environmental characteristics based on direct measurement as well as observer ratings. The model is intended for older people in general; although pilot respondents are no representative sample, they are members of a large segment of the older community–resident population. Results should be reported soon, to round out the three–quarter view and provide psychological "closure."

Acknowledgments

The authors gratefully acknowledge consultation with major figures in the field. M. Powell Lawton, Rudolph Moos, Milton Nehrke, and Eva Kahana were of particular assistance with respect to their own models and implications for ours; Jack Botwinick was most helpful regarding selection of cognitive competence measures; Victor Regnier, in respect to sources of objective items for assessment of the environment; and William Meredith, for statistical advice. We value their contributions and those of David Christensen who, as a Research Associate during the final two years of the project, bore particular responsibility for field testing and revision of the manual of procedures for collecting objective environmental data.

REFERENCES

Adorno, T. W., Frenkel-Brunswick, E., Levinson, D., & Sanford, R. M. *The authoritarian personality.* New York: Harper's, 1950.

Allport, G. W. *The nature of prejudice.* Cambridge, Mass.: Addison-Wesley, 1954.

Aloia, A. J. *Relationships between perceived privacy options, self-esteem, and internal control among aged people.* Unpublished doctoral dissertation, California School of Professional Psychology, 1973.

Anastasi, A. *Psychological testing.* New York: Macmillan, 1961.

Antunes, G. E., Cook, F. L., Cook, T. D., & Skogan, W. G. Patterns of personal crime against the elderly. *Gerontologist,* 1977, *17,* 321–327.

Appleyard, D., & Carp, F. M. BART Residential Impact Study: An Empirical Study of Environmental Impact. In T. G. Dickert & K. R. Domeny (Eds.), *Environmental Impact Assessment.* Berkeley: University of California Press, 1974, pp. 73–88.

Appleyard, D., & Lintell, M. The environmental quality of city streets: The residents' viewpoint. *Journal of the American Institute of Planners,* 1972, *38,* 84–101.

Aronson, E. Dissonance theory. In R. P. Abelson, E. Aronson, W. J. McGuire, T. M. Newcomb, M. J. Rosenberg, & P. H. Tannenbaum (Eds.), *Theories of cognitive consistency.* Chicago: Rand-McNally, 1968, pp. 5–27.

Barker, R. G. (Ed.), *The stream of behavior.* New York: Appleton-Century-Crofts, 1963.

Beattie, W. M., Jr. Aging and the social services. In R. H. Binstock & E. Shanas (Eds.), *Handbook of aging and the social sciences.* New York: Van Nostrand Reinhold, 1976, pp. 619–663.

Bell, W. G. The family life cycle, primary relationships and social participation patterns. *Gerontologist,* 1973, *13,* 349–354.

Bem, D. J. *Beliefs, attitudes, and human affairs.* Belmont, Calif.: Brooks/Cole, 1970.

Bohrnstedt, G. W. Observations on the measurement of change. In E. F. Borgatta (Ed.), *Sociological measurement.* San Francisco, Calif.: Jossey-Bass, 1969, pp. 113–133.

Botwinick, J. Intellectual abilities. In J. E. Birren & K. W. Schaie, (Eds.), *Handbook of the psychology of aging*. New York: Van Nostrand Reinhold, 1977, pp. 580–605.

Bradburn, N. M. *The structure of well-being*. Chicago: Aldine, 1969.

Brotman, H. Every tenth American. In M. P. Lawton, R. J. Newcomer, & T. O. Byerts (Eds.), *Community planning for an aging society*. Stroudsburg, Pa.: Dowden, Hutchinson & Ross, 1976, pp. 5–18.

Brunswick, E. *The conceptual framework of psychology*. Chicago: University of Chicago Press, 1955.

Butler, R. N., & Lewis, M. I. *Aging and mental health*. St. Louis, Mo.: Mosby, 1973.

Byerts, T. O., Prefatory remarks. In T. O. Byerts (Ed.), *Housing and Environment for the elderly*, Washington, D. C.: The Gerontological Society, 1973.

Byerts, T., Carp, F. M., Gertman, J. Guillemard, A. M., Leeds, M., Lawton, M. P. & Rajic, R. Housing. *Gerontologist*, 1972, *12*, 2, 3–10.

Campbell, A., Converse, P. E., & Rogers, W. L. *The quality of American life*. New York: Russell Sage, 1976.

Canter, D. An intergroup comparison of connotative dimensions in architecture. *Environment and behavior*, 1969, *1*, 37–48.

Cantilli, E. J., & Scmelzer, J. L. *Transportation and aging*. Washington, D. C.: USGPO, 1971.

Cantor, M. H., & Daum, M. Extent and correlates of mental health vulnerability among the inner-city elderly population. *Community care programs for the elderly*. New York: Community Service Society of New York, 1975.

Cantor, M. H., & Mayer, M. Health and the inner-city elderly. *Gerontologist*, 1976, *16*, 1, 17–24.

Carp, F. M. *A future for the aged*. Austin: University of Texas Press, 1966.

Carp, F. M. Attitudes of old persons toward themselves and toward others. *Journal of Gerontology*, 1967, *22*, 3, 308–312.

Carp, F. M. Differences among older workers, volunteers, and persons who are neither. *Journal of Gerontology*, 1968, *23*, 497–501.

Carp, F. M. Short-term and long-term prediction of adjustment to a new environment. *Journal of Gerontology*, 1974, *29*, 4, 444–453.

Carp, F. M. Housing and living environments of older poeple. In B. Binstock & E. Shanas (Eds.), *Handbook of aging and the social sciences*. New York: Van Nostrand Reinhold, 1976, pp. 244–271.

Carp, F. M. User evaluation of housing for the elderly. *Gerontologist*, 1976, *16*, 2, 102–111. (b)

Carp, F. M. Impact cf improved living environment on health and life expectancy. *Gerontologist*, 1977, *17*, 3, 242–249. (a)

Carp, F. M. Retirement and physical health. In S. Kasl & F. Reichsman (Eds.), *Advances in psychosomatic medicine (Vol. 9)*. New York: Karger, 1977, pp. 1–19. (b)

Carp, F. M. Effects of the living environment on activity and use of time. *International Journal of Aging and Human Development.*, 1978, *9*, 1, 75–91.

Carp, F. M. The effect of planned housing on life satisfaction and mortality of residents. In V. Regnier & J. Pynoos (Eds.), *Housing for the elderly: Satisfactions and preferences*. New York: Garland, 1983.

Carp, F. M., & Carp, A. Person-environment congruence and sociability. *Research on Aging*, 1980, *2*, 395–415.

Carp, F. M., & Carp, A. It may not be the answer; it may be the question. *Research on aging*, 1981, *3*, 1, 85–100. (a)

Carp, F. M., & Carp, A. Age, deprivation, and personal competence: Effects on satisfaction. *Research on Aging*, 1981, *3*, 3, 279–298. (b)

Carp, F. M., & Carp, A. A role for technical assessment in perceptions of environmental quality and well-being. *Journal of Environmental Psychology,* 1982, *2,* 171–191. (a)

Carp, F. M., & Carp, A. Perceived environmental quality of neighborhoods. *Journal of Environmental Psychology,* 1982, *2,* 295–312. (b)

Carp, F. M. & Carp, A. Age, situational deprivation, sense of personal competence, and coping style as predictors of domain satisfactions and well-being. *International Journal of Aging and Human Development,* 1983. (a)

Carp, F. M., & Carp, A. Relationships of social status, competence, and personality traits to activity, happiness, and adjustment. *Research on Aging,* 1983. (b)

Carp, F. M., & Carp, A. Age, deprivation, and personal competence: Effects on well-being across the adult life-span. *Journal of Personality and Social Psychology,* 1983. (c)

Carp, F. M., & Carp, A. Structural stability of well-being factors across age and gender, and development of scales unbiased for age and gender. *Journal of Gerontology,* 1983. (d)

Carp, F. M. & Christensen, D. *Residential quality: Development of objective measures.* (Research grant application submitted to NIH June, 1983).

Carp, F. M., Appleyard, D., Shokrkon, H., & Zawadski, R. *BART Residential Impact Studies, BART II: Rationale and procedure for the collection of pre-BART geographic, census and secondary data.* Institute of Urban & Regional Development, University of California, Berkeley, June 1973.

Carp, F. M., Carp, A., & Millsap, R. Equity and satisfaction among the elderly. *International Journal of Aging and Human Development,* 1982, *15,* 2, 151–166.

Cavan, R. S., Burgess, E. W. & Havighurst, R. *Your activities and attitudes.* Chicago: Science Research Associates, 1949.

Cooper, C. *Easter Hill Village.* New York: Free Press, 1975.

Corso, J. F. Auditory perception and communication. In J. E. Birren & K. W. Schaie (Eds.), *Handbook of the psychology of aging.* New York: Van Nostrand Reinhold, 1977, pp. 535–561.

Craik, K. H. Environmental assessment and situational analysis. In D. Magnusson (Ed.), *Toward a psychology of situations.* Hillsdale, N. J.: Erlbaum, 1981, pp. 37–48.

Craik, K. H., & Zube, E. H. The development of perceived environmental quality indices. In K. H. Craik & E. H. Zube (Eds.), *Perceiving environmental quality.* New York: Plenum Press, 1976, pp. 3–20.

Cronbach, L. J. Coefficient alpha and the internal structure of tests. *Psychometrika,* 1951, *16,* 297–334

Cronbach, L. J. *Essentials of psychological testing.* New York: Harper & Row, 1970.

Cronbach, L. J., & Furby, L. How we should measure "change"—Or should we? *Psychological Bulletin,* 1970, *74,* 1, 68–80.

Crowne, D., & Marlowe, D. *The approval motive.* New York: Wiley, 1964.

Cumming, E., & Henry, W. *Growing old: The process of disengagement.* New York: Basic Books, 1961.

Daniel, T. C., & Boster, R. S. *Measuring scenic beauty.* USDA Forest Service: Rocky Mountain Forest & Range Experiment Station Research Paper, 1976.

Dohrenwend, B. S., & Dohrenwend, B. P. (Eds.). *Stressful life events—Their nature and effects.* New York: Wiley, 1974.

Duke University Center for the Study of Aging & Human Development. *The older Americans resources and services multidimensional functional assessment questionnaire.* Durham, N. C.: Duke University, 1977.

Engen, T. Taste and smell. In J. E. Birren & K. W. Schaie (Eds.), *Handbook of the Psychology of Aging.* New York: Van Nostrand Reinhold, 1977, pp. 554–561.

Feldman, G., & Brandt, B. Working-class protest against an urban highway. *Environment and Behavior*, 1971, *3*, 1, 61–79.

Fines, K. D. Landscape evaluation–A research project in East Sussex. *Regional Studies* (U.K.), 1968, *2*, 40–55.

Firestone, I., Lichtman, C., & Evans, J. *Determinants of privacy and sociability among institutionalized elderly*. Paper presented at American Psychological Association meeting, Chicago, 1975.

Fishbein, M, & Adjen, I. *Belief, attitude, intention, and behavior*. Reading, Mass.: Addison-Wesley, 1975.

Fleishman, E. A. Dimensional analysis of movement reactions. *Journal of Experimental Psychology*, 1958, *55*, 438–453.

Fozard, J. L., Wolfe, E., Bell, B., McFarland, R. S., & Podolsky, S. Visual perception and communication. In J. E. Birren & K. W. Schaie (Eds.), *Handbook of the psychology of aging*. New York: Van Nostrand Reinhold, 1977, pp. 497–534.

Francescato, G., Weidemann, S., Anderson, J. R., & Cenoweth, R. *Residents' satisfaction in HUD - assisted housing*. Washington, D. C.: USGPO, 1979. (HUD-PDR-390)

French, J., Rogers, W., & Cobb, F. Adjustment as person–environment fit. In G. V. Coelho, D. A. Hamburg, & J. E. Adams (Eds.), *Coping and adaptation*. New York: Basic Books, 1974, pp. 316–333.

Griffin, K. Personal trust and the interpersonal problems of the aged person. *Gerontologist*, 1969, *9*, 4, 286–291.

Gifford, R. J. Judgment of the built environment as a function of individual differences and context. *Journal of Man-Environment Relations*, 1980, *1*, 23–31.

Goodchild, B. Class differences in environmental perceptions. *Urban Studies*, 1974, *11*, 157–169.

Grier, W. Social impact analysis of an urban freeway system. *Highway Research Record*, 1970, *305*, 63–74.

Gutman, G. M. Issues and findings relating to multi-level accomodation for seniors. *Journal of Gerontology*, 1978, *33*, 592–600.

Guttman, M. C., & Brown, H. Interaction of environmental factors and systemic arterial blood pressure: A review. *Medicine*, 1971, *50*, 543–544.

Hamovitch, M. B. Social and psychological factors in adjustment in a retirement village. In F. M. Carp (Ed.), *The retirement process*. Washington, D. C.: USGPO,, 1968, pp. 115–125.

Hamovitch, M. B., & Peterson, J. E. Housing needs and satisfactions of the elderly. *Gerontologist*, 1969, *9*, 1, 30–32.

Harrington, D. D. *The young driver follow-up study*. Sacramento, Calif: California State Department of Motor Vehicles, 1971.

Harris, L., & Associates. *The myth and reality of aging in America*. Washington, D. C.: National Council on the Aging, 1975.

Havighurst, R. J. A report of a special committee of the gerontological society. *The Gerontologist*, 1969, *9*, 4, part 2.

Havighurst, R. J., Neugarten, B. L. & Tobin, S. S. Disengagement and patterns of aging. In B. L. Neugarten (Ed.), *Middle age and aging*. Chicago: Univeristy of Chicago Press, 1968, pp. 161–172.

Hendricks, J. Leisure participation as influenced by urban residential patterns. *Sociology and Social Research*, 1970, *55*, 1.

Hershberger, R. A study of meaning and architecture. In H. Sanoff, & S. Cohn (Eds.), *Proceedings of the first annual Environmental Design Research Association conference*. Chapel Hill, N.C.: EDRA, 1970, pp. 86–100.

Holmes T. H., & Rahe, R. H. The social readjustment rating scale. *Journal of Psychosomatic Research*, 1967, *11*, 213–218.

Ittelson, W. H. *Visual space perception*. New York: Springer, 1960.

Jacobs, J. *The death and life of great American cities*. New York: Random House, 1961.

Kahana, E. A congruence model of person–environment interaction. In P. G. Windley, T. Byerts, & E. G. Ernst (Eds.), *Theoretical development in environments for aging*. Washington, D. C.: Gerontological Society, 1975, pp. 181–214.

Kahana, E., Liang, J., & Felton, B. J. Alternative models of person–environment fit. *Journal of Gerontology*, 1980, *35*, 4, 584–595.

Kaiser, E., Weiss, S., Burby, R., & Donnelly, J. *Neighborhood evaluation and Residential satisfaction*. Durham, N. C.: Center for Urban and Regional Studies, University of North Carolina, 1970.

Kaplan, R. Predictors of environmental preference: Designers and "clients." In W. F. E. Preiser (Ed.), *Environmental design research*. Stroudsburg, Pa.: Dowden, Hutchinson & Ross, 1973, pp. 265–274.

Kenshalo, D. R. Age changes in touch, vibration, temperature, kinesthesis, and pain sensitivity. In J. E. Birren & K. W. Schaie (Eds.), *Handbook of the psychology of aging*. New York: Van Nostrand Reinhold, 1977, pp. 562–579.

Kiyak, H. A. A multidimensional perspective on privacy preferences of institutionalized elderly. In W. E. Rogers & W. H. Ittelson (Eds.), *New Directions in Environmental Design, Research; Proceedings of the ninth annual conference of the Environmental Design Research Association*. Tucson: University of Arizona, 1978, pp. 79–91.

Klinger, E. *Meaning and void*. Minneapolis: University of Minnesota Press, 1977.

Krech, D., Crutchfield, R., & Livson, N. *Elements of psychology*. New York: Knopf, 1969.

Kreps, J. M. Intergenerational transfers and the bureaucracy. In E. Shanas & M. B. Sussman (Eds.), *Family, bureaucracy, and the elderly*. Durham, N. C.: Duke University, 1977.

Kuypers, J. A. Internal-external locus of control, ego functioning and personality characteristics in old age. *Gerontologist*, 1972, *12*, 2, 168–173.

Langner, E., & Rodin, J. The effects of choice and enhanced personal responsibility for the aged. *Journal of Personality and Social Psychology*, 1976, *34*, 191–198.

Lansing, J. B., & Marans, R. W. Evaluations of neighborhood quality. *Journal of the American Institute of Planners*, 1969, *35*, 195–199.

Lawton, M. P. Competence, environmental press, and the adaptation of older people. In P. Windley & G. Ernst (Eds.), *Theory development in environment and aging*. Washington, D. C.: Gerontological Society, 1975, pp. 13–83. (a)

Lawton, M. P. The Philadelphia geriatric center morale scale: A revision. *Journal of Gerontology*, 1975, *30*, 85–89. (b)

Lawton, M. P. The relative impact of congregate and traditional housing on elderly tenants. *Gerontologist*, 1976, *16*, 237–242.

Lawton, M. P. The impact of the environment on aging and behavior. In J. E. Birren & K. W. Schaie (Eds.), *Handbook of the psychology of aging*. New York: Van Nostrand Reinhold, 1977, pp. 276–301.

Lawton, M. P. Environmental change: The older person as initiator and responder. In N. Datan & N. Lohmann (Eds.), *Transitions in aging*. New York: Academic Press, 1980, pp. 171–193. (a)

Lawton, M. P. *Social and medical services in housing for the aged*. Rockville, Md.: National Institute for Mental Health, 1980. (b)

Lawton, M. P. *Environment and aging*. Belmont, Calif.: Brooks/Cole, 1980. (c)

Lawton, M. P. Residential quality and residential satisfaction among the elderly. *Research on Aging*, 1980, *2*, 309–328. (d)

Lawton, M. P. An ecological view of living arrangements. *Gerontologist*, 1981, *21*, 1, 59–66.

Lawton, M. P. Competence, environmental press and adaptation. In M. P. Lawton, P. G. Windley, & T. O. Byerts (Eds.), *Aging and the environment: Theoretical approaches*. New York: Springer, 1982, pp. 33–59.

Lawton, M. P., & Bader, J. Wish for privacy among young and old. *Journal of Gerontology*, 1970, *25*, 48–54.

Lawton, M. P., & Kleban, N. H. The aged resident of the inner city. *Gerontologist*, 1971, *11*, 277–283.

Lawton, M. P., & Nahemow, L. Ecology and the aging process. In E. Eisdorfer & M. P. Lawton (Eds.), *Psychology of adult development and aging*. Washington, D. C.: American Psychological Association, 1973, pp. 619–674.

Lawton, M. P., & Simon, B. The ecology of social relationships in housing for the elderly. *Gerontologist*, 1968, *8*, 108–115.

Lawton, M. P., & Yaffe, S. *Victimization of the elderly and fear of crime*. Philadelphia, Pa.: Philadelphia Geriatric Center, 1979.

Lawton, M. P., Brody, E. M., & Turner-Massey, P. The relationships of environmental factors to changes in well-being. *Gerontologist*, 1978, *18*, 133–137.

Lawton, M. P., Moss, M., Fulcomer, M., & Kleban, M. H. A research and service oriented multilevel assessment instrument. *Journal of Gerontology*, 1982, *37*, 91–99.

Lawton, M. P., Nahemow, L., & Teaff, J. Housing characteristics and the well-being of elderly tenants in federally assisted housing. *Journal of Gerontology*, 1975, *30*, 601–607.

Lewin, K. *Field theory in social science*. New York: Harper & Row, 1951.

Litwak, E. Extended kin relations in an industrial democratic society. In E. Shanas & G. Streib (Eds.), *Social structure and the family*. Englewood Cliffs, N. J.: Prentice-Hall, 1965, pp. 290–323.

Lopata, H. Z. Widows as a minority group. *Gerontologist*, 1971., *11*, 67–77.

Lord, F. M. Elementary models for measuring change. In C. W. Harris (Ed.), *Problems in measuring change*. Madison: University of Wisconsin Press, 1963, pp. 21–38.

Lowenthal, M. F., & Haven, C. Interaction and adaptation: Intimacy as a critical variable. *American Sociological Review*, 1968, *33*, 20–30.

Lowenthal, M. F., & Robinson, B. Social networks and isolation. In R. H. Binstock & E. Shanas (Eds.), *The handbook of aging and the social sciences*. New York: Van Nostrand Reinhold, 1976, pp. 432–456.

Lowenthal, M. F., Thurnher, M., & Chiriboga, D. *Four stages of life*. San Francisco: Jossey-Bass, 1975.

Lucas, R. C. User evaluation of campgrounds on two Michigan National Forests. St. Paul, Minn.: North Central Forest Experiment Station Research Paper NC-44, 1970.

Maas, H. S., & Kuypers, J. A. *Progress report on intergenerational studies—Aging study*. Berkeley, Calif.: Institute of Human Development, University of California, 1970.

Manheim, M. The impacts of highways on environmental values. *Highway Research Record*, 1970, *305*, 26–27.

Maslow, A. H. *Motivation and personality*. New York: Harper, 1954.

McNemar, Q. *Psychological statistics*. New York: Wiley, 1962.

Megargee, E. R. *The California psychological inventory handbook*. San Francisco: Jossey-Bass, 1972.

Messick, S., & Jackson, D. N. Acquiescence and the factorial interpretation of the MMPI. *Psychological Bulletin*, 1961, *58*, 299–304.

Michelson, W. An empirical analysis of environmental preferences. *Journal of the American Institute of Planners*, 1966, *32*, 6, 355–360.

Milbrath, L. W., & Sahr, R. C. Perceptions of environmental quality. *Social Indicators Research*, 1975, *1*, 397–438.

Mitchell, B. Behavioral aspects of water management. *Environment and Behavior*, 1971, *3*, 15–31.

Moos, R. H. Systems for the assessment and classification of human environments. In R. H. Moos & P. M. Insel (Eds.), *Issues in social ecology*. Palo Alto, Calif.: National Press Books, 1974, pp. 5–28.

Moos, R. H. *The human context: Environmental determinants of behavior*. New York: Wiley, 1976.

Moos, R. H., & Lemke, S. The multiphasic environmental assessment procedure. In A. Jegar & B. Slotnick (Eds.), *Community mental health: A behavioral ecological perspective*. New York: Plenum Press, 1980, pp. 357–371.

Moos, R. H., Lemke, S., & Clayton, J. Comprehensive assessment of sheltered care settings. *American Journal of Community Psychology*, 1981, *9*, 513–526.

Murray, H. A. *Explorations in personality*. New York: Oxford University Press, 1938.

Nahemow, L. & Lawton, M. P. Toward an ecological theory of adaptation and aging. In W. Preiser (Ed.), *Environmental design research* (Vol. 1). Stroudsburg, Pa.: Dowden, Hutchinson & Ross, 1973, pp. 24–32.

Nahemow, L. & Lawton, M. P. Similarity and propinquity in friendship formation. *Journal of Personality and Social Psychology*, 1975, *32*, 205–213.

National Heart and Lung Institute. *MRFIT (Multiple Risk Factor Intervention Trial) Inventory of Life Events*. Washington, D. C.: National Institutes of Health, 1974.

Nehrke, M. F., Turner, R. R., Cohen, S. H., Whitbourne, S. K., Morganti, J. B., & Hulicka, I. M. Toward a model of person–environment congruence. *Experimental Aging Research*, 1981, *7*, 363–379.

Neugarten, B. Personality and the aging process. *Gerontologist*, 1972, *12*, 1, 9–15.

Nuttall, R. L., & Fozzard, J. L. Age, socioeconomic status and human abilities. *International Journal of Aging & Human Development*, 1970, *1*, 2, 161–169.

Orleans, P., & Schmidt, S. Mapping the city. In W. J. Mitchell (Ed.), *edra 3*. Los Angeles: UCLA Press, 1972, pp. 1-4-1–149.

Palmore, E., & Luikart, C. Health and social factors related to life satisfaction. *Journal of Health and Social Behavior*, 1972, *13*, 68–80.

Pastalan, L. A. How the elderly negotiate their environment. In T. O. Byerts (Ed.), *Housing and environment for the elderly*. Washington, D. C.: Gerontological Society, 1973, pp. 21–34.

Payne, R., & Pugh, D. S. Organizational structure and climate. In M. D. Dunette (Ed.), *Handbook of industrial and organizational sociology*. Chicago: Rand McNally, 1976, pp. 1125–1174.

Pervin, L. A. Performance and satisfaction as a function of individual–environment fit. In R. H. Moos & P. M. Insel (Eds.), *Issues in social ecology*. Palo Alto, Calif.: National Press Books, 1974, pp. 569–587.

Pervin, L. A. Definitions, measurement and classifications of stimulus situations and environment. *Journal of Human Ecology*. 1978, *6*, 71–105.

Peterson, G., & Worrall, R. An analysis of individual preferences for accessibility to selected neighborhood services. *Highway Research Record*, 1970, *305*, 99–111.

Peterson, G. L., Bishop, R. L., & Michaels, R. M. Designing play environments for children. In G. Coates (Ed.), *Alternative learning environments*. Stroudsburg, Pa.: Dowden, Hutchinson & Ross, 1974, pp. 321–340.

Proceedings of the 1971 White House Conference on Aging. *Toward a national policy on aging* (Vol. 2). Washington, D. C.: Government Printing Office, 1973.

Radloff, L. S. The CES–D. *Applied psychological measurement*, 1977, *1*, 385–401.

Reader, L. R. Unpublished data gathered in the Los Angeles Metropolitan Area Survey by the UCLA Institute of Government & Public Affairs Survey Research Center, 1974.

Reid, D. W., Haas, G., & Hawkins, D. Locus of desired control and positive self concept of the elderly. *Journal of Gerontology*, 1977, *32*, 4, 441–450.

Rokeach, M. *The nature of human values*. New York: Free Press, 1973.

Rosenberg, G. S. *The worker grows old*. San Francisco: Jossey-Bass, 1970.

Rosow, I. *Social Integration of the aged*. New York: Free Press, 1967.

Rotter, J. B. Generalized expectancies for internal versus external control of reinforcement. *Psychological Monographs*, 1966, *80* (Whole No. 609), 1–28.

Rotter, J. Some problems and misconceptions related to the construct of internal versus external control of reinforcement. *Journal of Consulting and Clinical Psychology*, 1973, *43*, 56–67.

Saarinen, T. F. *Environmental planning: Perception and behavior*. Atlanta: Houghton Mifflin, 1976.

Schooler, K. K. A comparison of rural and non-rural elderly on selected variables. In R. C. Atchley & T. O. Byerts (Eds.), *Environments and the rural aged*. Washington, D. C.: Gerontological Society, 1975, pp. 27–33.

Schulz, R. Effects of control and predictability on the physical and psychological well-being of the institutionalized aged. *Journal of Personality and Social Psychology*, 1976, *33*, 563–573.

Schulz, R., & Brenner, G. Relocation of the aged. *Journal of Gerontology*, 1977, *32*, 3, 323–333.

Schultz, T. J., & McMahon, N. M. *Noise assessment guidelines*. Washington, D. C.: U.S. Department of Housing and Urban Development, 1971.

Seligman, M. E. P. *Helplessness: On depression, development, and death*. San Francisco.: W. H. Freeman, 1975.

Sells, S. B. Dimensions of stimulatus situations which account for behavior variance. In S. B. Sells (Ed.), *Stimulus determinants of behavior*. New York: Ronald, 1963, pp. 3–15.

Shanas, E., & Maddox, G. L. Aging, health, and the organization of health resources. In R. H. Binstock & E. Shanas (Eds.), *Handbook of aging and the social sciences*. New York: Van Nostrand Reinhold, 1976, pp. 592–618.

Shanas, E., Townsend, P., Wedderburn, D., Friis, H., Milhoj, P., & Stehouwer, J. The psychology of health. In B. L. Neugarten (Ed.), *Middle age and aging*. Chicago: University of Chicago Press, 1968, pp. 212–219.

Sherman, S. R. Provision of on-site services in retirement housing. *International Journal of Aging & Human Development*, 1975, *6*, 229–247.

Sherman, S. R., Mangum, W. P., Jr., Dodds, S., Walkley, R. P., & Wilner, D. M. Psychological effects of retirement housing. *Gerontologist*, 1968, *8*, 3. 170–175.

Simon, B. B., & Lawton, M. P. *Proximity and other determinants of friendship formation in the elderly*. Paper presented at the annual meeting of the Eastern Psychological Association, Boston, April, 1966.

Smith, R. E. Changes in locus of control as a function of life crisis resolution. *Journal of Abnormal Psychology*, 1970, *75*, 328–332.

Storandt, M., Wittels, I., & Botwinick, J. Predictors of a dimension of well-being in the relocated healthy aged. *Journal of Gerontology*, 1975, *30*, 97–102.

Sussman, M. B., & Burchinal, L. Kin family network. In B. L. Neugarten, (Ed.), *Middle age and aging*. Chicago: University of Chicago Press, 1968, pp. 247–254.

Taietz, P. Community complexity and knowldege of facilities. *Journal of Gerontology*, 1975, *30*, 3, 357–362.

Teaff, J. D., Lawton, M. P., Nahemow, L., & Carlson, D. Impact of age integration on the well-being of elderly tenants in public housing. *Journal of Gerontology*, 1978, *33*, 126–133.

Troy, P. Environmental quality in four suburban areas. Canberra: Urban Research Unit, Australian National University, 1971.

Ware, J. E., Jr. Scales for measuring general health perceptions. *Health and Services Research*, Winter, 1976, 396–415.

Welford, A. T. Motor performance. In J. E. Birren & K. W. Schaie (Eds.), *Handbook of the psychology of aging*. New York: Van Nostrand Reinhold, 1977, pp. 450–496.

Windley, P. G., & Scheidt, R. J. The well-being of older persons in small rural towns: A panel approach. *Educational Gerontology*, 1980, *5*, 355–373.

Windley, P. G., & Scheidt, R. J. An ecological model of mental health among small-town rural elderly. *Journal of Gerontology*, 1982, *37*, 235–242.

Winiecke, L. The appeal of age-segregated housing to the elderly poor. *International Journal of Aging & Human Development*, 1973, *4*, 293–306.

Wohlwill, J. F. The physical environment. In R. H. Moos & P. M. Insels (Eds.), *Issues in social ecology*. Palo Alto, Calif.: National Press Books, 1974, pp. 180–188.

Whyte, W. H. *The organization man*. New York: Simon & Shuster, 1956.

Ziegler, W. A. *Minnesota Rate of Manipulation Tests*. Minneapolis: Educational Testing Bureau, 1946.

Zube, E. H. Cross-disciplinary and inter-mode agreement on the description and evaluation of landscape resources. *Environment and Behavior*, 1974, *6*, 69–89.

Index